Philosophy and *Breaking Bad*

Kevin S. Decker • David R. Koepsell • Robert Arp
Editors

Philosophy and *Breaking Bad*

palgrave
macmillan

Editors

Kevin S. Decker
Eastern Washington University
Cheney, USA

Robert Arp
Independent Scholar
Overland Park, Kansas, USA

David R. Koepsell
Comision Nacional
de Bioetica, Mexico

ISBN 978-3-319-40342-7   (Hardcover)   ISBN 978-3-319-40343-4   (eBook)
ISBN 978-3-319-40665-7   (Softcover)
DOI 10.1007/978-3-319-40343-4

Library of Congress Control Number: 2016959579

Cover design by Samantha Johnson

Printed on acid-free paper

This Palgrave Macmillan imprint is published by Springer Nature
The registered company is Springer International Publishing AG
The registered company address is: Gewerbestrasse 11, 6330 Cham, Switzerland

For Suzanne, Vanessa, and Susan

TO W.W.
MY STAR, MY PERFECT SILENCE

CONTENTS

Contributors

Leslie A. Aarons, Ph.D. is Associate Professor of Philosophy at City University of New York LaGuardia Community College. She specializes in public philosophy, popular culture, and environmental ethics. Her more recent publications include "Underwood as Übermensch: A Postmodern Play of Power" in *House of Cards and Philosophy: Underwood's Republic* and "When a Charming Woman Speaks" in *Sons of Anarchy and Philosophy: Brains before Bullets*. She conducts specialized classes in environmental ethics and is currently writing a book on the subject.

J.I. Abbot, Ph.D. is Professor of English and Philosophy at Tunxis Community College in Farmington, CT. A poet, essayist, and translator with a focus on comparative Indo–Tibetan philosophies and their nexus to the philosophy of religion, philosophy of science, and poetics, Abbot completed an MFA in Literary Arts at Brown University, and his undergraduate work in Languages and Literature at Bard College. His collection of poems, *An Argument of Dreams*, will be published in 2017 by La Bohème, an imprint affiliated with the literary and political journal *Peripheral Surveys*.

Karen Adkins, Ph.D. is Professor of Philosophy at Regis University in Denver, Colorado. She has published articles in *Social Epistemology*, *Philosophy in the Modern World*, and *Synergies*. Her book, *Knowledge Underground: Gossip, Hypocrisy, Power*, is forthcoming from Palgrave MacMillan.

Robert Arp, Ph.D. is a research analyst working on models and simulations for the US Army at Ft. Leavenworth. He has interests in philosophy and popular culture. His more recent publications include *What's Good on TV? Understanding Ethics through Television*, a second edition of *Critical Thinking: An Introduction to Reasoning Well*, and *1001 Quotations to Enlighten, Entertain, and Inspire*. See robertarp.com.

Jennifer Baker, Ph.D. is Associate Professor at the College of Charleston in the Department of Philosophy. She looks to what is relevant in ancient accounts of virtue for use today. Her most recent work is the edited collection, *Economics and the Virtues*, for Oxford University Press.

Adam Barkman, Ph.D. is Associate Professor of Philosophy and Chair of the Department of Philosophy at Redeemer University College (Canada). He is the author of five books and the co-editor of another four, many of which have to do with the intersection between popular culture and philosophical themes. His most recent book is *Making Sense of Islamic Art & Architecture*.

Kimberly Blessing, Ph.D. is Professor of Philosophy at SUNY Buffalo State. Her interests include the meaning of life, philosophy of religion, existentialism, and early modern philosophy. She has recently written philosophy and popular philosophy on *Downton Abbey* and *Girls*.

Kevin S. Decker, Ph.D. is Professor of Philosophy at Eastern Washington University. He is the author of a number of published articles on American and Continental philosophy, applied ethics, political philosophy, and has edited or co-edited more than ten books in philosophy and popular culture. He is the author of *Who is Who? The Philosophy of* Doctor Who (I.B. Tauris, 2013).

Travis Dyk is an independent scholar who is interested in law, philosophy, and film.

Charlene Elsby, Ph.D. is Assistant Professor in the Philosophy Department at Indiana University-Purdue University, Fort Wayne, specializing in Ancient philosophy and realist phenomenology. She recently edited a volume, *Essays on Aesthetic Genesis* (with Aaron Massecar), published by University Press of America (2016). She is currently working on an analysis of how Aristotelian concepts found their way into the foundations of early phenomenology.

Kevin Guilfoy, Ph.D. is Assistant Professor of Philosophy at Carroll University in Wisconsin. His primary work is in medieval philosophy and social and political philosophy. He is co-editor of the *Cambridge Companion to Peter Abelard* and contributor to *Mad Men and Philosophy*, *The Philosophy of Viagra*, and *Terry Pratchett and Philosophy*.

Sheridan Hough, Ph.D. is Professor of Philosophy at the College of Charleston. She has also taught in the Honors College at the University of Houston and served as NEH Professor of the Humanities at Colgate University. Hough is the author of *Nietzsche's Noontide Friend: the Self as Metaphoric Double* and her most recent books are *Kierkegaard's Dancing Tax Collector: Faith, Finitude, and Silence* and the novel *Mirror's Fathom*, a work that explores the Kierkegaardian self. Her first volume of poetry, *The Hide*, was published by Inleaf Press in 2007. You can find more information about Sheridan at http://houghs.people.cofc.edu.

Christopher Ketcham, Ph.D. teaches business and ethics for the University of Houston downtown. His research interests are risk management, applied ethics, social justice, and East–West comparative philosophy. With Dr. Jean Paul

Louisot, he has co-edited *Enterprise Risk Management: Issues and Cases* and *Enterprise Risk Management: Developing and Implementing*. He has chapters in *Reconsidering the Meaning in Life* and *Commercial Space Exploration: Ethics, Policy and Governance*. He has recently published articles in *Philosophical Inquires*, *Per la filosofia*, *Leadership and the Humanities*, and *Journal of the Philosophy of Life*.

David Koepsell has a Ph.D. in Philosophy as well as a J.D. from the University at Buffalo. He has authored numerous scholarly books and articles, practiced law, and was Associate Professor of Philosophy at Delft University of Technology before becoming the Director of Strategic Initiatives for the National Commission of Bioethics (CONBIOETICA) in Mexico. He is also Advisor to the Rector at Universidad Autonoma Metropolitan—Xochimilco. See davidkoepsell.com.

Leigh Kolb is an instructor at a community college in rural Missouri, where she teaches English, journalism, and mass media. She has written film and TV criticism for *Vulture* and *Bitch* magazines. She wrote about the feminism of *Breaking Bad* at *Bitch Flicks*, and her chapter, "Mothers of Anarchy: Power, Control, and Care in the Feminine Sphere," appeared in *Sons of Anarchy and Philosophy: Brains before Bullets*.

Rob Luzecky is Lecturer in the Philosophy Department at Indiana University-Purdue University, Fort Wayne. When he is not busy running a car wash and trying to be the one who knocks, he specializes in the ontology of works of art, with particular reference to the thought of Roman Ingarden.

Joseph Mahon, Ph.D. was Lecturer in Philosophy at the National University of Ireland, Galway, until his retirement in 2013. His research and publications have concentrated on topics in Marxism, existentialism, feminism, applied ethics, and cultural policy. He is the author of *An Introduction to Practical Ethics*, *Existentialism, Feminism, and Simone de Beauvoir*, and *Simone de Beauvoir and Her Catholicism*.

James Edwin Mahon, Ph.D. is Professor and Chair of the Department of Philosophy at CUNY-Lehman College. His primary research interests are in moral philosophy, the history of moral philosophy, metaethics, and the intersection of law and applied ethics. Recent publications include "The Definition of Lying and Deception" in the *Stanford Encyclopedia of Philosophy* and "Innocent Burdens" in *Washington and Lee Law Review*.

Frank Scalambrino, Ph.D. is Senior Lecturer in Philosophy at the University of Akron, Ohio's Polytechnic University, and Associate Editor for the Taylor & Francis journal *Social Epistemology*. He has interests in social justice and philosophical psychology. His more recent publications include *Social Epistemology & Technology*, *Meditations on Orpheus*, and *Introduction to Ethics: A Primer for the Western Tradition*.

Sara Waller, Ph.D. is Associate Professor of Philosophy at Montana State University, where she teaches *Other Animals* and *Philosophy and Popular Culture*. She has published articles on philosophy of mind and cognitive neuroscience in journals such as *Synthese* and *Journal of Cognitive Neuroscience*, as well as on *Breaking Bad* and *House*. Her research interests include human and animal minds and measures of intelligence across species.

Introduction: Walt's Hero Journey

When the final history of TV has been written, when it is an obsolete art form replaced by god-knows-what 3-D-immersive, virtual-reality, 24-hour-per-day live spectacle to which we all can look forward, the first decades of the twenty-first century will be looked on as the culmination of the medium. The new Golden Age of Television is *now*—we are living through it. Not only a proliferation of channels, but also the reimagining of what it means to be a television network when cable and Internet allow us nearly unlimited viewing options have fueled its emergence. We think that many will likewise come to agree that among the very best offerings of this new Golden Age was *Breaking Bad*.

Breaking Bad is captivating and unusual TV for a variety of reasons. It is a long-form, self-contained, and limited serio-comic drama. It has a strong cast, but it is not, strictly speaking, an ensemble piece—there is one central character who emerges as a consistent, though changing, persona over the course of the show. What is more challenging to the audience is that we are meant to identify with this central character even as he becomes, essentially, a villain. And identify with him many of us certainly do, since *Breaking Bad* is one of the most loved and highly rated, critically acclaimed TV shows of all time. It is a success story many will likely attempt to recreate, but which sets a bar that may not be fully reached again.

Walter White has attained an international mythos, and his alter ego "Heisenberg" is a kind of heroic symbol, plastered on T-shirts like Superman or Iron Man. Given *Breaking Bad*'s mythic status, the complexities of the show's interpretations are varied, offering endless possibilities for discussion within any number of philosophical traditions. Vince Gilligan, the show's creator, has given numerous interviews about *Breaking Bad*, each of which provides evidence that he was working through some significant ethical issues in creating and writing it over five seasons. Because the central focus of the show is the gradual descent of an ordinary man into a criminal mastermind, much of the musing that exists about *Breaking Bad* focuses on ethics, but its moral territory is both deep and broad, and allows for approaches from a variety of ethical traditions. Numerous books and articles have already been published deconstructing, analyzing, and using *Breaking Bad* as a platform for discussion of topics both obscure and popular, often from a philosophical point of view. Among popular culture artifacts, the show is not unique in this regard, but is especially useful and fruitful as a source of inspiration for philosophical inquiry because of its clear, self-conscious philosophical standpoint. *Breaking Bad* will provide us all with opportunities for fresh philosophical musings for some time to come.

Perhaps what is most intriguing about Walter White's moral arc is that we are somehow compelled to sympathize with him, to root for him against his foes, even when his foes are the "good guys" and it has become clear that he has fallen completely into the depths of depravity. Vince Gilligan has perhaps perfected the *anti*-hero's journey, in stark contrast to the hero's journey described by Joseph Campbell in his 1949 work, *The Hero With A Thousand Faces*.[1] The hero takes the basic steps shown in Fig. 1, which include Call to Adventure, Supernatural Aid, Threshold Guardian, Threshold, Helper Mentor, Temptation, Revelation, Abyss, Death, Rebirth, Transformation, Atonement, and Return.

David Corbett includes Walter White in a list of modern anti-heroes and briefly describes the anti-hero's journey in *Bright Ideas* magazine, but *Breaking Bad* differs from the anti-hero that Corbett traces back to ancient Greek epic to *Mad Men* and *The Sopranos*. Corbett sums up Walt this way:

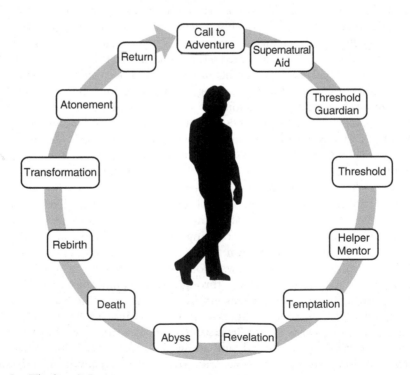

Fig. 1 The hero's journey

Like the tragic hero, the antihero stands before a vast, impersonal force—not God or fate, but hypocrisy, or the end of an era. Unlike the tragic hero, he avails himself the weapon of amorality, plumbing the darker aspects of his nature. This provides an excellent means to dramatize the seemingly endless struggle between the proud, resourceful individual and the corrupt society that would gladly crush him. And though his turn toward the darkness may help him survive, it also taints whatever victory he manages to secure.[2]

Walt's final act is not "tainted" any more than Odysseus's triumph is. Campbell's description of the hero's journey is morally neutral. We can see this in various well-delineated phases of Walt's transformation in each of these stages. For example, it is arguable that Tuco is a threshold guardian of sorts, and his death in Walt's inferno is the latter's crossing of a threshold (other threshold points may be argued, and this analysis could well have been another chapter). And perhaps Gus is best seen as a helper mentor, and Walt's realization of his expendability and defeat of Gus is his transformation, while his defeat of the white supremacists, scheme for delivering the money to his family, and confession of his true love for what he did as his motivation are all part of his return home and atonement. Walt has, by the end of *Breaking Bad* in Season Five, taken the hero's journey in full.

Yet heroes in heroic epics do terrible things. Consider that, upon his return, Odysseus murders dozens of Penelope's suitors, whose attentions Penelope has been fending off as she awaits his return. Or think of Luke Skywalker, a pretty clear-cut hero and one modeled consciously by George Lucas on the hero of Joseph Campbell's works. Let's assume for the sake of argument that the million or so Imperial forces on the first Death Star were all clearly evil, and none of them were mere functionaries with families and children, etc. (a pretty big assumption). As Kevin Smith's characters in the film *Clerks* argued, many of the deaths in the second Death Star's explosion (in *Return of the Jedi*) were murders, plain and simple. Contractors who were still hard at work building the destructive weapon were incinerated with Luke's help in its destruction, though the final shot is Lando Calrissian's. In any case, it is surely arguable that our hero, Luke Skywalker, is instrumental in the murders of thousands of innocent workers, maybe more.

What is it in Walt's journey that "taints" his final victory? In fact, he has attempted to avoid killing those he deems innocent, though with the notable exception of the poisoning of Brock (who survives). His victims are, more or less, all wrapped up in the dangerous and immoral (or amoral) world of drug manufacturing and dealing. Even Gale Boetticher is not innocent—he knows for whom he works, and what they do, and while he justifies his actions with a libertarian perspective, he is enmeshed in a dangerous, criminal scheme.

We are meant to disdain Walt and to cast judgment on his deeds and motivations. He is certainly no role model, but then few epic heroes are. But it is the journey that is important. The possibility of the hero's transformation and reemergence as someone more than he once was, the ability to overcome and triumph over death itself, to become the subject of songs and inspiration of some sort—these are the marks of the hero. Walt was a nobody who becomes a legend, his alter-ego's name whispered in hushed tones, spray painted on walls, and in the real world, iconic and ubiquitous. There is little sense in distinguishing Walt from other heroes whose histories are spotted with violence and death. The world that he leaves behind is not worsened, and the lives of his children improved by his actions. Numerous criminal drug lords are left dead in his wake, as well as a clutch of nasty white supremacists and a couple crooked business people, too.

Perhaps Walt is not a hero as such, but his journey is undeniably the hero's journey, and his appeal to us is similarly undeniable. If he ended the show as merely "evil," we would have lost interest or felt betrayed. We feel instead a sense of justice in the final act. Whether we admire Walt or not, see him as a hero or anti-hero, we relish something about the satisfying end of the show, a satisfaction few literary works achieve in the context of such moral ambiguity.

The editors of *Philosophy and Breaking Bad* come to bury Walt, though, not to praise him, and to examine his life and the world of *Breaking Bad* philosophically, from a number of different angles. It is rich territory and we would do well to set aside our prejudices. The careful examinations in the following chapters offer fresh perspective on this epic tale, the journey Walt takes, and his victims and triumphs. A number of themes remain constant throughout, in this book and others like it, but fresh takes emerge with each new examination. Each new viewpoint of the show offers similar bounty. The world of *Breaking Bad* continues in the spin-off *Better Call Saul*, which will no doubt spawn its own philosophical examinations, but we return here to the source text, the founding documents of that world, and the heroic journey of its protagonist, Walter White.

PART 1

"We Tried to Poison You": Breaking Evil

CHAPTER 1

What's Stopping Me: *Breaking Bad* and Virtue Ethics

Jen Baker

Morality is not a common theme in a television series. We are accustomed to writers creating characters, perhaps ones with notable quirks, who respond to external challenges that interfere with their everyday, relatable, plans. When morality is itself the theme, as it is in shows that are truly great, critics note the difference. Emily Nussbaum writes that many shows that attempt a moral theme by presenting an anti-hero, in comparison to *The Sopranos* and *Breaking Bad*, are but "lesser imitators." They offer "anti-hero cupcakes with moral ambiguity sprinkles." These shows remain in "the old style of television," which will "always snap back to titillation, determined to please, not to challenge."[1]

Breaking Bad instead delivers on its title. Critics immediately recognized it as a "morality tale."[2] It was described as "Old Testament at its core," even in its early stages.[3] As Elijah Siegler writes, *Breaking Bad* might even amount to "the end of the anti-hero genre, not only taking the trope as far it can go (in Walter White's journey from mild mannered high school teacher to mass-murdering drug kingpin, all accompanied by lies and rationalization)" but by rejecting "moral relativity" in favor of "an uncompromising theological vision."[4] Television critic Todd VanDerWerff claims that it is "a religious show," noting that,

---

For indeed none can love freedom heartlie, but good men; the rest love not freedom, but license. –John Milton, *The Tenure of Kings and Magistrates* (John Milton, *The Tenure of Kings and Magistrates*, ed. William Talbot Allison, (New York: Henry Holt and Co., 1911), 10)
You are the devil! –Marie Schrader ("Blood Money")

J. Baker (✉)
College of Charleston, Charleston, SC, USA

© The Author(s) 2017
K.S. Decker et al. (eds.), *Philosophy and Breaking Bad*,
DOI 10.1007/978-3-319-40343-4_1

Walter White isn't just a sinner. He's a man who pushes further and further into his dark heart, who unleashes all manner of destruction upon the world, both at large and in his own home. He is a murderer, many times over; he is a man who abuses his wife; and he is a force of fear for everyone who sees his true face. He is, for lack of a better word, Satan… He gives in to his selfishness and pride, his rage and resentment. He becomes the devil, and he is punished accordingly. He lived in something like heaven, and he chose to create something far more like hell. *Breaking Bad* argues that that is a choice too many of us make, every day of our lives.[5]

But what do these critics take morality to be? What do these descriptions mean? What is the lesson of *Breaking Bad*'s morality tale, and does it apply to all of us? What exact choices do we face every day? What is Old Testament-like about Walt's exploits and fate?

We should not expect television critics to answer these questions. They end their essays with questions (whether "Walt's power to transform his basic character, the extremity of his self-determination, calls into question" our "foundational notions about good and evil.").[6] They often demonstrate our current popular discomfort with the issue of morality. Forgetting that a significant portion of *Breaking Bad*'s potential audience still regards the Old Testament as relevant, initial reviews puzzled over whether the show's writers could pull off "biblical categories of good and evil" in a "culture like ours."[7] Vince Gilligan's own claim that viewers (still) desire "for wrongdoers to be punished" was treated as a kind of paradox, given that our society is overly "individualistic" and lacks the necessary "metaphysical" backdrop.[8] As *The New York Times* pondered: "This moral dimension might explain why 'Breaking Bad' has yet to achieve pop cultural breakthrough status."[9] Other critics put forward banalities instead of engaging with moral psychology or ethical theory. Their non-explanations include the idea that Walter White was merely "essentially" evil, like the villains in Old Westerns, or as Chuck Klosterman blandly concludes: morality, in *Breaking Bad*, "seems to be a continually personal choice."[10]

In contrast, the *L.A. Review of Books* published two very fine analyses that pointed out the many parallels between *Breaking Bad* and John Milton's *Paradise Lost* (1667).[11] Yet, not even these critics assessed the show's fidelity to that account of morality. No one wants our media critics to be ethical theorists, of course. But *Breaking Bad* poses a fundamental question about morality, one that the show's creator sees like this: "I find atheism just as hard to get my head around as I find fundamental Christianity. Because if there is no such thing as cosmic justice, what is the point of being good? That's the one thing that no one has ever explained to me. Why shouldn't I go rob a bank, especially if I'm smart enough to get away with it? What's stopping me?"[12]

I would like to attempt to answer Vince Gilligan's question, using the answers ethical theory makes available. Gilligan and the other writers of *Breaking Bad* do more than reflect a Miltonic account of evil, they continue and improve upon the very argument Milton was making in *Paradise Lost*, expertly dramatizing it (as Milton did), but applying it to mortals like us. Yet, I want to suggest that, in the end, virtue ethics, and not Miltonic ethics, offers a better answer to the question "Why be moral?" than the answer: "Or you will end up like Walter White."

MILTONIC ETHICS

Milton's work can be read for many reasons. At times he addresses us with moral arguments directly, clearly making a case for why we should resist the censorship of books and allow for divorce.[13] And then there is the dense poetry of *Paradise Lost* and *Paradise Regained* that tosses up perspectives, lays out tricky narrations and offers up allegories and rich, verbally depicted visuals. Yet he again tells us, directly, that with these poems he intends to "justify the ways of God to men."[14] Milton's challenge was to make sense of the type of evil that the Biblical story depended upon. Pious Milton completed the account where the Bible did not. He answers the questions the Bible raises about evil in his depiction of Satan.

Milton's Satan is a personification of a characteristically Christian account of evil. I want to emphasize how original and particular the Christian notion is. In Milton's hands, evil is a consciously given alternative to the account of moral psychology the older Greek accounts provide. The basic narrative Milton creates is this: Satan was once an angel, the most beautiful of them all, serving alongside God. Yet he began to resent God's power, arguing that the terms of his service were somehow unfair (angels are self-begot, so why should they always serve under God?). Satan came to resent being replaced in God's affection by Christ.[15] But by the time *Paradise Lost* begins, we know for sure only that Satan hates the sun for the way in which it reminds him of what he once was. He also knows God will never trust him, because, even though his war against God failed, he will always resist and resent God.

As all-powerful, God is more puissant than Satan, and Satan is always aware of this. He convinces a third of the angels to rebel with him, though he is always aware they will, in the end, lose. We are likely familiar with depictions of his verbal manipulation of Eve: her will was free, but her happiness depends on obedience (just as it did with the angels). Yet she disobeys God's one rule for her, because Satan tells her to: "taste this, and be henceforth among the Gods/ Thy self a Goddess, not to Earth confined."[16] Having gotten humans expelled from the Garden of Eden, Satan returns to Hell, expecting to be congratulated for accomplishing what he set out to do (and it was no small feat).[17] Instead, he is greeted by hisses: God has punished the rebellious angels by turning them into serpents, the disguise Satan had adopted in seducing Eve. And Satan, too, falls to his belly and becomes a "monstrous Serpent." "His Arms clung to his Ribs, his Legs entwining/Each other [...] A greater power/Now ruled him, punished in the shape he sinned [...] He would have spoke/But hiss for hiss returned with forked tongue/To forked tongue."[18]

The writers of *Breaking Bad* were, I imagine, not consciously imitating Milton's story. Yet we need no more evidence than what follows to suggest that they share the same account of moral psychology as the great thinker. Albert Kuo and Michelle Wu, in their 2012 essay, point out four parallels between Milton's Satan and Walter White. Kuo and Wu begin by denying the assertion of other critics that Walter represents an ineffable destructive force. Instead, he is, like Milton's Satan, "terrifying because he is recognizably human: he exhibits ambition, pride, desire for freedom, and injury at being undervalued. Like Milton's Satan, Walter is an anti-hero, burningly intelligent and reeking of lust for power."[19]

Second, both Walter and Satan are looking to exert control and gain power: "Walt's dilemma is the same as Satan's: how to assert a modicum of control—of free will—against forces larger than oneself. Satan rages against a tyrannical, unjust, uncaring God; Walt battles against the inexplicability of his cancer and a broken health-care system."[20]

Third, they each offer rationalizations for their behavior. "Like Milton's Satan, Walt seeks to reason and justify his rebellion. He invokes art, science, free market rationality, protection of one's family."[21] We are left uncertain as to the extent they believe their own arguments. One of Walt's most frequent explanations is that he needs to make money to leave his family. Yet not only does he regularly risk the money *and* put his family's life at risk *for it*, but in the end, they don't even want the money (more on this later).

Fourth, both Walt and Satan are bold and knowingly take risks, despite the odds against them. "Walt risks all to feed a ceaseless, self-destructive desire to be king. For Milton's Satan, ruling Hell means liberty; for Walt, selling meth means being no one's bitch. As Milton's Satan says of Hell, "Here at least/ We shall be free."[22] In the script for the first episode of *Breaking Bad*, Gilligan describes Walter White as the kind of guy we wouldn't "pay attention to if we passed him on the street." But when Walt in the pilot yanked off his gas mask, escaping the RV full of poisonous gas he used to kill Crazy-8 and his cousin, we'd step right "out of his way" ("Pilot"). And even here we see the thesis of this masterwork in moral psychology unfold: we may not *begin* bad. We may be meek and typical, and go along with the flow. But we can transform into someone to be feared if we only… If we only *what?*

Before I answer, let me add three more parallels. Milton's devil does not use physical force. Instead, his view is that "…who overcomes/By force, hath overcome but half his foe."[23] With his manipulative stories and flattering words, he convinces others to rebel in ways they had not previously considered. Walter White at times harms others with his physicality, but the show's writers typically depict it as his last resort. One example is in the episode "A Handful of Nothing," when Walt gets Tuco to back down using nothing but his words. When Walt has a final showdown with his wife, she does not beg him to not hit her. Instead, she demands he not "say one more word."

Sixth, neither Walt nor his wife shows any enjoyment of their material gains. In a shot since they become famous, they merely stare upon their hidden stacks

of money. Walt buys one sports car, but he cannot be said to revel in the pleasures such a purchase brings. Milton's Satan is similarly bereft of normal joy.
"In misery," he says "such joy ambition finds."[24] This allows us to assume that
for both Satan and Walt, the actual motivation, the reason for overthrowing
heaven or burning with spite on seeing a happy couple, is just spite itself. There
is no further end ("The more I see/Pleasures about me, so much more I feel/
Torment within me...").[25] Foreshadowing an explanation of the morality of
Breaking Bad in terms of virtue ethics, note that Aristotle would have considered this type of commitment unusual, classifying it as "vice." The vicious
person, Aristotle tells us, is unlike most of us. We mostly fail to do the right
things because we lack the moral strength. The vicious person *decides* to act
immorally, and on following through, enjoys it. Aristotle thinks a vicious person is irredeemable, having transformed himself or herself into someone who
finds pleasure in such ways.

Seventh, as Kuo and Wu correctly predicted, Walter stays unrepentant and
yet is also diminished in the end. They wrote, "In *Paradise Lost* the origin of
Satan's fall is his own free will. At the start of the epic, Satan is seductive, brilliant, and brimming with human desires. By epic's end, he is irredeemable."
If *Breaking Bad* stays loyal to the universe that it has created, Walt will be as
well.[26] Walter died unrepentant. It may seem a further parallel that Walt also
became exposed for what he was and gained new infamy for it (the hissing is
there). And Walt finally acknowledges (to others and perhaps also to himself)
that "It was for me. I liked it. I was good at it. And I was really—I was alive"
("Felina"). But I want to suggest that, in fact, he was not diminished in the
way Satan was.

But let us also consider some disanalogies. Walt dies; Satan is rendered
unable to speak, losing his ability to recruit and manipulate, but kept alive (he
is an immortal and cannot die). Yes, Walter loses that ability, too, but Walt
does not live with this loss. As the show made clear from the first episode,
White was going to die anyway, so he had much less to lose than Satan. To take
out the possibility of living forever in heaven is to remove the "metaphysical
backdrop" and look to Gilligan's question as he posed it. Why should non-
believers, unafraid of losing heaven, be moral? Why shouldn't we rob a bank, if
we are smart enough to get away with it?

A seeming similarity that nonetheless becomes a difference is that Satan,
having brought down mankind, seems to have achieved something. Entering
the Garden of Eden was no simple task. But God is merely using Satan, as Satan
also knows, for greater good. Yet, when Walter also dies (with no small amount
of success), evil is shown as not altogether impotent. Many viewers still think,
after all, that Walt's craftiness in getting the money to his family demonstrates
his genius. His family was not killed and is not shown to be at risk of suffering.
Critic Emily Nussbaum was bothered by this, to the point that she suggests
the finale ("Felina") is a dream sequence, Walt's own fantasy of the best-case
outcome. She writes, "It's not that Walt needed to suffer, necessarily, for the
show's finale to be challenging, or original, or meaningful: but Walt succeeded

with so little true friction—maintaining his legend, reconciling with family, avenging Hank, freeing Jesse, all genuine evil off-loaded onto other, badder bad guys—that it felt quite unlike the destabilizing series that I'd been watching for years."[27] In other words, where are the actual consequences for Walt? Satan's were these: "Far as he could see there were flames, but they burned dark instead of bright, and they only revealed sorrow and hopelessness. These fires would never go out and the torture would never end. This is the place Justice made for those who rebel against God. It was as far from Heaven and Heaven's light and as different from Heaven as it could be."[28]

Walt's literal hell is easily imagined: the endless physical torture of his wife and children. He was never forced to experience that. He imagines it, when recognizing the significance of not letting Crazy-8 live ("...And the Bag's in the River"), but the torture of hell is our ongoing experiences in it. I want to argue that this is how the show offers a crucial update to Milton. By removing the Biblical backdrop and leaving us with just Milton's moral psychology, *Breaking Bad* offers an answer to the question of "why be moral?" other than "or be condemned to hell." Satan's story will not provide answer for mortals. Walter White's might. And I think the show makes it clear that an extended Miltonic moral psychology does not explain how those who "break bad" will lose all worldly gains and truly suffer, in their lives, for their evil. *Breaking Bad* exploits the dramatic potential of this. As with all mortals, death will anyway end pleasures or sufferings.

No one stops you from "breaking bad," should you choose it. And since we are going to die anyway, in a life filled with indignities, bad luck and a lack of respect, we might instead take control. If this is the answer *Breaking Bad* provides, and if morality is not justified, this would be to confirm Nussbaum's reading: "The story ended by confirming Walt's most grandiose notions: that he is, in fact, all-powerful, the smartest guy in the room, the one who knocks."[29] God is not just rendered impotent because heaven is not on the table. God lacks the power or desire, in *Breaking Bad's* universe, to torture Walt for his sins while he was alive. Prior to "breaking bad," Walt is described as plodding through life "like he's marching to Bataan" ("Pilot"). Yet, Walt's baseline misery, before he broke bad, doesn't eliminate the possibility that he could be tortured in more extreme ways, but it is a baseline which makes later rationalizations that much easier to make.

It would also be to agree with Jesse Pinkman's impression of Walt's prowess. As Jesse memorably puts it in "Rabid Dog," "You two guys are just guys. OK. Mr. White—he's the devil. He is smarter than you, he is luckier than you. Whatever you think is supposed to happen, I'm telling you, the exact, reverse opposite of that is going to happen." Is Jesse voicing the actual view of the show writers here?

One problem with this interpretation is that it works against Gilligan's stated intention. He is quoted as saying, "If there's a larger lesson to 'Breaking Bad,' it's that actions have consequences." He continues, "I like to believe there is some comeuppance, that karma kicks in at some point, even if it takes years or decades to happen." And he adds, "My girlfriend says this great thing that's become my philosophy as well. 'I want to believe there's a heaven. But I can't not believe there's a hell.'"[30] How do we reconcile Gilligan's lesson with its conclusion? Jesse Pinkman is once again useful. With a different outlook than White, though with the ability to do what amounts to the same kind of harm to others, Pinkman expresses his frustration at the mollifying approach being taken in a group therapy session. He says (perhaps mimicking Gilligan's own frustrations), in response to the group leader casually telling him there is no judgment in the group:

> Why not? Why not? [...] The thing is, if you just do stuff and nothing hap-
> pens, what's it all mean? What's the point? All right, this whole thing is about
> self-acceptance [...] So no matter what I do, *hooray for me,* because I'm a great
> guy? It's all good, no matter how many dogs I kill—what, I do an inventory, and
> *accept?* ("Confessions")

What Pinkman does not realize, and what the writers must, is that this is indeed Christian philosophy. All of our sins can be forgiven. This is part of the nature of sin. Yet, I want to next argue that the concept of sin is inadequate to an account of moral psychology that can justify living a good and ordered life and that the extension of Miltonic philosophy in *Breaking Bad* works as a very able critique.

SIN VERSUS VICE: TWO TRADITIONS

We have two dominant traditions that inform our explanations for evil today. The popular imagination's focus on Tony Soprano is support for how one of these, the ancient Greek conception of bad character, continues to seem plausible. In the ancient world, Medea was the equivalent of Tony Soprano: a larger-than-life character who fascinated people due to her extraordinary pow-ers; ancient ethicists carefully argued that Medea was an example to us all. We may not kill our children, but we seethe and rage and lose control in our small ways. They urge us to watch the play and think of the damage we too can do, if we refuse to control our emotions and order our lives.

The Christian narrative has a different and much easier idea to sell: why wouldn't we want to seek eternal life? There is little more necessary to make eternal life appealing. Instead, Christians warn about the everyday temptations that catch us unaware, distracting us from what is obviously in our best, long-term interest. But *Breaking Bad* is not John Bunyan's *Pilgrim's Progress.* When Walt joins a former student in the meth trade, this is not Christian inattention to the long-term goal. Instead, this is the decision by Milton's Satan to rebel. Walter White deliberately turns from the good. This is far better explained by an Aristotelian account of ethics than a Miltonic one.

The connection between Christian philosophy and Greek philosophy is easily traced, yet in the very early Christian work we can see the significant departures.[31]

Once an interventionist God is put at the center of a moral account, we are no longer considered wholly responsible for ourselves. We must have faith to purify a moral psychology that we can only partly work and transform. Similarly, our lives are not wholly ours to control. To procrastinate, to a Christian, is to put off preparation for heaven, and to think about worldly chores is to misunderstand our true obligations. This is not so for the Greeks, to whom our most common failing is not the failure to love God. According to Aristotle, we often fail despite being able to recognize what we *ought* to do. We fail practically, through procrastination; we experience *akrasia* or a failure of self-control; we act impetuously, or are weak.[32] We give in to lesser impulses and do not engage in the moral behaviors we think we should. As a result of this, we come to distrust ourselves, and our morality becomes increasingly less efficacious. We will not, the Greek philosophers explain, be able to experience the happiness that a person who is efficacious does.

The ancient Greek tradition in ethics was committed to an understanding of happiness (*eudaimonia*) as our highest good.[33] Many things followed from this determination. We were, as a result, best off if we organized our aims around the happiness of our lives as a whole, rather than around shorter-term aims. Power, wealth and fame were, the ancients argued, not resources that could reliably guarantee happiness. This was a matter of our psychology, which, they pointed out, would not be satisfied with any level of fame or power. But it was also a matter of the goods themselves. They never really become part of us, as much as we might want them to. They could so easily be taken away. Their care could so easily consume us with worry and attention.

On the other hand, a life lived for the sake of being moral was something that would psychologically satisfy (once the hard work of becoming committed to such a life is over, at least). And a life lived for the sake of being moral would make the (inevitable) losses of any lesser goods easier, in a sense, to prepare for. The consequence of committing oneself to such a life would be the development of the virtues. The ancient schools (Platonic, Aristotelian, Stoic, Epicurean) were all convinced that the process of developing virtue would have to be active and acutely self-conscious. In other words, no one is surprised to find herself virtuous; this is not the sort of thing you could attain without being aware of as your primary agenda. To be naturally brave is not to be truly brave, on the ancient account, because bravery requires awareness of the point of applying the virtue of courage to your activities. Without this, your actions are still not virtuous, as they do not meet the criteria for this type of behavior. And to meet this criteria in the case of courage (to understand why and when it is appropriate) means that you will surely also have an understanding of when, for example, courage is appropriate. This is to say that good behavior will be marked by understanding and bad behavior will be marked by confusion. In stark contrast to Christianity, the traditional virtue ethicists regard the *motives* of a person acting badly to be almost completely uninteresting. They are missing the mark in any number of ways, and yet this can be explained simply: they are pursuing short-term goals rather than their long-term, *eudaimonistic* aims.

Now, if Walter White's psychology had been modeled on one of the ancient Greek accounts, we would expect several differences. For one thing, a virtue ethicist would find it odd that Walt does not enjoy his money, since most people who have renounced or ignored standard ethics would be doing so in order to indulge in base desires. It seems unusual, to a virtue ethicist, that Walt would be so controlled in one area and not in another. For another, we would anticipate Walter's confusion about his own motives. The character Tony Soprano is again a neat contrast to Walter White, as Soprano confessed to benefitting from being out of control; White does nothing of the sort. A virtue ethicist would read Walter White's confidence as some type of rationalization, because even his verbal commitments to his family (he does secure them the money), his own self-regard and his aim of accumulating money are confused. He has failed to recognize the one way to integrate these interests: by becoming moral.

If an ancient description of our nature seems implausible, it can be helpful to see that it is actually reflected back at us today in the work of contemporary behavioral scientists and others working on the neuromechanics of choice.[34] They have found evidence for some of what the ancient eudaimonists emphasized: that we all regularly experience *akrasia*, or the inability to do what we believe to be right. Some approaches invoked to supplement ethics, such as rational choice theory, fail to problematize motivation enough to acknowledge how often we are akratic. Identifying the "inconsistent propositions" involved in *akrasia* is the same focus that traditional virtue ethics has always taken. Behavioral scientists also point out that it is our brains that themselves generate rewards, and therefore it is not always external rewards themselves that provoke some regular response.[35] Traditional virtue ethics has always insisted that reliable reward structures are internal. If we fail to recognize that we often "appoint" rather than "discover" value, we could assume that an agent would choose in the same way over time until she got some new information. But neither animals nor humans do this. Instead, as the psychiatrist and behavioral scientist George Ainslie writes, while making a choice, we "try out scenes before entering them." In doing so, "a scenario competes for our engagement against alternatives such as preparing coffee, taking a nap, or imagining something else."[36] We entertain self-determined and *prospective* rewards—dessert before or feeling self-controlled later—just as the ancients described.

The ancient eudaimonists also depict us as internalizing personal rules. If we violate these rules, they believed we would experience negative psychological feedback: "those who do not attend to the disturbances in their own soul" are "inevitably in a state of unhappiness."[37] The idea that there are psychological consequences to violating a personal rule is something scientists also confirm. They are attempting to determine how we decide which choices we've made constitute lapses of personal rules. If you catch yourself lying to a client, you may never get caught, but there may be a psychic cost and an impact on your agency in the form of a loss of self-trust. As Ainslie puts it, we succeed at following our own rules only if we convince ourselves we "can't get away with cheating" and that our "current compliance" gives us "enough reason not to cheat subsequently." The more doubtful we become that we can maintain our personal rules, the more likely we are to violate them. "Personal rules," Ainslie explains, "are a recursive mechanism; they continually take their own pulse, and if they feel it falter, that very fact will cause further faltering."[38] This will sound familiar to students of the ancients.

If the Greek account is applied to Jesse Pinkman, the cognitive dissonance he suffers can be put in a moral context. He thinks of himself as a decent person, yet cannot stop doing things he does not think are right. This makes him lose moral efficacy, and the cycle continues. He cannot be happy as a result (which he cannot deny, no matter how much money he accrues). Exactly as a virtue ethics would predict, Pinkman cannot abide by—he stands outside of (*ekstatikos*)—the conclusions of his own moral reasoning.[39] But virtue ethics applied to Walter White is not so simple. Like Satan, White has disavowed standards of pleasures and happiness. In such cases, the Aristotelian concession to the possibility of there being "vicious persons" is relevant. Little discussed in contemporary virtue ethics, Aristotle's vicious person is one who is not just weak or indulgent; instead, he is actually committed to being a person who pursues evil. Aristotle did not think this would be common (I read him as thinking it is just a theoretical possibility). But Walt would represent such a case. This implies a life of "hell on earth" for Walt.

Yet, Walt's hell need not be the very domestic life (one unironically called "heaven" by critic Todd VanDerWerff) that Walt uses to justify his murders. The tedium and the emasculation he experiences with his disinterested wife would not explain his motivation to provide for this family, or to fool himself into thinking "you've done it all for them." The domestic and career orderliness of his prior life are not representative of a foundational category of good, anyway. Instead, they are a sham moral category, one bereft of any real (or at least secular) justification. The idea is advanced by Max Weber: morality can be seen as absurd apart from specific religious beliefs about who is chosen for the afterlife.[40]

Walt's hell is also not his felt compulsion to provide for his family. Walt's fans suggest that his life circumstances and poor health insurance pointed to violent and illegal routes to earn a tremendous amount of money; this reasonably looks like his most appealing option. The claim is that because his intentions were good, his single-minded focus can be forgiven, even though it involved immoral means. I want to suggest that the notion that Walt is not to blame is ruled out by his confession of having enjoyed the experiences he had, dangerous and deadly as they were.

No, instead, Walt's hell is the one the ancients described: it is a lack of happiness. This lack made itself felt in his domestic setting, but it was not that setting itself. It was because of the economy, but it was not his economic situation itself. His hell is *himself*, making him live with someone he can't stand. His motives are complex by design, intended to hide his own disappointment with himself; they make no sense for this reason. He's out for vengeance, to prove something, but what? To whom? For what? He's rebelling, and even the Stoics would admit that we can admire this. It takes a great soul, like Medea's, to do spectacular things. But again, against what is he rebelling? We know Walt is not religious. He's always said he did what he did for his family, even when that was no longer making any sense. As Lanham puts it, "On the surface, Walt appears to pursue power and money for the protection of his family with a cold and calculated rationality. His actions seem to make sense. On closer inspection, however, Walt's motives begin to appear paradoxical, as his simultaneous desires for power and family intertwine and compete until they are literally at cross purposes. As a result, Walt's intentions and emotions remain unreadable."[41] I would add: they are unreadable to Walt himself, too.

Lanham compliments this condition, as if Walt is empowered by it. He speculates that "Walt is never subject singly to any one desire, so he seems to choose his own motivations, as if he's free not only to decide what to do next, but to control what desires will shape his very character."[42] Yet, consider what this depends upon in order to be a realistic description. If the Miltonic account of moral psychology is right, any of us can break bad at any moment. A Greek account finds this wildly implausible. Virtue ethics will always expect there to be psychological explanations that go far back in a person's history. So I disagree strongly with VanDerWerff: *Breaking Bad* does not argue that Walt's "is a choice too many of us make, every day of our lives."[43] And I also disagree with Lantham (and Jesse, too): Walt is not a mastermind. He does not choose his own motivations. He is no freer than Satan. He is, instead, rebelling against his very own internalized moral norms. And he is constrained by his commitment to a particular preference: "*Better to reign in hell, than serve in heav'n.*"[44] Or as Aristotle writes, the soul of the vicious man "is in conflict, and on account of being vicious, when he is restrained part of him is in pain, part is pleased; one side pulls this way, the other that, as if he is being torn apart."[45] Such a man is "full of regret," not about actions he wishes he had taken, but about the person he has become. To find distraction, such people "flee from themselves."[46] Aristotle warns us that they may even "do away with themselves," as they do not care for their own lives (and we imagine, they care no more for the lives of others).[47] This explains Walt, and the rest of us, far more than does the example of Satan. This is what stops us from getting away with breaking bad.

NOTES

1. Emily Nussbaum, "The Closure-Happy 'Breaking Bad' Finale," *The New Yorker*, last modified September 30, 2013, http://www.newyorker.com/culture/culture-desk/the-closure-happy-breaking-bad-finale; on anti-heroes in television see Elijah Siegler, "Television," in *The Routledge Companion to Religion and Popular Culture*, ed. John C. Lyden and Eric Michael Mazur, (New York: Routledge, 2015), 41–64.

2. David Segal, "The Dark Art of Breaking Bad," *New York Times*, last modified July 6, 2011, Web.
3. Albert Kuo and Michelle Wu, "In Hell We Shall be Free: On Breaking Bad," *Los Angeles Review of Books*, last modified July 13, 2012, Web.
4. Siegler, "Television," 41.
5. Todd VanDerWerff, "*Breaking Bad* Ended the Anti-hero Genre by Introducing Good and Evil," *A.V. CLUB*, last modified September 30, 2013, Web.
6. Andrew Lanham, "Walter White's Heart of Darkness," *Los Angeles Review of Books*, last modified August 11, 2013, Web.
7. Segal, "The Dark Art of Breaking Bad."
8. Ibid.
9. Ibid.
10. Chuck Klosterman, "Bad Decisions," *Grantland*, last modified August 2, 2011, Web.
11. Lanham, "Walter White's Heart of Darkness."
12. Segal, "The Dark Art of Breaking Bad."
13. John Milton, *Aeropagitica and Other Political Writings of John Milton*, ed. John Alvis (New York: Liberty Fund, 1999). *Aeropagitica and Other Political Writing of John Milton* (Indianapolis: Liberty Fund, 1999); also "The Doctrine and Discipline of Divorce," *The John Milton Reading Room*, last modified January 15, 2016, Web.
14. John Milton, *Paradise Lost*, *The John Milton Reading Room*, last modified January 15, 2016, Web, Book 1.26.
15. Scholars such as Scott Poole have begun to suggest that all evil comes from being replaced in a parent's affection, in this type of manner; see Scott Poole, *Monsters in America* (Waco, TX: Baylor University Press, 2014).
16. Milton, *Paradise Lost*, 5.77–78.
17. Ibid., 10.505–10: "[H]e stood expecting/Their universal shout and high applause/To fill his ear when contrary he hears/On all sides form innumerable tongues/A dismal universal hiss, the sound/Of public scorn."
18. Ibid., 10. 509–515.
19. Kuo and Wu, "In Hell We Shall be Free: On Breaking Bad."
20. Ibid.
21. Ibid.
22. Milton, *Paradise Lost*, 1. 268–269.
23. Ibid., 1. 648–649.
24. Ibid., 4. 89.
25. Ibid., 9.119–121.
26. Kuo and Wu, "In Hell We Shall be Free: On Breaking Bad."
27. Nussbaum, "The Closure-Happy 'Breaking Bad' Finale." "If, instead, we were watching Walt's compensatory fantasy, it was a fascinating glimpse into the man's mind," she writes.
28. Milton, *Paradise Lost*, 1.
29. Nussbaum, "The Closure-Happy Finale of 'Breaking Bad.'"
30. David Segal, "The Dark Art of Breaking Bad."
31. Sarah Broadie, *Nature and Divinity in Plato's* Timaeus (New York: Cambridge University Press, 2012).
32. Aristotle, *The Nicomachean Ethics*, trans. W. D. Ross (Oxford: Clarendon Press, 1925), 1147a10–24.

33. Examples of contemporary but classically styled virtue ethics include Daniel Russell's *Practical Intelligence and the Virtues* (Oxford University Press, 2009); Julia Annas's *Intelligent Virtue* (Oxford University Press, 2011); Lawrence Becker's *A New Stoicism* (Princeton University Press, 2001); Rosalind Hursthouse's *On Virtue Ethics* (Oxford University Press, 2001); Mark LeBar's *The Value of Living Well* (Oxford University Press, 2013).

34. Paul W. Glimcher, "Choice: Towards a Standard Back-Pocket Model," in *Neuroeconomics: Decision Making and the Brain*, ed. Paul W. Glimcher (Amsterdam: Elsevier, 2009), 503–522.

35. In his recent work, George Ainslie has been drawing on the implications of behavioral scientists having come to agree on the basic neural mechanics of choice. Multiple studies of monkeys entertaining choices in their intraparietal cortex indicate they are engaging in "vicarious trial and error." When we, too, do this, we are not just considering the route to greater rewards; we "bring up a memory so as to relive a scene, or a plan so as to anticipate one, or another person's experience so as to model one, and may stay engaged with any of them for a considerable time without necessarily being moved to any actual behavior." See "Money as MacGuffin: A Factor in Gambling and Other Process Addictions," in *Addiction and Self-Control: Perspectives from Philosophy, Psychology, and Neuroscience*, ed. Neil Levy (Oxford: Oxford University Press, 2013), 25–26.

36. Ibid., 26.

37. Marcus Aurelius, *The Meditations*, trans. G. M. A. Grube (Indianapolis: Hackett Publishing, 1983), 13.

38. George Ainslie, *Break-down of the Will* (Cambridge: Cambridge University Press, 2001), 88.

39. Aristotle, *Nicomachean Ethics*, 1145bll-14, 1150b27-28 and 1151a20-22.

40. *Max Weber, The Protestant Ethic and the "Spirit" of Capitalism and Other Writings*, ed. Peter R. Baehr and Gordon C. Wells (New York: Penguin, 2002).

41. The acting is particularly good in this regard! "With potently ambiguous expressions and body language, Cranston refuses to show us the inner life that Gandolfini [Tony Soprano of *The Sopranos*] doled out so generously, and we are as in the dark about Walt's true intentions as someone he is about to murder. Perhaps the most enjoyable (and disturbing) part of the show is trying to decipher what's going on behind Walt's craggy visage"(Lanham, "Walter White's Heart of Darkness").

42. Lanham, "Walter White's Heart of Darkness."

43. Todd VanDerWerff, "*Breaking Bad* Ended the Anti-hero Genre by Introducing Good and Evil," *A.V. CLUB*, last modified September 30, 2013, Web.

44. Milton, *Paradise Lost*, 1. 258–63.

45. Aristotle, *Nicomachean Ethics*, 1166b20-23

46. Ibid., 1166b25 and 1166b14.

47. Ibid., 1166b13.

CHAPTER 2

Eichmann in Albuquerque

Karen Adkins

Hannah Arendt's dissection of the banality of evil in *Eichmann in Jerusalem* (1963) has immediately established itself as a philosophical classic. But while "banality of evil" gets regular use outside of her book, its applications are variant enough that it is sometimes difficult to see evil as meaningfully banal. While Eichmann's actions and culpability get regular historical and philosophic reexamination,[1] the fact that he was part of such a catastrophic genocide as the Holocaust makes it difficult to usefully apply Arendt's ideas in less extraordinary settings. Despite the distressing continuation of genocide in the post-Eichmann world, most people living in the global north lead lives relatively detached from the reality, experiences and dilemmas accompanying genocide. And while Arendt herself resisted philosophical implications to her analysis, there are also clear hints in the text that her "report" is not merely singular, and that its analysis can and should be extended. I suggest that the paradoxical nature of banal evil is strikingly difficult to apply effectively, in such a way that is actually productive for practical ethical discussion.

Adolf Eichmann is a banal bureaucrat; his actions are typically modest or technical. He organizes the logistics of the evacuation of victims to concentration camps, so he is removed from the direct consequences of his actions. His persona is ordinary and modest; he does not attract attention with his demeanor or his behavior. And yet his actions, in their banality, are still evil. They are predictable; it is not difficult to imagine that managing the transportation of tens of thousands of people to concentration camps will result in their deaths. The consequences are seriously harmful to many. Finally, they are avoidable; as Arendt shows in her text, Eichmann's choice to join the SS and move up its ranks was not a coerced choice. Recognizing and analyzing the ways in which

K. Adkins (✉)
Regis University, Denver, CO, USA

© The Author(s) 2017
K.S. Decker et al. (eds.), *Philosophy and Breaking Bad*,
DOI 10.1007/978-3-319-40343-4_2

small, modest and technical actions can lead to predictable, avoidable and serious harms is challenging. Contemporary applications of Arendt tend either to the highly formalistic and removed from daily life, such as the Stanford Prison Experiment, or the dangerously loose, as in Ward Churchill's comparison of dead Wall Street workers after 9/11 to "little Eichmanns."[2]

Despite its fictional nature, I would propose that Vince Gilligan's *Breaking Bad* actually helps us to see the paradox of banal evil in its full flourishing, and in ways that invite ethical engagement and discussion. Most basically, while few people are drug dealers let alone manufacturers, the sheer pervasiveness of the drug trade across the globe means that many people have direct or indirect exposure to it. Importantly, the character trajectory of Walter White fleshes out what Arendt's text only hints at—the way in which an agent gradually becomes acclimatized and indifferent to banal evil. Reading *Breaking Bad* against Arendt helps us to see the way in which a tendency toward indifferent and instrumental thinking can develop.

"STAY OUT OF MY TERRITORY…"

The crucial concept I want to focus on will be Arendt's account of *empathy*, and its centrality in the development of thought and judgment. The absence of empathy is an organizing concept for Eichmann's personality; it seems to facilitate his banally evil actions. Notwithstanding Walter White's better qualities, he also displays an absence of empathy toward those not in his direct family. This lack of empathy, initially only tangentially present, gradually dominates depictions of his personality and perspective. Despite the ostensibly redemptive close to the series, the ways in which Walter White is revealed as incapable of meaningful ethical reflection about his actions are instructive. Indeed, it is the manner of ethical thinking that Gilligan's series so regularly engages with. Ultimately, the series depicts the ways in which restrictive thinking—a failure of ethical imagination, in which Walter White cannot meaningfully recognize, respond to or respect other perspectives, or even the obvious consequences of his actions—is so destructive. This detailed depiction, I would argue, is a useful contemporary analog to Arendt's argument.

The use of empathy in Arendt's work as a theoretical framework might seem counter-intuitive, given that she is notoriously critical of the concept of empathy in several of her writings.[3] However, following Giunia Gatta, I want to suggest that her most critical portrayals of empathy, such as in *On Revolution*, are caricatures, and render it merely a mute, emotional response to generalities.[4] Rather, her account of Eichmann's cognitive failing, in my view, more truly captures empathy as we more traditionally understand it: an intellectual orientation toward specific people to whom one has concrete relations, or what Gatta describes as "a modality of appreciation for the other as other."[5]

I will unpack these claims. First, Arendt's criticism of empathy characterizes it closer to ESP than what is commonly understood as empathy (the ability to understand or identify with another's thoughts, feelings or experiences). In a representative passage, she describes it as knowing "what actually goes on in the mind of all others."[6] But the phrasing of that claim is too strong; knowing what it is in another's mind suggests knowing things that are unvoiced or unsaid, things for which there is no rational or linguistic evidence. This is not typically an attitude we describe as empathic, but is instead psychic. More to the point, Gatta notes that Arendt's version of empathy is oddly generic, for knowing about the minds of *all* others is self-defeating. "Either we are encountering real others, with real—and possibly deeply conflicting—stances, or we are making up differences out of our own minds."[7] Arendt's version of empathy, in addition to being receptive and supernatural—one simply and effortlessly penetrates others' consciousness—is unconnected to any concrete encounters with any real people. Common use of the term empathy or describing a person as "empathic" undermines this, since empathy requires a specific orientation, otherwise it lacks any content. There would be no specific thing to be understood, recognized or with which to identify. Gatta persuasively offers a more recognizable concept of empathy that is proposed by Karl Jaspers. Jaspers' concept of empathy is epistemological, reflexive and humble; when I empathize with another, I recognize that my access to their experience is limited (comprising only that which they present to me, linguistically and bodily) and reflexive; I cannot escape my representation of their experience.[8] This version of empathy, which is a far cry from Arendt's passive immersion into another's inner life, is actually more politically useful for Gatta; she argues that a reflexive, interactive and humble empathy is world-making, and criticizes Arendt's exaggerated empathy as world-erasing, because it makes the world generic and unspecified.[9]

In using this version of empathy as a starting point for considering Eichmann, I would contend that it actually comes closer to what Arendt praises in setting the historical context for *Eichmann in Jerusalem* as well as other writings, but criticizes about Eichmann's cognitive and moral failings. For instance, Arendt praises the Greeks for their ability to engage in specific and diverse viewpoints. "[T]he Greeks discovered that the world we have in common is usually regarded from an infinite number of different standpoints, to which correspond the most diverse points of view.... Greeks learned to *understand*—not to understand one another as individual persons, but to look upon the same world from one another's standpoint."[10] She values a cognitive orientation that engages specific, differing positions on the same topic. In *Eichmann and Jerusalem,* she criticizes Adolf Eichmann for exactly those cognitive failings. She doesn't worry about his lack of immersion into others' lives; she witheringly dismisses him for his specific and repeated unwillingness to acknowledge the differences between others' experience of forced emigration and execution and his own career ambitions and frustrations.

Indeed, examining her criticism of Eichmann during the trial demonstrates that his weakness wasn't an inability to imagine the generic mind of others, but rather a particular inability—or more damningly, unwillingness—to imagine experiences of specific others: the people whose condemnation and transportation to death camps he so capably directed. Arendt repeats twice in two pages

Eichmann's inability to think or examine the world from another's point of view; such repetition is unusual for her.[11] These observations arrive in the midst of discussion of specific failures of specific engagements with inconvenient concerns of others (his brutal handling of forced emigration of Viennese Jews in 1938). More tellingly, her second iteration of this formula renders it a specifically cognitive failing; it was "obvious," she contended, that "his inability to speak was closely connected with an inability to *think*, namely, to think from the standpoint of somebody else."[12] This is consistent with her later writings on thought, which stress the ways in which thinking is interpersonal.[13] Thought's construction in speech rejects solipsism; speech is other-dependent (while we sometimes think, and speak, to ourselves, we do not always do so). Indeed, Arendt's regular invocation of a Kantian disinterested "enlarged mentality" as a challenging goal for morally and politically autonomous people in her rehearsals only comes after being able to work through different positions. "The more people's standpoints I have present in my mind while I am pondering a given issue, and the better I can imagine how I would feel and think if I were in their place, the stronger will be my capacity for representative thinking and the more valid my final conclusions, my opinion."[14] It's worth noting, however, that this orientation isn't merely cognitive, but emotive as well; it is instructive for us to be able to think *and feel* as if we were in another's place, should we want to draw sounder conclusions about difficult and controversial ideas.

But even leaving aside whether Arendt allows for the possibility of an emotive empathy, the purely cognitive empathy she lauds in her writings is clearly something Eichmann does not possess or pursue. Eichmann's decision to join the SS is described as thoughtless; "Why not?" Eichmann replies to a friend of the family and Nazi higher-up, upon invitation to join the party.[15] Eichmann provides no reasons, meaningful or clichéd, for his decision. Arendt clearly juxtaposes this decision with Eichmann's general desire to advance himself socially and economically. Dire consequences and the perspectives of those targeted by the SS weren't considered and dismissed, according to Arendt; they simply weren't considered at all.

"OH WELL, *HEIL* HITLER, BITCH!"

Eichmann's inability to think leads to his inability to judge, and ultimately his refusal to act. Arendt notes that Eichmann favorably compares himself to Pontius Pilate after the 1942 Wannsee Conference (in which the Final Solution was definitively settled upon as strategy); he was free of guilt (apparently because genocide was formulated as policy) and thus had no rule of judgment.[16] Given that he acquitted himself of the responsibility for genocide, it was probably predictable that he would describe himself as refusing to see the consequences of his actions. In his testimony regarding his inspection of the Chelmno camp, Arendt stresses his pride in his deliberate refusal to watch as Jews were marched to gas chambers: "I cannot tell how many Jews entered, I hardly looked. I was much too upset... [my supervisor] did not get much profit out of my report...

[then, after following the transportation of corpses to a ditch] I was off—jumped into my car and did not open my mouth any more… a physician in white overalls told me to look through a hole into the truck while [the corpses] were still in it. I refused to do that. I could not. I had to disappear."[17] Arendt's selection of testimony focuses on Eichmann's repeated inaction, his refusal to see or witness and his representation of this action, perversely, as therapeutic; it preserves his feelings. His active refusal to see and witness consequences of his actions is a necessary consequence of his lack of empathy; it preserves his sense of his innocence. Actually seeing the consequences of his transportation plans would make it difficult for him to continue with his chosen career. This shows that for Arendt lack of habit empathy isn't simply a casual or accidental personality weakness; it is a habit that is actively reinforced by refusal to engage with the others around whom one is engaged. Our intellectual habits (in particular, habits of intellectual laziness, by refusing to consider the viewpoints of those not in our immediate group) lead to moral laziness (refusal to judge) and apathy (indifference to action). Adolf Eichmann is a banal villain because his intellectual and moral laziness should be shamefully recognizable to us, even and especially in smaller acts or inaction.

Initially, none of this might appear to fit *Breaking Bad*'s Walter White. The introductory sequence focusing on domestic Walt shows him as a modest and tamed husband, carefully and quietly getting out of bed early so as not to disturb his sleeping wife with his before-work exercise ("Pilot"), and as a man with underappreciated brilliance. The camera pauses at the two awards on his wall—most prominently, recognition for his research and leadership in the Los Alamos lab that contributed to a Nobel prize (the camera zooms into this award, tracking Walt's eyes). The much smaller award from the Albuquerque public schools for teaching is off to the side, and unnoticed. He wears pastels, sweaters, and chinos throughout the first few episodes—he presents as an unthreatening, middle-class professional man. When we see him teaching, the camera juxtaposes his impassioned lecture on chemistry as change—growth and decay, dissolution and solution—with the faces of his students (whose reactions vary between interested, balancing pencils on their glasses and snuggling). White is entirely other-oriented in these early scenes.

And yet, despite this modest appearance and behavior, his considerations about whether to cook meth for profit are noteworthy primarily for their immediate, material orientation. There is no evidence of Walt thinking about anything other than the technicalities about cooking meth, and certainly no evidence of him weighing whether the production of drugs is an ethical act or not. Walt rushes into the decision to cook, according to the logic of the pilot, less by thought than by impulsive and egoistic reaction. His second job at the car wash is humiliating; his boss forces him to wash the car of one of his wealthy students, Chad, who ignores his teaching and mocks him for his part-time job ("Pilot"). We see Walt seethe, and it's no coincidence that the next time he's at work, he quits this part-time job. His cancer diagnosis provides a dilemma: he will need money (far more than he can get between both jobs) for costly treatment. The money in meth is clear to White—his brother-in-law, DEA agent Hank Schrader, gives him some figures—and the chemistry is easy. So he approaches his former student and dealer Jesse Pinkman, offering an appeal both rational (Pinkman needs a lab and a partner) and coercive (Pinkman says yes or White turns him in to the DEA). But it's striking that nowhere in the pilot do we see any inclination that White thinks about his choice as a choice, or considers choosing differently.

Indeed, tellingly, White several times describes his choice to cook meth as more of a forced choice; he regularly describes it throughout the series as something he's done for his family. But this is a banal rationalization. Eichmann's choice to join the SS is indeed a free choice, as Arendt demonstrates; his stated claim that refusing to follow orders would have compelled him to commit suicide or be executed is undermined by the evidence of numerous party members who resigned from the party or their positions without death.[18] White is in a similar situation. He regularly appeals to his financial need due to his cancer diagnosis, as well as his absolute valuing of his family as his motivations for acting. And his rhetoric echoes famous ethical dilemmas, such as the man stealing an expensive drug for his desperately sick wife, that have been used by theorists like Lawrence Kohlberg and Carol Gilligan, such as the scenario of "Heinz," a man contemplating stealing an expensive drug for his desperately sick wife. Yet, while some people may find themselves in similarly dire straits when it comes to a cancer diagnosis, White is not nearly so desperate. It is clear that White's in-laws, Hank and Marie Schrader, have money, and they variously pledge and demonstrate generosity toward the White family. White's wife Skyler makes a brief reference to White's mother and a likely inheritance ("Cancer Man"). Finally, and most notoriously, White's former business partners are millionaires, who first offer White a job and then to pay the coverage for his treatment. White rejects all of these options, thus emphasizing the way in which his actions are both banal and evil; cooking meth is an unnecessary way to secure his family's future (indeed, he clearly imperils their future), and his rationale that he's merely a manufacturer is transparently deceptive and thoughtless.

"It Is the Purest, Most Chemically Sound Product on the Market, Anywhere…"

What White does think about, by contrast, is the minutiae of how one cooks meth successfully and profitably. Banality and absence of empathy are revealed in Eichmann and White alike by their ability to absorb themselves in technicalities elevated to misleading importance, a way of abstracting from the gruesome and harmful details and consequences of their actions. The technicalities are often expressed in actions. Eichmann's pleasure at making the forced emigration of Jews efficient is remarkable for its tone-deafness; he organizes all the steps of emigration precisely so that desperate people seeking to leave a dangerous and deadly regime can rid themselves of all their worldly belongings and savings in a time- and space-efficient manner. When the visiting Jewish dignitaries are shown this model, Eichmann is astonished that they are appalled; he had imagined that his innovation "would do justice to both parties," as if the Jews and Nazis were negotiating a difficult contract.[19] White demonstrates a similar excitement for the chemistry and minutiae of meth production; he giddily shows Pinkman the paraphernalia he's stolen from the high school, lectures Pinkman on his incorrect use of equipment and calls Pinkman's produced meth "shit" and "garbage" ("Pilot"). White savors the opportunity to display his prowess. "We will not make garbage," he affirms. "We will produce a chemically pure and stable product that performs as advertised" ("Pilot"). The camera regularly echoes this absorption; we are repeatedly treated to extended scenes of the cooking of meth, and the growing sophistication of the labs White and Pinkman use.

White's absorption into technicalities is as tone-deaf as Eichmann's. When White and Pinkman are trying to figure out what to do with the corpses of Krazy-8 and Emilio, White proposes "chemical disincorporation," or dissolving the bodies in strong acid ("The Cat's in the Bag"). His pedantic explanation meets with disgust from Pinkman, who is no stranger to the realities of the drug industry. "That's messed up," he suggests. More tellingly, after Tuco beats one of his associates to death in front of White and Pinkman, White's immediate response is to calculate in his head how much money he must earn from the meth to secure his family's freedom, and thus how long he must be involved with Tuco ("Seven Thirty-Seven"). By contrast, the less-educated Pinkman worriedly fingers his *memento mori* skull keychain and sighs disbelievingly when White contends that they only need to do this for 10 more weeks. Pinkman, who is portrayed almost clownishly in the early episodes of *Breaking Bad*, here and henceforth demonstrates a keener sense of the dangers of their enterprise than his sophisticated and better-educated partner. Indeed, Pinkman later anguishes over threats not just to himself but to those he values (his girlfriend and her son) as well as to innocent bystanders (the boy in "Dead Freight"), and will act to avoid those dangers (most notoriously by quitting cooking meth during Season Five). By contrast, White's breaking up of an unbearable and difficult task into mechanistic increments (weeks, dollars, pounds) is a way of disingenuously abstracting from the direct and threatening violence to which he has volunteered himself and, by extension, his family.

For Eichmann, the misleading technicalities are often retreats into gauzy clichés and misconstructions of his actions and their context. He comically contorts Kant's moral theory to suggest that his actions are morally defensible by the categorical imperative, proudly designs an assembly-line model of forced deportation and utilizes business language, saying that "officialese is my only language."[20] In these words and actions, Eichmann is compatible with the Nazi party, which, as Arendt notes, uses corporate "language rules" euphemisms to disguise murder and deportation as apparently palatable yet dishonest "medical matters" or "change of residence."[21] Similarly, Walter White swiftly and consistently uses corporate language to disguise his actions. He describes himself as a "silent partner" of the meth-production enterprise ("Crazy Handful of Nothin'"), requests a "capital investment" from psychopathic drug distributor Tuco ("A No-Rough-Stuff-Type of Deal") and regularly uses corporate language as a way of abstracting from the real harms and risks to themselves and others. When he and Pinkman are trying to solve the problem of working with a dangerous psychopath such as Tuco, White raises numerous objections to Jesse's proposed solution of killing Tuco, then replies "we'll put a pin in that" repeatedly. It's as if they are at a corporate strategy meeting trying to figure out a successful marketing approach as opposed to trying to figure out how to avoid being murdered by the man who distributes their meth ("Seven Thirty-Seven"). When rival dealers kill Pinkman's friend Combo, Walt's concerns are all corporate: "We need infrastructure," he moans about their dilemma ("Mandala"). For a man as intelligent as White, his use of corporate language can descend into cliché just as much as Eichmann's; when he is motivating a panicked Pinkman into staying with their meth-cooking enterprise, he offers up a crude and empty motivational speech, declaring that "this is the first day of the rest of your life" ("A No-Rough-Stuff-Type of Deal"). White's proud description of his meth as "a chemically pure and stable product that performs as advertised" ("Pilot") is a direct instantiation of the Nazis' language rules; it could describe Tylenol as well as White's meth. Indeed, the banal lies that White's clichés represent are even more apparent than Eichmann's; immediately after complaining about the absence of "infrastructure" in his and Pinkman's business, he defines their needs in the clichéd language of the drug industry: "foot soldiers, street dealers, muscle" ("Mandala"). Being able to effortlessly leap from the tired truisms of the corporate boardroom to the clichés of the drug world apparently does not register for White, but the aural juxtaposition is striking.

White uses this technical and clichéd language as a way of absolving himself of direct ethical engagement with the facts on the ground; his response to a plane crash is clearly connected to his meth-dealing academic. He intently studies historical data on the likelihood of fatal plane crashes, and the diffuse nature of their causes ("No Más"). Supplying enough technical details, for both Eichmann and White, means that their actions are part of a diffuse network of actors and accountability is similarly dispersed. Because White is from the beginning portrayed as a highly educated and intelligent person, his absolution can be explicit as well as implicit. When his wife Skyler confronts him with his activities by accusing him of dealing drugs, his response is to engage in semantics and dissembling. "I'm a manufacturer. I'm not a dealer, per se... There are a lot of angles to this. It's complicated" ("No Más"). His response hearkens back to his initial request to be a silent partner; seeing himself as merely a manufacturer means that he can be disengaged from the direct act of putting the drugs into the hands of those who consume them. They become distant and disconnected from his world; he doesn't have to see them. A complicated situation with many angles is hard to parse ethically, and this is to the benefit of the "manufacturer's" moral hygiene.

The ability of both Eichmann and White to use technical or corporate language as a way to avoid seeing the specific people damaged by their actions has a direct parallel: both characters also, at various places, directly refuse to acknowledge their actions and their likely effects. Most plainly, when White initially works to establish himself as the silent partner in the meth-cooking enterprise, he cordons off of his behavior from the reality of street violence. "As far as our customers go, I don't want to know anything about them. I don't want to see them, I don't want to hear from them. I want no interaction with them," and absurdly suggests that he will avoid bloodshed and violence ("Crazy Handful of Nothin'"). But, of course, White's words acknowledge the reality of the customers and their traffic in his attempt to deny them. It is directly similar to Eichmann's refusal to look through the hole in the van at the Chelmno executions; saying you refuse to see violence does not wish the violence away, but merely makes plain the cowardice of refusing to recognize the consequences of actions.

Ignoring or erasing those who coexist with us is a dominant theme in both texts. The ignoring can be cognitive in nature. When White defends his return to the meth-cooking business in Season Three, he uses oddly academic language. "I simply respect chemistry. The chemistry must be respected" ("Más"). White's wording here echoes Eichmann's "idealism," which Arendt sardonically explicates as being "prepared to sacrifice for his idea everything and, especially, everybody."[22] A preternatural fidelity to an idea (or an academic discipline) for both of these men has a way of making actual, lived human beings and their needs fade into the shadows. The ignoring or erasing can also be more sadly prosaic. When one of their dealers, Combo, is violently killed by a bike-riding child foot soldier of competing dealers, Jesse, in palpable distress, informs White ("Mandala"). White's tentative response is revealing, considering that he has met all three of their street dealers. "Which one is he?" he asks. The simple question reflects the way in which Combo isn't a person worth attending to; he is simply an instrument of White's financial need. This is made plain when White later minimizes Combo's death as "a bit of a setback," which provokes a violent disagreement from Pinkman ("Mandala").

"I Woke Up. I Found Her. That's All I Know..."

We can ignore by our lack of action as much as direct action. We have seen examples of Eichmann's inaction, most notoriously his refusal to witness camp deaths. His inaction is justified by a curious metaphysics; while writing his memoirs in 1960, he describes "the Norn [fate] of misfortune, spinning threads of grief and sorrow into my life," and describes his choice to join the Nazi party in similarly passive terms; "being swallowed up by the Party... it happened so quickly and suddenly."[23] Eichmann's agency is entirely governed by impersonal forces of misfortune, or political institutions. White's inaction is equally quick and sudden, but hardly metaphysical. He fails to stop the death of Jane Margolis, Jesse's girlfriend ("Phoenix"). After giving Pinkman his share of the proceeds from their deal with Gus Fring (which White disingenuously describes as extortion), White is troubled by their fight (during which Margolis accurately describes him as someone who's using Pinkman for his own benefit) and decides to return to Pinkman's house. Breaking in, he finds Jesse and Margolis unconscious from drugs. He tries to shake Pinkman awake, which rolls Margolis onto her back. When she begins vomiting in her sleep, White's initial impulse is to save her. "No, no no," he says, rushing to her. But he catches himself, clearly recognizing the business value of her death (Pinkman will no longer have divided loyalties), and stands back impassively. He is notably calm; his lips quiver a bit when she dies, but he sheds only a single tear. There are no whispers of "I'm sorry." And most tellingly, it is his inaction that causes her death. He stands by, watches her die, and then leaves Jesse to sleep next to a corpse (another absence of action that reveals a lack of empathy).

This scene is particularly striking, given that at this point in the series White is starting to see Pinkman as a family member and feels some sense of obligation toward him. But his willingness to treat someone as important to him as Pinkman as instrumental to his own ends demonstrates absence of empathy. This instrumental treatment of others isn't isolated. White learns during a family poker game that the school janitor is being blamed for the missing chemistry equipment that White stole. Hank Schrader tells White that the janitor, Hugo (who cares about Walt and is well liked in the school), will lose his job and spend months in jail. As Schrader challenges White on his play, he asks, "You going to man up or puss out?" White responds, "I'm all in," which is prescient of the plot as it unfolds; he will say nothing as Hugo's life is upended for White's actions, and will himself turn to violence as needed ("Crazy Handful of Nothin'").

Seeing others as simply instruments isn't just demonstrating an absence of empathy; it demonstrates a perverse centrality of the ego. We can treat others as mere means (as Kant says), in part because our own ends are the only ones that have merit. Arendt disdainfully identifies a boastfulness in Eichmann; despite his trappings of modesty and his clichés, he brags about his knowledge of Zionism, portrays himself as a philosopher and, ultimately, fosters his own conviction out of a desire to be recognized as notorious. Despite the pedestrian nature of his behavior and personality, a longing for fame and recognition drives Eichmann. White's ego is more narrowly focused on his area of expertise, chemistry, but it is no less excessive or destructive. The camera provides many quick hints of White's suppressed ego. His comically absurd vandalism of a car is entirely unjustified ("Cancer Man"); he is irritated both by the man's taking a parking spot (a momentary and trivial irritation), but mostly because of the man's demeanor—the salesman boasts of his business and financial prowess, while White struggles to fund his doctor visits. White is deeply motivated by financial envy and resentment; this is clearest when he comes into contact with his former graduate school friends Elliott and Gretchen Schwartz. White gasps when he enters Elliott's book-lined study, and the pause of admiration for Schwartz's *Scientific American* cover shots and articles posted to the wall stands in clear contrast to White's own achievements ("Gray Matter"). When Gretchen Schwartz visits the Whites, Walt pauses to look at her Bentley with the vanity plate and visibly grimaces ("Peekaboo").

White's ego is apparent to other characters. Schwartz's offer of a job, while clearly aimed at funding White's treatment, is cannily presented to appeal to White's ego ("Gray Matter"). Elliott acknowledges the decades since Walter's lab work, but argues that a fresh perspective can help them see things differently. The camera shows White tempted and pondering, but the rapid movement toward an agreement is suddenly reversed when it's clear that Elliott knows about White's cancer diagnosis. The sudden change in White's mien and attitude, as he abruptly refuses the job, is stark. It's the injury to Walt's pride that is decisive; the fact that a job offer would be charitably offered is impossible for White to bear. When Gretchen Schwartz discovers Walt has lied to his family about the Schwartzes funding his treatment, the situation descends quickly into an argument about egos; he again dismisses their offer as unworthy charity ("Phoenix"). Indeed, he challenges her honesty, and suggests that she and Elliott Schwartz deliberately cut him out of the profitable business the trio co-founded. Schwartz's response that she feels sorry for Walt is climactic; he swears at her, leaves, and later tells his wife that the Schwartzes refuse to fund his treatment any more because they are having money troubles. "They're broke … they're prideful people," he says to Skyler ("Phoenix").

But Walt is also drawn by the lure of his competence being recognized and respected (however, pseudonymously). Early on, he relishes in his alter ego of "Heisenberg," an alias based on the groundbreaking theoretical physicist, and adopts a more fearsome look to go along with his new name. He takes pride in the success of his methamphetamine: "my formula," he regularly calls it, and at one crucial turn in the series, needlessly returns to the meth-cooking business apparently out of spite because of a meth patent infringement. White's discovery that Pinkman has started cooking "his" formula of meth for Gus Fring enrages him; he makes a deal with Fring to replace Pinkman, and throws his preferential status in Pinkman's face. "Gus was only using you to get to me," he tells Pinkman. "Don't even think about using my formula" ("Más"). He revels in the wealth his formula produces; he complains to his lawyer Saul Goodman that he has so much money he has to weigh it on the bathroom scale, but he can't spend any of it, and that his friends and family think he's on the verge of bankruptcy ("Phoenix"). His fame and financial success, however subterranean, are sources of deep and nourishing pride.

This is because his success is direct and material evidence that he has outsmarted so many people: his law-abiding former colleagues, his family and his brother-in-law, the DEA agent. When he is briefly confronted with someone who can outthink and strategize even him, White is briefly, and tellingly, undone. White's pivotal and dangerous confrontation with Jesse ("End Times") over who poisoned the boy Brock results in their deciding, falsely, that Fring is the villain, and thus must die. White's choice of language in persuading Pinkman reveals more about how White sees himself in comparison to Fring than anything else. What he accuses Fring of in this conversation—killing children for his own competitive advantage, not seeing them as people—is an accusation aimed at himself. Indeed, his next line, the bitterly delivered "[Fring] has been ten steps ahead of me at every turn," demonstrates the real issue for White. Fring has shown himself to be the intellectual and strategic equal, if not better, of White; Heisenberg's sense of himself as brilliant is fatally compromised by this. But as a person motivated by loyalty and emotion, Pinkman doesn't care about who's smarter.

One of the striking ironies of comparative analysis is that Walter White is formally an extremely intelligent man, whereas Arendt pulls no punches in displaying Eichmann as a dim-witted clown. Indeed, White's sense of his intelligence and his lack of a level of success in accord with his brilliance drive the plot of the show. It is why he begins cooking meth in the first place, it is why he kills Gus and it is ultimately why he returns to cooking meth the final time. This contrast between someone with high technical intelligence and complete absence of empathy, rather than weakening my case, actually strengthens the Arendtian analysis. Walter White can think very clearly and effectively about subatomic particles and their interactions; he knows their traits, and can predict how they will interact. When it comes to complicated, living human beings with desires, beliefs, principles and experiences, he has much less success. Advanced schooling is no guarantee of intellectual or ethical substance. Indeed, Walter White in this respect is closer to the version of Eichmann seen in more recent scholarship that is critical of Arendt's portrayal of Eichmann.[24]

White's ego, though, isn't grounded merely in his material or intellectual success or lack thereof; his regular and deep appeals to his identity as a family man (routinely cited as the motivation for his behavior) are at bottom ego-driven. When Skyler discovers his meth-cooking and presents him with divorce papers, he fails to distinguish his family's needs from his own. "This is punitive, is what this is. We are happily married. I am happily married. I am happy," he says ("No Más"). He easily slips from the first-person plural to the first-person singular; they are equivalent in his view. When Walt Jr. creates a fund-raising Web site for Walt that Goodman uses to launder drug money, White is less relieved than distressed ("ABQ"). His son's receiving credit for the money Walt has earned troubles him. A television interview with Walt Jr., in which the son repeatedly praises his father as a universally admired and worthy man, visibly discomforts White. It is a momentary indication that White recognizes that he has become someone so lacking in empathy that he resents credit not going his own way, even if the credit is going to his own son, who has lovingly created a Web site to support his father in a time of dire need. His family is more an idea than a collection of real, loved beings who have specific needs and demands of him.

"You Are Not the Guy…"

That absence of empathy is something that is developed, not something intrinsic or static within us, is also present in Arendt's work on banality of evil. Humans may have natural "desires and inclinations" against murder or robbery, or what Arendt tellingly calls "temptations" at one point, as if the inclination to be non-violent or non-aggressive was a dangerous lure. "But God knows," she writes of most Germans, "they had learned how to resist temptation."[25] It's the fact that they *learned* to do this that is worth emphasizing; they became attenuated to indifference to their fellow citizens (indeed, to begin seeing them as less than full citizens, or less than humans).

We see a similar progression, or rather devolution, in Walter White. Early on, Walt is troubled by the inevitably violent results of his work. Walt and Pinkman imprison rival dealer Krazy-8 in their basement after Krazy-8 threatens to kill them, but White responds to Krazy-8's demand for recognition. "Look at me," Krazy-8 pleads. "I wouldn't do this to my worst enemy. This is degrading" ("The Cat's in the Bag…"). White responds accordingly—providing food, water and then crustless sandwiches made according to Krazy-8's preferences. White and Krazy-8 talk, and they share that they have both made tradeoffs of personal desires for material security in their lives. Krazy-8 wanted to study music but got a business degree for practicality's sake (the unstated implication is that the turn to the drug trade is a similar move). White abandoned Los Alamos for a pregnant wife. White agonizes over his task to kill Krazy-8, and it is only here that we see him doing anything that resembles ethical deliberation. But the resemblance is slight: he compiles a pro–con list in Jesse's bathroom. The cons are a mixture of ethical appeals ("it's the moral thing to do," "murder is wrong!" "Judeo/Christian principles") and appeals to enlightened self-interest ("post-traumatic stress," "he may listen to reason," "won't be able to live with yourself," "you are not a murderer"). There is only one pro ("he'll kill your entire family if you let him go"). While he plans to release Krazy-8, his hand is forced when it's revealed that Krazy-8 has hidden a sharp sliver of a broken plate to use against White. The murder is intimate on camera; we see their struggle, their physical intimacy (they are clutching each other around a pole in the basement) and their effort. This pairing, along with their parallel life trajectories, and White's earlier lecture on chirality (mirrored images following different paths) emphasize the way in which White could as easily be the victim as the aggressor. White is devastated by his actions. He sobs and repeats "I'm sorry," as he chokes Krazy-8 with the bicycle lock ("And the Bag's in the River").

By contrast, as we've seen, White's response to his participation in Jane Margolis' death is minimal; this is clearly a clinical decision on his part. Similarly, when partner Todd shoots an innocent boy during a daring theft of 1000 gallons of methylamine from a train, White responds entirely clinically both to the boy's death, and to Pinkman and Mike Ehrmantraut's attempt to leave the partnership ("Buyout"). Immediately after witnessing the entirely unnecessary shooting of a preteen boy and the partners' "chemical disincorporation" of the boy's body and motorbike, White delivers a motivational business talk to Jesse, focusing on the personal pride he feels from building a meth empire. Walt has become thoroughly detached from even the most immediately violent results of his actions. While the dramatic resolution to the series—White sacrificing himself to save Jesse—suggests some redemptive possibilities for those lacking in empathy, they are tepid at best. The high body count of the series and the emotional toll on families suggest that empathy is worth cultivating as a habit. The costs of apathy can be both unforeseen and stark.

One scene in particular merits close attention: "Face Off" provides arresting visual evidence of the gap between White's sense of empathy (and hence ability to think) and that of more complicated or admirable human beings. In this episode, White has deceived Pinkman into joining him in assassinating Gus Fring by falsely representing Fring as a threat to both of their lives, not simply White's (Walt goes so far as to poison Brock, the young son of Pinkman's girlfriend, to reinforce this threat). This scheme, which goes wrong in ways typical to the series, culminates in Walt needing to get money from his watched and unsafe house very quickly so that he can get Pinkman out of legal trouble White has caused. He calls his elderly neighbor and asks her to check his house (also on false pretenses). The scene in which he watches from down the street as his neighbor enters his house is structurally and grammatically similar on many fronts to the pivotal scene in Alfred Hitchcock's *Rear Window*, in which Jeff Jefferies watches Lisa Fremont enter and search the apartment of suspected murderer Lars Thorwald.[26]

The similarities and the differences are both ethically and personally telling. White's neighbor, Rebecca Simmons, is an elderly woman; she carries a cane and walks a bit tentatively. By contrast, Hitchcock's Lisa Fremont is young and vibrant; she scales the fire escape in a cocktail dress and heels, and climbs along the outside of the apartment building to attempt to escape Lars Thorwald. White's calmness as he sends Simmons into unknowing peril is striking: "There you go," he mutters calmly to himself as she walks next door. By contrast, Jeff is nervous the instant Lisa leaves the apartment with the camera, pausing to register his anxiety. We are voyeurs to the White household as we are to the Thorwald household; we regularly see the action in both scenes from the perspective of the watchers (often via binoculars). In both scenes, crucial action happens out of our view, because it is behind curtains or blocked by exterior walls, or at one point, because Thorwald extinguishes the light. We do not fully hear what is happening in either household, which increases the tension for the viewers. White remains impassive when Gus Fring's thugs show up to his house, and does not warn Simmons (by, for instance, calling her on her cell phone, which, it's clear, she has in her hand). By contrast, Jeff not only trembles in terror, he can't bring himself to look. Hitchcock's movie, which puts on display the all-too-human temptation of voyeurism in most of us (and demonstrates the ethical frailty of all of its major characters) nonetheless presents Jefferies as much more ethically sympathetic than the analogous scene in *Breaking Bad* does for Walter White.

The major ethical difference between the two cases centers on consent, deceit and culpability. Lisa Fremont knows she is taking a risk and she both comes up with the idea and chooses to do it (indeed, even over protests from Jefferies). By contrast, Rebecca Simmons assumes she is doing a harmless and momentary favor for a neighbor. Indeed, White's lie about a fire on his unattended stove even makes Rebecca Simmons' act foolish *not* to do—she thinks she is acting in her own interest as much as in White's. Crucially, Lisa Fremont volunteers to do a task Jeff Jefferies, in a wheelchair with a broken leg, is himself physically incapable of accomplishing. By contrast, Rebecca Simmons is volunteered against her knowledge for a physically dangerous act, and her frailty means that she is ill-equipped to handle any complications that may arise. The fact that White later enters the house and is then able to escape detection by hiding in his basement crawl space emphasizes the way in which he casually and indifferently exposes a longtime neighbor to unnecessary risk and harm. Lastly and importantly, Lisa Fremont does something ethically and legally problematic (spying on and breaking into a neighbor's house) in an attempt to gain further evidence that Thorwald has murdered his wife, a theory the police refuse to take seriously. By contrast, White's efforts to get Pinkman out of legal trouble don't compare. This one brief scene, particularly in juxtaposition to a famous cinematic predecessor, devastatingly illustrates White's instrumental thinking, his egoistic motivation and his immunity to others' experience, for avoidable and predictably harmful ends. It is a distillation of the absence of empathy.

CONCLUSION

While the case for White's absence of empathy is clear, some may suggest that the extreme scenarios of the drug trade, as portrayed in *Breaking Bad*, leave viewers as ethically removed from White's absence of empathy as Eichmann's banality is to those disconnected from the Nazi genocide. But I think there is good evidence to suggest that the contemporary drug trade is, sadly, a likely candidate for banal evil.

In the first place, the pervasiveness of the drug trade renders it banal. While it is certainly true that most of us are not chemistry prodigies who can viably start up meth-cooking enterprises, the problem of drug addiction and the drug trade, particularly for seriously addictive drugs, is growing in the United States. While numbers of meth addicts are relatively small, percentages have been growing in the last few years, particularly for adolescents.[27] The size of the meth industry and meth seizures from Mexico has increased every year since 2007.[28] In addition, overprescription of opioid pain relievers like Oxycontin has increased dramatically, and has been linked to increased rates of heroin addiction.[29] Rates of heroin users aged 12 and more were higher in 2014 than in most of the preceding 11 years.[30] Opioids function similarly to methamphetamine—they are highly addictive, and have similarly serious physical and psychological effects. Meth and opioids are present and abused in all 50 states, in rural as well as urban areas, and across ethnic and age groups. Opioid use, abuse and its connection to heroin addiction is such a common subject that several US presidential candidates spoke of their family connections to it during the 2016 election. The harms of these drugs are well established; they are highly addictive, can be easily abused or can lead to fatal overdoses and routinely lead to physical, financial and emotional damages that are long-lasting for users and their intimates.

Yet, surprisingly, these pervasive but harmful effects are rarely shown in *Breaking Bad*. The violence that *Breaking Bad* does show is rarely directly connected to the *consumption* of meth. The deaths and beatings we see onscreen, often with lascivious visual and auditory detail, are largely attributed either to those who deal in meth or purely innocent bystanders (the plane passengers, the boy in "Dead Freight"). Other than our brief view of a meth house that Jesse goes to drug himself into unconsciousness after Jane's death in Season Three, the fact that they are dealing a highly addictive and destructive drug gets arm's-length treatment from the series creators. Indeed, Hank Schrader reminds us early in the first season that meth used to be legal, a momentary reminder that our views of what is harmful or not are hardly historically static.

Appropriately, neither *Eichmann in Jerusalem* nor *Breaking Bad* lingers on the violence in their stories; they regularly and relevantly return to the everyday moments in our lives as overlooked, yet pivotal. The revelation and punishment of both Eichmann and White come from their overconfidence and result from impulsive decisions any of us can easily imagine making. Arendt stresses that Eichmann is brought down by his need to be recognized as smarter than he really is; he grants an interview to a journalist, who publishes articles in major magazines that give crucial assistance to Israeli secret services.[31] White's undoing is far more prosaic; while looking for toilet reading, Hank Schrader happens upon White's copy of *Leaves of Grass*, tellingly inscribed to him by the dead lab assistant Gale Boetticher ("Gliding Over All"). The ultimate pointlessness of both Eichmann's and White's courses of action are dramatically illustrated: Arendt drily stresses that despite Eichmann's stated intention of joining the Nazi party and focusing on career enhancement to secure his family's future, his postwar life in Argentina looks all too much like his prewar life. He lives relatively modestly, and works a series of odd jobs with no meaningful career enhancements.[32] White, who has similarly trumpeted his desire to provide for his family as a constant justification for his actions, gets an even starker response. After going into hiding, he returns to Albuquerque ("Blood Money") to find his home empty, sealed off and vandalized, with his alter ego "Heisenberg's" name spray-painted across the living room: local kids are using the drained swimming pool as a skateboarding arena. The seat of family bliss has been revealed as empty, ugly and trashed. The cost of his choices is made plain to him: prediscovery. White cheerfully greets neighbor Carol with a cordial hello. Shortly after his discovery, White, unshaven and filthy, has left his fenced-off house only to greet neighbor Carol, who wordlessly drops her groceries in utter terror ("Blood Money"). He still outwardly behaves as the same, ordinary neighbor we might meet on the street, but his actions have led him to an unrecognizable place. White stands as a warning figure to those of us who can be tempted by the ease of instrumental thinking, or by the momentary erasure of the lives and values of others.[33]

NOTES

1. Most recently, Bettina Stangneth, *Eichmann Before Jerusalem: The Unexamined Life of a Mass Murderer* (New York, Vintage, 2015) and Deborah Lipstadt, *The Eichmann Trial* (New York, Shocken, 2011). Their historical and archival challenges to Arendt's portrait of Eichmann do not undermine, in my view, the *philosophical* argument Arendt makes about the role of apathy in evil. This philosophical defense of Arendt against the history is well articulated by Seyla Benhabib, in "Who's on Trial, Eichmann or Arendt?" *The New York Times*, last modified September 21, 2014, Web.

2. For the Stanford Prison Experiment, see Philip Zimbado, *The Lucifer Effect: Understanding How Good People Turn Bad* (New York: Random House, 2008); Ward Churchill's essay, "'Some People Push Back': On the Justice of Roosting Chickens," *Cryptome*, last modified September 12, 2001, Web. While much fruitful academic and popular analysis has examined the relationship between American foreign policy and the rise of the Taliban and al-Qaeda, Churchill's quick equivocation of all workers in the financial industry—even those who simply worked in the towers serving meals or cleaning bathrooms—to the foreign policy establishment, in its usage of Arendt, ignores her clear rejection of the idea of "collective guilt" as ethically empty; see Stangneth, *Eichmann Before Jerusalem*, 295–296.

3. For relevant passages, see her *Lectures on Kant's Political Philosophy*, ed. Ronald Beiner (Chicago: University of Chicago Press, 1989), 42 as well as *On Revolution* (New York: Penguin, 1991 [1963]), 61–82.

4. See Giunia Gatta, "Visiting or House-Swapping? Arendt and Jaspers on Empathy, Enlarged Mentality and the Space in Between," *Philosophy and Social Criticism* 40, no. 10 (2014): 997–1014.

5. Ibid., 1004.

6. Arendt, *Lectures on Kant's Political Philosophy*, 42.

7. Gatta, 1003.

8. Ibid., 1005.

9. Ibid., 1010.

10. Hannah Arendt, *Between Past and Future: Eight Exercises in Political Thought* (New York: Penguin, 1977), 51.

11. Arendt, *Eichmann in Jerusalem*, 48–49.

12. Ibid., 49.

13. Arendt, *The Life of the Mind* (New York: Harcourt Brace, 1971), 32.

14. Arendt, *Between Past and Future*, 241.

15. Arendt, *Eichmann in Jerusalem* 33.

16. Ibid., 114.

17. Ibid., 87–88.

18. Ibid., 91.

19. Ibid., 48.
20. Ibid., 135–136, 45–46, and 48, respectively.
21. Ibid., 48 and 69.
22. Ibid., 42.
23. Ibid., 27–28, 33.
24. Stangneth, *Eichmann Before Jerusalem*, 6–7, 220, 363.
25. Arendt, *Eichmann in Jerusalem*, 150.
26. Alfred Hitchcock, *Rear Window*, film (Los Angeles: Paramount, 1954).
27. Center for Behavioral Health Statistics and Quality. *Behavioral Health Trends in the United States: Results from the 2014 National Survey on Drug Use and Health* (HHS Publication No. SMA 15-4927, NSDUH Series H-50), 2015, last modified February 25, 2016, Web.
28. Henry H. Brownstein, Timothy M. Mulcahy, and Johannes Huessy, *The Methamphetamine Industry in America* (New Brunswick: Rutgers University Press, 2014), 23.
29. See Samuel Quinones, *Dreamland: The True Tale of American Opiate Epidemic* (London: Bloomsbury, 2015).
30. Center for Behavioral Health Statistics and Quality, 1.
31. Arendt, *Eichmann in Jerusalem*, 238.
32. Ibid., 236–237.
33. Thanks to Kevin Decker and David Koepsell for their helpful suggestions for revision.

CHAPTER 3

Empathy and Evil: Drug-Dealing Murderers Are People Too

Charlene Elsby and Rob Luzecky

Gustavo Fring has just had his face blown off, and chunks of Hector Salamanca are sizzling in the flaming remains of an overpriced nursing home ("Face Off"). Walter White is on the roof of a parking garage smoking a cigarette and savoring his victory. He turns to the camera and smiles. We smile with him because we empathize with him. But what exactly does that make us? It is clear that Walter White feels no remorse for his actions, but should we feel guilt when we identify with his victories? *Breaking Bad,* hailed as the ultimate representation of the anti-hero, leaves us with a lot of questions regarding our own moral standing: if I'm happy to see Walter White succeed in killing (sometimes innocent) people, if I'm glad that his drug empire is expanding, what does this mean? Am I a horrible person?

In short, our answer is no. By examining philosophical notions of empathy, including those of Edith Stein in *On the Problem of Empathy*, as well as Maurice Merleau-Ponty's writing on our experience of ourselves and other subjects in *Phenomenology of Perception*, we can provide an alternate explanation for why we empathize with anti-heroes and rejoice in their successes. We comprehend Walt's motivations and actions given his situation; we relate to his deliberations and ultimate actions, even if, after the fact, we reflect on them and come to the conclusion that they are objectively evil. We can still say that if we had been in his situation, we might have done the same thing. We comprehend, for example, that Gale Boetticher has to die, and we hope that Jesse succeeds in pulling the trigger ("Full Measure").

Breaking Bad gives us the opportunity to experience the trials and tribulations of the anti-hero. As a form of indirect experience, Walter White's exploits are a non-primordial form of experience, and therefore similar to experiences

C. Elsby (✉) • R. Luzecky
Indiana University-Purdue University, Fort Wayne, Fort Wayne, IN, USA

© The Author(s) 2017
K.S. Decker et al. (eds.), *Philosophy and Breaking Bad*,
DOI 10.1007/978-3-319-40343-4_3

of memory, expectation and fantasy. We empathize with Walter White to the extent that we take on his perspective. This is only possible insofar as we have some immediate recognition of him as another subject, but one whose intentions are similar to our own. The fact that he is the protagonist of the show demands that we take his perspective; positioning his character as the protagonist results in our habituating ourselves to his mode of existence, such that a relation of *empathy* is the natural result.

This leaves us with the problem, though, of why we never seem to reject this empathic relation when Walter White does something that's *just too evil*. We propose that our empathic relation to the character extends as far as we conceive his actions as within a realm of possibility for us. Where we might run into discord is when we realize that, even if we *were* in his situation, we would not do the same thing. This discord often factors into our evaluation of good and bad television. But *Breaking Bad* is good television; we just find murder comprehensible.

To make sense of this, we must figure out what exactly it means to empathize with someone. In her all-too-often overlooked doctoral dissertation, Edith Stein presents a robust phenomenological account of the nature of empathy. First, we elaborate on Roman Ingarden's ontologies of works of art and Stein's analysis of empathy to demonstrate that though Walter White is a fictional character, we can and do empathize with him. Next, we propose that Merleau-Ponty's concept of the phenomenal body accounts for the fact that we perceive Walter White as another subject with intentions more similar to ours than dissimilar. In a final section, we look at the ethical implications of empathy and the possibility of the indirect experience of evil.

STEIN'S ACCOUNT OF EMPATHY

To propose that we can empathize with Walter White seems problematic in the sense that Walter White is not actually a human being. It's not that Walter White's actions are so immoral that we no longer regard him to be human. Rather, the problem is that he is a fictional character, and whatever mode of existence fictional characters enjoy, it is radically different than the one we humans enjoy when we order a pizza and specifically do not throw it on the roof of the garage[1] ("Caballo Sin Nombre"). From the outset, we can identify two clear means of differentiating fictional characters from humans: the latter are composed of flesh and bone, and also have the capacity to respond when we ask them why, for example, the pizza is on the roof of the garage. Of course, it's wrong to claim that fictional characters lack any sort of material component—the pixels on our TV screens are just as material as the corpuscles of blood running through our veins. That both fictional characters and human characters have a material ontic base, however, doesn't imply that they are the same sort of things. Different kinds of material arrayed in different ways can yield fundamentally different kinds of entities. That fictional subjects cannot be enough like us based on differences in their material constitution is the topic of our second section. The second claim, that fictional entities lack the capacity to respond to our queries, seems much more problematic. I can walk over to the science building and ask a chemistry professor how to make wonderfully pure meth, and while I might not like the answers or the police officers who subsequently come knocking on my door, I can be sure that both the chemistry professor and the police officers are beings like me because they have the capacity to respond to my actions. And yet through all five seasons of *Breaking Bad*, Walter White never once answered my question of why he seemed to prefer to wear tighty-whities.

In *On the Problem of Empathy,* Edith Stein points out that we can feel empathy toward an entity under two conditions: if it fits into our phenomenal world, and if it demonstrates a capacity to communicate with us. Walter White fulfills both of these conditions. We are transfixed by his descent from a fine upstanding school teacher to the morally reprehensible drug czar who allows his partner to be tortured by white supremacists ("Ozymandias," "Granite State," "Felina"). Elaborating on the nature of the "individual" with whom we empathize, Stein notes:

> ...[T]his living body is not given as a physical body, but as a sensitive, living body belonging to an "I," an "I" that senses, feels, and wills. The living body of this "I" not only fits into my phenomenal world, but is itself the center of my orientation of such a phenomenal world. It faces this world and communicates with me.[2]

While we cannot merely identify a fictional character with a "living body," we should note that an object of our empathy need only exist in the phenomenal world and engage in acts that the audience can recognize as meaningful. Though he is clearly different from us in all sorts of substantive ways, we can empathize with Walter White because he exists as something to be encountered, which does seem to amount to a form of communication, in the sense that information is conveyed to the viewer.

In particular, fictional entities exist in the phenomenal world but have no particular spatio-temporal extension, no location in time and space. Roman Ingarden makes this point when he illustrates the absurdity of asking questions about the location of a work of art. Ingarden writes:

> What is it supposed to mean, for example, that Beethoven's sonata, opus 13, is "here"? Where is "here"? In this room, or in the piano, or in the section of space over the piano? And if the sonata is performed at the same time in ten different cities, is one and the same sonata then supposed to be in ten different places? That is an obvious absurdity.[3]

Like the characters appearing in various works of art that may function as subjects we can empathize with, our empathetic acts are not a species of our perception of the external world (i.e., our outer perception). We cannot identify empathy with outer perception because anything perceived as a part of the world external to consciousness has a very specific spatio-temporal localization. Empathy, on the other hand, defies any attempt to localize its object.[4] While there may be a subject in the world external to consciousness that I empathize with, the process of my empathizing may expand to refer to other spatiotemporal objects. That empathetic acts are not part of our perception of the world external to consciousness implies that empathy might be a sort of *inner* perception. In characterizing empathy in this way, we need to be careful to distinguish it from our memories: none too happy with the identification of empathy and memory, Stein clarifies the nature of memory:

> The memory of a joy is primordial as a representational act now being carried out, though its content of joy is non-primordial. This act has the total character of joy which I could study, but the joy is not primordially and bodily there, rather as having once been alive (and this "once," the time of the past experience, can be definite or indefinite). The present non-primordiality points back to the past primordiality. This past has the character of a former "now." Accordingly, memory posits, and what is remembered has being.[5]

When we remember something, the act of remembering is present with us as something right here and now, but also points to something in the past. When we remember a trip to the Georgia O'Keeffe museum in Santa Fe, for example, this memory is not primordial in the sense that its content is only here with us now as something that has already come and gone. In other words, the act of memory is dependent on the existence of some prior event, and this is why the act of remembering is not primordial. Though our memories may seem real, they are really more akin to Badger's meth-induced delusions of grandeur, which no matter how vivid and how profound, derive their entire measure of reality from something else. While our memories might take us out of the dark places we end up, and, like in Walt's case, might provide some measure of comfort on those cold and lonely New Hampshire nights, these memories merely posit the existence of actual acts and events. Our memories are just the unreal things we summon and metaphorically cling to in order to give our lives a small degree of happiness, as in Jesse's case, for example, when our business partner has betrayed us and our lover is dead.

When we are empathizing with Walt's plight as he gets his initial cancer diagnosis, this act is performed in our present lived experience. Elaborating on the nature of empathy and the content of empathetic acts, Stein explains:

> [I]t [the content of our empathizing] arises before me all at once, it faces me as an object (such as the sadness I "read in another's face"). But when I inquire into its implied tendencies (try to bring another's mood to clear givenness to myself), the content, having pulled me into it, is no longer really an object. I am no longer turned to the content but to the object of it, am at the subject of the content in the original subject's place. And only as successfully executed clarification, does the content again face me as an object.[6]

When we empathize with Walt, we are drawn into what we imagine his psyche might be based on his words and gestures. Our empathic connections with Walt blur the ontological boundaries between subject and object to such a degree that we identify with him. Only once this identification has occurred do we come to realize that Walt is a *violent* other with whom we empathize. For example, the joy that we feel when Walt seems to truly become "the one who knocks" does not come from us, but from his own sinister glee. Our process of empathizing is distinct from the process of remembering, in the sense that remembering is specifically a remembrance of a past which has obtained as something real, and when we empathize with Walt, he is something that obtains in our present.

MERLEAU-PONTY'S CONCEPT OF THE PHENOMENAL BODY AND OTHER SUBJECTS

Merleau-Ponty's concept of the phenomenal body provides further conceptual tools to strengthen the analogy between ourselves and fictional characters. The difficulty Merleau-Ponty overcomes is the objection that, given that fictional characters are themselves intentional rather than material beings, how can we, as material beings, empathize with a screen image or a book character, the physical manifestation of which is nothing more than graphic marks on paper? The answer is that the body that engages in empathy is, for us, just as immaterial. The "phenomenal body," constituted by the body's possible interactions with a world, is not material in a narrow sense; it has an intentional form of being akin to that of the fictional character.

The phenomenal body is what engages with the world in a *meaningful* fashion. The concept treats the human form as something existing beyond its material properties. In fact, the concept of the body as merely a material thing (or the "objective" body, in Merleau-Ponty's terminology) is an abstraction from how the body is actually experienced—that is, as a locus of possible actions. The phenomenal body is constituted of possible interactions with a world, that is, intentional relations with the world and with other subjects. What unites me with Walter White and makes my empathy for him possible is that we both seem to engage with our respective worlds with the same meaningful actions. We have far more in common with Walt than the superficial characteristics of being Americans or family members; our commonalities of being bipedal mammals whose faces are full of perceptual holes are far more important to the phenomenal body. We exist along with Walter White insofar as he too can open doors by rotating his hands, which he uses for gripping things, that he has a certain horizon of perception by being approximately two meters tall and bipedal and, in general, *all* that human beings share that makes us far more analogous to one another than not. The intentional relations toward a world of possibilities provided by our phenomenal body lend the basis for an empathic connection. And these intentional relations are also independent of the actual material stuff that makes up our respective bodies.

The objective body is differentiated from the phenomenal body because the phenomenal body includes the capacity for *action* in its definition, something which we tend not to ascribe to the body as a mere material object. We admit, of course, that we can conceive of a material body as a possible object for other subjects; however, my experience of my own body is never as just an object, but as a subject capable of action. Merleau-Ponty explains, "It is never our objective body that we move, but our phenomenal body, and there is no mystery in that, since our body, as the potentiality of this or that part of the world, surges towards objects to be grasped and perceives them."[7] The phenomenal body "rises towards the world... the consciousness of the body invades the body, the soul spreads over all its parts, and behaviour overspills its central sector."[8]

The phenomenal body is that which is capable of actions, the actions that indicate to us the existence of a subject with motivations, either similar or dissimilar to our own. The objective body, on the other hand, is a fiction we use to describe the materiality of ourselves and others, but we must remember that this is an abstraction. We only experience ourselves and others merely as objects insofar as we imagine bodies devoid of intentionality. But *everything bodies do* provides a counterexample to this conception. Insofar as Walter White exists in a world in which he makes deals, threatens people and, of course, cooks meth, he is a possible other subject with whom we can empathize, and the idea that he is not a proper object of empathic identification based on the material of which he is constituted alone (pixels on a screen) is based on a misguided abstraction which is proved suspect every time he demonstrates intentional action.

The point to take home from this analysis of Merleau-Ponty's concept of the phenomenal body is this: no matter whether our intentions coincide with someone else's or not, we still conceive of the actions of others as *meaningful*, regardless of any particular meaning they might have. We are both subjects engaging meaningfully with a shared world.

THE ETHICAL COMPONENT OF EMPATHY

Mary Whiton Calkins opens her 1918 *The Good Man and the Good* with the following observations:

> What we most need to know about any man is surely this: whether he is good or bad. To be sure, we seldom put the question so crudely. Indeed we often affect a scorn for mere goodness, persuading ourselves that we are more concerned with a man's breeding, his intellectual vigor, his artistic skill or his practical efficiency, but in the end we all admit, implicitly or explicitly, that we are more deeply interested in his honesty, his courage and his justice—in a word, in his goodness—than in his intellectual or creative endowment, his upbringing, or his possessions. All this amounts to saying that the most significant way of grouping human beings is as good or bad.[9]

Calkins describes an attitude she believes is commonplace, that people place a value on goodness itself. She implies that an ultimate evaluation of persons would be based on their goodness or badness, such that the good is conceived of as superior to the bad. It is implied that we must differentiate good from bad men just so that we may accept the good ones and reject the bad. This view seems intuitively correct; however, it doesn't go far enough.

We argue that while we as subjects do seem to care about the goodness or badness of other subjects with whom we interact and empathize, this attitude is not enough to render the actions of an other, even if portrayed as evil, to be foreign to us. More basic than goodness or badness are the freedom with which we engage in ethical decisions, the comprehensibility of a desired end, and engagement in deliberation toward those ends. Still, we left off exploring Merleau-Ponty's phenomenal body with the nagging suggestion that the fact someone has arms and uses them for mutually comprehensible purposes may not be enough for us to treat them as if they are a subject worthy of moral consideration. The key factor, though, is not a judgment of goodness or badness, but merely one about habit.

An implied conclusion of the previous section is that it is possible for us to treat other individuals as objects and not subjects. The so-called objective body, that is, a material thing without intention, is what we perceive when we see other people as an object to our subject. Rather than empathizing with them, we can take the stance that they are but objects to us. If other people are objects and not subjects, then we can justify doing things to them that we would never do to another subject—that is, a person engaging in meaningful existence in our shared world. But if we find some excuse to exclude them from the realm of subjects, then our moral duty toward them diminishes. An example of this phenomenon takes place at the end of the film *Dawn of the Planet of the Apes*. The intelligent chimp Koba tries to save himself by reminding the ape leader Caesar of the commandment, "Ape not kill ape." Caesar responds, "You are not ape," and tosses him off the precipice to his inevitable death.

The same kind of thing happens in *Breaking Bad* when Walt finds clever ways to take down members of various criminal organizations. In the first season, for instance, Walt eliminates quite a few drug dealers, using more and more sophisticated methods as he becomes accustomed to his new lifestyle. At some level, we decide this is fine: while we ourselves aren't running around dissolving drug dealers in our bathtubs ("Cat's in the Bag…"), we care more for the success of Walter White, the chemistry teacher, than we do for the lives of his new associates. We posit that this is because there is a general societal norm of treating criminals as objects. At a very basic level, of course, they maintain the same intentional relations with the world and therefore should be seen as other subjects, but this awareness is overridden by the habit of assuming that people like Emilio Koyama aren't really humans and are therefore not worthy of ethical consideration. Along the way, however, something happens to our concept of what is good and bad. Sometimes Walt acts as if people we perceive as subjects of equal ethical standing must be treated badly in order to ensure his success. The most extreme example the show offers is the murder of Gale Boetticher ("Full Measure").

The point of this analysis is not to determine whether the murder of Gale Boetticher is right or wrong. If we were to ask anyone who wasn't currently ensconced in a blanket on their twenty-seventh straight hour of a *Breaking Bad* marathon, whether it's okay to shoot your colleagues in the face to ensure your continued usefulness to an organization, the vast majority would reply in the negative. Even as we grapple with the horror of the act itself, though, we recognize that this decision is Walter White's best shot at saving himself. This brings up another ethical trope, the intuitively valid ethical excuse, "It was either him or me." We tend to think that an action is less blameworthy when it serves the sake of continued survival; we take survival to be a *universal* goal. If someone is a human, then they should aim at survival. (On the flip side, this is also why we think that those who sacrifice themselves for the sake of another or many others are morally superior beings.)

Gale Boetticher, on the other hand, is a lovely man with an aptitude for chemistry who poses no threat to Walter White except that he may be, in the eyes of Gus Fring, a possible substitute for him. We cannot excuse his murder under any guise: he is neither an object among subjects nor is he an existential threat. Still, we may find Walter White's actions against him (and the unfortunate involvement of Jesse) justifiable *in a sense*.

The case of Gale Boetticher brings ethics into conflict with empathy, and the point we've been working toward in this chapter is that *they are not the same thing*. Rather, as was noted by the existentialists, we live in a way that now, more than ever, shows we are aware of our own paradoxical condition. Simone de Beauvoir claims,

> Men of today seem to feel more acutely than ever the paradox of their condition. They know themselves to be the supreme end to which all action should be subordinated, but the exigencies of action force them to treat one another as instruments or obstacles, as means… Each one has the incomparable taste in his mouth of his own life, and yet each feels himself more insignificant than an insect within the immense collectivity whose limits are one with the earth's.[10]

While empathy takes place on the level of the individual, ethics is supposed to provide universally valid principles for action. The reason that Gale Boetticher's murder is so disturbing is that it forces us to come to terms with the fact of our ambiguous condition: we can no longer escape to the conceptual safety of either an empathic relation to Walter that would justify the elimination of his competitors, or to a universally valid ethical principle that would ban shooting nice chemists in the face. We feel committed to *both* viewpoints.

The goal of an existential ethics is to come to terms with this condition of ambiguity, wherein we find ourselves constantly demanding the transcendence of the subjective viewpoint while at the same time failing miserably at all attempts. The subjective viewpoint tells us that Walter White is an individual whose justification for murder we have taken on as we indirectly experience his life through the medium of TV. The abstracted, universal viewpoint tells us that he is morally reprehensible, and that by empathizing with him, we too are monstrous.

The advantage of an existential ethics, according to Beauvoir, is that it is the only way to account for the real role of evil in the world. In our ambiguous condition, we can empathize with Walter White, and in doing so become accustomed to the realization that he is not so different from us and that we too are capable of great evils. At the same time, existential ethics is not meant to justify evil; rather, it provides an optimistic counterpoint to the real existence of evil because it is only in response to real evil that an ethics is even necessary. As Beauvoir maintains,

> Existentialism alone gives—like religions—a real role to evil, and it is this, perhaps, which makes its judgments so gloomy. Men do not like to feel themselves in danger. Yet, it is because there are real dangers, real failures and real earthly damnation that worlds like victory, wisdom, or joy have meaning. Nothing is decided in advance, and it is because man has something to lose and because he can lose that he can also win.[11]

The failure we perceive in Walter White is his failure to survive without sacrificing Gale. Instead, he is in a position of treating Gale as an obstacle whose existence threatens his ability to flourish, and in that we perceive that there is some kind of real failure. Only in the face of this real failure do we attempt to escape by resorting to universal principles, and only with respect to the universal principles does his situation constitute a failure. Were the world actually governed by ethical laws, then no such failures would exist.

CONCLUSION

We smile when Walt has his victories, and we empathize with Jesse when he has his defeats. Both these characters act in decidedly evil ways, and, at least for "the one who knocks," there is a self-identification with evil. But our empathizing with these characters does not entail that we are morally evil. We empathize with these anti-heroes, but we don't have to hang our heads in shame and neither do we have to go jump into a plastic tub filled with hydrofluoric acid in an attempt to pay for our moral transgressions. There is nothing morally wrong with empathizing with the bad guys.

We can empathize with Walt because he presents us with a phenomenal body, and this body communicates meaningful actions to us. Even though he is not a bodily thing like you and I, we can still recognize him as a subject of our empathetic acts, because he can act. While we regard most of his acts as morally reprehensible, we can still feel empathy for Walt, because his actions have meaning as actions that could be performed by a human like us.

NOTES

1. Roman Ingarden presents the claim that fictional entities enjoy an intentional sort of "life" in *The Literary Work of Art*, trans. George G. Grabowicz (Evanston, IL: Northwestern University Press, 1973). On reading a draft of *The Literary Work of Art*, Stein noted that Ingarden's section of the life of the work of art and all its represented objects was quite underdeveloped; Edith Stein, *Self-Portrait in Letters: Letters to Roman Ingarden*, trans. Hugh Candler Hunt, ed. Maria Amata Neyer (Washington, DC: ICS Publications, 2014), 299. Jeff Mitscherling elaborates extensively on the intentional life of the literary work of art in *Roman Ingarden's Ontology and Aesthetics* (Ottawa: University of Ottawa Press, 1997) and "Concretization, Literary Criticism, and the Life of the Literary Work of Art," in *Existence, Culture and Persons: the Ontology of Roman Ingarden*, ed. Arkadiusz Chrudzimski (New Brunswick: Ontos Verlag, 2005), 137-158. In what follows, we elucidate Stein's phenomenological account of the empathy to clarify the intentional mode of existence of fictional entities.

2. Edith Stein, *On the Problem of Empathy*, trans. Waltraut Stein (Washington: ICS, 1989), 5.

3. Roman Ingarden, *Ontology of the Work of Art: The Musical Work, the Picture, the Architectural Work, the Film*, trans. Raymond Meyer and John T. Goldthwait (Athens, OH: University of Ohio Press, 1989), 35–36. Though Ingarden's example addresses the musical work of art, the claim that works of art have no particular spatio-temporal location extends to all works of art.

4. Stein clarifies in *On the Problem of Empathy*, 7: "[t]hus empathy does not have the same character as outer perception, though it does have something in common with outer perception: In both cases the object itself is present here and now. We have come to recognize outer perception as an act given primordially. But though empathy is not outer perception, this is not to say that it does not have this 'primordiality'."

5. Ibid., 8.

6. Ibid., 10.

7. Maurice Merleau-Ponty, *Phenomenology of Perception* (New York: Routledge, 2005), 121.

8. Ibid., 87.

9. Mary Whiton Calkins, *The Good Man and the Good* (New York: MacMillan, 1918), 1.

10. Simone De Beauvoir, *The Ethics of Ambiguity* (New York: Citadel, 2000), 8–9.

11. Ibid., 34.

PART 2

"I Am the One Who Knocks": The Shadow of Death and the Meaning of Life

CHAPTER 4

In the Shadow of the Sickness Unto Death: Walter White's Transformation into the Knight of Meth

Frank Scalambrino

Death erases all distinctions...

—*Søren Kierkegaard, Works of Love*[1]

This chapter philosophically examines the transformation of "Walter White" into "Heisenberg," as depicted in *Breaking Bad*, in terms of Søren Kierkegaard's "stages of life" and Carl Jung's "process of individuation." Though Walt's transformation is an oft-discussed topic regarding *Breaking Bad*, there has yet to appear in the philosophical literature an examination of this transformation in terms of Kierkegaard and Jung. Such an examination is important since it also addresses a number of the questions regarding the shift in Walt's moral compass given his terminal prognosis. That is to say, Walt's transformation into Heisenberg in terms of Kierkegaard and Jung provides a moral account of his decisions without having to sacrifice a notion of his free will or forcing us to accepting the imminence of death as justification for the perpetration of evil.

It is, of course, not a requirement of "existentialism" that it be atheistic. In fact, Kierkegaard famously understood human experience at the level of the individual to be one of "constantly dying," despite "not being able to die" until the individual's existential relation to God is established.[2] This relation is of such importance that Kierkegaard used it to characterize an individual's existence in terms of all the possible "stages along life's way."[3] What is more, just as an individual's relation to God determines the individual's stage of life, so too the stage of life determines the meaning of the existential aspects of life, such

F. Scalambrino (✉)
Duquesne University, Pittsburgh, PA, USA

© The Author(s) 2017
K.S. Decker et al. (eds.), *Philosophy and Breaking Bad*,
DOI 10.1007/978-3-319-40343-4_4

as "love" and "death."[4] In other words, how an individual relates to their own existence and the existence of others may be understood as a development of the individual's relation to God.

Whereas Kierkegaard's examination of human existence provides a contextual understanding for an individual's psychological relations, Jung's in-depth examination of an individual's "process of individuation" highlights the more dynamic aspects of an individual's psychological development. So by using Jung's vocabulary, we come to understand Walt's transformation into Heisenberg stemming from his existential crisis of love and death. Walt's terminal prognosis of "inoperable lung cancer" presents him with a dilemma that reveals him as being either Kierkegaard's "Knight of Infinite Resignation" (KIR) or "Knight of Faith" (KOF). *Breaking Bad* depicts Walt as the Knight of Infinite Resignation; in this stage, Walt's relations with various villains account for the manifestation of his shadowy Persona "Heisenberg," at least in terms of Jung's psychodynamics.

Finally, we will look at Jung's adoption of the vocabulary of "philosophical alchemy," which allows us to tie the parallel depictions of chemistry and transformation in *Breaking Bad* together with Jung's notion of individuation and Kierkegaard's Knights. As we will see, the difference between the Knights in Kierkegaard is determined by whether the Knight attaches its identity to the changing world or to an unchanging God. It is as if Walt's (infinite) resignation expresses itself as an understanding of the world and his relations to others within it (e.g., "Crazy 8," "Tuco," "Gus" and "Saul") with an unstable identity. Thus, Walt's existential situation is a catalyst for his own change—combining and bonding in interesting ways with the various villains of *Breaking Bad*. In this way, this chapter not only offers an existential reading of *Breaking Bad* but also speaks of a number of philosophical issues including concerns about personal transformation, personal identity over time, Walt's morality and moral duties and the oft-discussed question of Walt's alter-egos, also known as "Heisenberg's Uncertainty."

FROM THE SICKNESS UNTO DEATH TO FINDING THE DRUG LORD IN THE DESERT

Kierkegaard famously characterized despair as the "sickness unto death." Clearly, Walter White is in despair, but how would Kierkegaard have understood this despair? According to Kierkegaard, there are three kinds of despair, and each of these corresponds with a stage along life's way. The three stages are the aesthetic, the ethical and the religious.[5] Because the aesthetic stage (associated with the perennial "libertine and seducer" Don Juan, depicted, for example, in Mozart's 1787 opera *Don Giovanni*) may be characterized in terms of a willingness toward self-destruction, Kierkegaard suggests this is not "despair in the strict sense." Thus, there are two forms of despair in the strict sense. The first coincides with the ethical stage, and an individual in this stage is known as the "Knight of Infinite Resignation" (KIR). The second coincides with the religious stage, and such an individual is known as the "Knight of Faith" (KOF).

Kierkegaard's explication of these two forms of despair provides his understanding of the "self." According to Kierkegaard,

> A human being is spirit. But what is spirit? Spirit is the self. But what is the self? The self is a relation that relates itself to itself or is the relation's relating itself to itself in the relation; the self is not the relation but is the relation's relating itself to itself. ... thus under the qualification of the psychical the relation between the psychical and the physical is a relation. If, however, the relation relates itself to itself, this relation is the positive third, and this is the self. [Lastly,] such a relation that relates itself to itself, a self, must either have established itself or have been established by another. (Kierkegaard, 1980: 13).

We want to be clear on three points from the above. First, Kierkegaard indicates two different answers regarding the identity of the self. On the one hand, the self is a relation that relates itself to itself. This will be the first strict form of despair and the KIR. On the other hand, the self may be the relation that relates itself to itself while in relation to an absolute unchanging dimension. Whereas both types of selves may relate to others, only the latter enters into a relation with a being that does not change, that is, God.[6]

Second, because Kierkegaard understands human being to be spiritual, the relation between the "soul" and the "body" is "under the qualification of the psychical." In other words, the body ultimately expresses the soul and the soul's activity; therefore, concern for the soul takes primacy over concern for the body. Though it is true that for Kierkegaard, "Death erases all distinctions...,"[7] the soul retains the quality (developed through embodied existence) of its relation to the absolute.[8] Third, then, to the extent that the relation does not relate to the absolute, then the self has either "established itself" or allowed itself to be "established by another."

What does this mean for Walt? With the terminal prognosis functioning as a kind of catalyst, it is as if Walt's relations to the world and others become volatile, that is, de-stabilized. This crisis manifests as despair for Walt; however, he will ultimately need to choose which kind of despair it will be. Because he determines *the meaning* of his existential crisis in non-absolute terms, his self must be established by the "either/or" of itself or another. This is not the "lowest" third form of despair because he is not in despair that he has a self. Rather, he is "in despair not to will to be oneself." In other words, Walt's self may be characterized from a non-absolute perspective as a mild-mannered high school chemistry teacher and "family man." Walt's decision to understand his existential situation in terms of the effect his death will have on his family ultimately constitutes his position as the KIR. That is, Walt resigns himself infinitely to tasks for, and duties to, others that have been established by his roles as a chemistry teacher and family man.

What would it look like for Walt to be characterized from the absolute perspective? This would entail his thinking of himself in terms of his relation to God, thereby accepting the primacy of that relation over worldly embodied concerns. This is, of course, easier said than done. Had Walt understood love and death absolutely in terms of harmonizing his will with the absolute, that is God willing his death, he would have taken the position of the KOF and could have understood his death as an act of absolute love. That is to say, in the *religious* stage the self is established in absolute terms by its relation to God, but in the *ethical* stage the self is established in relative terms in relation to worldly beings. In the *aesthetic* stage the self is characterized nihilistically in terms of its resistance or reluctance to be characterized at all, that is, it is neither the KIR nor the KOF.

The ambiguity, and perhaps even the ambivalence, of the aesthetic allows for it to be understood as a resistance to both the KIR and the KOF. But if the aesthetic is characterized in terms of "de-stabilization," then it would be appropriate to characterize it as the "shadow" of the KIR, not of the KOF. This is important not only because the KOF may also be understood as a de-stabilization of the KIR, but rather because in echoing the aesthetic as the "lowest" type of despair (non-strictly construed), it allows us to recognize the KIR as the "shadow" of the KOF. Thus, as the KIR, Walt resigns himself to a position in the shadow of the KOF, and in this shadow, Walt decides to cook methamphetamine.

According to Kierkegaard, had Walt occupied the aesthetic stage, he would have spent the remainder of his time merely pleasing himself without excessive concern for the well-being of others. Had he occupied the religious stage he may have understood his situation in terms of the "idea so frequently stressed in Holy Scripture for the purpose of elevating the lowly and humbling the mighty, the idea that God does not respect the status of persons." [9] Yet, in the religious stage, Walt could not have justified the emergence of Heisenberg and his actions in relation to the worldly concerns of his family, since, "only when the single individual fights for himself with himself within himself and does not unseasonably presume to help the whole world to obtain external equality, which is of very little benefit," [10] for example, reading "external equality" here as referring to the desire to make his family materially equal to some social status. In other words, as the KIR, Walt could not have justified the emergence of Heisenberg and his actions in *relation* to the worldly concerns of his family. Thus, rather than appropriately directing his love to God, Walt becomes "melancholically enamored" as Heisenberg and "pursues one of anxiety's possibilities, which finally leads him away from himself." [11] We will re-visit this theme after approaching Walt's transformation in terms of Jung's psychodynamics and philosophical alchemy.

Hence, from the perspective of Kierkegaard's stages, it is as if Walt assumes the KIR position by understanding his self, his death and his love for his family in relative and worldly terms. According to Kierkegaard, the "infinite" aspect of this relation, though ultimately still in regard to the relativity of the world, makes the individual aware of the possibility of an absolute relation. It is as if the KIR is the "shadow" of the KOF's relation to the absolute, and so in full light of the absolute, the resulting ego-stabilization would even allow our protagonist to see "Walt" as merely a relative worldly characterization of himself.

ADAPTING IN THE SHADOW OF UNCERTAINTY

To explicate the transformation of Walter White into Heisenberg in terms of Jungian psychodynamics, we need to consider several of Jung's terms: "adaptation," "individuation," "ego," "Persona," "Shadow" and "Self." The last three terms are capitalized to illustrate their technical use as "archetypes." Jung believed that "Before [individuation] can be taken as a goal, the educational aim of adaptation to the necessary minimum of collective norms must first be attained."[12] Though Jung understood adaptation to be continuous, "The constant flow of life again and again demands fresh adaptation. Adaptation is never achieved once and for all"[13]; once a sufficient amount of adaptation occurs, an individual is able to individuate itself in relation to social norms in authentic ways. Thus, individuation "is the process by which individual beings are formed and differentiated; in particular, it is the development of the psychological individual as a being distinct from the general, collective psychology."[14] Further, it has two principle aspects: "an internal and subjective process of integration, and in the second it is an equally indispensable process of objective relationship."[15] In other words, individuation involves an individual's relating internally to itself and externally to others.

According to Jung, "The ego, the subject of consciousness ... is constituted partly by the inherited disposition (character constituents) and partly by unconsciously acquired impressions and their attendant phenomena."[16] The ego manifests through adaptation in a kind of "constellation" of both conscious and unconscious aspects of an individual. The Persona, Shadow, and Self may be understood, then, in regard to this "constellation." Jung held that

> ... the Persona is a complicated system of relations between individual consciousness and society ... a kind of mask, designed on the one hand to make a definite impression upon others, and, on the other, to conceal the true nature of the individual.[17]

Thus, the Persona participates in the constellation, sustaining a person's ego and functions by concealing the aspects of adaptation deemed necessary to conceal. The process of individuation, then, refers to the individual's re-conciliation with his concealed aspects, integrating them into the constellation in a more harmonious way than was possible through initial adaptation. Further, "though [the Persona] is not pathological in nature, if an individual identifies too much with the Persona, then their relation to the world and others may become severely unbalanced and pathological."[18]

Jung characterizes the initial concealment in the process of adaptation in terms of the Shadow archetype. In this way, "the shadow is cast by the conscious mind and is as much a privation of light as the physical shadow that follows the body."[19] Consistent with Kierkegaard and the Western philosophical tradition's use of the figurative phrase "privation of light," Jung noted, "the psychological shadow with its moral inferiority might also be regarded as a privation of good."[20] The Shadow "proves to be a darkness that hides influential ... autonomous [and unconscious] factors."[21] Initially, the externally relating Persona conceals the "inner personality," which is "the way one behaves in relation to one's inner psychic processes," that is, an "attitude ... toward the unconscious."[22] As a "characteristic face," this attitude also participates in the constellation sustaining a person's ego. Hence, whereas "Walter White" faced outward to society, it was as if his inner-facing attitude toward the unconscious were latently, that is, chaotically and clandestinely, characterized by "Heisenberg" and, thereby, participated in the Shadow portion of Walt's constellation.

Finally, Jung characterized the goal of the process of individuation in terms of "integration" and "harmony," and, sounding like Kierkegaard, characterized the culmination of an individual's integrating and harmonizing conscious and unconscious aspects of its psychology in terms of teleology. Thus, "The aim of individuation" is "nothing less than to divest the Self of the false wrappings of the Persona on the one hand, and of the suggestive power of primordial [unconscious processes] on the other."[23] Harmony of the Self requires an individual's more developed relation to its Persona, since "when the ego is not differentiated from the Persona, it can have no conscious relation to the unconscious processes..."[24] Understanding the integrated harmonized constellation as participating in the wholeness of the Self archetype and from the perspective of such wholeness, Jung used the term "entelechy" to suggest that the process of individuation may be understood as a natural teleological process of human psychological development. Jung "called this consciousness-transcending wholeness 'Self.' *The purpose of the individuation process is the synthesis of the Self* [emphasis added]. From another point of view the term 'entelechy' might be preferable to 'synthesis'."[25] Further,

> ... why "entelechy" is, in certain conditions, more fitting: the symbols of wholeness frequently occur at the beginning of the individuation process ... This observation says much for the *a priori* existence of potential wholeness, and on this account the idea of entelechy instantly recommends itself. But insofar as the individuation process occurs, empirically speaking, as a synthesis, it looks, paradoxically enough, as if something already existent were being put together.[26]

Hence, characterized as a kind of natural teleology, Jung's process of individuation isomorphically relates to Kierkegaard's stages along life's way. That is to say, achieving psychological harmony coincides with the KOF.

The culmination of the stages along life's way in the KOF constitutes a kind of "salvation" for Kierkegaard; because of this, we may refer to the soteriological aspect, in addition then to the teleological aspect of individuation. Further, since Jung's way of discussing this may be surprising, we quote him at length:

> When a summit of life is reached, when the bud unfolds from the lesser the greater emerges, then, as Nietzsche says, "One becomes Two," and the greater figure, which one always was but which remained invisible, appears to the lesser personality with the force of a revelation. He who is truly and hopelessly little will always drag the revelation of the greater down to the level of his littleness, and will never understand that the day of judgment for his littleness has dawned. But the man who is inwardly great will know that the long expected friend of his soul, the immortal one, has now really come, "to lead captivity captive"; that is, to seize hold of him by whom this immortal had always been confined and held prisoner, and to make his life flow into the greater life – a moment of deadliest peril! ... Christ himself is the perfect symbol of the hidden immortal within the mortal man.[27]

On the one hand, Jung stresses the themes of risk, death and liberation. He emphasizes a view of adaptation in which movement to integration, wholeness and harmony liberates the "immortal" into awareness. On the other hand, Jung sounds strikingly like Kierkegaard when he characterizes participation in the "Christ archetype" as the soteriological goal and teleological culmination of the process of individuation: the "Christ-image concentrates upon itself the characteristics of an archetype – *the archetype of the Self* [emphasis added]."[28]

THE MYSTERIOUS CONJUNCTION OF LOVE AND DEATH

Before employing these ideas to Walt's case, two points should be clarified. First, though it may seem most appropriate to characterize Kierkegaard as avowedly Christian and Jung as avowedly pagan, we may clarify their relationship by look at the archetype of Christ from a pagan perspective. Along such lines, the ancient Greek "love gods," relate to the ancient Greek words for love: *Eros, Philia,* and *Agápē,* and these gods, namely, "Dionysus," "Orpheus" and "Christ," are also all gods of "voluntary death."[29] Thus, as if describing the KOF, Jung noted, "In the light of eternity ... [death] is a wedding, a *mysterium coniunctionis.* The soul attains, as it were, its missing half, it achieves wholeness. On Greek sarcophagi the joyous element was represented by dancing girls ..."[30] The separation of Persona from the ego-complex and the subsequent integration of the Shadow allow for the adapted "one" to emerge into awareness as "two," that is, as conscious and unconscious aspects. Finally, the mysterious and harmonious conjunction of these two constitutes a kind of "dying to the world," what Kierkegaard might have referred to as being reborn into the life of Christ. In fact, in a chapter titled, "The Soul and Death," Jung refers to a "withdraw from the life-process, at least psychologically," and explained we should accept *the necessity* of our own death, noting that "only he remains vitally alive who is ready to *die with life*."[31] Recalling a phrase from Heraclitus, it is as if the *mysterium coniunctionis* refers to the soul's conjunction with life as it continues to live through the death of this one of its individual incarnated expressions.[32]

Of course, Walt did not approach his death this way. His focus was on the world and the worldly consequences of his dying without leaving a legacy for his family. Rather than see his death in terms of the *mysterium coniunctionis* of Jungian psychodynamics or the Kierkegaardian KOF, he seems incapable of separating his Persona from his ego-complex. As we will discuss below, from the very beginning of *Breaking Bad*, Walt's ego appears threatened as his Persona of chemistry teacher and family man is scrutinized and ridiculed. Had Walt brought his individuality to consciousness, Jung suggests that he would have integrated his Shadow, rather than continued to struggle with the uncertainty of his Persona's inferiority and its reflection upon his undifferentiated ego. According to Jung,

> The psychic individuality is given *a priori* as a correlate of the physical individuality, although, as observed, it is at first unconscious. A conscious process of differentiation, or individuation, is needed to bring the individuality to consciousness … If the individuality is unconscious, there is no psychological individual but merely a collective psychology of consciousness.[33]

In this way, the harmony of the Self coincides with a conscious awareness of oneself as individuated and differentiated from one's Persona and, just as importantly, from the Shadow it casts on one's ego-complex. Regarding this, Jung was quite clear,

> Individuation cuts one off from personal conformity and hence from collectivity. That is the guilt which the individual leaves behind him for the world, that is, the guilt he must endeavor to redeem. He must offer a ransom in place of himself, that is, he must bring forth values which are an equivalent substitute for his absence in the collective personal sphere. Without this production of values, final individuation is immoral and – more than that – suicidal. The man who cannot create values should sacrifice himself consciously to the spirit of collective conformity.[34]

On the one hand, Walt's personal conformity reveals he has not "brought forth values" that would individuate him from a KIR relation to existence or allow his personal individuation from societal conformity. On the other hand, since his ego-complex is guided more by the Persona than the Self, his ego must struggle unconsciously with his Shadow, and—this is the decisive moment—in relating to himself within the KIR relation to existence, Heisenberg emerges by overshadowing the Walt Persona. In other words, it is as if the Heisenberg Persona represents the non-individuated, and thereby non-integrated, Shadow guiding the ego-complex.

Toward the Alchemy of *Breaking Bad*

Alchemy tends to be depicted as either a forerunner of chemistry or as a practice of spiritual purification. Whereas the former refers to the infamous practice of transforming lead to gold, the latter refers to the transformation of the individual practicing the art.[35] Jung famously invoked these thoughts of the medieval alchemists about psychological transformation as similar to his own.[36] In this way, the alchemical quest for "gold" or the "philosopher's stone" becomes a quest to transform oneself into a higher, more purified form of being.[37] Though Jungians today tend to characterize the understanding of alchemy in terms of spiritual or individual transformation as "philosophical alchemy," the language of chemistry and its transformation of base elements are retained in figurative form. This, of course, coincides well with the language of chemistry in *Breaking Bad*, such that these discussions, whether in Walt's High School classroom or in the meth lab, could figuratively refer to the transformation of Walt into Heisenberg. Thus, these three interpretative elements—Kierkegaard, Jung and philosophical alchemy—provide a philosophical account of Walt's transformation.

Intriguingly, the pilot episode of *Breaking Bad* reads as if it were written for the very purpose of establishing the base and trajectory of the main character Walt according to this kind of account. For example, in the initial classroom scene, Walt enthusiastically notes:

> Chemistry is the study of ... change ... Now, just think about this ... they change their energy levels... change their bonds... Elements, they combine and change into compounds. Well, that's all of life, right? ... It's the cycle. It's solution, dissolution. Over and over and over, it is growth, then decay, then transformation! ("Pilot").

As the episode progresses, the next several scenes all reinforce the theme that Walt is neither respected nor admired in his Persona as High School chemistry teacher and family man. This lack of respect manifests for him through those who point out he doesn't have enough money and those who ritually demean him in front of his friends and family. Of course, this is underscored by the fact that Walt did not receive the rewards due from his contributions to Nobel Prize winning work. Walt then receives his diagnosis of inoperable lung cancer and decides to break bad.

When Jesse Pinkman sees the purity of Walt's methamphetamine for the first time, he notes, "This ain't chemistry. It's art!" ("Pilot"). Twice we hear in the first episode that Walt's "heart" is "in the right place," and in terms of philosophical alchemy "the heart" is that which survives dismemberment.[38] Thus, Walt seems primed to become the KOF as his prognosis tears his relation to the future apart. "Best case scenario, with chemo, I'll live a couple more years...," Walt numbly parrots back to his doctor ("Pilot"). Instead, Walt transforms into Heisenberg. The transformation is signaled in the first episode when we see him standing in the desert, believing the sirens he hears signify his imminent arrest, Walt attempts suicide. He pulls the trigger, but, the gun's safety is on, and it does not fire. Finally, Walt returns home from the desert already swelling with what will be his transformation into Heisenberg, and with an ego already inflated with more shadowy primal unconscious winds he presents himself to his wife Skylar. The episode ends with her asking, "Walt, is that you?"

In his Jungian book *Anatomy of the Psyche: Alchemical Symbolism in Psychotherapy*, Edward Edinger provides the following vocabulary with which to organize the process of spiritual, or philosophical, alchemy: *calcinatio, solutio, coagulatio, sublimatio, mortificatio, separatio* and *coniunctio*. For Edinger, each of these operations involves a system of symbols, and these "central symbols of transformation ... provide basic categories by which to understand the life of the psyche, and they illustrate almost the full range of experiences that constitute individuation."[39] Notice, the last two "stages" refer to separation and then conjunction. Of course, conjunction echoes Jung's *mysterium coniunctionis* from the previous section and Kierkegaard's KOF. However, here we will meditate on separation. This separation is necessary for the perfection and completion of the purification and of the appropriate transformation; however, it is also associated with "blackness," "loneliness" and "despair."

Ultimately, we must all face death alone. No matter who is there with you, no matter who may be holding your hand, when it is your time to die, no one can encounter your death for you.[40] This separation, the way in which being-toward-death isolates an individual psychologically, reveals the horizon of what the alchemists called the "black sun," a symbol associated with despair.[41] Yet, because death must be faced alone, it is also possible to think of the alchemical stages as trials on a quest to find the spiritual gold of the mysterious conjunction with a higher spiritual being. Thus, "Mediaeval tales and legends often refer ... most frequently of all to a black knight."[42] Further regarding the significance of colors in alchemy, recall how the infamous blue meth leads to both money and Heisenberg, so that "it can be said that the descending scale would be from blue to green... These two colors stand for the celestial, and the natural or terrestrial factors. Furthermore, black is associated with sin, penitence, the withdrawal of the recluse, the hidden..."[43] It is as if the elements of Walt's psychological constellation have "changed their energy levels" and "changed their bonds," and, yet, alchemically speaking and as emphasized by the clear association of the color black with Heisenberg, Walt's transformation to Heisenberg forestalls the purification and completion of Jung's *mysterium coniunctionis* or the absolute relation of Kierkegaard's KOF.

In fact, Kierkegaard's discussion of the Knight of Infinite Resignation and the Knight of Faith also emphasizes the connection with isolation, despair and darkness. According to Kierkegaard,

> It is possible to become lost in possibility in all sorts of ways, but primarily in two. The one takes the form of desiring, craving; the other takes the form of the melancholy-imaginary (hope/fear or anxiety). Legends and fairy tales tell of

the knight who suddenly sees a rare bird and chases after it ... and when *night* comes, *he finds himself separated* from his companions *and lost* in the wilderness... Instead of taking the possibility back into necessity, he chases after possibility – and at last cannot find his way back to himself [emphases added].[44]

Kierkegaard's second way of "becoming lost" entails an individual being "melancholically enamored," who, therefore, "pursues one of anxiety's possibilities..." (Ibid.). In Walt's case, his diagnosis represents his finding himself separated. Just as the bewilderment of being lost is associated with this stage alchemically, Walt becomes "melancholically enamored" with his ego's new darkened vision. Seeing himself in the darkness of his own Shadow, he transforms into Heisenberg. For Kierkegaard, Jung and in the terminology of philosophical alchemy, had Walt taken "the possibility [of Heisenberg] back into necessity," that is, the necessity of his own finality as a mortal being, he could have turned to the golden light in the darkness and completed the mysterious conjunction with what the KOF understands as a higher "celestial" dimension of being.

FROM LOVE IN DESPAIR TO THE LOVE OF DESPAIR: HEISENBERG AND THE DANGER *PARTICIPATION MYSTIQUE*

Fans of *Breaking Bad* have astutely pointed out that Walt's transformation into Heisenberg seems to be aided by his taking on aspects of the identities of the nefarious drug lords he bests, like Tuco and Gus Fring. From the perspectives of Kierkegaard, Jung and philosophical alchemy, this insightful fan-observation is philosophically fruitful. The follow-up episode to the pilot, "The Cat's in the Bag...," provides us with content from one of Walt's lectures for context.

Describing the concept of "chirality," Walt notes, "So too, organic compounds can exist as mirror images of one another." He clarifies what he means by "mirror image," explaining,

> Just as your right and your left hand... are identical, yet opposite; well, so too organic compounds can exist as mirror image forms of one another all the way down at the molecular level. But, although they may look the same, they don't always behave the same.[45]

Philosophers familiar with Plato or Derrida may recognize the relevance of his clarification to the ancient Greek term *pharmakon*.[46] Just as *pharmakon* can mean either "medicine" or "poison," and without context may be left undecidable which is the true meaning, so too the true meaning of Heisenberg's emergence seems uncertain. The concrete example from Walt's lecture is "thalidomide," which he describes, in terms of chirality, as, on the one hand, a medicine and, on the other hand, a poison. The scene concludes with Walt mishearing a student's use of the word "midterm" as "murder," illustrating the chirality of Walter White and Heisenberg. Memorably, in this same episode, Walt declares, "I haven't quite been myself lately" ("The Cat's in the Bag...").

In the next episode, "...And the Bag's in the River," Walt deliberates on whether to kill Krazy-8 or not. He creates two columns, and in the "Let him live" column, we find: "Moral thing to do," "Judeo-Christian Principles," "You are *not* a murderer," "He may listen to reason," "post-traumatic stress," "Won't be able to live with yourself," "Murder is wrong!" In the "Kill him" column, we find: "He'll kill your entire family if you let him go..." Of course, Walt kills Krazy-8, and so we see the beginning of a pattern. That is, if we think of Walt and Heisenberg in a chiral relation to one another, with Walt initially participating as his Persona and the emergence of Heisenberg as the elements unconsciously participating in the Shadow archetype, then it is as if "Walt's" ego-constellation, that is, the non-individuated elements participating in the Self archetype, defends itself by turning to the Shadow, as opposed to turning to an absolute dimension through the Self. In other words, the transformation of the *Breaking Bad* protagonist moves along an ego-defensive spectrum, which may be characterized in terms of the exchange of dominant Persona, from Walter White to Heisenberg, but also in terms of the psychological elements "changing their bonds," "combining" and "changing into compounds"; the defensive spectrum thus crosses the chiral threshold and becomes an offensive spectrum.

The concept of chirality is also at work in the scene in which Walt first uses the name Heisenberg ("Crazy Handful of Nothing"). Just after shaving his head, and hearing his son note in response "Bad ass dad," Walt goes to visit Tuco. When Tuco asks him for his name, Walt announces "Heisenberg." In the context of chirality, this is a quite interesting and complicated scene. Playing on the "uncertainty" associated with both chirality and Heisenberg's famous principle, we may extract four insights here. First, when Tuco refers to the chemical compounds Walt brought to the meeting as "meth," Heisenberg corrects him, ultimately noting that, though it "looks just like" meth, it's actually "fulminated mercury," a highly volatile and explosive substance. Second, the individual speaking "looks just like" Walt, though behaving in a way quite unlike Walt. Third, though Tuco looks very different from Walt, his out-of-control behavior "looks just like" some of the behaviors exhibited by Heisenberg later in the series. For example, the "I am the danger!" and "Say my name" scenes come to mind. Finally, we can envision the relation between Heisenberg and Tuco in terms of Jung's Shadow and chirality. It is as if just by being in the presence of Tuco chirally, so to speak, Walt's ego-constellation is enlivened by Tuco to become the drug-dealing "Bad ass" previously unconscious and participating in the Shadow of Walt. In this way, the Jungian psychodynamics resonates with the (al)chemical metaphors to account for the manner in which Walt, as Heisenberg, seems to "take on" the characteristics of the shadowy drug lord characters with whom he interacts. Jung's technical term to describe circumstances when one individual may "take on" the characteristics of a different individual is participation mystique.

Jung characterized the individuation process in terms of participation mystique and "projection." Basically, the ego de-stabilized by the mobilizing animation of adaptation and individuation must re-stabilize itself in relation to the person's internal dynamics and the external environment. As just noted in terms of chirality, Walt enters into the participation mystique of the dangerous world of methamphetamine manufacturing and distribution. According to Jung, participation mystique

> connotes a peculiar kind of psychological connection with the object wherein the subject is unable to differentiate himself clearly from the object to which he is bound ... Among civilized peoples it usually happens between persons ... it is a so-called state of transference, in which the object obtains a sort of magical, i.e. unconditional, influence over the subject.[47]

By the end of the series we hear statements, characteristic of Heisenberg, such as, "Everyone has a death sentence" and "I am the one who knocks." These claims reveal his ego-identification with the aspects of the various drug lords he has killed. It is as if nefarious characters like Krazy-8, Tuco and Gus provided ideals for the elements of Walt's psychological make-up for the sake of emerging as a coherent Persona. Hence, Heisenberg could emerge from the Shadow through a kind of participation mystique with such offensive characters.

It is worth noting that in Kierkegaard's terms, the defensive spectrum may be thought of as a movement from *love in despair* to the *love of despair*. Recall Kierkegaard's reference to the idea that despair can be rooted in an individual's being "melancholically enamored." What began as a KIR's pursuit of "one of anxiety's possibilities" related to the non-absolute dimension of Walt's family's worldly concerns, chirally turns into pursuit of "one of anxiety's possibilities" related to the non-absolute dimension of Heisenberg's drug-world kingpin concerns.

CONCLUSION

The two key existential determinants for Walter White are death and love. The five seasons of *Breaking Bad* essentially show his progression from prognosis of terminal cancer to violent unnatural death. However, this progression seems like it is also driven by love, initially love of family and later the love of something darker. When Walt takes matters into his own hands, and with each subsequent destructive situation he cooks up, he is further eclipsed by Heisenberg. The *Breaking Bad* protagonist chooses to understand his existential crisis in what Kierkegaard described as the relative dimension of worldly concerns. For Kierkegaard,

It holds for everyone that when he comes to death's door ... he must discard all pomp and glory and wealth and worldly esteem and starred medals and emblems of honor – whether bestowed on him by kings and emperors or by the crowd and the public – discard them as totally irrelevant and superfluous.[48]

However, Walt's motivation to cook methamphetamine reveals his deep concern to leave a legacy for his family. So, at first look we may think that the above statement from Kierkegaard may not apply to Walt since he ultimately is concerned with the security of those who will remain living after he dies.

Yet, understood through Kierkegaard's stages of life, the realization that death erases all distinctions is supposed to prompt us to consider an absolute dimension to which we may relate ourselves. Such a relation stabilizes an individual so they are truly able to die. That is to say, whether understood in Kierkegaard's Christian-influenced manner or a more ancient pagan manner inspiring Jung, an individual may realize the meaning of their existence as if it were the expression of a universal immortal life by discovering a relation to that which does not change. By doing so, the individual may experience their death as the destruction of merely the individual mortal-expression of immortal life.

In terms of Jungian psychodynamics and philosophical alchemy, we saw how the process of individuation through which individuals develop initially involves adaptation, that adaptations may involve participation mystique and that a level of psychological harmony and integration is reached when an individual is able to live as the individual mortal-expression of immortal life. Jung characterized this in terms of the *mysterium coniunctionis* indicating harmonious participation in the Self archetype. This coincides with the pursuit of spiritual purification associated with medieval alchemists. Through Kierkegaard, Jung and philosophical alchemy, we provided a reading of the transformation of Walter White into Heisenberg.

The distinction between the KIR and KOF stages of life in Kierkegaard helped us locate the concerns for relative and absolute dimensions of existence, respectively. So too Jung's vocabulary in his psychodynamic account of individual development helped us to understand the psychological activity taking place in the non-individuated shadow of the KIR, as a shadow of the KOF. Interestingly, this coincided with various key discussions of chemistry taking place in *Breaking Bad* as foreshadowing for Walt's transformation into Heisenberg. These discussions were, in turn, related to traditional themes in philosophical alchemy, so that by touching on the theme of "knights" we were able to combine all of these integral elements into a harmonious constellation, as it were, philosophically characterizing the transformation that constituted the emergence of Heisenberg in *Breaking Bad*.

NOTES

1. Søren Kierkegaard, *Works of Love*, trans. H. V. Hong and E. H. Hong (New York: Harper & Brothers, 1962), 74.
2. See Søren Kierkegaard, *The Sickness Unto Death*, trans. H. V. Hong and E. H. Hong (Princeton: Princeton University Press, 1980); *The Point of View*, trans. H. V. Hong and E. H. Hong (Princeton: Princeton University Press, 1998); *"The Moment" and Late Writings*, trans. H. V. Hong and E. H. Hong (Princeton: Princeton University Press, 2009).
3. Søren Kierkegaard. *Stages on Life's Way*, trans. H. V. Hong and E. H. Hong (Princeton: Princeton University Press, 1988).
4. Søren Kierkegaard. *The Concept of Anxiety*, trans. H. V. Hong and E. H. Hong (Princeton: Princeton University Press, 1981); *Fear & Trembling and*

Repetition, trans. H. V. Hong and E. H. Hong (Princeton: Princeton University Press, 1983); *Eighteen Upbuilding Discourses*, trans. H. V. Hong and E. H. Hong (Princeton: Princeton University Press, 1992).

5. Kierkegaard, *Fear & Trembling and Repetition; Either/Or, Vol. I,; Stages on Life's Way.*

6. Paul Martens and Tom Millay, "'The Changelessness of God'" as Kierkegaard's Final Theodicy: God and the Gift of Suffering," *International Journal of Systematic Theology* 13, no. 2 (2011): 170–189.

7. Kierkegaard, *Works of Love*, 74.

8. Frank Scalambrino. "The Temporality of Damnation," in *The Concept of Hell*, ed. Benjamin W. McCraw and Robert Arp (New York: Palgrave, 2015), 66–82.

9. Søren Kierkegaard. *Upbuilding Discourses in Various Spirits*, trans. H. V. Hong and E. H. Hong (Princeton: Princeton University Press, 1992), 143.

10. Ibid.; also *Fear & Trembling and Repetition; Either/Or, Vol. I.*

11. Kierkegaard. *The Sickness Unto Death*, 37; also *The Concept of Anxiety.*

12. C. G. Jung. *Psychological Types*, trans. R. F. C. Hull, in *The Collected Works of C.G. Jung*, vol. 6, ed. H. Read et al. (Princeton: Princeton University Press, 1971), 449.

13. C. G. Jung. *Structure & Dynamics of the Psyche*, trans. R. F. C. Hull, in *The Collected Works of C.G. Jung*, vol. 8, ed. H. Read et al. (Princeton: Princeton University Press, 1970), 73.

14. Jung. *Psychological Types*, 448.

15. C. G. Jung. *Practice of Psychotherapy*, trans. R. F. C. Hull, in *The Collected Works of C.G. Jung*, vol. 16, ed. H. Read et al. (Princeton: Princeton University Press, 1985), 234.

16. C. G. Jung. *Development of Personality*, trans. R. F. C. Hull, in *The Collected Works of C.G. Jung*, vol. 6, ed. H. Read et al. (Princeton: Princeton University Press, 1971), 91.

17. C. G. Jung. *Two Essays on Analytical Psychology*, trans. R. F. C. Hull, in *The Collected Works of C.G. Jung*, vol. 7, ed. H. Read et al. (Princeton: Princeton University Press, 1967), 192.

18. Frank Scalambrino. *Meditations on Orpheus: Love, Death, and Transformation*, 31; cf. Frank Scalambrino. "The Vanishing Subject: Becoming Who You Cybernetically Are."

19. C. G. Jung. *Aion: Researches into the Phenomenology of the Self*, trans. R. F. C. Hull, in *The Collected Works of C.G. Jung*, vol. 6, ed. H. Read et al. (Princeton: Princeton University Press, 1969), 266.

20. Ibid.

21. Ibid.

22. Jung. *Psychological Types*, 467.

23. Jung. *Two Essays on Analytical Psychology*, 174.

24. Jung. *Psychological Types*, 470.

25. C. G. Jung. *Archetypes and the Collective Unconscious*, 115.

26. Ibid., 116.

27. Ibid., 121; cf. Jung. *Aion*, 69.

28. Ibid., 68.

29. Scalambrino. *Meditations on Orpheus*, 247; cf. R. Gordon Wasson, Albert Hofmann, and Carl A. P. Ruck. *The Road to Eleusis: Unveiling the Secret of the*

Mysteries; cf. Günther Zuntz. *Persephone: Three Essays on Religion and Thought in Magna Graecia.*

30. C. G. Jung. *Freud & Psychoanalysis*, 314.

31. Jung. *Structure & Dynamics of the Psyche*, 407.

32. cf. Scalambrino. *Meditations on Orpheus*, 181–3; cf. Scalambrino. *Full Throttle Heart: Nietzsche, Beyond Either/Or*; cf. Karen-Claire Voss. "The Hierosgamos Theme in the Images of the *Rosarium Philosophorum.*"

33. Jung, *Psychological Types*, 448; cf. Kierkegaard, *The Sickness Unto Death*, 13).

34. C. G. Jung. *The Symbolic Life: Miscellaneous Writings*, 450.

35. cf. Lyndy Abraham. *A Dictionary of Alchemical Imagery*; Stanton J. Linden. *The Alchemy Reader: From Hermes Trismegistus to Isaac Newton.*

36. cf. C. G. Jung. *Symbols of Transformation*; C. G. Jung. *Alchemical Studies*; C. G. Jung. *Psychology and Alchemy*; James Hillman. "Alchemical Blue and the *Unio Mentalis.*"; James Hillman *Alchemical Psychology.*

37. cf. Scalambrino. *Meditations on Orpheus*; Allison Courdet. *Alchemy: The Philosopher's Stone.*

38. Carl Kerényi. *Dionysos: Archetypal Image of Indestructible Life*; cf. George E. Mylonas. *Eleusis and the Eleusinian Mysteries*; Scalambrino, *Full Throttle Heart.*

39. Edward F. Edinger. *Anatomy of the Psyche: Alchemical Symbolism in Psychotherapy*, 15.

40. cf. Jung, *Structure and Dynamics of the Psyche*, 404–415.

41. cf. Marie-Louise von Franz. *Alchemy: An Introduction to the Symbolism and the Psychology*; Stanton Marlan. *The Black Sun.: The Alchemy and Art of Darkness.*

42. J.E. Cirlot, *A Dictionary of Symbols*, 170.

43. Ibid., 171.

44. Kierkegaard, *The Sickness Unto Death*, 37

45. Ibid.

46. cf. Plato. *Phaedo*; Jacques Derrida. "Plato's Pharmacy."

47. Jung. *Psychological Types*, 572–573.

48. Kierkegaard. *The Point of View*, 68.

CHAPTER 5

Death Is Easy If You're Dead

Christopher Ketcham

There have been many philosophical inquiries into the issue of death. No less than the Buddha, Plato, Aristotle, Epicurus, Saint Augustine, Marcus Aurelius, Thomas Hobbes, Immanuel Kant, George W.F. Hegel, Soren Kierkegaard, Martin Heidegger, Emmanuel Levinas, George Luis Borges and many other philosophers, authors and theologians have commented on the subject of death.[1] Many questions have been asked, including: why is death bad?[2]; is death evil?[3]; is life absurd because there is death?[4]; is life but a game?[5]; what has death to do with the meaning of life?[6]

I will contend with Martin Heidegger that since we cannot experience our own death, the existential mode of the meaning and experience of death is unavailable to us. Rather than try to extrapolate what death means, this chapter will consider issues associated with the phenomenology of existence through the experiences of Walter White who, in *Breaking Bad*, has been given a near-certain date of death in the very first episode. In other words, I will be pursuing answers to the question, "What does existence mean to one man who knows that his death is near?"

Martin Heidegger took from his mentor Edmund Husserl that experience occurs in the world. Phenomenology therefore is limited to experience of being in the world. Phenomenology is on the surface straightforward—as observation, free of preconceived ideas, and free from the "natural attitude" (that our ego is separate from the world) which pervades our everyday view of the world. The science of phenomenology seeks to bracket and set aside that which we preconceive (the natural attitude) to look at what we *actually* see for further analysis and consideration. In other words we [bracket] any theory or meaning attributed to our previous experience of or observation of the object

C. Ketcham (✉)
University of Houston Downtown, Houston, TX, USA

© The Author(s) 2017
K.S. Decker et al. (eds.), *Philosophy and Breaking Bad*,
DOI 10.1007/978-3-319-40343-4_5

and set it aside until we observe the intentional object before us without pre-conception. The idea of mindfulness comes to mind in the phenomenological method Husserl posits, because it requires us to be in the moment with the intentional object and not elsewhere. I will attempt to show Walter White from the moment we see of his experience in the episodes of *Breaking Bad*.

Todd May suggests four important lines of inquiry to pursue this chapter's question, "What does existence mean to one man who knows that his death is near?" In his book, *Death*, May first explains that death is the end of us and of our experience, and second, there is no goal called death—only an ending, a full stop. Third, death comes to everyone, but we do not know when it will come with any certitude. Given these three, May derives a fourth: what meaning could we reasonably ascribe to our lives when death is the cessation of meaning as we understand it?[7] May builds upon thinkers such as Martin Heidegger, who said that *Dasein* (the human way of being) is *being toward death*.[8] *Dasein* is the one being that understands its own mortality, and this affects its way of being in the world. In between birth and death, we are thrown into the world; we are beings in the world alongside and with others, finding affordances and constraints around us.

Ultimately, *Dasein* is no more; it ceases. It is more correct for Heidegger to say that *Dasein* does not die, *per se*, because *Dasein* cannot experience its own death. Death could never be a condition of *Dasein*; could what follows death be *Dasein*? No, because the condition that follows the event of *Dasein* ceasing to be is without experience; therefore, it is not *Dasein*, because *Dasein* is a being that experiences.

Following May and Heidegger, to summarize: there is an existence in time for *Dasein*, and *Dasein* experiences in the world. Only from experience in the world can *Dasein* derive any personal meaning. Others may posit meaning in my life, but it is not my meaning. As Emanuel Levinas says, the other is infinitely alterity or different from me.[9] I can never know the other in itself, and *vice versa*. Therefore, any meaning that you may posit in me is colored through your phenomenological experience of yourself, experience that is most likely incomplete and possibly even wrong.[10]

DEATH DATE CERTAIN

The title of this chapter, "Death is Easy If You're Dead," represents one aspect of the phenomenological experience of existence and meaning in life when one person—the fictional character Walter White—is confronted with death that is no longer temporally uncertain. To some, fictional characters and scenarios may not provide evidence to demonstrate anything in reality. However, there are counterexamples that can serve to refute this. Derrick Bell, for example, developed his critical race theory through the use of fictive counternarratives to explain the plight of African Americans in American society. Richard Delgado explains, "Critical race theory scholarship is characterized by frequent use of the first persona storytelling, narratives allegoric interdisciplinary treatment of law, and the unapologetic use of creativity."[11]

Delgado's discourse is centered within the law. What about philosophy? Martha Nussbaum explains that, "a view of life is *told*"[12] The story that is told steps out of its words into a context that resonates with the reader as told by the storyteller. The storyteller guides the reader into the world of the character at a specific moment in time that will exemplify the character's trial or dilemma. We join Walter White as he makes the transition from school teacher to cancer sufferer and from that diagnosis to meth cooker. How he comes to metamorphose is detailed in the richness of his life that, as Nussbaum said, is *told*. I suggest that the fictive narrative can be used to help describe some aspects of the phenomenology of being "a dead man walking," that is, Walter White, who is facing the imminent temporal end of himself as *Dasein*.

Stories, plays, novels and poems have all been used by humans since the dawn of civilization to represent the experiences of people in different situations who face various decisions or challenges. The difference between the *Dasein* who experiences and the character who experiences is one of depth. This is because the fictional character may be complex, but all we have of the character is what is written and performed. We might think of the fictional character in terms of a hologram. A hologram is a two-dimensional object, but contains the light image of a three-dimensional object. Thus, the hologram provides information about the shape and surface of its original, but does not give us any insight to what is within the outline of the three-dimensional form.

Certainly the character was created in the mind of the author, playwright or poet, but we cannot experience the character as it exists in the creator's mind. Much like the biblical idea of a God who creates *Dasein*, we cannot peer into the mind of God; we have only *Dasein* to consider. Once the character is unleashed upon the world, we are left only with the character as written and performed, and the hermeneutical experience of the reader or critic; that is, his or her attempt to understand the character in its expressive nature.[13]

What a great author does is to bring to us what the *author* believes is necessary for us to vicariously experience what the character is experiencing. We are left to ride along with the character and consider what meaning we derive from the character's experience. In many respects we approach the problem *with* the character, providing our own personal commentary or critique that relates to what we might have learned from riding vicariously along with our rather limited view of the character's experience.

Yet, the fictional character is not *Dasein*, and can never be *Dasein*. If anything, the character's mythology is created in our minds from whatever information is provided about its potentiality for being, including the actor's performance. The character is what has been written, and in the case of television and film, recorded. We can speculate about whether there might be something deeper if the character were real, but we have only what is presented to us—which, admittedly, is not only a bare set of facts but also our interpretation of the writing or recording.

Thus, the phenomenological task is simpler with a fictional character because its dimensionality is foreshortened by its fictional incompleteness. Themes and theories are necessarily constrained by the limitations of the text or phenomenon, which is all we have of the character. At best, we can say that a character is an *impression* of *Dasein*, not *Dasein* itself. Two additional challenges emerge when we attempt to develop meaning from a fictional character. First, we have limited information about the character's past: we are given temporal boundaries in which to confine our analysis. Second, we are often left not knowing what happens to the character after the story concludes. We do know, however, with Heidegger that if *Dasein*, as expressed by a character, dies, the end of experience for the fictional *Dasein* has occurred. What we experience of the story after the death of a fictional *Dasein* is not that *Dasein*'s own experience, but that of others. The phenomenological experience of *Dasein* is always up and until the death of *Dasein*.

For *Dasein*, life is an experiential continuum in time. Rather than lay out the full continuum of the real *Dasein*, an author generally portrays a short time-frame in a fictional character's life. Certainly, there are stories told of characters from birth to death, but even in these, periods are often skipped over or otherwise not accounted for. Instead, the author lingers where the *author* believes it is necessary to frame dilemmas that the character, as developed phenomenologically and experientially, tries to solve. We are then asked to consider what meaning that character may derive from existence in these rather brief moments of its life. This meaning we test against our own to find harmony or various degrees of divergence.

Walter, You Can't Take It with You

In the first episode of *Breaking Bad*, we are told that Walter White has been given two years to live from doctors who have diagnosed him with Stage III cancer. These are two years in his immediate temporal horizon.

Why is this important? Heidegger's thesis in *Being and Time* is that we must understand "the interpretation of *Dasein* in terms of temporality, and the explication of time as the transcendental horizon for the question of being."[14] What *Dasein* does with its time is an important consideration for the understanding of being itself. We all will die. We just do not know when. What if we knew a fairly good date certain we would die, not at the firing squad tomorrow, but with a horizon that Walter White has of two years? What the story of *Breaking Bad* does is provide us with insight as to what Walter White sees and experiences as he progresses ever closer to a death date certain. The story isn't only about his descent into criminality, but it is also about the way he begins to evolve and how he views the world and his own self in relationship to others. If the story is well told and adequately detailed, it may provide us with a better phenomenological insight of the being toward death.

Walter White is but one character in the drama of *Breaking Bad*. But the story of Walter White is important, not only because he represents an attempt to portray what the author hoped would be a believable character but also because he attempts to influence the being of others in the world after the end of his experience, the end of *Dasein*. How he does this is the central theme of the entire story. The composition of the "after-*Dasein*" is not *Dasein* but the objects and people once experienced by *Dasein* which have been left for survivors to deal with. Just as important is what Walt hypothesizes about the world after *Dasein*, beyond experience, because it shows some meaning he ascribes to *Dasein*'s existence before he faces inevitable death. While Walt, our fictional *Dasein*, may derive meaning from preparing the world for the after-*Dasein*, *Dasein* must do so, Heidegger says, through processes associated with practical considerations of being-in-the-world.

At the moment of his cancer diagnosis, Walt becomes the poster child for the life insurance industry. Even the best savers, the best retirement planners cannot complete their plan for leaving a legacy if they do not have time. The life insurance policy replaces time with a lump sum of money to complete the saver's plan. Unfortunately, Walter White has neither saved for retirement nor purchased insurance. To add to this fiscal scenario, his cancer treatments will likely take whatever savings he has accumulated…but toward what end? He believes he will die in two years regardless of the treatments he receives. Barring some miracle remission, he is doomed and his family will be destitute. However, Walter has time to do something to resolve the dilemma of a penniless family after he is gone. He has a skill: chemistry. He determines that the quickest way to riches through chemistry is to use this skill to cook and then sell meth.

Of course, quick riches, whether through speculation or illicit activities, involve more risk than the methodical accumulation of wealth. Meth trafficking is especially dangerous because of the volatility of chemicals. The trafficker's life in the drug business is typically "solitary, poor nasty, brutish and short," as Thomas Hobbes might have said.[15] Meth cooks and innocent bystanders including children and law enforcement have been injured in volatile explosions of labs.[16] Some jurisdictions consider meth dealers to be the primary source of all drug problems, and a recent study in Mexico noted that the life expectancy of men in Mexico is on the decline due to drug wars.[17] Alone, and without experience, Walter White would likely not make it in this business, but he chooses a partner, Jesse, who has networks and some insight into how the business operates. Walter White is an excellent meth cook, becomes as ruthless as his peers and survives to amass a sum of money that far exceeds the amount he needed to meet his original goals.

The Deconstruction of the Unsaid: Care

Any project of understanding *Breaking Bad* and Walter White would be complex and lengthy, needing to encompass five full seasons of hour-long episodes. Rather than try to discover meaning through engagement with each script, we should consider a single unsaid word which pervades Walter White's phenomenal experience after he receives his death sentence: *care*.[18] Heidegger said:

Being-a-whole for *Dasein*, then this would give phenomenal confirmation for the thesis that "care" is the ontological term for the totality of *Dasein*'s structural whole. If, however, we are to provide a full phenomenal justification for this principle, a *preliminary* sketch of the connection between Being-towards-death and care is not sufficient; We must be able to see this connection above all in that concretion which lies closest to *Dasein*—its everydayness.[19]

Though Heidegger posits that care provides a structural whole for the idea of *Dasein*, he remains uncomfortable with the concept of care until the phenomenology of *Dasein*'s everydayness can be shown. What is care?

Heidegger says "that care is the basic state of *Dasein*."[20] He explains:

Care is Being-towards-death. We have defined "anticipatory resoluteness" as an authentic Being towards the possibility which we have characterized as *Dasein*'s utter impossibility. In such Being-towards-its-end, *Dasein* exists in a way which is authentically whole as that entity which it can be when "thrown into death." This entity does not have an end which it just stops, but it exists *finitely*. The authentic future is temporalized primarily by that temporality which makes up the meaning of anticipatory resoluteness; it thus reveals itself as *finite*. But "does not time go on" in spite of my own no-longer-*Dasein*? And can there not be an unlimited number of things which still 'lie in the future' and come along out of it?[21]

Walter White, once a being toward a death with an uncertain date, has become a being toward death with a fairly certain date. He grapples with the idea of death and his everydayness as care for the people he loves. Initially, the object of his care is financial security for his family.

In Walt's case, the everydayness of care also requires a deconstructive reversal. The reversal of care for Walt is not care, but *obsession*. However, obsession is technically not a reversal of care, rather it is an *excess* of care. Care quickly becomes obsession for Walter White. Obsession exceeds the everydayness of care. The object of the obsession is "bracketed" (*epoché*) within experience as Edmund Husserl explained, but not bracketed in order to search for meaning without precondition as Husserl's phenomenological method would indicate. Rather, its precondition is bracketed to make its meaning even stronger. This bracketing excludes all other considerations and totalizes meaning in such a way that no other meaning is possible. As has been said, at the beginning of Walter White's journey, the object of his care is money to support his family after he dies. As time goes by, though money remains the intentional object of care, his obsession evolves. The obsession becomes more complex, shifting gradually away from money toward being "good at the game" of drug trafficking. He doesn't stop when there is enough money; he's fueled by the excitement of the business and his new found ability to thrive within it as ruthlessly as others in the story, like Gustavo Fring and Mike Ehrmantraut. Walter White says, "I did it for me. I liked it. I was good at it. And I was really...I was alive ("Felina")."

Why did Walt become obsessed with the game, and what is Walter White's game? Bernard Suits defines game as:

> To play a game is to engage in activity directed toward bringing about a certain state of affairs, using only means permitted by certain rules, where the means permitted by the rules are more limited in scope than they would be in the absence of the rules and where the sole reason for accepting such limitation of means is to make possible such activity.

The rules of the drug trade are these. First, there is a recipe for making meth. Second, the drug trade is an established business with certain implicit rules of commerce. Within a paradigm of power, ruthlessness is fundamental to the playing of the game. Secrecy is equally important because the other threat to the trafficker is the law. Any detention of Walter White means the end of the game for him because he will die before he gets out of jail.

Suits suggests there can be a game where the goal is to maximize pleasure. Walter White begins the story as a chemistry teacher; he is no James Bond. However, despite the obvious dangers and moral implications of the game and the tension and anxiety it causes him, he begins to enjoy the game itself and all the activities associated with it. He becomes high on success.

Suits suggests, "The way we choose to die, accordingly, becomes the way we chose to live." We wonder whether the pleasure Walter White is maximizing as he becomes better and better at the game is toward a moment where his death will be sudden and painless. Is he running from the eventual pain he will suffer as the cancer progresses? He plays the game like the Spartans who thwart the Persian advance at Thermopylae—with determination, skill and the knowledge that their death is inevitable and near. Like the Spartans, Walter White wants to be successful in the game until he can guarantee the security of his people. Like the Spartans, Walter White pushes back the oncoming rush of his enemies; but unlike the Spartans he amasses a fortune beyond anyone's dreams.

"Life is a Game," said Suits. The meth game has become Walter White's life. He cannot stop until the game experience stops: the end of *Dasein*. Unless something intervenes, Walter will continue the game until he dies, however that should occur. In a short conversation at the end of Season Four in the episode "Face Off," Walter White's wife Skyler has heard much news about deaths of people she knows are associated with her husband—was it him and what does it mean, she asks. He says in response, "I won." The question that arises from Walter's obsessive playing of the game is how might we define his experience of care.

Heidegger says we reveal ourselves as care; however, "we must distinguish it from phenomenon which might be proximially identified with care, such as will, wish, addiction and urge. Care cannot be derived from these, since they themselves are founded upon it."[22] In this game Walter White begins by playing on behalf of "the other" in the guise of his family. He soon finds that he is pushing others away—first others involved in the drug trade, and then his own family. His obsession has bracketed him, in other words contains his focus within [brackets] to where he cannot see outside the playing of the game to understand that he once had a goal in mind to benefit his family. Once this goal is accomplished, does Walter need to play the meth game anymore? What began as care to provide for his family itself becomes Walt's addiction to build an increasingly greater fortune. Ironically, he becomes an addict of the craft to provide substance for addicts to continue their existence as addicts.

Perversely, with his fiscal goal achieved, he does not stop. His obsession requires a new outlet, and that is the danger high he receives from playing the game. Heidegger calls this inauthenticity, or being ready for enjoyment. He says:

> As modes of Being, *authenticity* and *inauthenticity* (these expressions have been chosen terminologically in a strict sense) are both grounded in the fact that any *Dasein* whatsoever is characterized by mineness. But the inauthenticity of *Dasein* does not signify any "less" Being or any "lower" degree of Being. Rather it is the case that even in its fullest concretion *Dasein* can be characterized by inauthenticity—when busy, when excited, when interested, when ready for enjoyment.[23]

"Care" for Heidegger is the everydayness mode of existence for *Dasein*. It is bi-directional: toward self and others. It is caring about the world and about others in the world. Obsession distorts that world. As Heidegger says, "In determining itself as an entity, *Dasein* always does so in the light of a possibility which it *is* itself and which, in its very Being, it somehow understands."[24] The pure possibility for Walter White is no longer a vague horizon; it is now a bright line for *in itself as Dasein* with an expiration date virtually certain. In his obsession, Walt has transformed into what Emmanuel Levinas sees as the dangerous center of his critique of Husserl's phenomenology.

Levinas's complaint about Husserl's phenomenological method is located within the idea of the *grasp*—the holding on to the other, possessing the other. He sums up his critique of Husserl:

> Consciousness as a conscious grasp is a possession of the Other by the Same; the I dominates the Other and is in position to withdraw itself through an epoche of all engagement in being which it rediscovers as an intentional object, "bracketed" and entirely at its disposal.[25]

"To grasp" means to take and hold, to reach out and make something mine. Walter has assumed that Skyler will want what he wants for her—a secure financial future. However, he really doesn't understand her. Skyler says to him, "Walt …I want my kids back. I want my life back. Please tell me…how much is enough? How big does this pile have to be? ("Gliding Over All") The locus of Walt's grasp is the "I." He may be able to touch the face of his wife but he cannot ever grasp her infinite alterity: her otherness. Yet by the grasp, he has captured the being of his wife with his phenomenal hand, bracketed by obsession. He does not see her, only the money. His obsession becomes a drawing inward more toward him than the original other of his care: his family. Their needs and wants are no longer important; only his needs are, even if his focus of care appears obliquely toward his family after he is gone. Within his obsession, his family is objectified, concretized and schematized in the process of a perverse Husserlian bracketing. Walter White's phenomenal reduction strips away alterity and produces: "what it is for" for Walt, not his family. That which has been bracketed has become part of Walter White's dwelling-in in himself and his enjoyment, his inauthenticity.

Walt's obsession produces an ontological totality that does violence to the other—his family—by defining his family as a bracketed object of intentionality. Conversely, said Levinas, the other should be celebrated for otherness. Walter White's wife Skyler implores him to back out of his obsessive "mineness." In another episode, he makes his mineness clear, saying, "We're done when I say we're done." ("Live Free or Die").

Walt's possession of the other in this manner does violence to them in a way that he does not understand. He becomes a dwelling-in in his bracketed obsession that devolves from a legacy for others to the personal high he obtains from playing the game—the highly dangerous, illegal and ethically bankrupt game of meth trafficking.

IMMORTAL OR ETERNAL

In Jorge Luis Borges's short story, "The Immortals," the deathless Troglodytes care not so much to be in the world.[26] They know that if something could happen, it eventually will happen…why rush the inevitable? The immortals are beyond experience. They are no longer *Dasein*. This is death, the permanent state of being other than *Dasein*.

Todd May writes, "To exist in eternity is to be immune to time, if only for a little while."[27] One aspect of care is being toward death, according to Heidegger, but this being is most often the being who does not know when *Dasein* will die. Walter White knows when he will die. He has bracketed care in order to become the eternal, the eternal who has the maximum experience of being *Dasein*. Is this what Heidegger was seeking? Is the authentic *Dasein* Walter White, meth cooker? Walter White, the being toward death who knows when he will die, is eternal, but not immortal like the troglodytes. With his death sentence he understands that his experiences are forever for him, and the more he experiences, the more he experiences the eternality of *Dasein*. Death, the beyond-experience, the world of the troglodytes, is meaningless to him as it is to them. Walter White, the meth cooker, is all about the experience. This is in contrast to the Walter White, the chemistry teacher, who, as Kimberly Baltzer-Jaray, says that Walter White, "sees himself as defined completely by others."[28] What we have to ask ourselves is whether in his transformation to meth cooker do we believe he redefines himself "authentically" or lets the meth "other" redefine his life in a way that is as completely controlling as the others who defined his life before his cancer diagnosis?

We have seen how Walt's care has devolved into obsession. We see him descend into this fixation, first to build a fortune for his family, then later, to keep the game going to feed the high he receives from his gaming addiction. He is living the life of an eternal, not as *Dasein* who has all the time to build a fortune for his family, but an eternal for whom there is no risk he can take that will prevent his death in two years. He is a walking dead man; there is no worrying about his mortality. He will do anything he can to keep the game going until the end of *Dasein*.

Eternality, obsession, and death become intertwined in the experience of Walter White. While we follow Walt's story as he enters and attempts to master the game, we wonder whether this is something that could happen to us should we be confronted with the certainty of our own death date. We likely do not have to look far.

Many of us, for example, give over our lives to the corporate game. The corporate game provides some measure of personal satisfaction in addition to income. At times the objectives set by corporations are, as in Walter White's case, too aggressive to be met by legal or ethical means within the available timeframe. A good example is the recent Volkswagen emissions scandal. In order not to suffer the consequences of failing to meet impossible corporate goals, engineers allegedly rigged equipment so that during emissions tests diesel vehicles would meet standards that were not possible during normal operation. The corporate game is a harsh mistress, requiring that one meet goals before a prescribed deadline or face the metaphorical death sentence of termination. Why do they call it a deadline, after all?

What triggers the change of the meaning of *Dasein* as the being who cares to *Dasein* who obsesses? It's difficult to say. Walter White begins by bracketing money as the object of his care. At first he disguises this in the building of a fortune for the family that will survive him. However, as he says, he begins to like being the eternal who thrives on the intense experience of being *Dasein*, the being toward death. He discovers a surplus of care in his obsession, when not only does he become good at the game, but it wholly becomes what he believes is his "authentic" existence. Before his death sentence, he was, like the rest of us, plodding along like the troglodytes, waiting for whatever might come along. However, we understand that his later "authenticity" has been bracketed by his obsession. His authentic being toward death is therefore an illusion of authenticity.

Conclusion

We are all going to die. Heidegger complains that we don't think enough about death because death can shape our very lives, yet as Todd May says, "we don't reflect on it, don't take it into account in considering the shape our lives take."[29] However, as we have seen, Walter White shapes his life not only in preparation for death but for the time he has remaining as an eternal *Dasein*. It isn't only his death that gives his life new meaning, but the period of life he is permitted which reorganizes his thinking about being in the world.

As Todd May and others have explained, we put death out of our minds in the center of our everydayness and continue with our lives like the troglodytes. We muddle along thinking we have time to care until we have none anymore. Most who are given a death sentence like Walter White do not become drug traffickers; not every employee who is confronted with an impossible deadline makes untoward choices. The chapter's title "Death Is Easy If You're Dead" begins to ring true when temporal horizons are foreshortened. Care can become obsession; obsession may create a Walter White, or it may turn the bucket list into a whirlwind world tour, or it may become time spent in a pure phenomenal experience of a favorite place.

Care for Walter White transforms into obsession when the end time for *Dasein* is certain; obsession brackets goals and can bracket methodologies that fit the timeframe regardless of their effects upon society. For Walt, actions that had been wrapped in altruism begin to be carried out both unethically and illegally, and in the end the only one he can ever try to satisfy is himself.

However, he begins his journey toward death, trying to be responsible to the other: his wife and family. Rather than, as Levinas suggests, to understand the others in his life as being infinitely different from him, he begins to bracket them into a concretized other who, without his skillful playing of the game, will be destitute. He makes the others in his family poor to justify his obsession with the game. We see with his wife Skyler that this is not the case. She wants what she had before his obsession even though it will eventually not include Walter. However, his obsession begins to bracket her own thinking about who Walter is and she begins to distance herself from him. What began in the responsible response to Skyler's needs, Walter has transmogrified into his own. He has become what he didn't want to be—irresponsible, not because he would leave his family destitute of money; rather, he has produced more money than they will ever need (up and until the last episode), but he has become irresponsible because he has not seen what his wife really needs— love. His care has been turned around from being focused on Levinas's alterior other, to himself: narrowly defined as meth game master. His everydayness has become an obsessive mineness, ultimately feeding his excess of care, care for himself in the form of the game.

We have ridden with Walter on his red-knuckle journey toward death in this chapter, but we have just scratched the surface of the Walter White phenomenon of care that has become obsession. There is much more to learn about death date certain, authenticity and obsession for *Dasein* who is ontologically structured as care—a being toward death.

NOTES

1. Andrew Alexandra, "'All Men Agree on This...' Hobbes on the Fear of Death and the Way to Peace," *History of Philosophy Quarterly* 6, no. 1 (1989); J. L. Borges, *The Aleph and Other Stories*, (London: Penguin Books, 2000); V. J. Bourke, *Saint Augustine: The City of God* (New York: Doubleday, 1958); John

Burbidge, "Man, God, and Death in Hegel's Phenomenology," *Philosophy and Phenomenological Research* 42, no. 2 (1981); Richard A. Cohen, "Levinas: Thinking Least About Death: Contra Heidegger," *International Journal for Philosophy of Religion* 60, no. 1/3 (2006); Kai Draper, "Epicurean Equanimity Towards Death," *Philosophy and Phenomenological Research* 69, no. 1 (2004); C. J. Ducasse, "Demos on "Nature, Mind, and Death"," *The Review of Metaphysics* 7, no. 2 (1953); John Martin Fischer, "Epicureanism About Death and Immortality," *The Journal of Ethics* 10, no. 4 (2006); Sigmund Freud, *Beyond the Pleasure Principle*, trans. James Strachey (US: Pacific Publishing Studio, 2010); Lawrence J. Hatab, *Nietzsche's Life Sentence: Coming to Terms with Eternal Recurrence* (New York: Routledge, 2005); G. Hays, *Marcus Aurelius: Meditations* (New York: Modern Library, 2002); Martin Heidegger, *Being and Time*, trans. John MacQuarrie and Edward Robinson (New York: HarperCollins Publishers, 1962); I. Kant, *Practical Philosophy*, trans. M. J. Gregor (Cambridge Univ Pr, 1999); Soren Kierkegaard, *The Essential Kierkegaard*, trans. Howard V. & Edna M. Hong Hong (Princeton, NJ: Princeton University Press, 1997).
2. Anthony L. Brueckner and John Martin Fischer, "Why Is Death Bad?," *Philosophical Studies: An International Journal for Philosophy in the Analytic Tradition* 50, no. 2 (1986).
3. Harry S. Silverstein, "The Evil of Death," *The Journal of Philosophy* 77, no. 7 (1980).
4. See Quentin Smith, "Concerning the Absurdity of Life," *Philosophy* 66, no. 255 (1991).
5. See Bernard Suits, "Is Life a Game We Are Playing?," *Ethics* 77, no. 3 (1967).
6. See Levine 1987.
7. Todd May, *Death* (Stocksfield, UK: Acumen Publishing Limited, 2009), 22.
8. Heidegger, *Being and Time*, 277, H34.
9. Emmanuel Levinas, *Totality and Infinity: An Essay on Exteriority*, vol. 1 (Springer, 1979), 34.
10. Leah Kalmanson and Sarah Mattice, "The De of Levinas: Cultivating the Heart-Mind of Radical Passivity," *Frontiers of Philosophy in China* 10, no. 1 (2015): 128.
11. Richard; Jean Stefancic Delgado, ed. *The Derrick Bell Reader* (NY and London: New York University Press, 2005), 78.
12. Martha Craven Nussbaum, *Love's Knowledge: Essays on Philosophy and Literature* (New York: Oxford University Press, 1992), 5.
13. Said Hans Georg Gadamer on hermeneutics or the interpretation of texts, "The task of hermeneutic is to clarify this miracle of understanding, which is not a mysterious communion of souls, but sharing in a common meaning." Hans Georg Gadamer, *Truth and Method*, trans. Joel Weinsheimer and Donald G. Marshall (New York: Crossroad/Continuum, 1989), 292.
14. Heidegger, *Being and Time*, 63, H39.
15. Thomas Hobbes, *Leviathan* (London: Andrew Cooke, 1651), 78.
16. The Center for Disease Control reported that in the period 2001–2012, more than 1300 chemical incidents related to meth labs were recorded in five states: Louisiana, Oregon, Utah, New York and Wisconsin. This included 162 injuries and two deaths. The report did not include the cost of damage from pollution caused by meth wastes or fires as a result of meth lab explosions or the tearing

down of structures contaminated by meth lab poisons. See: Injuries from Methamphetamine-Related Chemical Incidents—Five States, 2001–2012.

Weekly August 28, 2015/64(33);909–912, http://www.cdc.gov/mmwr/preview/mmwrhtml/mm6433a4.htm

17. For information on the statistics of the methamphetamine problem in the USA, see: Rachel Gonzales, Larissa Mooney, and Richard Rawson, "The Methamphetamine Problem in the United States," *Annual review of public health* 31 (2010). For information about the change in mortality rates in Mexico correlated with the drug wars there see: *Mexico's murder rate has led to decrease in men's life expectancy, UCLA-led study shows*, Enrique Rivero, Last modified January 05, 2016, Web.

18. Deconstruction is a term attributed to Jacques Derrida. Gayatri Spivak explains that deconstruction serves, "To locate the promising marginal text, to disclose the undecidable moment, to pry it loose with the positive lever of the signifier; to reverse the resident hierarch, only to displace it; to dismantle in order to reconstitute what is always already inscribed" Jacques Derrida, *Of Grammatology*, trans. Gayatri Spivak (Baltimore: The Johns Hopkins University Press, 1976), lxxvii. The marginal text that is being deconstructed in context of Walter White is the word care. Care we will reverse hierarchically into obsession and try to reconstitute what the word care and its hierarchical excess called obsession mean in context of Walter White's experience of being before a death date certain.

19. Heidegger, *Being and Time*, 296, H52.

20. Ibid., 293, H49.

21. Ibid., 378, H 30.

22. Ibid., 227, H182.

23. Ibid., 68, H43.

24. Ibid.

25. Emmanuel Levinas, *Emmanuel Levinas Basic Philosophical Writings*, ed. Adriaan T. Peperzak, Simon Critchley, & Robert Bernasconi (Bloomington, In: Indiana University Press 1996), 18.

26. Borges, "The Aleph and Other Stories," 13.

27. May, *Death*, 52.

28. Kimberly Baltzer-Jaray, "Finding Happiness in a Black Hat," in *Breaking Bad and Philosophy: Better Living through Chemistry*, ed. David Richard Koepsell and Robert Arp (Chicago: Open Court Publishing, 2012), 44.

29. May, *Death*, 35.

CHAPTER 6

Cosmic Justice in *Breaking Bad*: Can Sociopaths and Antiheroes Lead Meaningful Lives?

Kimberly Blessing

There is a long history of the art of depiction of suffering being inflicted on sinners. But this kind of suffering, along with the notion of sin, has fallen out of favor.[1] A case in point: television's "New," or "Third Golden" Age.[2] Fans were notoriously disappointed with the conclusion of *The Sopranos*. We never knew if mob hit man Tony Soprano—the first of the male antiheroes of this "Golden Age"—lived or died. More recently, fans were critical of *Mad Men*'s finale. Sixties ad-man Don Draper is a selfish and self destructive, womanizing drunk. After hugging some hippies are we to believe that he found spiritual enlightenment or came up with what is arguably the greatest commercial ever created (the 1971 "hilltop" Coca-Cola commercial)?[3]

Standing in sharp contrast to these morally ambiguous postmodern tales is Vince Gilligan's highly acclaimed television series, *Breaking Bad* (a Southern expression for "raising hell"). Gilligan, a former writer for, and producer of, *The X-Files*, was raised Catholic but describes himself as agnostic. Yet, a decidedly theistic conception of life's meaning can be detected in *Breaking Bad*. Cosmic justice reigns in the fictional universe Gilligan has created. Make no mistake, Walt ends up in Hell.

Gilligan tells us that the "larger lesson" to *Breaking Bad* is that "actions have consequences." "If religion is a reaction of man, and nothing more, it seems to me that it represents a human desire for wrongdoers to be punished. I hate the idea of Idi Amin living in Saudi Arabia for the last 25 years of his life. That galls me to no end."[4] In the same interview with the *New York Times*,

K. Blessing (✉)
SUNY Buffalo State University, Buffalo, NY, USA

© The Author(s) 2017
K.S. Decker et al. (eds.), *Philosophy and Breaking Bad*,
DOI 10.1007/978-3-319-40343-4_6

Gilligan continues, "I feel some sort of need for biblical atonement, or justice, or something. I like to believe there is some comeuppance that karma kicks in at some point, even if it takes years or decades to happen."[5] He tells us that his girlfriend would describe his philosophy as follows: "I want to believe there's a heaven. But I can't not believe there's a hell." Gilligan admires director Woody Allen. "Allen may be right. I'm pretty much agnostic at this point in my life. But I find atheism just as hard to get my head around as I find fundamental Christianity." He explains why he finds atheism so unsatisfying. "[I]f there is no such thing as cosmic justice, what is the point of being good? That's the one thing that no one has ever explained to me. Why shouldn't I go rob a bank, especially if I'm smart enough to get away with it? What's stopping me?"[6]

In what follows I will use Gilligan's storyline and characters to explore various theories about the meaning of life. I shall argue that we can plausibly read a theistic theory of life's meaning into *Breaking Bad*. By "theism" I mean belief in God or gods, where "God" refers to the Judeo-Christian God or the God of classical theism. Gilligan believes that in order for life to be meaningful, actions must have consequences, specifically wrongdoers must be punished. If wrongdoers are not punished, then there is no point to being good. In other words, in order for life to meaningful there must be justice. As Gilligan acknowledges, cosmic justice could be accounted for in non-theistic theories of meaning, such as Eastern religious views that include some notion of karma. Since these theories are not addressed in the philosophical literature on the meaning of life, however, I will focus attention on theism, which is a theory of life's meaning that can accommodate cosmic justice. It is this brand of justice that reigns in the world of *Breaking Bad*.

COSMIC AND TERRESTRIAL MEANING

If we think of life's meaning in terms of *kinds*, we can distinguish between *terrestrial* and *cosmic* meaning.[7] Terrestrial meaning addresses meaningfulness *in* an individual human life; it answers the question, "What condition(s) would, if satisfied, make an individual's life, or some aspect of that life, meaningful?"[8] Cosmic theories of meaning are additionally looking for the meaning *of* life which includes all human life or humanity in general. These theories include broader mystery of existence-type questions: "What is the point of it all?" "Is my life part of some bigger narrative or cosmic plan?" "Why are some lives meaningful and others not?" and so on.

Whether we are talking about the terrestrial or cosmic variety, meaningfulness is an intrinsic and final good that varies and comes in degrees. Meaningfulness applies only to human life, whether we are considering the whole or some part of that life, including an individual action or set of actions, project, or endeavor. As a category of value, meaningfulness is distinct from both morality and happiness or well-being. For example, Hitler's immoral and unhappy life would count as meaningful if, say, Hitler's finding his life fulfilling is sufficient for meaningfulness. Finally, meaningfulness is closely related to purpose. But the lives of an immoral dictator or soldier suffering from PTSD (Post Traumatic Stress Disorder) have purpose, and they are not necessarily meaningful.

When we are looking at *theories* of life's meaning, we can divide them into two camps: *subjective* and *objective*. Subjective theories of life's meaning can account only for terrestrial meaning. Most objective theories of life's meaning likewise focus only on terrestrial meaning. This is because the vast majority of philosophers who write about the meaning of life approach it from an atheistic or naturalistic perspective, and hence they do not address the larger, mystery-of-existence type questions. In their more narrowly defined discussions of terrestrial meaning, these philosophers offer any number of objective conditions that, if satisfied, could render an individual life, or some aspect of that life, meaningful. Some examples include transcending the limits of the self (Robert Nozick)[9]; pursuing maximally non-hedonist goods, such as friendship, beauty, and knowledge (Peter Railton)[10]; exercising or developing rational nature in exceptional ways (Thomas Hurka,[11] Alan Gewirth[12]); substantially improving the quality of life of people and animals (Peter Singer)[13]; overcoming challenges that one recognizes to be important at one's stage of history (Ronald Dworkin)[14]; rewarding experiences in the life of the agent or the lives of others the agent affects (Robert Audi)[15]; altruism (Julia Baginni)[16]; leaving traces upon one death (Brooke Alan Trisel)[17]; family relationships (David Velleman)[18]; and life plans (David Heyd).[19]

Any one of these theories is worth considering in terms of whether or not the life of Walter White (or other characters from *Breaking Bad*) could be considered meaningful on objective grounds. They will not, however, be taken up in this discussion because none of these terrestrial accounts of meaning can provide an account of cosmic justice. Only theistic theories of meaning, which by definition claim objectivity, can explain our life in a just cosmos in which goodness prevails and those who raise hell end up in Hell. I will now consider two varieties of subjective theories of meaning, what I call *hard* and *soft* meaning-subjectivism. According to the former it may be argued that Walter White's life was meaningful, while under the latter it was not. But first, let's look at Walt's confession.

Breaking Bad takes off when Walter White awakes from the slumber of his unfulfilling life as a nerdy high school chemistry teacher working two jobs with crummy health insurance, a baby on the way, a broken water heater, and a Pontiac Aztek in the driveway of his Albuquerque split-level. A diagnosis of terminal lung cancer gives rise to this awakening.[20] Walt realizes that he will be unable to pay for his treatments, much less provide for his family after he is gone. Hence, Walt comes up with an ingenious solution and consequently finds his passion: using his science skills to cook meth in a dilapidated RV. Parked in the middle of a New Mexico desert, Walt transforms into Heisenberg, a badass drug lord; in the words of the creator of *Breaking Bad*, this is a story "about a man who transforms himself from Mr. Chips into Scarface."[21]

As far as drug lords go, Heisenberg is a real success story. This genius entrepreneur figured out how to cook the most coveted meth that local dealers have ever known—96 % pure. As Jesse Pinkman would say, "Yeah *science*, Bitch." Throughout six seasons Walt was single-minded and purposeful in all his actions, creating Heisenberg with a specific goal in mind. It was even a laudable goal, that is, to leave a nest egg for his son Walt Jr. and pregnant wife Skyler after cancer takes his life. Walt even gave up getting credit for it, letting his wife think his hard-earned cash was a gift from Gretchen and Elliott Schwartz, co-owners of Gray Matter Technologies. In the final episode, however, Walt finally told the truth about his motivations and desires in creating his alter ego Heisenberg, first to Skyler and then to Jesse. Walt did it all for himself, because he *enjoyed* it. Because he was "good at it." "I did it for me. I liked it. I was good at it. And… I was really… I was alive" ("Felina").

HARD MEANING-SUBJECTIVISM

Once Walt was doing what he enjoyed, he felt alive, that is, his life had purpose and meaning. This view that it's the thinking and feeling of a subject that determines whether or not life is meaningful reflects one camp of theories about the meaning of life: *meaning-subjectivism*. Historically, existentialists embrace a subjective view of life's meaning. The father of existentialism, Søren Kierkegaard, maintained that "subjectivity is truth" and "truth is subjectivity." This viewpoint points to passion as the most precious thing; it motivates and sustains our actions. Similarly for Friedrich Nietzsche, "Without passions you have no experience whatever."[22] Nietzsche thinks that meaning arises from the creative, passionate *process* of an activity, not by achieving goals. If you live in the moment with passion simply for what it is, as if you could repeat the same exact moment for eternity, then life can be meaningful. More recently, Harry Frankfurt has argued that deeply loving or caring for something is sufficient for a life to be meaningful.

In his "Felina" confession to his wife, Walt tells us that what made him feel alive and finally gave his life meaning is that he found something he enjoyed doing. In short order Walt discovered that he was good at cooking meth. As he told Jesse, "being the best at something is very rare." Like many of us would do, Walt took great pleasure from doing something at which he excelled. As the series goes on we see that Walt additionally felt deep satisfaction in pulling off the sting. It required nothing short of criminal genius. It must have felt so good for Walt to finally be able to exercise his intellect and talents and then reap the rewards. Walt is deeply resentful that his former girlfriend Gretchen and her husband Elliot stole Walt's research to launch the highly successful company Gray Matter (the name came from a combination of the two's last names. *Schwartz* means "black" in German, and combined with "White," makes gray.) He confesses to Jesse that he checks the company's valuations weekly, torturing himself with what could have been. But now Walt can derive deep satisfaction, and make a whole lot of money, from something that is all his own creation: Heisenberg. This satisfaction that Walt experiences as Heisenberg is what finally gives him a sense of meaning and purpose in his otherwise meaningless existence.

This view of meaningfulness understood in terms of fulfillment or desire-satisfaction is best captured by Richard Taylor, who offers the most influential account of meaning-subjectivism, or what I am calling "hard meaning-subjectivism."[23] Taylor uses the Myth of Sisyphus as the iconic case of a meaningless existence. He then asks us to imagine that the gods took pity and injected Sisyphus with a drug that gives him the desire to roll rocks up a hill only to fall down again. The pointless nature of his existence remains the same, but now Sisyphus *wants* to do this. He has found his passion. Sisyphus now loves rolling rocks. Now that it fulfills him, the pointless task is meaningful.

Long before Kierkegaard or Nietzsche or Taylor came on the scene, however, eastern sage Confucius advanced this same view of meaningfulness. Even if it is hard to imagine him talking about "jobs," he is credited with the following advice: "Choose a job you love, and you will never have to work a day in your life." This view is widely reflected in contemporary popular culture. Talk-show-host-turned-spiritual-guru Oprah Winfrey preaches: "Follow Your Bliss." Winfrey is a fan of Joseph Campbell, an American mythologist. In his best seller, *The Power of Myth*, Campbell explains that his general formula for his students is "'Follow your bliss.' Find where it is, and don't be afraid to follow it."[24]

But hard meaning-subjectivism is perhaps best articulated by one of the most successful entrepreneurs of the modern era, Steve Jobs. The creator of Apple offered the following advice to the Stanford University class of 2005: "You've got to find what you love. And that is as true for work as it is for your lovers. Your work is going to fill a large part of your life, and the only way to be truly satisfied is to do what you believe is great work. And the only way to do great work is to love what you do."[25] Instead of mythical gods injecting magical serum into our veins, Jobs tells us that we can do it ourselves. It's simple: if you want to be truly satisfied or fulfilled, "Do What You Love." "DWYL" has become a favorite mantra for Apple's largest market: Millennials. Indeed, this is a view that resonates with a great many people. A large supermarket chain in the state of New York, Wegmans, boasts of having made *Fortune Magazine* list of the "100 Best Companies to Work For" since 1998. As of March 2016, they have posters hanging all over their stores: "Do What You Love."

Hard meaning-subjectivists believe that any individual can find or create meaning in any situation or life. In creating Heisenberg, Walter White transformed himself from a pathetic high school chemistry teacher—a real loser—into a god-like super villain. "By the end of the series," Kristin Magaldi writes, "you're almost *happy* Walter became the badass that he did; he represents the small man taking back his dignity to become the knocker instead of the knocked. You wish you had that courage..."[26] At the very least, we no longer feel sorry for him.

At first glance the idea that a meaningful life is within anybody's reach is empowering, liberating, and egalitarian. That is, just as long as the individual in question has the opportunity, means, and good fortune to be able to pursue his or her passionate interests. But as Henry David Thoreau observes, there are masses of people who "lead lives of quiet desperation." When we first meet Jesse he seems to be just this sort of character—destined for misery and failure no matter how many times he tries to set his life straight. Even Skyler could be viewed as someone who was quietly living out a life that lacked passion and meaning. Meaning subjectivists might argue that this is expressly the point: the more a person hates his or her life, the more he or she is unsatisfied or unfulfilled, the more meaningless it is. They would likely agree that misfortune or the lack of means or opportunity precludes some people from living meaningful lives, and that this is lamentable. If this is true, however, then it is not the case that just *any* individual can find or create meaning in his or her life. Instead, this model of meaningfulness favors those who are powerful, even cunning, like Walter White, and leaves weaker and more desperate characters like Jesse or Skyler at a serious disadvantage. Even if Sisyphus, the iconic case of a meaningless existence, could find a way to love rolling rocks up a hill, it's not clear that all of us would be able to push the rocks up the hill in the first place. Some of us just might not have it in us. Hence, hard meaning-subjectivism is not necessarily liberating, empowering, or egalitarian.

The strongest objection to hard meaning-subjectivism is that if anything counts as meaningful, then not only obviously trivial things like counting bottle caps or hairs on one's head—or say spending an entire day trying to kill a fly—could be meaningful. But dastardly deeds would also have to count. As Walt further immerses himself in the amoral criminal underworld, his family, friends, and all the structures that formerly gave his life meaning and worth are destroyed before his eyes. Subsequently, he is able to find meaning in the amoral sociopath he has created in Heisenberg. But how could the life of an amoral sociopath be more meaningful than, or at least as meaningful as, the life of a dutiful father and family man who makes an honest living teaching chemistry?

Most philosophers writing about the meaning of life reject subjective accounts of meaningfulness. Eric Wielenberg offers a clever *reductio ad absurdum* argument to illustrate what is deeply wrong with meaning-subjectivism. He asks us to consider a grinning pianist and a grinning excrement-eater. "A grinning excrement-eater who passes up a pianist's life for the sake of eating excrement is a fool… No matter how great his passion, no matter how big his grin as he spoons it down, he should be an object of pity rather than envy."[27] The fact that hard meaning-subjectivists would have to grant that the lives of the excrement eater and pianist are equally meaningful suggests a very good reason to reject hard subjectivism. Even if we were to grant that both of these lives are equally meaningful, it becomes harder to swallow when we consider deeply immoral lives, like that of Walter White.

John Kekes argues that countless dedicated Nazi and Communist mass murderers, committed terrorists, "people whose rage, resentment, greed, ambition, selfishness, sense of superiority or inferiority give purpose to their lives

and lead them to inflict grievous unjustified harm on others… may be successfully engaged in their projects, derive great satisfaction from them, and find
their lives as scourges of their literal or metaphorical gods very meaningful."[28]
Kekes acknowledges that this point of view "outrages our moral sensibility."
But he believes it must be accepted if one is to "[do] justice to the plain fact
that many evil and morally unconcerned people live meaningfully."[29]

This is not a pill that Gilligan is willing to swallow. Even if Walt does find
meaning and fulfillment *in* his deeply immoral life, this is not sufficient to
account for the meaning *of* life. For Gilligan, in order for life in general or the
human experience to be meaningful, Walt must get his comeuppance "even if
it takes years or decades." Gilligan assures us that if he were a god, "I wouldn't
be a particularly vengeful one. I've realized that judging the character is not
a particularly fruitful endeavor on my part, and yet I have done that. I've lost
sympathy for Walter White, personally." He goes on to say:

> But this is not a show about evil for evil's sake. Walt has behaved at times in what
> could be regarded as an evil fashion, but I don't think he's an evil man. He is an
> extremely self-deluded man. We always say in the writers' room, if Walter White
> has a true superpower, it's not his knowledge of chemistry or his intellect, it's his
> ability to lie to himself. He is the world's greatest liar. He could lie to the pope.
> He could lie to Mother Teresa. He certainly could lie to his family, and he can lie
> to himself, and he can make these lies stick. He can make himself believe, in the
> face of all contrary evidence, that he is still a good man. It really does feel to us
> like a natural progression down this road to hell, which was originally paved with
> good intentions.[30]

The fact that Walt is written as being on the road to Hell distinguishes
Gilligan's attitude from hard meaning-subjectivists like Kekes who believe we
simply have to accept the idea that evil or self-deluded antiheroes can live
meaningfully.

Although hard meaning-subjectivism is widely accepted in popular culture,
it does not hold up to philosophical scrutiny. Even Taylor later rejects this
view and comes to think about meaningfulness in terms of creativity.[31] Still
some philosophers believe that even if it's not sufficient, desire-satisfaction or
fulfillment is at least *necessary* for meaningfulness. I will refer to this as "soft
meaning-subjectivism."

Soft Meaning-Subjectivism

Susan Wolf, in her well-regarded book *Meaning in Life and Why It Matters*, is
a soft meaning-subjectivist. Wolf explains that the popular "fulfillment view"
suggests that the reason we should find our passion or follow our bliss is
because in doing so our lives will have a particular type of good feeling.[32] The
fulfillment a person may experience from following his or her passion is not,
however, sufficient for a meaningful life, according to Wolf. A person has to be

passionate about the right kinds of things; "the things one loves must be good in some independent way."[33] Hence, Wolf's "fitting fulfillment" view says that meaningfulness amounts to "loving objects that are worthy of love."[34] This hybrid view of meaningfulness can be expressed in a pithy phrase: "meaning arises when subjective attraction meets objective attractiveness."[35]

Wolf acknowledges that not everyone cares about meaningfulness.[36] It may be that the desperate people Thoreau had in mind are too busy trying to survive to worry whether or not their lives are meaningful. But what about those unfortunate people who do care? Take the life of a single mother of three who hates her work as a maid. She is painfully aware that she is not living out the life she envisioned for herself. On the other hand, consider a DINK (double income, no kids) philosophy professor who loves her work. She found her passion early in life and is overall content with her relatively worry-free existence. On Wolf's model, each of these women is equally devoted to worthy pursuits: motherhood and professorship. Yet, simply by virtue of the fact that the philosopher gets to do what she loves, her life is more meaningful than the life of the struggling single mother.

This is just another version of Wielenberg's excrement test. In this case, however, we are not comparing two individuals who are equally fulfilled yet engaged in different kinds of projects (piano player and excrement eater), one worthy and the other one not. Instead, we are comparing two equally worthy projects or lives that are yielding different levels of satisfaction or fulfillment (mother and professor). It may be argued that the maid in question is in fact fulfilled, for she is deriving deep satisfaction from the fact that she is able to support her children. But in this case, is it the feeling of fulfillment or desire-satisfaction that is bestowing meaning? Or is it something more in line with duty or virtue? In reality, there are many relatively desperate people living quiet lives of virtue and self-sacrifice despite the fact that they do not derive enjoyment from doing so. Wolf would have to say that these noble yet unsatisfying lives are not meaningful. Moreover, what about cases in which we compare unlovable and lofty pursuits, such as teaching chemistry to adolescents who hate chemistry, to a loveable yet more lowly pursuit, such as Skyler making breakfast for Walt Jr.? As worthy as any project or life may be, it will not pass Wolf's test unless the individual in question is experiencing that good feeling of fulfillment or satisfaction.

A second objection to the objective side of Wolf's theory is that she is an elitist in her choice of intrinsically meaningful activities. These include highbrow pursuits such as art, philosophy, and other scholarly activities. Some of her examples of meaningless lives seem far-fetched, such as the person who spends all day gazing at gold fish or smoking pot—although many of Jesse's loser associates like Badger and Skinny Pete may fit the bill for the latter. But Wolf also discusses more realistic cases such as the assembly line worker, conscripted soldier, and alienated housewife—Skyler or her shop-lifting sister Marie come to mind. These individuals may know their work is valuable but they are not emotionally engaged, which means their lives are not meaningful or at least not as meaningful as they could be. If, on the other hand, they could find work that they love or find a way to love their work, say in the way Walter White loves cooking meth, their lives would be more meaningful.

Wolf defends herself by saying that she does not dismiss entire lives as meaningless. Still, her view does degrade and devalue work that is not done from love. This would include socially necessary work, which is often carried out by the blue-collar working class, not to mention the working poor who often find themselves doing work that is very far from loveable—take, for instance, our maid or, say, a coal miner. On Wolf's model, there are two opposing classes of work: (i) that which is lovable (creative, intellectual, socially prestigious such as art of philosophy), and (ii) that which is not (repetitive, unintellectual, undistinguished such as assembly line worker or housewife).

First-generation immigrants would likely laugh at the idea that a person needs to love what she does. Instead, these men and women often make great sacrifices so their children can live better lives. It is doubtful that the children of these immigrants would view their parent's lives of self-sacrifice as less meaningful than their own simply because their parents did not feel fulfilled by their work. Instead, these children would admire and be grateful to their ancestors for the opportunity they were provided to follow their dreams. If Wolf is right, however, we are left in a counter-intuitive position. We would have to say that a more noble life devoted to others—like Hank, the dutiful and heroic DEA agent who struggles with feelings of inadequacy at work—is less meaningful than a life that is less noble and selfish—the cocky badass drug lord Walter White.

A third objection to Wolf's theory has to do with how we assess the overall worthiness of a project or endeavor. Wolf insists that for something to count as meaningful, that thing we love must be "good" in some way independent of the subject. On the one hand, when we consider the consequences of Walt's very successful career as a drug kingpin, they immediately strike us as unlovable or bad. His actions will most certainly wreak havoc and misery in many people's lives, including his own family, meth dealers, and especially meth addicts. On the other hand, Walt's original intention for embarking on this ignoble career was to provide for his family once cancer had taken his life. This pursuit seems more loveable or good. Moreover, what are we to do in cases where there are mixed motives? Perhaps Walt wants to help his family (loveable), and he wants to experience the satisfaction of doing something that he is good at (selfish and unlovable).

For all of his considerable efforts, Walt does end up leaving his family a ton of money (good or loveable). Yet, as Gilligan observes, Walt's been "looking through the wrong end of the telescope" (bad or unlovable). "For years now, he thought if he makes his family financially sound—that's really all he has to do as a man, as a provider, and as a father. They're going to walk away with just shy of 10 million in cash, because of Walt's machinations with Gretchen and Elliott."[37] On the other hand, Walt's family is emotionally scarred forever. "So it's a real mixed message at the end. Walt has failed on so many levels, but he has managed to do the one thing he set out to do, which is a victory. He has managed to make his family financially sound in his absence, and that was really the only thing he set out to do in that first episode. So, mission accomplished."[38] Could the ends justify the means on Wolf's view? Would Wolf consider success or accomplishment as something that is "good" in some independent way? It becomes apparent that one weakness of Wolf's theory, which she shares with many others who adhere to objective theories of terrestrial meaning, is that there is nothing built into her theory to specifically bar immoral actions or evil intentions from being meaningful.

Even if we were to ignore the problematic aspects of soft and hard meaning-subjectivism, they are both inadequate for Gilligan's epic. This is because any terrestrial theory of life's meaning will be unable to address Gilligan's deepest worry, namely, that antiheroes and bad guys like Walter White might not end up suffering for their sins. If sin does not lead to suffering, how are we to understand the meaning *of* life? Furthermore, if there is no guarantee that more saintly lives, or aspects of a life, will end up being meaningful, then what is the point of being good? This is precisely what the agnostic Gilligan finds unintelligible about atheism. If there is no cosmic justice, then there is no point to being good. It is for this reason that Gilligan creates a universe in which those who raise hell end up in Hell. There is only one grand narrative that can make this promise.

THEISTIC THEORIES

Only a theistic theory of meaning is adequate to understanding the moral world of *Breaking Bad*. John Cottingham, in his book *On The Meaning of Life*, articulates the chief problem with secular humanism. It lacks something objectively *good*—not simply objective—to ground meaning. Thus, a meaningful life reduces to nothing more than "an engaged life in which the agent is systematically committed to certain projects he makes his own, *irrespective of their moral status*."[39] It would not matter, for example, that the artistic genius is a selfish philanderer, the great athlete is a thug, or that the brilliant engineer cheats on his taxes.[40] Or that a brilliant chemist is cooking meth.

In contrast to secularism, a religious point of view provides "a model of fulfillment that would locate our human destiny within an enduring *moral* framework."[41] Instead of thinking of our lives as a "cosmic accident" or a "by-product of blind forces," they would be seen as having a purpose—"that of attuning ourselves to a creative order that is inherently good."[42] It is not that theism provides the only final end or purpose or fulfillment that matters, for this could be accomplished from an atheistic point of view, at least regarding meaningfulness *in* individual lives, or terrestrial meaning. For example, Singer's terrestrial theory that life's meaning is to be found in "substantially improving the quality of life of people and animals" could do the same.

Instead, Cottingham's point is that God's plan can guarantee that its adherents find their purpose and fulfillment in something which is inherently good.

Only theism guarantees that the meaning *in* life that is found in the pursuit of worthwhile activities will contribute to some overall good, namely, cosmic justice. In a just cosmos, immoralists and antiheroes like Walter White and the many other cretins we meet over six seasons of *Breaking Bad* will pay for their sins, and innocents and victims like Walt's children, Skyler, Hank, and Marie will end up all right.

A key to Cottingham's view is his emphasis on the fact that the worth of our activities and projects is, to some degree, success-oriented. At the same time whether or not our sincere pursuit of worthwhile activity yields a meaningful life "will be open to chance."[43] This is what Cottingham refers to as the "problem of the frailty of goodness." "The lucky ones on whom fortune smiles will be able to look back at the end of their lives and pronounce them meaningful, while those who are, by birth, or upbringing, or ill-health, or lack of resource, or accident, unable to pursue worthwhile goals, or prevented from reaching them, will just have to lump it."[44] Cottingham finds this point of view "ethically repugnant" because it goes against a long "compassionate" and "egalitarian" tradition that suggests that every human being is eligible for salvation.[45] It is also "psychologically indigestible" because it unrealistically expects us to pursue the good with no hope or assurance that we will succeed.[46] Theism, on the other hand, "encourages us with hope" that the very difficult and demanding task of being virtuous contributes to some sort of moral order that the cosmos was created to realize.[47]

Cottingham explains that religious claims about "the buoyancy of goodness" are commonly misunderstood. "[T]he hope involved here is closer to an emotional allegiance to the idea of the power of goodness than to the cognitive attitude of expectation that outcomes will be, on any given occasion, or in general, favorable..."[48] The "resilience of goodness... is not a matter of any magical tendency to bounce back or win through, but rather a matter of something in the human spirit which can respond to the deepest stress and weakness in ways that are transforming."[49] Likewise, philosopher of religion John Hick argues that all world religions offer a "cosmic optimism" that has little to do with a cheery disposition or frame of mind. Instead, it offers "an ultimate trust and confidence, even in life's darkest moments of suffering and sorrow."[50]

According to Cottingham's vaguely Pascalian-Wittgensteinian view, what is central to Christian life is not "reaching an intellectual decision" but "the adoption of a framework of understanding and praxis."[51] For Cottingham, it is "the practices of spirituality" which stem from the Christian tradition that give meaning to the lives of those who adopt them. "[N]ot in virtue of allegiance to complex theological dogmas but in virtue of a passionate commitment to a certain way of life."[52] Similarly for Pascal, it is not sufficient to wager on God, but a person has to also participate in the rituals of Christianity. It is through practice that one can become a sound, believing Christian.

Despite his expressed agnosticism, Gilligan seems to adopt a Christian framework of understanding, at least in writing his fictional narrative *Breaking Bad*. It is as if writing and producing this television series is his own kind of spiritual exercise. At the very least it is a way for him to exorcise his demons. Lucky for us, Gilligan's spiritual exercises resulted in something that is good, maybe even beautiful, in terms of artistic mastery. When asked how such a "benign-seeming person" can come up with such malign tales, Gilligan quotes Flaubert: "I'm not going to get this exactly right, but it's something like, 'You should be neat and orderly in your life so you can be violent and original in your work.'"[53]

We see the goodness of *Breaking Bad*'s creator expressed in Gilligan's decision to spare Jesse. Gilligan admits that every one of his writers just loved Jesse, who they viewed as in a way over his head.

> When you think of it, he didn't really have a chance in the early days. Walt said, 'You either help me cook meth and sell it, or else I'll turn you in to the DEA.' So this poor kid, based on a couple of really bad decisions he made early on, has been paying through the nose spiritually and physically and mentally and emotionally. In every which way, he's just been paying the piper, and we just figured it felt right for him to get away. It would have been such a bummer for us, as the first fans of the show, for Jesse to have to pay with his life ultimately.[54]

Indeed, it would have been a "bummer" of cosmic proportions if Walt would have ended up killing Jesse. Instead, given the problem of the frailty of goodness, Gilligan lets Jesse go to a better place. "…[H]e's got a long road to recovery ahead, in a sense of being held prisoner in a dungeon for the last six months and being beaten to within an inch of his life and watching Andrea be shot. All these terrible things he's witnessed are going to scar him as well, but the romantic in me wants to believe that he gets away with it and moves to Alaska and has a peaceful life communing with nature."[55]

In an interview with Steven Colbert, Gilligan admits that he fashioned his ending after John Ford's classic Western, *The Searchers*.

> The wonderful western *The Searchers* has John Wayne looking for Natalie Wood for the entire three-hour length of the movie. She's been kidnapped by Indians and raised as one of their own, and throughout the whole movie, John Wayne says, 'I need to put her out of her misery. As soon as I find her, I'm going to kill her.' The whole movie Jeffrey Hunter is saying, 'No, we're not – she's my blood kin, we're saving her,' and he says, 'We're killing her.' And you're like, 'Oh my god, John Wayne is a monster and he's going to do it. You know for the whole movie that this is the major drama between these two characters looking for Natalie Wood. And then at the end of the movie, on impulse, you think he's riding toward her to shoot her, and instead he sweeps her up off her feet and he carries her away and he says, 'Let's go home.' It just gets me every time – the ending of that movie just chokes you up, it's wonderful.[56]

Whether the idea for the finale was borrowed or invented, it reflects the kind of cosmic optimism that permeates *Breaking Bad* and demonstrates the extent to which Gilligan's narrative reflects a theistic theory of life's meaning. Gilligan cashes in on theism's guarantee, namely, that its adherents will find meaning—their purpose and fulfillment—in something that is inherently good. But theism also motivates its believers toward the difficult task of pursuing that good. When we look at Jesse or Skyler or Walt's son or Marie or Hank, and all the other people who had the misfortune of coming into contact with Walter White, we see that misfortune, desperate circumstances, and the bad decisions of others do indeed prevent some individuals from finding meaning in their lives. Only theism offers a remedy. It guarantees that good will ultimately triumph over evil because the theist believes that the things over which we have no control are guided by a divine power that is working for the good.

Richard Norman describes an "attractive additonal gloss" that theists can put on the human experience, as well as a "pattern to the theist's extras." "The belief that a personal power in nature and in our own lives is working out some purpose, obscure to us but ultimately making for the triumph of good, provides the theist with a grand narrative, an overall story into which can be fitted the myriad of more particular stories which makes sense of our lives."[57] While some atheists and agnostics may be able to recognize the appeal of being able to have such a feeling, it presupposes beliefs an atheist or agnostic cannot accept. Contrary to what some theists argue, however, this does not mean that atheists and agnostics cannot find meaning *in* life, that is, terrestrial meaning.[58] This variety of meaningfulness is perfectly sufficient for many non-believers. But not for Vince Gilligan.

CONCLUSION

In one interview in which Gilligan is asked whether Walt's death means that he ultimately pays for his sins, Gilligan uncharacteristically backs off from his romanticism. He suggests that it is in the eye of the beholder. He astutely points out that mere death is not necessarily a way to pay for your sins. "I certainly hope it's not, because the nicest people that have ever lived are going to die eventually."[59] For those fans who want to argue that Walt *did* get away with it, they will point out that "he never got the cuffs put on him. [There was] the one time with Hank."[60] But Walt had already passed away when the cops showed up.

They're rolling in with the sirens going and the lights flashing and he just doesn't give a damn. He's patting his Precious, in *Lord of the Rings* terms. He's with the thing he seems to love the most in the world, which is his work and his meth lab and he just doesn't care about being caught because he knows he's on the way out. So it could be argued that he pays for his sins at the end or it could just as easily be argued that he gets away with it.[61]

Perhaps the kind-hearted Gilligan is being charitable to his beloved fans, leaving open multiple interpretations of his masterful finale. But from the creator's point of view, we have to believe that Walt will get his comeuppance and that Jesse will move on to something better. Otherwise, what *is* the meaning of life in *Breaking Bad*?

Gilligan and his writers considered any number of ways to write their finale, which Gilligan describes as "nothing if not a definitive ending to the series."[62] In more than one interview, Gilligan, along with the key actors in the series, expresses his satisfaction with the ending they ultimately chose. "I guess our gut told us that it would feel satisfying for Walt to at least begin to make amends for his life and for all the sadness and misery wrought upon his family and his friends. Walt is never going to redeem himself. He's just too far down the road to damnation. But at least he takes a few steps along that path."[63]

Indeed, it is too late for Walt. The definitive ending to this epic tale of good and evil is for Walt to end up in Hell. Walt did not spend his final moments struggling with guilt. Instead, he was remembering the good times he'd had as a crystal-meth kingpin. He had a chance to bid farewell to his sleeping daughter. But Walt's "last loving caress was for the lab equipment"[64]—the one thing that made him feel alive. Unlike his peers, Gilligan wrote a deeply satisfying finale. It is satisfying because he did not give in to the ubiquitous postmodern trope: moral ambiguity. In Gilligan's world, Walt will pay for his sins. Revealing the traces of his Catholic upbringing, the creator of this television masterpiece even has the audacity to leave us with hope.

NOTES

1. David Segal, "The Dark Art of *Breaking Bad*," *New York Times*, last modified July 6, 2011. Web.
2. Todd Leopold, "The New, New, New TV Golden Age," CNN, last modified May 6, 2013. Web.
3. "I have never been clear, and I have always been able to live with ambiguities," said Mathew Weiner. "In the abstract, I did think, why not end this show with the greatest commercial ever made? In terms of what it means to people and everything, I am not ambiguity for ambiguity's sake. But it was nice to have your cake and eat it too, in terms of what is advertising, who is Don and what is that thing?" See Tim Goodman, "'Mad Men': Tim Goodman on Pairing Up and Partnering Off as Change Announces Its Arrival," *Hollywood Reporter*, last modified April 27, 2015. Web.
4. Segal, "The Dark Art of *Breaking Bad*."
5. Ibid.
6. Ibid.
7. Thaddeus Metz, "The Meaning of Life," *The Stanford Encyclopedia of Philosophy*, last modified June 3, 2013. Web.
8. Thaddeus Metz suggests using a family resemblance model such that questions about the meaning of life include a variety of closely related but not entirely overlapping questions, such as, "What should we strive for besides achieving happiness and being moral? How can we do something worthy of great esteem or admiration? What is particularly worthy of love and allegiance?" See "The Meaning of Life."
9. Robert Nozick, *Philosophical Explanations* (Cambridge, MA: Harvard University Press, 1981).

10. Peter Railton, "Alienation, Consequentialism, and the Demands of Morality," in *Consequentialism and Its Critics*, ed. S. Scheffler, 93–133 (Oxford: Oxford University Press, 1988).
11. Thomas Hurka, *Perfectionism* (Oxford: Oxford University Press, 1993).
12. Alan Gewirth, *The Community of Rights* (Chicago: University of Chicago Press, 1998).
13. Peter Singer, *Practical Ethics* (Cambridge: Cambridge University Press, 1993).
14. Ronald Dworkin, *Sovereign Virtue. The Theory and Practice of Equality* (Cambridge, MA: Harvard University Press, 2000).
15. Robert Audi, "Intrinsic Value and Meaningful Life," *Philosophical Papers* 34 (2005): 331–355.
16. Julian Baggini, *What's It All About? Philosophy and the Meaning of Life* (Oxford: Oxford University Press, 2005).
17. Brooke Alan Trisel, "Futility and the Meaning of Life Debate," *Sorites* (2002): 70–84; also "Human Extinction and the Value of Our Efforts," *The Philosophical Forum* (2004): 371–391.
18. David Velleman, "Well-Being and Time," *Pacific Philosophical Quarterly* (1991): 48–77.
19. "David Heyd and Franklin G. Miller, "Life Plans: Do They Give Meaning to Our Lives?" *Monist* 93, no. 1 (2010): 17–37.
20. *Huffington Post*, "Breaking Bad Dedicates Premiere To Kevin Cordasco, 16-Year-Old Who Lost Battle With Cancer," *Huffington Post*, last modified August 14, 2013. Web.
21. Paul MacInnes, "*Breaking Bad* Creator Vince Gilligan: The Man Who Turned Walter White from Mr. Chips into Scarface," *The Guardian*, last modified May 18, 2012. Web.
22. Friedrich Nietzsche, *Human, All-Too-Human*, tran. Helen Zimmern and Paul V. Cohn (Mineola, NY: Dover Publications, 2006).
23. Richard Taylor, *Good and Evil* (New York: Macmillan, 1970).
24. Joseph Campbell, *The Power of Myth* (New York: Anchor Doubleday, 1988).
25. *Stanford News*, "'You've got to find what you love,' Jobs," *Stanford News*, last modified June 14, 2005. Web.
26. Kristin Magaldi, "White to Don Draper: The Science Behind Our Love of Antiheroes," *Medical Daily*, last modified March 26, 2015. Web.
27. Erik Wielenberg, *Value and Virtue in a Godless Universe* (Cambridge: Cambridge University Press, 2005).
28. Metz, "The Meaning of Life."
29. Ibid., 34.
30. Lane Brown, "In Conversation: Vince Gilligan on the End of *Breaking Bad*," *Vulture*, last modified May 12, 2013. Web.
31. Metz, "The Meaning of Life."
32. Susan Wolf, *Meaning in Life and Why It Matters* (Princeton: Princeton University Press, 2010).
33. Ibid., 27.
34. Ibid., 30.
35. Ibid., 9.
36. Ibid., 109.
37. Dan Snierson, "'Breaking Bad': Creator Vince Gilligan Explains Series Finale," *Entertainment Weekly*, last modified September 30, 2013. Web.

38. Ibid.
39. John Cottingham, *On the Meaning of Life* (London: Routledge, 2003).
40. Ibid., 62.
41. Ibid., 62.
42. Ibid., 62
43. Ibid., 69.
44. Ibid., 69.
45. Ibid., 69.
46. Ibid., 70.
47. Ibid., 72.
48. Ibid., 73.
49. Ibid., 74.
50. Joseph Runzo and Nancy M. Martin, eds., *The Meaning of Life In The World Religions* (Oxford: Oneworld Publications, 2000).
51. Cottingham, *On the Meaning of Life*, 90.
52. Ibid., 91.
53. Segal, "The Dark Art of *Breaking Bad.*"
54. Snierson, "'Breaking Bad': Creator Vince Gilligan Explains Series Finale."
55. Ibid.
56. Ibid.
57. Norman goes on to suggest that the theist is also likely to believe "that our responsiveness to beauty in art and nature, and our responsiveness to moral values, are imitations of the presence of that same transcendance by personal power. See Richard Norman, "The Varieties of Non-Religious Experiences," *Ratio* (2006): 493.
58. See William Lane Craig, "The Absurdity of Life Without God," in *The Meaning of Life: A Reader,* ed. E. D. Klemke (Oxford: Oxford University Press, 2008), 41: "[I]f there is no God, then life itself becomes meaningless. Man and the universe are without ultimate significance... if God exists, then there is hope for man. But if God does not exist, then all we are left with is despair." If we grant that atheists are able to live robustly meaningful lives, it's not clear what the atheist would lose in conceding that atheism might not offer the greatest meaning possible for any human being. It is not the case that the theist's life is really meaningful and the atheist's is not. They are just meaningful in different ways.
59. Snierson, "'Breaking Bad': Creator Vince Gilligan Explains Series Finale."
60. Ibid.
61. Ibid.
62. Ibid.
63. Ibid.
64. Molly Wilson O'Reilly, "Breaking Bad #516: "Felina"," *Commonweal,* last modified September 30, 2013. Web.

CHAPTER 7

Law and Morality in *Breaking Bad*: The Aesthetics of Justice

David Koepsell

WALT FOUGHT THE LAW

Walter White is an average, middle-class American who has apparently no history of breaking the law, much less any norms or conventions of civil society at the beginning of *Breaking Bad*. In a short time, through pressures both external and internal, Walter becomes a lawbreaker, and slips well into the abyss of both criminal and moral degradation. Walt's journey affords us an opportunity to investigate the relations, if any, between what we refer to as "morality" (the pursuit of the good) and the law. Of course, the law is the secular, civil institution that is often considered to be properly used to enforce shared moral principles. The project is aided by the fact that built into its narrative are characters and situations in which tensions between what is right and what is legal are made explicit, notably including the relationship between Walt and his brother-in-law, Hank, who happens to be a Drug Enforcement Agency (DEA) agent, and who is also unwittingly searching "Heisenberg," his brother-in-law Walt's notorious alter-ego. Later in the series, we gain additional insight into distinctions and vagueness between the good and the legal through the character of attorney Saul Goodman, whose evolution into a shady lawyer is now the subject of its own series. Indeed, as I argue in this essay, literary or dramatic figures like Walt and Hank may offer us some insight into the tricky problem of understanding the notion of justice, perhaps even better than do various theories of justice.

One of the philosophical questions at the heart of *Breaking Bad* is, "Do the moral justifications for Walt's actions outweigh the illegality of what he has chosen to do?" Wrapped up with this question are dozens of related practical

D. Koepsell (✉)
UAM-Xochimilco, Mexico City, Mexico

© The Author(s) 2017
K.S. Decker et al. (eds.), *Philosophy and Breaking Bad*,
DOI 10.1007/978-3-319-40343-4_7

and philosophical problems that complicate the answer to the fundamental question of Walt's ethics, just as in the real-world the discussions of the relations of law to morality are dynamic and complex. Fiction and life are filled with questions about the contrasts or intersections of law and morality, such as Victor Hugo's epic treatise in the form of *Les Miserables*, in which we are forced to confront the injustice of blind obedience to law against the backdrop of eventual, violent revolution.

Breaking Bad's backdrop is more mundane: recessionary Middle America, pre-Obamacare and in the midst of a mid- and south-western meth epidemic. Walter White is no Jean Valjean, a character who, following an unjust and long jailing for a minor theft, attempts to walk the straight and narrow and succeeds for years. Rather, the legal and social climate that Walt inhabits, as well as various cultural baggage, leads him from a nebbishy family life to drug kingpin. We might well ask whether the circumstances Walt was faced with, both personal and cultural, suggest some ambiguity about Walt's ethical choices in light of the legal climate and its various problems. In order to put this into the context of the age-old philosophical debate, let's first examine some theories about the relationship between law and morality in the context of the central dilemma posed by the series.

THERE'S WHAT'S RIGHT AND THERE'S WHAT'S RIGHT

When diagnosed with terminal lung cancer, Walt has few practical options for the rest of his life and especially his medical care. Like most Americans, he lacked sufficient savings. He also had no adequate medical insurance. The legal context in which someone might be faced with bankruptcy because of the onset of a sudden and terminal illness was part of the national debate over Obamacare, which is still far from meeting the standards in most developed countries. Elsewhere, universal healthcare simply doesn't present the threat to patients like Walt whose family will be destitute if he receives treatment. The morality by which we first must judge Walt's decision is bracketed by this legal/moral context, in which the poor, or even the working poor/middle class, must choose between essentials like food and shelter, or medical care, but not both. Indeed, a vast literature examining the morality of this context exists, weighing the libertarian arguments that individual health and well-being are not the responsibility of the state against the care ethics that suggests that we should provide certain minimum levels of healthcare for everyone regardless of their financial means.

Like the case of Jean Valjean, who stole bread to help feed his family, should we judge Walt less harshly for his choice to break the law and enter the drug trade because the existing legal and social climate is such that his family will likely become homeless or worse due to his illness? Just as the law that, regardless of means to acquire food, forces Valjean into making the choice to steal and face the risks so that his family won't starve, so too does Walt disregard the law that prohibits making meth in order to provide for his family. In another legal regime, no such choice might be necessary: in a welfare system, medical care or food would be available so that the choice of committing a crime need not be the only path for people like Walt.

Our choices about how to view Walt in relation to both the law and some form of morality hinge in part on our view of the nature of law itself, and whether it is somehow related to "the good," or whether this relation obtains naturally or simply by virtue of human design.

THE EMERGENCE OF POSITIVISM

Walt's musings about the nature of law and morality arise several times during the course of the series. The idea of "positive law" arises for the viewer when he and his brother-in-law, DEA agent Hank Schrader, are smoking Cuban cigars at a family barbeque. Cuban cigars were, at the time, illegal, and this prompts Walt to remark about the social and temporal contexts of substance prohibitions. Of course, at the time Walt has already begun his drug manufacturing sideline ("A No Rough-Stuff Type Deal"). Walt concludes that the prohibition against meth and other substances is essentially "arbitrary" and Hank, puffing his Cuban, warns him that a lot of guys in jail had the same attitudes. Walt is correct about meth, as shown by the evidence that in the early 1900s, drugs like cocaine and heroin were also legal. When prohibition of alcohol was enacted into law in the USA, Hank would have been an illegal manufacturer of the same sort as his brother-in-law Walt simply by making his home-brew "Schraderbrau."

Until recently, legal systems were generally based upon a presupposition that morality (generally defined by the state's church) and law were one and the same, or at least intimately connected. For more than a thousand years, legal rules were devised by sovereigns who were themselves held to be divinely imbued with moral authority for rule-making. Of course, with the spread of the Enlightenment and the fall of various sovereigns at the hands of liberal revolutions, the basis for valid, moral rule-making and enforcement began to shift. The foundations of modern liberalism included a notion of natural law. Devised Locke, Rousseau and other modern liberal political theorists a new vision of the basis for natural law, one that extended natural law theory beyond the simplistic, sovereign-based dogma of old, to a more consistent set of tenets. Natural law, it was argued, grounded the validity of legal rules in duties and obligations dictated by the fabric of nature (whether or not one accepted its origins in a deity), and even sovereigns were subject to the dictates of nature's laws. This shift in thinking reflected a shift in scientific and theological thought, roughly reflecting the move from an involved, acting creator, to a distant, detached, clock-maker creator, who sets the world in motion and then steps back. The revolutions sparked by Locke et al. were seen as legitimated by the violation of subjects' naturally endowed rights to life, liberty and property, and these natural rights formed the basis for modern liberal democracies, both in their constitutions and in their laws. In a world in which just law derives from nature, there is a solid connection between law and morality. But a new trend emerged in the late Enlightenment, when philosophers and political theorists began to question the foundations of just law, as well as to reformulate approaches to ethics and justice themselves. In the nineteenth and early twentieth centuries, the natural foundations of law began to be challenged, especially in Anglo-Saxon legal scholarship.

The British philosopher Jeremy Bentham moved away from natural law theory in arguing against deontology as the foundation of ethics. Bentham, seeking to make more scientific the study of ethics, rejected nature as a foundation of duties, and formulated the modern ethical approach we call utilitarianism. He is well known for calling natural law theory "nonsense upon stilts." His objections to natural law were epistemological, as he argued we could never rightly suppose we know the intentions of a creator, nor can duty-based theories of ethics like those of Immanuel Kant ever provide a sufficient justification for accepting the obligation to any particular duty *a priori*. Indeed, a central weakness of deontology is found in reconciling the existence of certain duties with contradictory duties, or converse duties that appear to arise in exceptional situations. Utilitarianism does not presuppose the existence of categorical duties, but rather argues that the ethical compulsion lies not in intent or duty, but rather in consequences. The epistemological argument is clear: consequences can be measured *post hoc* and from this, more or less predicted using Bentham's "hedonic calculus." Yet intentions can never be similarly measured. In the scientific vein of the time, Bentham sought to make the pursuit of legal and ethical theory calculable, and viewed a solid, measurable basis for judging an action as being found only in its consequences, namely, the amount of net happiness produced. For Bentham, the good can be judged based solely upon whether it increases net happiness, and duties, intentions or other epistemologically unapproachable matters need not be consulted. The implications for legal rule-making are obvious, and in the absence of a natural foundation for just laws, legal theorists began to reimagine the role and scope of legal theory.

According to John Austin, the validity of legal rules can only be judged according to the proper foundation of their enactment by a sovereign. A sovereign is one who is recognized as such by a majority, and the laws are the sovereign's enactments, backed by sanctions. This means that there is no basis external to a legal system by which rules can be judged to be right or wrong, morally speaking. Rule-making is valid so long as the sovereign is the majority-recognized sovereign, has no higher sovereign and so long as the rules are backed by the promise of sanctions in case of their violation. Even while a continental positivism of a sort was being formulated by Hans Kelsen, in which at least some solid basis for recognizing a valid sovereign is posited (a *Grundnorm*), the Anglo-Saxon school of positive law becomes solidified with the work of H.L.A. Hart. Hart nicely categorizes types of rules, distinguishing among primary rules (which direct action) and secondary rules (which address procedures). But in direct opposition to Kelsen, Hart rejects the theory of *Grundnorm*, and does nothing to resolve what seems now to be a significant gap in positive legal theory: reconciling rules with a notion of *justice*. As opposed to the approach of John Rawls, a neo-Kantian and the twentieth century's most prominent political philosopher outside of the positivist tradition, legal positivists do not see inquiring into the *just* foundations of legal rules—outside of the valid enactments of sovereigns according to established procedures—as a coherent area of inquiry.

Ours is a hybrid culture of sorts in which laws are taken not as founded solely upon nature, nor justice found only in the strict adherence to law, but in which we are nonetheless largely positivist in our conceptions of justice. Walt avoids the legal system, partly because he finds a lawyer who helps him navigate it. Justice is a game, of sorts, that can be navigated by bending the rules and by working around its edges, but there is still some sense of justice beyond mere following of rules, a sense that is hinted at in our sympathies for both criminals and lawmen caught up in a drug war and an economy that are beyond their control. How do we deal with issues of justice aside from our aesthetic sense of what is just? In trials, jurors still may reach verdicts based solely upon their *sense* of justice—they can act according to what feels right, even while supposedly acting in accordance with "the law." The notion of jury nullification is based upon this, the jury is the final arbiter, not lawyers or judges. Yet, by and large, legal systems depend largely upon a positivist approach to what is legal without regard to what is good or even just.

Legal positivism is the political extension of the ethical theory of utilitarianism. With legal positivism, we need not concern ourselves with metaphysical questions of right or wrong, just or unjust, but can focus instead on epistemological questions regarding the results of our actions and whether they accord with our preferences. Legal positivism is the dominant theoretical paradigm in Anglo-Saxon law schools, and it is bolstered by various trends in politics, including concerns with pluralism and multiculturalism. Natural law theory is vulnerable to critique where various cultural, religious, ethnic or philosophical backgrounds confront problems from differing viewpoints. Adopting the natural law justification for a rule that contradicts some religious, ethnic, cultural or philosophical viewpoints means arguing for the error of someone's point of view. But as we live in increasingly pluralistic societies, with ever more multicultural populations, asserting one paradigm of values to be correct risks eroding what many conceive to be a foundation of liberalism: the freedom of conscience. A basic tenet of our modern liberal democracies is necessarily that people are entitled to their opinions, points of view and to express their beliefs. Thus, states ought not to criticize the foundations of those beliefs or force citizens to ascribe to a particular point of view. Because positive legal theory embraces the notion that a law is valid so long as it is enacted by a sovereign and backed by sanctions, then there is no further basis to question the validity of a validly enacted rule. The freedom of conscience of those who either support or defy the rule is preserved, because no judgment about the underlying *justice* of that rule may be made. We can only classify people as "rule followers" or "rule breakers," not as "just" or "unjust," and the basis of valid rules need not be traced to any natural, immutable source. A rule breaker cannot be judged to be immoral, and rules we do not like can be changed without reflection upon metaphysical issues of justice or *the good*. Pluralism and multiculturalism are preserved both within nations and among them, as ethics and rules are completely divorced. Lawmaking can be scientifically accomplished by looking at a list of projected consequences, and applying those rules that maximize the consequences we prefer.

But legal positivism is vulnerable to attacks based upon histories of failing to divide ethics from rules, and thus upon cultural, national and international reactions to perceived injustices within sovereign states, as well as between them. These same attacks are consistent with criticisms of utilitarian ethical theory: if we are only guided by consequences for the majority as a guide to action, then on what moral basis could minorities be protected? In utilitarianism, as in legal positivism, there is no theoretical basis for protection of minorities. In classical utilitarianism, the right thing to do is that which increases happiness (maximizes utility) overall. Positive legal theorists similarly must recognize the validity of an enactment if it is enacted by a valid sovereign (supported by a majority) and backed up with sanctions. Countless examples of potential injustices can be named, both historical and hypothetical. Positivism fails us too in a deep examination of the tension between ethics and rules in a number of works, including *Breaking Bad*, as we shall see in greater detail below.

I will argue that these analytic accounts of justice fail because the connection between law and the "good" is not founded upon logic nor derived from nature. Rather, we have an aesthetic sense of judgment most closely captured by art (including our religious works) rather than through rigorous analysis of the "good" or its foundations. As it turns out, justice is experienced phenomenally, not analytically, and so is like obscenity, which we cannot define but "know when we see it." *Breaking Bad* puts us in a position to realize this through Walt's rigorous analysis of the good, his frequent justifications for acting in ways that we likely see as unjust and by his efforts to contrast these justifications with contextual injustices that challenge our traditional, legal and religious conceptions of justice. In the end, we are meant to see Walt's moral arc as concluding with a form of justice, regardless of its contrast with our typical views of the good, and despite its clearly unlawful path.

WALT'S POSITIVELY WRONG

Walt has been forced to consider issues of right and wrong from the beginning of the series, notably when confronted with the quandary of whether to kill Krazy-8 when his initial attempt at poisoning him goes awry. Trapped in a basement, chained to a pole, Krazy-8 is recovering from his injuries and seems likely to regain his health and live. Walt and Jesse flip coins to decide who will kill him, and Walt loses. Faced with the decision to take a life more directly, with his own hands, Walt is conflicted. He makes his now-famous list of reasons to either spare Krazy-8's life or to kill him. Outweighing the moral prohibition on murder is Walt's love for his family. Killing Krazy-8 is still murder, and not even justifiable homicide in the eyes of the law.

Walt is almost convinced by the moral or perhaps the legal arguments against murder, until the exigency of Krazy-8's own murderousness forces Walt to take his life. Swayed by the utilitarian necessity of protecting himself and his family, Walt overcomes both morality and the law and arguably saves his and his family's lives. The audience witnesses Walt's first murder and perhaps sympathize, understanding that some higher duty may overcome the legal or moral prohibitions Walt has violated, agreeing that somehow the duty to protect one's family, especially against a murderous criminal, may somehow mitigate against the moral or legal harm. Will Krazy-8 even be missed? Won't there be good consequences if there is one less violent drug dealer on the streets?

There are good reasons, during the course of *Breaking Bad*, to question the positivistic outlook; a character who seems to have embraced it is Saul Goodman, the sleazy lawyer who helps Walt navigate several legal issues, but who also hooks him up with important figures in the dark underworld of the Albuquerque drug trade. DEA agents who defy or break the law, both for personal reasons (they like Cuban cigars) or in the furtherance of an investigation (as Gomez and Schrader seem routinely inclined to do) make the fact of lawyers working hand in hand with criminals less surprising. On this view, the law is a flexible barrier to achieving various goals, and both cops and lawyers, better than anyone, understand how it functions and how to work around it. In light of this, Walt's cooking meth seems somehow more innocent, driven by the need to fund his cancer treatments and build a nest egg for a family living paycheck to paycheck. Is the net result to illuminate some higher form of "justice" outweighing the obvious rule-breaking? Does some good transcend that which is defined both by typical morality and the law, and has Walt effectively sought and achieved it, or is the show in its entirety an indictment of the very concept of justice?

PROBLEMS OF JUSTICE

Positive legal theory leaves open the difficult problem of determining when a particular action or intention is morally 'wrong'. In fact, none of these theories make the notion of "moral wrongness" comprehensible. Things may or may not be acceptable in specific contexts, or may be valued for increasing general utility (assuming it can be measured or is measurable), but notions of right or wrong, as the terms are traditionally used in ethical theory, are not *per se* applicable. Although students of ethics are taught about utilitarianism, and both ethics scholars and applied ethicists must resort at time to the hedonic calculus in resolving ethical dilemmas, the end result of this work will always be a determination about what one should do in order to increase general utility (happiness), and not clearly what we typically consider to be an ethical judgment about a category of actions that are *right* or *good* in a *moral* sense.

This is because each decision is necessarily contingent, and hypothetical, as opposed to decisions made according to deontological theory, which are *categorical* and apply to every such action or intention. The weaknesses of utilitarian-based systems of justice are noted by John Rawls and other neo-Kantian scholars of law and ethics. These weaknesses make it difficult to argue that positive legal theory, or utilitarianism, can lead a society to a state fairly called *just*. This is because "justice" implies some connection with notions of morality. In modern constitutional parlance, there are two forms or aspects of justice: substantive and procedural. Procedural justice means simply that for every person who becomes involved in a criminal or civil judicial matter, the procedures used are employed equally and fairly, their content is transparent and purposes clear. Substantive justice is more complex, and the notion implies some accord with some higher law. Substantive justice is a measure by which both constitutions and legislation may be judged, and according to which they may fail. If a law fails to fulfill the requirements of substantive justice, it may justly be struck down. Procedural justice, on the other hand, refers to how a legal process accords with the non-substantive, but largely bureaucratic, elements of achieving justice, although the two forms may be intertwined. The difference between the two is like the difference between the "letter" of the law and the "spirit" of the law.

Given the weaknesses of positive legal theory in providing a solid context in which justice can be evaluated, or by which just legal systems and their rules could be imposed, why does the positivist approach continue to thrive in legal scholarship and political theory? One explanation may be that legal and political scholars have abandoned Kantian notions of categorical right and wrong, and have embraced a utilitarian world view. It seems to be that in so doing, and in simultaneously accepting the Rawlsian notion of *distributive* justice (as indeed some of these same scholars and theorists seem to do), they are trapped in a contradiction. Rawlsian distributive justice depends upon accepting the notion of categorical duties, including the duty to treat everyone as an end, and not merely as a means to an end. Another categorical duty under Rawls is to treat everyone with equal dignity. But Rawls simply accepts the Kantian explanation for the existence of these duties, arguing that we would arrive at these duties in forming a society if we place ourselves in the "original position" behind his hypothetical "veil of ignorance" from which vantage point we have no idea of who we might be in a society. Kant's categorical imperative is arrived at by a different heuristic, but the content is the same: we must be able to successfully universalize an imperative without contradiction in order for the rule to be moral. Neither Rawls nor Kant judge the morality of a rule according to consequences, and Rawls is thus generally classed as a neo-Kantian, as he himself at times agrees.

If justice becomes contingent upon actually or potentially existing laws, as it must under a utilitarian/positivist perspective, then rule-making will be similarly contingent. Just as Bentham insisted, the link between lawmaking and morality must be completely severed, and decisions about the *justice* of rules must be limited to procedural matters. As a result, no coherent system of substantive justice could be based upon utility as a measure or standard by which just laws could be created. The barriers to a substantive sense of justice compatible with utilitarianism are epistemological (the calculus cannot be carried out to sufficient exactness, either over and across populations, or through time) as well as ontological: the calculus does not tell us what is *good* or *right*, but merely what we should do in a certain situation to maximize happiness. And despite Bentham's rejection of deontology, the demand to maximize happiness relies upon a categorical rule, one which cannot be adjudged scientifically, namely, happiness is a sound basis for moral decision-making. Because of this and similar problems with utilitarianism, and the unacceptable practical consequences of accepting a pure utilitarian basis for ethical decision-making, legal positivism stands on similarly shaky ground. The fact is that neither rule makers nor ordinary people function as though there is no grounding for just rules other than utility. There are clear, historical instances of both individuals and states committing acts that are clearly *unjust*, regardless of their effect on general utility. The reasons why we consider certain intentional states and actions to be wrong in themselves are beyond the scope of this chapter, but the fact that we do consider them wrong is recognized in constitutions and in courts. The general recognition that, despite the arguments of legal positivists, there are certain categorically *wrong* actions and intentions, is what has enabled constitutional change as well as liberal revolutions, and it is what has made these historical moments *good*. That unjust laws are possible provides the impetus behind the slow march toward greater freedom and more perfect systems of justice.

In the absence of theory of justice, how does law work? What enables us to have some confidence in systems of law, or the discretion of lawyers and judges? We see various "injustices" all the time, come to some consensus about them and adjust of institutions and their administrators on occasion, but what guides that process? In the absence of clear, guiding principles of what constitutes the good and the just, how do we determine who wears the white hat and who wears the black, porkpie hat? *Breaking Bad* makes it evident that the inquiry goes much deeper than traditional analysis allows.

It is clear there is no "good guy" in *Breaking Bad*. Even the lawmen are tainted by the desire to achieve goals that fly in the face of moral and legal prohibitions, and so justify their rule-breaking at least to themselves. In pursuit of some higher "justice," positivists and utilitarians agree: the ends may justify the means. But isn't this the exact lesson of Walt's endeavors, and hasn't he justified in its conclusion his descent into "evil?" Innocents may have perished along the way, but has Walt found justice in his demise?

The Transcendent, Aesthetic Justice of *Breaking Bad*

In the absence of some divine or natural morality, our legal codes cannot be grounded in anything but exigency, and so the very notion of justice as some higher ideal is suspect. Walt shows no apparent interest or belief in the divine, nor does he seem to believe that nature is a foundation for the good. His own "good," with reference to caring for his family, is the measure of his actions.

The justice system is all but powerless because of human frailties, and its failures drive the five seasons of *Breaking Bad*. As we have seen, the injustice of society in failing to provide healthcare is part of what drives Walt to his criminal pursuit. Justice is as dead as God, and so Walt and those around and involved with him must forge their own paths to seek whatever justice they can, whatever nexus between their desires and some sort of "good" they can assemble from a meaningless and indifferent universe. Let's return to some contrasts between Walter White and Jean Valjean, and contrast the themes and characters in both to another work, Dostoevsky's *Crime and Punishment*, and the characters of Raskolnikov and Porfiry, to examine the possible role of a transcendent justice beyond mere exigency in *Breaking Bad*'s moral landscape.

What analytic philosophy fails to accomplish in the field of "justice," literature achieves. In other worlds, none of the approaches to the connection between law and morality undertaken as a philosophical project succeeds in confirming any relation between the two except connections that are ineffable and transient. Yet, in depictions of heroes, both tragic and noble, we may sense justice, however fleeting and intangible, through their ordeals.

Les Miserables presents us with Valjean and Javert, a pair of characters similar to Walt and Hank. Valjean, the (former) criminal, is pursued relentlessly by the tenacious lawman Javert. Similarly, parallel characters and themes emerge in *Crime and Punishment* in which the criminal Raskolnikov is doggedly pursued by attorney/detective Porfiry Petrovitch. In all three dramas, the conception and the attainment of "justice" differs. Ultimately, once we see that Walt believes that he has somehow achieved justice in the show's resolution, we can see in *Breaking Bad* a particularly modern view of justice.

Jean Valjean has done his time and more, having served 19 years in jail for stealing some bread to save his family from starvation. When released, he essentially "skips parole," tosses out his "yellow passport" which branded him as an ex-con and assumes a new name and life. Along the way, he steals from a bishop, but is saved from the police, and then pursues a life of goodness after he is "converted" by the religious figure. He becomes a mayor and a factory owner, a respectable, wealthy man under cover of his new identity and guided by his converted spirit. Still, Javert tracks him down. When Javert finds him and realizes that Valjean is his former prisoner working and living under a new identity, he disregards the goodness of the station which Valjean has attained, focusing solely upon the law that has been broken it.

Javert is the perfect positivist. The law has been broken and this must be rectified. There is no exclusion in the positive law for violating the yellow passport rule, and Jean Valjean's new life is a legal lie that must be corrected. Justice is, after all, abiding by man-made rules. The moral of *Les Miserables*, though, is that the law fails to suffice. The conditions that "required" or at least drove Jean Valjean to his initial theft were beyond his control. Javert's use of the law was disproportionate and unfair, though perfectly valid from a positivist viewpoint. Javert is eventually so conflicted between his compulsion to see that "justice" is done and his eventual respect for Valjean as a reformed, good person, that he kills himself, his sense of justice unable to comport with justice as a purely legal concept.

Blind adherence to the law, disregarding moral qualities such as virtue, forgiveness, salvation, is literally deadly for Javert. Despite our philosophical failures in targeting the foundations of justice through analytic means, our aesthetic of justice is clear: Javert is wrong, though he abides to the law, and Valjean is right, despite his defiance of the letter of the law. Justice is defined, we feel aesthetically, by something more than the written law. Victor Hugo pits law against love as the main values we might adhere to, and love must win in the end. It is the same aesthetic sense that at first draws us into sympathy with Walter White. His character is compelling in part because we do not abhor him. Rather, we identify with Walt, or at least sympathize with him, as we do with Valjean, understanding that we too would be tempted to do what Walt chooses in order to refrain from bankrupting his family, and perhaps even leave a little something for them in the process. A certain necessity, due to the injustice of the social context, seems to make his choice acceptable at first, though later we will become appalled by future choices that stem from his meth-cooking path.

As with Javert, Hank's insistence of blind adherence to the law is distasteful at first, and the hypocrisy of it made clear in relation to his own preference for illegal cigars and his wife's kleptomania. Moreover, Hank and Gomez pursue their legal targets with a fair amount of disregard for legal process, defying rules of evidence, privacy and other restrictions of police process throughout the series. The law is not the equivalent of justice in *Breaking Bad* or *Les Miserables*.

Justice in *Les Miserables* is realized in the confluence of the students' rebellion and the death of Javert by his own hand. Javert recognizes the disjunction between the legal, positivist view of justice that affords no exception to laws against theft and that can condemn a man like Valjean despite his salvation and pursuit of a new life. Jean Valjean perseveres and triumphs. He attains justice. Javert can only do so through death.

Contrast this now with the criminal/pursuer duo from *Crime and Punishment*. Unlike the criminal protagonist of *Les Miserables*, Raskolnikov murders a pawnbroker out of anger and nihilism. Although he does indeed owe his landlady back rent, his major purpose in killing her is to see what it is like out of a morbid, philosophical curiosity founded in nihilism: the belief that there is no meaning to life. Without a god to judge, Rodion Raskolnikov is free to do what he will in pursuit of his own purposes, much as Walt, who in calculating the makeup of the human body concludes we have no "soul," is free to embark upon his criminal pursuits to attain a materially sustainable existence for his family. But Raskolnikov's murders (he also kills the sister of the pawn-broker in the course of the crime) eat at him afterward, plunging him into both mental and physical sickness. Finally, his mental torture and the gentle but persistent questioning of the detective Porfiry, who is convinced of Raskolnikov's guilt but lacks evidence, bring Raskolnikov to the point of confession.

Porfiry uses psychology rather than a badge or gun to get inside the head of Raskolnikov and extract a confession. Raskolnikov is then sentenced to eight years of labor in Siberia and thus justice is served. Profiry has operated under the assumption that he could bring on Raskolnikov's confession and thus lead him toward a path of redemption. As with the bishop who nudges Jean Valjean toward a life of virtue, Raskolnikov's confession and incarceration bring a form of justice no other act could. Unlike Javert's pursuit of Valjean, Porfiry pursues Raskolnikov with love, and so his eventual justice is not tinged with the unbending legalism that dooms Javert. The sense of justice served differs from *Les Miserables*, in which the criminal protagonist is "saved" well before he is caught by the law.

Walter White differs from these two literary bad guys. He is never saved. His pursuer, his own brother-in-law, will die in a shoot-out that Walt tries to avoid, and this despite entreaties to the white supremacists to spare him, not because it is right, but just because he is his brother-in-law. Walter White's justice will neither come from incarceration nor personal salvation and triumph. He must die. But he must die having achieved something, having overcome the obstacles that both the law and other criminals have erected. Walt's death at the end of the series could be viewed as tragic, but his death was effectively preordained in the series opener. He was dying of cancer, a man with no prospects and nothing to leave for his family, a man who might be mourned, but never in his absence materially missed. By the end of the series he has left a legacy. He successfully manufactures not just Blue Sky meth, a much-desired and imitated product, but a legacy. Heisenberg and his legend will be told for generations, but more importantly for Walt's sake, he has achieved what he set out to do: secure the comfort for his family after his death, something he could hardly have done had he walked the straight and narrow. The aesthetic beauty of the justice he attains, though clouded by murder and mayhem, addiction and scandal, is undeniable. It is satisfying. Justice is a form of satisfaction, as evidence by these three stories. It is not the adherence to some legal code, nor the abidance of some natural law. Rather, justice involves something a bit more ineffable, but made clear through stories about justice, crime, deceit and love.

Walt sums it up when he refuses to apologize for what he has done and who he has become. He has found something he lacked before *Breaking Bad* began: a love for something, a love for himself and a way to satisfy his love for his family in the only way possible. "I did it for me. I liked it. I was good at it. And, I was really…. I was alive." Walt has overcome two deaths and must succumb to the third. The death that cancer threatened, and the death that his undistinguished everyday middle-class existence embodied are trumped by his criminal adventure. In the end, his death in exacting vengeance on those who killed his brother-in-law, and securing safety and comfort for his family, are the best justice he could hope for. Like Javert, death by his own design solves the problem of conflict between the good and the just.

Whether the justice achieved in *Breaking Bad* is morally good or not cannot be analytically proven. It does not comport with standard theories of justice, it violates conceptions both of natural law and positivism. The justice Walt gets is purely an aesthetic one. We are left satisfied, like Walt, with the hint of a smile on our lips as the dust settles on the horror that has transpired. It is finished, and we feel a sense that it has ended as it should.

PART 3

"I Will Put You Under the Jail": The Tragedy of *Breaking Bad*

CHAPTER 8

The Crumbling Patriarchy and Triumphant Feminist Ethic of Care in *Breaking Bad*

Leigh Kolb

When Jake and Amy were presented with Heinz's dilemma in Lawrence Kohlberg's research on morality,[1] the children's differing answers helped illustrate a dichotomy between justice and care presented in Carol Gilligan's groundbreaking text *In a Different Voice: Psychological Theory and Women's Development*. Gilligan challenges the notion that Jake's black and white, justice-based answer was more "developed" (according to Kohlberg's scale) than Amy's much less certain answer, which acknowledged a moral gray area and focused on the possible effects on the relationships involved.[2] Heinz's dilemma involves the question of whether a man should steal expensive prescription drugs to save his wife, and the Walter White dilemma in *Breaking Bad* starts with a question of whether a man should make illegal meth for profit to pay for his own cancer drugs and to ostensibly provide for his family.

Had Jake and Amy been faced with the central conflicts presented throughout *Breaking Bad*—methamphetamine production and distribution, murder, familial deception, and disloyalty—their reasoning and logic would likely mirror Walter White and Jesse Pinkman's, respectively. Throughout the series, Walt, the flailing patriarch, is contrasted with Jesse, the sensitive young man who is largely unconcerned with the trappings of traditional masculinity that Walt attempts to embody. Walt's patriarchal rise and fall represents a crumbling of empire (both his meth empire and the more expansive societal empire of patriarchal control and violence). Yet, Jesse consistently lives within a feminist ethic of care, and while he suffers greatly, he is ultimately triumphant. Through the decisions of Walt, Jesse, and various ancillary characters,

L. Kolb (✉)
East Central College, Union, MO, USA

© The Author(s) 2017
K.S. Decker et al. (eds.), *Philosophy and Breaking Bad*,
DOI 10.1007/978-3-319-40343-4_8

Breaking Bad promotes a feminist ethic of care over the violent, patriarchal empire-building of the past.

"Who's in Charge? Me"

During the pilot episode, Walt delivers a lesson to his high school chemistry class. He says that chemistry is the study of matter, but he prefers to see it as "the study of change." It's his fiftieth birthday, and it's quite clear that he's celebrating this milestone amid the resentment of a life he had not imagined for himself. A plaque shows that he contributed research to Nobel Prize-winning work. Yet he's teaching in a public high school classroom, a profession that is not regarded with prestige either by reputation—as his disengaged students or peers remind him constantly—or financial gain, as his after-school job at a car wash signifies. At his surprise birthday party that night, his brother-in-law Hank, a Drug Enforcement Agency (DEA) agent, hands Walt his Glock; Walt says that it's heavy, and Hank responds, "That's why they hire men." Walt acts sheepish, another example in a day full of moments reminding him that his is not a life of power or strength.

Of course, the opening flashback scene shows the audience that Walt will indeed get his chance. As he speaks to a camera to record a message to his family, his life clearly in danger, he chokes back sobs and tells them how much he loves them. "No matter how it may look, I only had you in my heart," he says. Sirens approach, and his look turns sinister as he confidently points a gun forward.

This moment is important, as it immediately introduces a viewer to a man who is much more comfortable with violence and desirous of power than he would have those around him believe. Walt, in his deepening resentment over any instance of emasculation in his life (perhaps originally stemming from Gray Matter Technologies' success without him), attempts to become Nietzsche's Superman (*Übermensch*) and build an empire.

In *Thus Spoke Zarathustra*, Zarathustra says, "For today all petty people have become lord and master: they all preach submission and acquiescence and prudence and diligence and consideration and the long et cetera of petty virtues. What is womanish ... that now wants to become master of mankind's entire destiny—oh disgust! disgust! disgust!" He goes on, encouraging men to "overcome" to become higher men, "And rather despair than submit."[3] By the end of the pilot, Walt has literally risen from the ashes and is on his way toward embracing the path of least submission as he clamors to gain power over his life and his family's life, though under the guise of protecting them.

In "On Violence," Hannah Arendt says, "It is, I think, a rather sad reflection of the present state of political science that our terminology does not distinguish among such key words as 'power,' 'strength,' 'force,' 'authority,' and finally, 'violence'—all of which refer to distinct, different phenomena and would hardly exist unless they did."[4] She goes on to delineate between these terms (which Walt would certainly conflate), and reaches this point: "Violence can always destroy power; out of the barrel of a gun grows the most effective command, resulting in the most instant and perfect obedience. What never can grow out of it is power."[5] Walt sees violence as a necessary way to increase his power. He tends to view violent acts as claims of justice: violence is used to save his own life, to save his family's life, to keep his territory, or—sometimes most importantly—to preserve and guarantee his flow of money. Since Walt's resentment apparently stems from Gray Matter's success, his cancer diagnosis gives him an excuse to attempt to seek "power, strength, force, [and] authority," using means that his society has made synonymous with those terms: money and violence.

In *The Deepening Darkness: Patriarchy, Resistance & Democracy's Future*, Carol Gilligan and David A.J. Richards argue that looking at the ancient Roman empire can give us deep insights into our current society, particularly its patriarchal tendencies: "Patriarchy is an anthropological term denoting families or societies ruled by fathers. It sets up a hierarchy ... in which the priest, the *hieros*, is a father, *pater*. As an order of living, it elevates some men over other men and all men over women; within the family, it separates fathers from sons ... and places both women and children under a father's authority."[6] Walt's desire to be the patriarch inside and outside of his home adds to hierarchy's destructive force. *The Deepening Darkness* asserts that throughout history, we see patriarchy (private and public) as mostly accepting of violence, since domination and power are the ultimate goals.

Hank Schrader's masculinity takes traditional forms: he carries guns, works in an authoritative position in law enforcement, and boasts beer-making, barbecuing, and Cuban cigar-smoking as hobbies. As Walt's brother-in-law, his role with the DEA is a central conflict. His masculinity also serves as a threat to Walt, especially in the early seasons. Walt Jr. appears to idolize Hank and listens to his stories of drug busts with reverence and excitement. However, as the series progresses, as Hank is pushed to become even more masculine, he becomes more emotionally and physically disabled. When he kills Tuco and gets his grill as a prize from his coworkers, his anxiety increases. He's done what he's supposed to do, and what he's supposed to be proud of, but it haunts him. When Tortuga is killed and beheaded in the desert and Hank sees his colleagues killed and dismembered, he cannot seem to recover emotionally. In "I.F.T." Hank takes Steven Gomez to a bar and sees a drug deal; he wants to take care of it himself, and for a dangerous moment, he leverages his masculinity, leaving his gun in the vehicle to go back in against Gomez's advice to corner the dealers. When he is almost killed by the Cousins, he is left unable to walk, helpless and vulnerable. Hank's trajectory shows that the more patriarchal violence a man enacts, witnesses, and internalizes, the more harmed he is, literally and figuratively. Hank as the figure of justice, also signifies that an adherence to justice without emotional intelligence or a sense of care is destructive. This justice-obsession hurts him personally: he coldly whips out a recorder to take Skyler's statement and calls Jesse a "junkie murderer," wanting his confession and seeing the upside to having his murder on tape. It also hurts him professionally, as he's consistently asked to redirect his efforts from his apparent obsession with the blue meth. *Breaking Bad* shows that an inability to empathize and communicate selflessly—to embody and perform traditional masculinity and patriarchal authority—is tragic. Walt's signature blue meth, and his all-consuming desire to create it, parallels his gendered desire to be a patriarch in public and private life. Hank's parallel obsession with chasing the blue meth also symbolizes his masculine goals. The gendering of the color blue is significant, as is the fact that it destroys the men who are obsessed with it.

In the introduction to *The Deepening Darkness*, Virginia Woolf's words are summoned to describe how patriarchal systems have left us with "dead bodies and ruined houses" scattered throughout our history.[7] So also does *Breaking Bad* leave us with those exact images, remnants of the destruction of patriarchy and the violence it encourages.

"A Man Provides"

The night that Walt will watch Jane Margolis die, he sits in his living room and hears Skyler singing "Hush Little Baby" to newborn Holly over the monitor while a show about elephants plays on the television. The narrator notes that elephants are matriarchal in social order ("Phoenix"). He tells Jesse later that this moment in the living room was his perfect moment—the moment he should have died, when his family would have still missed him ("Fly"). His last memory of his own father was of a sick, weak, and miserable man. He wants his family to miss him and remember him in a positive light. He knows at this point that that won't happen. Had Walt not left the house that evening, he would have been submitting to a kind of domestic comfort—even a matriarchy—that he clearly wasn't ready to embrace. A representation of matriarchy on screen, his wife's voice on the monitor—he looked content, but he was not yet satisfied. When he watches a young woman die while his wife sings lullabies to his daughter, Walt transforms into something that has been within him the whole time: a desperate Superman.

After Walt leaves to pick up diapers that night, Jane's father Donald tells Walt in a chance meeting at a bar that family is everything and that the best thing he can do for his daughter is to love her. However, Walt is not driven by love (for his own daughter or anyone else). Instead, Walt follows the Gus Fring parenting manual. Gus tells Walt, "A man provides. And he does it even when he's not appreciated, or respected, or even loved. He simply bears up and he does it. Because he's a man" ("Más"). While Gus's family (or lack thereof) is never shown, and it's suggested that he could be gay, his power, strength, force, authority, and violence (socially accepted as intertwined) instill fear and motivation in Walt. Walt is mildly threatened and annoyed by Hank's masculinity; he wants to become Gus—respected, in control, and awash in money. Gus is the new face of patriarchy; unlike Hank, he is emotionally intelligent, communicative, and highly educated. He cooks, having no problem navigating domestic spaces. Yet he operates under this principle: "A man provides.

... Because he's a man." This transactional relationship suggests dominance versus submission, and this "responsibility" notion of patriarchy still leads to an acceptance of violence. And Gus certainly must accept and promote violence.

When Walt wakes up in a hospital after escaping the Salamanca home in the desert ("Bit by a Dead Bee"), he sees a painting on the wall; a man is rowing away as his family is on the shore. But presence is not what Walt sees as valuable in his relationships. Even when he's at his most believable, doing what he does "for his family," money is the priority, even if it means he's absent from his daughter's birth or his son's birthday. Conversely, in the feminist ethic of care that *Breaking Bad* ultimately promotes, the old model of "patriarch as absent wage-earner" is replaced with a model of closer relationships and communication. Walt's stubborn adherence to illegal trade in a patriarchal professional and domestic structure is destructive to all around him.

"SOMEONE HAS TO PROTECT THIS FAMILY FROM THE MAN WHO PROTECTS THIS FAMILY"

In Simone de Beauvoir's *The Second Sex*, she writes about "woman": "She is occupied, but she does nothing; she does not get recognition as an individual through her functioning as a wife, mother, housekeeper. The reality of man is in the houses he builds, the forests he clears, the maladies he cures..."[8] Skyler White's role—as Walt's wife, antagonist, and partner—is complicated. As Beauvoir describes woman as the Other, so is Skyler's role often the subject of infamous audience scrutiny (fans holding up Walt up as a Superman, a hero, treated Skyler—who at times attempted to stop him—not only the Other, but also the enemy).

Carol Gilligan's analysis of Amy's response to the Heinz dilemma posits that the multiple angles of Amy's response—which relied on looking closer at communication and relationships—are not less developed than Jake's response, which relied on strict logic and justice. Indeed, there are numerous times throughout *Breaking Bad* that Skyler's approach to problem-solving saves lives and businesses. Her idea to purchase the car wash and to attempt to negotiate the price, her performance with the IRS to save Ted (and herself), her attention to details in the storytelling that she and Walt had to agree upon, and her maneuvers to keep Walt Jr. and Holly out of harm's way oftentimes proved her to be a more effective and shrewd parent and business-person than Walt was. His primary concern—as he admits in the finale—was himself, what he considered as his rights and what he considered just. Her primary concern was her family's safety and navigating and repairing the convoluted web that Walt snared them in. Skyler appears to have the most fulfilling experiences when she goes back to work as a bookkeeper and when she gives birth to Holly vaginally without anesthesia. She is capable and successful in the public and private spheres, yet even those moments are marred by the incompetence and criminal actions of the men whose realms she inhabits.

Carol Gilligan frequently mentions Woolf's concept of "the Angel in the House." This "Angel" would whisper to women to be what women should be: "sympathetic," "tender," "pure," and to "never let anybody guess that you have a mind of your own." Woolf goes on to say, "I turned upon her and caught her by the throat. I did my best to kill her. My excuse, if I were to be had up on a court of law, would be that I acted in self-defense. Had I not killed her she would have killed me."[9] Gilligan uses this quote to illustrate the need for resistance to patriarchal systems, and Skyler too had to break free from both external social pressures and also Walt's pressures to do as he says to decide whether or not to go back to work so quickly after Holly's birth. As she feels more and more like a hostage in her home, she lashes out not to seek self-satisfaction, but to dismantle the patriarchal grip that Walt tries to hold her hostage in. She tells her therapist that her affair with Ted, she suspects, is just to make Walt leave her. She momentarily gets pleasure from the affair, but she's really just looking for a means of escape. When she feigns drowning herself at a family picnic, she does so to ensure Hank and Marie take the kids. She's self-sacrificing, but she grows stronger by utilizing care and communication in her actions. She refuses, above all, to allow her children to live in a home where drugs and murder are simply "shit [that] happens" ("Fifty-One"). Yet, the vitriol that Skyler's character received online by fans was illustrative of the hurdles that still remain when women attempt to resist patriarchy.[10]

Marie is affected by the feminine expectations of Woolf's "Angel" for physical and domestic perfection, and although Hank is, on the surface, the patriarchal ideal, Marie is powerful in the home. She gets the best possible care for Hank, even if it means borrowing from Walt and Skyler, and she has professional success as a radiologist. However, her habitual kleptomania echoes Beauvoir's sentiments that the woman's "...unique personality is expressed in her clothes and her 'interior'; she builds up a double that is often sketchy, but sometimes constitutes a definite personage whose role the woman plays for life."[11] Indeed, Marie typically steals feminine or domestic objects: black heels, an expensive tiara for Holly, a Hummel figurine, a spoon, a family photo as she attempts to take ownership of her own passive and isolated life with rebellious, illicit acts of control. As Walt's guilt comes to light, Marie's total consumption in the need for justice and revenge is noteworthy. Hank knows that his career will be in jeopardy as soon as he reveals Walt; they know Walt's cancer has come back and that he will probably die soon; however, Marie seeks a swift justice no matter whom it might hurt. *Walt must pay.* Marie embodies a masculine sense of logical justice here, even though those around her ask for other considerations (Hank out of pride, Skyler out of compassion). Here, Marie desires the rules and order of justice and patriarchy. After all, patriarchy dictates that some men are above other men, and she wants it to be clear that Hank is above Walt.

"I'm Not Your Wife. I'm Your Hostage"

The sexual relationship between Skyler and Walt represents the changing dynamic of their marriage as Walt becomes more enamored with his own authority. In the pilot episode, Skyler manually stimulates him as she watches an eBay auction (her for-profit hobby at the beginning of the series) and he talks about taking a drive to visit the Mars Rover. The banal orgasm (punctuated by her cries to "Keep it going!" "Yes!"—in response to the eBay auction) illustrates their incredibly comfortable and boring existence. By the end of the episode, Walt has cooked meth, gotten a pile of cash, and killed two men. He comes home and grabs Skyler's face, kissing her and initiating intercourse: "Oh Walt, is that you?" she says. This initial rush of what he had been missing—a feeling of patriarchal control—makes him feel virile. Later in the season, in "A No-Rough-Stuff-Type Deal," Walt acts confidently and powerfully at a public school meeting, stroking Skyler's leg and going up her skirt during the meeting. They have sex in his Aztek in the parking lot; Skyler asks why it was so good, and Walt says "because it was illegal." At this point, his body count and cash flow had increased. He's facing death with his cancer diagnosis, but he's reclaiming some idealized form of patriarchal life, which includes taking initiative during sex; this is a positive development, sexually, until it turns into ownership. In "Seven Thirty-Seven," Walt comes home from a deadly meth deal. Pregnant in a bathrobe and a fresh, green face mask, Skyler makes Walt a plate of food—the picture of domesticity and femininity. He bends her over, her face slamming against the refrigerator, until she screams at him to stop and he finally listens. The inherent subjugation of women and violence of patriarchy, which Walt has become more and more enmeshed in, physically hurts Skyler. When Walt Jr. arrives home later, he sees but doesn't consciously understand the meaning behind the remnants of her green mask on the refrigerator, a sort of signifier of patriarchy from father to son.

When Walt lavishes in outward displays of masculinity, he becomes more of a hero to Walt Jr. Muscle cars, alcohol, "gambling"—all of these objects or narratives gain Walt Jr.'s respect, and Walt is more and more into the destructive empire he has built for himself. At the beginning of the series, when Skyler's ultrasound indicates she will have a girl, Walt says, "That's exactly what I was hoping" ("The Cat's in the Bag..."). If Walt is still to be considered a father figure, this baby—Holly—is one last chance for him to succeed. The advice of Jane's father—"to love"—was lost on Walt as he watched Jane die (out of shock, fear, and, ultimately, concern for his own future and well-being if she was alive). But if Walt Jr. is his biological son, whom he attempts to parent with gifts, Jesse Pinkman is his surrogate son, a former student and business partner whom he cares about, yet who he consistently berates and belittles. Their relationship begins, of course, with a threat: Walt tells Jesse that they will partner up to make meth, or he will turn him in ("Pilot"). Jesse's role in

Breaking Bad is that of Walt's partner and Walt's foil; Jesse is a man who is not bound by patriarchal constraints, and he offers a view of the alternative to the patriarchal "justice" that is sought after by Walt and Hank. He eschews muscle cars for hatchbacks, which points to his eschewing symbols of masculinity. Jesse embodies the future man, who can transcend the past by embracing a feminist ethic of care.

"Live Free or Die"

In *The Elements of Moral Philosophy*, James Rachels and Stuart Rachels begin the chapter on "Feminism and the Ethics of Care" by pointing out that the assertion that men and women think differently has historically been used to subjugate women:

> Aristotle said that women are not as rational as men, and so women are naturally ruled by men. Immanuel Kant agreed, adding that for this reason women "lack civil personality" and should have no voice in public life. Jean-Jacques Rousseau tried to put a good face on it by emphasizing that men and women merely possess different virtues; but, of course, it turned out that men's virtues fit them for leadership, whereas women's virtues fit them for home and hearth.[12]

They go on to point out that while a "principles" (justice) perspective and a "caring" perspective are not, of course, inherently male or female, they are typically framed in that way. As mentioned before, the "caring" perspective, as illustrated by Amy's response to the Heinz dilemma, was seen by Kohlberg as evasive or lacking in development according to his Stages of Moral Development, a fact which itself proves the bias toward traditionally "masculine" approaches to ethical dilemmas. In *Gender Trouble*, Judith Butler points out that "gender proves to be performative."[13] *Breaking Bad* does not fall into the trap of constructing characters out of tired molds. Archetypes are present, yet the characters' complexities and motivations suggest a dismantling of the framework by which we normally view male and female characters. The feminism of *Breaking Bad* exists in examining the ways patriarchy is destructive and how an ethic of care is ultimately the triumphant way to approach public and private life. Gilligan and Richards say:

> Patriarchy's error lies in wedding us, men and women alike, to a false story about human nature and then characterizing our resistance to this story as a sign of pathology or sin. ... But it is by looking through a gender lens that we are able to see the problem whole: not as a problem of women or men, or of women versus men, but rather a problem with the framework we have used in thinking about these questions.[14]

Skyler's aforementioned ethic of care—her focus on communication, details, connectivity, and selflessness—is accompanied by intelligence and logical thought. She has a sense of justice, certainly, but not the blind mathematical justice that is so often fueled by pride and revenge. These qualities that represent an ethic of care are often delineated as "feminine" qualities, yet these qualities are not reserved for women. Feminist philosophers suggest that abilities for justice and for care are not opposed to one another, but can work together as a more robust approach to moral reasoning.[15] The patriarchal demand to separate and subjugate the feminine has historically diminished this approach, in which traditionally masculine qualities—in personality, behavior, and thought—are regarded as superior. Rachels' commentary on the historical de-valuing of women's voices (or feminine thought in general) contrasted with Skyler's characterization help illuminate the abject hatred that many male fans directed toward Skyler.

Other characters offer more complicated combinations of justice and care. Mike Ehrmantraut is most alive with his granddaughter, Kaylee. While he attempts to make sure she's financially taken care of, he also spends a great deal of time with her, caring for and playing with her. This is what is exemplified as love. Lydia Rodarte-Quayle's actions—her attention to detail and her willingness to have anyone in her way killed (though she will hide her eyes)—are framed as being driven by her role as a mother. If she dies, she wants her daughter to find her body so she knows she didn't abandon her ("Madrigal"). Lydia makes Walt swear on his children's lives that she won't be hurt, because she refuses to have her daughter go to some "group home" ("Dead Freight"). Walt, unmoved by her pleas, kills her eventually. The marriage of justice and care in these characters illustrates the attention that we must pay to the interconnectedness of lives—especially, in their cases, their care of children.

"WE MAKE POISON FOR PEOPLE WHO DON'T CARE"

Throughout *Breaking Bad*, Jesse Pinkman represents a breaking down of the framework of patriarchal structures and the prescribed places of men and women within that structure. During the penultimate episode, "Granite State," the Neo-Nazis watch Jesse's tearful confession video: "Does this pussy cry through the entire thing?" Jack asks. While Jack was talking about the confession video, Jesse does indeed cry throughout the entirety of *Breaking Bad*. In his early 20s, Jesse has made an illicitly comfortable life for himself as "Cap'n Cook," a small-time meth cook. For the first few seasons, Jesse is notorious for making homophobic slurs against Walt, and for using terms like "faggot," "homo," and "pussy" as pejoratives, and most famously, "bitch" as a punctuation mark. The slurs fade as the series progresses and he matures, but from the beginning, he is clearly sensitive and compassionate.

Jesse's aunt died from cancer, and he helped care for her while she was ill. He lives in her home now, which is still decorated somewhat effeminately. Jesse's role as caretaker and his relationship to the domestic space are highlighted early on. When Walt suffers the effects of chemo, Jesse fans him to cool him down, and asks about his radiation dot. He advises him to put an ice pack on his head during chemo to help hair loss ("Crazy Handful of Nothin'").

In contrast, Hank calls Jesse a "junkie murderer," and Walt belittles him for his lack of education and addiction at every turn. Walt consistently tells Jesse that his life is less important because he doesn't have a family; however, Jesse shows more familial care and empathy than any other character.

Jesse's relationships are always shown as incredibly important to him. When Combo is killed, Walt coldly asks, "Which one was that?" and incenses Jesse. He is smarter than Badger and Skinny Pete, but he treats them with respect and kindness. He's polite to those in positions of authority—real or imagined—as he always calls Walt "Mr. White" and treats Skyler with an almost humorous level of respect, complimenting her "lovely home" and delicious green beans that have "slivered almonds" (she retorts that they are from the deli) ("Buyout").

When Jesse rents a duplex, he excitedly shows his friends around and shares his plans for the decor. He shows them where the TV is going, and where he'll place seating, candles, and a fountain. Badger talks about how a 3D TV would be great for porn, and Combo says that women will "cream up real nice for candles and shit" ("Breakage"). Jesse shows no interest in either of their comments; he's attempting to set up a home.

When he and Jane meet, she's drawing an angel. As they develop a relationship, she suggests they go to Abiquiú to see a Georgia O'Keeffe exhibit. While Jane playfully promises paintings that look like vaginas, they focus on the painting "My Last Door" ("Abiquiú"). This visit happens in Jesse's flashback while he is struggling with her death. Before Jane starts using again, and Jesse uses heroin, they had a promise of a future, highlighted by these feminine spaces of domesticity and art. Jesse would cook for her, and they imagined a different life. The first time Jane wanted to visit the O'Keeffe exhibit, Walt called Jesse and demanded he join him for a binge cooking session.

Jesse is a natural caretaker with children. In "Peekaboo," Jesse has to go to the home of two addicts who held up Skinny Pete. He was willing to chalk up the loss to "breakage," but Walt says, "What you call breakage is just you making a fool of yourself." Jesse breaks into their house and has a gun pointed, nervous and terrified as he prepares to confront the thieves. A tiny boy emerges from the disgusting mess of the home and crawls up on the couch to watch TV. Jesse asks, "Don't you want to watch Mr. Rogers?" but there are only shopping channels. He makes a sandwich for the child and plays peekaboo with him, putting him to bed and tucking him in when he hears the couple approaching. He even takes the boy with him outside after calling 911 because of Spooge's death under the ATM. "You have a good rest of your life, kid," he says. His discomfort and utter terror in the face of demands to enact violence and his compassion and care for the little boy show Jesse's character. He convinces himself that he is the "bad guy" as the series progresses, but Jesse's core ethic of care is the consistent heartbeat of the show. His relationship with Andrea's son, Brock, also exemplifies his natural connection to children. The instances in which Jesse becomes intensely vengeful and violent are related to harm caused to children: when Andrea's little brother is used and then killed by a gang that works for Gus, when Todd kills Drew Sharp, and when he figures out that Walt poisoned Brock. Jesse is selfless and self-deprecating, but will risk everything if a child is hurt.

When Jesse kills Gale (on Walt's command), he is transformed ("Full Measure"). Gale softly says to him, "You don't have to do this," but Jesse feels compelled to save Walt since Walt had saved him. Walt/Gus and Jesse/Gale are certainly reflexive pairs, with Walt ultimately responsible for Gus's death and Jesse responsible for Gale's death. While these are ostensibly business decisions, considering these characters through the lens of gender provides support for *Breaking Bad*'s commentary on gender complexity and anti-patriarchy. Gale's sexuality is never mentioned, but he is a man who's not constrained by gender expectations. He's making tea and singing when Jesse knocks on his door. He sings "Major Tom (Coming Home)" on karaoke (which Hank berates), a song based upon David Bowie's character; he loves Walt Whitman (Bowie and Whitman both defy gender expectations and were sexually fluid). Of all the characters in the meth business, Gale and Jesse were the most sympathetic; perhaps their lack of adherence to patriarchal expectations and their ethics of care intensified our sympathy. After Jesse kills, he slips into isolation and addiction; violence doesn't give him the virile power that it gives Walt.

Capitalism is closely aligned with patriarchal thought and action. Certainly Walt's efforts to build an empire (to psychologically and financially make up for his "lost empire" in Gray Matter Technologies) to gain power and money, which capitalism and patriarchy as we know it see as bedfellows. Jesse, however, makes clear early on his disdain for this system. In "Gray Matter," he is in a suit, attempting to get a job. What he thinks is a sales job is actually an advertising job—dressing up as a dancing dollar bill on the street. He refuses. Meanwhile, Walt and Skyler attend a birthday party for Elliott Schwartz (he and his wife, Gretchen, who Walt had dated, now run Gray Matter). Walt and Skyler are dressed gaudily and do not fit in, and Walt's pride is compromised at every turn. When Walt is faced with what he considers shame or affront to his pride, he doubles down. He will make more money; he will become more powerful. Jesse does not operate in that framework. The more money and power he has, the more uncomfortable he seems. In his darkest moments, he seeks to make more money (Season Three), but quickly finds emptiness. When he's given bags of money in the final season, he attempts to give it to the family of Drew Sharp and to Kaylee Ehrmantraut after Walt kills Mike. When Saul refuses to let him, he throws money into the yards of strangers. Jesse realizes that money will not make him whole. In "Felina," he flashes back to a story he had told his therapist: he loved woodworking in high school, and worked hard to make a beautiful wood box. He had traded it for weed, but the flashback shows the love and care—and beautiful craftsmanship—that Jesse is capable of.

"The Clinching Interlocking Claws, a Living, Fierce, Gyrating Wheel"

For most of the series, Jesse is certainly a prisoner of toxic masculinity and patriarchy. First, he must work under Walt, then he's literally a prisoner of Todd, Jack, and the Neo-Nazis. When he breaks free at the end—killing Todd with his chains, but not having to kill Walt because he'd already been shot—he speeds out of the Nazi compound, breaking through the gates to leave his past behind.

As Walt dies, he strokes a tank in the meth lab lovingly, leaving a bloody handprint. Jesse didn't want that life; Skyler didn't want that life. Walt's insistence on empire building and his greed take them all down with him, but at least they survive. Walt admits to Skyler that he had done it for himself: "I did it for me. I liked it. I was good at it. And I was really, I was alive" ("Felina").

In Marty Robbins' "El Paso," the singer is in love with a woman named "Felina." In *Breaking Bad*, Walt's love isn't a woman. It's not his wife; it's not his children. It's his power and his money—the empire that he built with blue meth. Robbins' line "A bullet may find me" foreshadows what will happen to Walt. He has, purposefully or not, killed himself. His own gun, his own ricocheted bullet, did find him. At the end, his desperate need for power, to be a man, killed him–and many others in his path.

> In "On Violence," Arendt says, Neither violence nor power is a natural phenomenon, that is, a manifestation of the life process; they belong to the political realm of human affairs whose essentially human quality is guaranteed by man's faculty of action, the ability to begin something new. And I think it can be shown that no other human ability has suffered to such an extent from the progress of the modern age, for progress, as we have come to understand it, means growth, the relentless process of more and more, of bigger and bigger.[16]

Like a cancer, the patriarchal structures of capitalism and violent means of control lead to destruction. The survivors in these scenarios are those for whom an ethic of care—a compassionate and complicated moral code not governed by man-made codes of justice—is the driving force behind decisions that are concerned with relationships and trust.[17] In "Moral Orientation and Development," Gilligan writes:

> As a framework for moral decision, care is grounded in the assumption that self and other are interdependent ... Seen as responsive, the self is by definition connected to others, responding to perceptions, interpreting events, and governed by the organizing tendencies of human interaction and human language. Within this framework, detachment, whether from self or from others, is morally problematic, since it breeds moral blindness or indifference—a failure to discern or respond to need.[18]

This morality, which pulls in the "different voice" of feminine ethics, is the morality that *Breaking Bad* ultimately espouses.

In "Ozymandias" (which shares its title with one of the last episodes of *Breaking Bad*), Percy Bysshe Shelley writes, "Two vast and trunkless legs of stone/Stand in the desert. ... And on the pedestal these words appear: 'My name is Ozymandias, King of Kings: / Look on my works, ye mighty, and despair!'"[19] Walter White is primarily concerned with his role as a monument, as a king. However, he and his empire crumble, and likewise, in the future, personal and social ethics must move away from patriarchal violence and control and toward interconnectedness and care. Nietzsche's Superman is dead.

NOTES

1. Lawrence Kohlberg, *Essays on Moral Development, Vol. I: The Philosophy of Moral Development* (San Francisco, CA: Harper & Row, 1981).
2. Carol Gilligan, *In a Different Voice: Psychological Theory and Women's Development* (Cambridge, MA: Harvard University Press, 1982), 26–29.
3. Friedrich Nietzsche, *Thus Spoke Zarathustra*, trans. R. J. Hollingdale (London: Penguin Books, 1961), 298.
4. Hannah Arendt, "On Violence," in *Crises of the Republic* (San Diego: Harcourt Brace, 1972), 142.
5. Ibid., 152.
6. Carol Gilligan and David A. J. Richards, *The Deepening Darkness: Patriarchy, Resistance, & Democracy's Future* (New York: Cambridge University Press, 2009), 22.
7. Ibid., 5.
8. Simone de Beauvoir, *The Second Sex*, trans. Constance Borde and Sheila Malovany-Chevallier (New York: Vintage, 1949), 641.
9. Gilligan and Richards, *The Deepening Darkness*, 241.
10. Anna Gunn, "I Have a Character Issue," *The New York Times*, last modified Aug. 23, 2013.
11. de Beauvoir, *The Second Sex*, 645.
12. James Rachels and Stuart Rachels, *The Elements of Moral Philosophy* (Boston: McGraw-Hill, 2007), 160.
13. Judith Butler, *Gender Trouble* (New York: Routledge, 1990), 34.
14. Gilligan and Richards, *The Deepening Darkness*, 197.
15. Alison M. Jaggar, "Caring as a Feminist Practice of Moral Reason," in *Justice and Care: Essential Readings in Feminist Ethics*, ed. Virginia Held (Boulder, CO: Westview Press, 1995), 184–185.
16. Arendt, "On Violence," 179–180.
17. Annette C. Baier, *Moral Prejudices: Essays on Ethics* (Cambridge, MA: Cambridge University Press, 1994), 183–202.
18. Carol Gilligan, "Moral Orientation and Moral Development," in *Justice and Care: Essential Readings in Feminist Ethics*, ed. Virginia Held (Boulder, CO: Westview Press, 1995), 36–37.
19. Percy Bysshe Shelley, "Ozymandias," in *The Complete Poetical Works of Percy Bysshe Shelley*, ed. George Edward Woodberry (Boston: Houghton Mifflin Company, 1901), 356.

CHAPTER 9

What Bad Is Not: *Breaking Bad*, Apophatic and Dramaturgic Continua from Creator to Viewer, and a Poetics of the Philosophy of Religion

Jesse Abbot

What can Walter White, a man who is convinced "[t]here's nothing here but chemistry," teach us about the potential phenomenology and texture of spiritual realities? Are there human possibilities that find their best descriptions in the realms of aesthetics, poetics, and discussions about literature? Does language fail us to an equal degree when we employ the vocabularies of verification-driven science and philosophy on the one hand and the often specialized language of religious thinkers, on the other?

If indeed there is nothing here but chemistry, we might brazenly ask, what is chemistry, really? And what might the nothing that is here be, but for the presence of that same chemistry?

It is certainly possible to view *Breaking Bad* meaningfully without doing or asking any such esoteric things. But Vince Gilligan is by many accounts a trickster, a man of disarming Southern gentlemanliness and charm who shocks his actors and writers with ingenious, yet often horrifying, ideas. Said his mother, Gail Gilligan, to David Segal of the *New York Times* in 2011, "Vince was an acolyte in the Catholic Church," though, as she followed up, he also played *Dungeons and Dragons*. "There was certainly a lot of evil in that game," she said, "but it never seemed to affect him adversely."

At the intersection of these two worlds, entertain for just a moment J.R.R. Tolkien's mystical concept of the holiness of the creative author: "Man, Sub-creator, the refracted light/through whom is splintered from a single

J. Abbot (✉)
Tunxis Community College, Farmington, CT, USA

© The Author(s) 2017
K.S. Decker et al. (eds.), *Philosophy and Breaking Bad*,
DOI 10.1007/978-3-319-40343-4_9

White/to many hues, and endlessly combined/in living shapes that move from mind to mind."[1] With Tolkien, we might conceptualize a site for the existence of a creative universe that can accommodate "a lot of evil" without necessarily succumbing to it.

I have long been preoccupied with the redemptive properties of tragedy: not solely to isolate what constitutes Aristotelian *kátharsis* through art (e.g., viewing theater and film, or literary reading as a subset of poetics as a formal study), but also the nearly inevitable tragedy of an academic discourse that often yields to argumentative litigation, something purely eristic. The Buddhist traditions identify aggression as a principal identifying feature of being human, so redemption is not likely to be achieved in a heresiology that successfully roots out all purely emotive appeals, but rather in a constant recognition of this human state. Tragic figures are people obsessed, women and men possessed. They are invariably fanatical and humorless.

An earlier and more provisional discussion of the currents of this chapter appeared in an op-ed of the *Jerusalem Post*, when *Breaking Bad* was ending in October 2013. I was teaching my seminar in the philosophy of religion, and my students' interest in the show coincided fortuitously with our exploration of the use of literature as a mediator between philosophical and scientific reasoning, on the one hand, and typical arguments advanced to support truth claims in faith traditions, on the other.

We were conceiving of the possibility of a poetics sharing territory with the terrain of philosophy (a vexed issue arguably already driven by a role of poetics in Continental circles) and religion; this "poetics of the philosophy of religion" could also benefit from the ambiguity of whether the "of" is subjective or objective. So this can be a poetics that speaks principally to the questions of the philosophy of religion, but with its own agenda.

Our seminar took on such complexities, with surprising alacrity. The central, often interlocking, themes that drove our discussions for a week, as well as the op-ed in the *Jerusalem Post*, included the existence of God, overlaps between scientism and religious literalism, negative theology as a possible response to reductionism, a moral aesthetic, genius, the imagination, "creating a monster" in a lab, Vince Gilligan's worldview and aesthetics, and Schleiermacher's views on art as a diplomat to religious experience. I will again present and further develop several themes here. To these, I will add and address three more: Gus, demiurges, and the problem of evil; Walter Blanco, *Metástasis*, and Hugh Everett's Many Worlds Interpretation (MWI) of quantum mechanics; and social and political implications of these inquiries.

As a branch of philosophy, the philosophy of religion continues to bear the imprint of logical positivism, which utilized the third step of Hume's Fork in treating religious statements as nonsense. The latter half of the twentieth century allowed for some alternatives to this verdict; nonetheless, most of us who teach in this area still (appropriately) value some version of the thematic question: "Is this particular religious truth claim logical and supportable by reasonable evidence?" We ask questions such as "Can it be reasonable to conclude, as Christians have, that God has three persons?" Or "Does sound reasoning support the *Quran* permitting a man to marry up to four women, assuming he treats them equally, when the scripture does not permit a woman under any circumstances to marry more than one man, let alone up to four?" Or "Is it sound logic to conclude, as Buddhists do, that there exists no intrinsic permanent entity we might fairly call a 'self'?" Or, as we might only half-jokingly ask, given the publicly verifiable literalistic beliefs of sects such as the Westboro Baptist Church in Kansas... "Does gay sex cause tornadoes and earthquakes?" However, at least a second line of questioning is also appropriate for a lot of us: "Is philosophical logic the *only* acceptable path to what a given religion conceives as truth?"

THE EXISTENCE OF GOD

The emerging "Religion and Science" movement by turns excites thinkers in a variety of disciplines or unnerves them, depending on their respective levels of commitment to finding common ground of some potential truth versus engaging in the bloodlust of eristic winner takes all. Show-stopper debates between figures such as the late Christopher Hitchens and William Lane Craig invariably prompt atheists to lionize Hitchens for his perceived conquest of the Christian philosopher and, alternatively, evangelical Christians to perceive their representative as the unequivocal victor. But a number of prominent thinkers have concluded that we really should be having a discussion about religion *and* science rather than the necessity of a false dilemma of religion *or* science.

Art itself—and certainly, a prime example is *Breaking Bad*—can also become a laboratory for investigating the philosophy of religion when the artist is preoccupied with the same problems. Raised Catholic and now an agnostic who, as he says, "would like to believe that there is... more than just us in this universe," Gilligan has stuffed the five seasons of his show with all manner of religious images: a pair of Mexican cartel leaders making offerings at a macabre shrine to Santa Muerte, patron saint of death, Buddhist monks chanting surreally in a gangster's hideout, and many more.

In my seminar, Gilligan joined our imagined discussion table of Jewish, Christian, and Muslim philosophers, such as Maimonides (the Rambam), Thomas Aquinas, and Ibn Sina, on the subject of whether God exists. The majority, but not all, of my students knew the series but had to weave and bob to make use of the show's riveting situations while protecting some class members from spoilers; we considered what the world, according to Walter White, had to say compared to these thinkers. At the end of the story, what lesson was Gilligan trying to present us in offering up a dead antihero who is only partially redeemed? No fixed answer to the last question emerged; it became clear that any response could only be arrived at by each viewer, working along the fine line between meaning and meaninglessness that the show occupies. Happily, there is a lot of "DNA evidence" sprinkled throughout the five seasons of the show that allows us to trace Gilligan's basic "moral aesthetic," if we may call it that, and gather some clues. In a flashback scene in "…And the Bag's in the River," White asks his ex-flame Gretchen a vexed question about the human condition: "Doesn't it seem like something's missing?" In response, she offers a perennial religious query: "What about the soul?" "The soul?" Walter replies, "There's nothing here but chemistry." White's scientistic and materialist worldview is a potent force in the series, but one challenged at every turn by a vast web of non-linear causes and effects that often bear signs of being moral retribution. In one of several haunting examples of this, two passenger jets collide directly over White's house in the finale of Season Two ("ABQ"). That calamity is clearly intended to present to viewers the indirect but undeniable result of a series of choices White has made. Such decisions comprise a disastrous closed system representing White's attempts to protect the interests solely of himself and his immediate family.

Maimonides (1135–1204) stands as a helpful mediator between his Islamic predecessors (such as Ibn Sina, 980–1037)—who attempted to prove God's existence using creation as the evidence—St. Thomas Aquinas (1225–1274)—who, depending on which Thomist one talks to, either accepted this Islamic argument or didn't—and, say, a modern non-believer….perhaps Walter White. A jurist in training and disposition, Maimonides meticulously argues that while it's impossible to show the world was created specifically to prove God's existence, the concept of creation itself is more plausible and spiritually preferable to its alternatives. Maimonides, or the Rambam, was a pillar of a theological approach known as negative theology, an orientation to this field that denies it is possible to claim positive attributes for God—since language and human concepts such as "God is wise" could not possibly be faithful to the infinite nature and oneness of God—and thus engages in negation (or, in the case of Maimonides, often silence) as a means of approaching God. Aquinas, on the other hand, was not entirely won over by the Rambam's methodology.

POETICS OF THE PROBLEM OF EVIL AND GILLIGAN'S THEODICY: RAISING THE STAKES

My interest in the minds of artistic creators—including authors, show runners on television programs, screenwriters, and directors—lies in teasing out a deeper wisdom from their comments, the implications of which they may not have considered despite the very real insights resulting from their creations. During *Breaking Bad*'s run, I found myself speculating that Gus Fring was the show's answer to what God might be. The nagging ideation of Gus as God is plausible only because he's always several moves ahead of Walt to a terrifying degree (much as the character of O'Brien is depicted in Orwell's *1984* in relation to Winston Smith). It is almost as if Gus's mind *contains* Walter's inside of it. Shortly after considering such aesthetic intention, I saw that one participant in an online threaded discussion on the program was zealously evangelizing "Gus Is God!"—prompting me to retreat from such a crude teleology. But it didn't help that in Season Three's "Más," as Walt descends for the first time into an obvious subterranean hell of a meth lab designed just for him, glimmering white equipment greets his and our gaze, and eerie celestial strings trill ironically.

Gilligan confirms that such a finalistic religious vision, however ironic, really isn't his style:

> Every now and then in the writer's room we say to ourselves "Gus seems to be getting a little close to Darth Vader…" and we pull him back and say to ourselves, we don't want this guy to be all knowing and all powerful, he's still a human with feet of clay. He has his flaws but he is also very smart. He's a chess player.[2]

OVERLAP OF SCIENTISM AND RELIGIOUS LITERALISM

Scientists typically don't care for the term "scientism," just as religious literalists don't favor the word "fundamentalist" (except occasionally in jest, as is sometimes the case with the humorous evangelical insiders' word "fundie"). Most of us would not like to be reduced to mere reductionists.

Strikingly, when Walt first approaches Jesse to blackmail him into partnering with him, Jesse knows something is awry, and offers, "I mean, if you're planning on giving me some bullshit about getting right with Jesus by turning myself in…" ("Pilot"). Although Jesse may not have perfect pitch, he recognizes some timbre of reductionism. The noted Heideggerian interpreter of Tibetan Buddhism, Herbert V. Guenther, perfectly sums up the common descent of imaginative thinking into unimaginative dogmatism:

> Actually, any intellectual system—philosophical, religious, political, or any other kind—is geared to reductionist ways of thinking and is bound up to end up in the utter stagnation and rigidity of a tyrannical dogmatism. Buddhist philosophy, in this regard, is no exception. The much vaunted Madhyamaka philosophy, particularly in its Prāsaṅgika version, is the ultimate in reductionism, and its manifestation as dogmatic intolerance in Tibetan history is well-known….
>
> Despite its reductionist quality, however, system or model building is itself a creative process, one through which we attempt to develop a generalized world view out of observations and valuations. Unfortunately, we then impose this world view on our dealings with the physical, social, and cultural-spiritual aspects of our environment, with the inevitable result that the free play of creative imagination is strangled.[3]

Because Gilligan and his team nudge us throughout the series with religious imagery and/or references, it's no small irony that Walt responds to Jesse's inquiry whether Walt is crazy or depressed by saying, "I am awake." This echoes the purported response of the historical Buddha to inquirers curious whether he was a celestial being, a god, magician, etc.[4] While White early on equates subjective existential freedom with objective truth, his preoccupation with scientific puritanism reaches its culmination in the so-called bottle episode of the third season entitled "Fly."

In that installment, Walt's inability to tolerate even an infinitesimal impurity or contamination results in his protracted search for a tiny, winged heretic or infidel, leaving audiences earnestly wondering if his lung cancer has metastasized to his brain, or if he has slipped into genuine psychosis (i.e., other scientists, namely, psychiatrists, could readily commit him on the basis of his behavior in this episode). Aficionados of absurdist theater may note resonance with the works of Becket, particularly *Waiting for Godot*. Upon airing, "Fly" was maddening to many fans, perhaps because, in the words of *Godot*'s Estragon, in the containment of archetypal insomnia and claustrophobia, "Nothing happens. Nobody comes, nobody goes. It's awful."[5]

Negative Theology: Antidote to Reductionism? A Path of Redemptive Tragedy?

I am going to assert here—probably much to the consternation of classical philosophers of religion and perhaps also philosophers of science convinced of something similarly sacrosanct in their enterprise—that models of thinking and examined living which apply methods like the Socratic *elenchus* as therapeutic cross-examination of one's conceptual and imaginative certainty *just don't sell as well as models that affirm something*. In such methods I would include key strains of Judaic thought and philosophy from Maimonides through Levinas; much of Chan thought in China and its variations as Seon and Zen in Korea and Japan (with "Only Don't Know" serving as a key Korean Seon response to, or deconstruction of, a more kataphatic, or affirmative mystical apparatus like the mantra in Buddhist praxis); Orthodox Christian traditions whose theology typically at least wishes that the kataphatic be subordinated to the apophatic; and in the sciences, Popperian falsificationism *contra* repeated trials with controls.

Thinking that recognizes conceptual fanaticism, literalism, and idolatry in the habit of affirming, more than asking good questions, takes longer to foster, to cultivate, or (if you will) to cook. Maimonides is much more cautious about kataphatic theological models than is Aquinas, who does use some negative theology but not to the same degree as his Jewish philosophical forebear. Western thought simply isn't as comfortable with the *via negativa* as some other traditions, except in its esoteric reaches.

In one sense, recognizing the inner reductionist or fanatic is a healthy point of departure for any inquiry, whether secular-materialist or religious. Perhaps clinging to the image or idol of certainty is the most fundamentally addictive predicament of mortal persons. We are driven by different circumstances, but also by needs for certainty that differ by character. I long ago struggled with the concept of "mystical fundamentalism" to refer to the tendency of figures vaunted as saintly figures of great spiritual subtlety—that is, "round characters" who avoid many of the obvious pitfalls of a given spiritual path—to succumb to a hardening of such subtlety into formula: luminous dogma. A secular-materialist analogue to "mystical fundamentalism" might be "urbane scientism." At first glance, Walter White is a heroic, urbane "badass." But his reduction of the universe to chemistry that he can manipulate, oblivious to his own inner poisoning—a catastrophic chemical reaction—frames the entire series.

And this is quite consciously portrayed by Gilligan, who in a 2010 interview told Jovana Grbić, chemist and editor of the online journal *ScriptPhD*, "First and foremost to me, the show is a character study about a man who is undergoing a radical transformation. He's transforming himself from a protagonist to an antagonist. The whole show, in that sense, is an experiment to continue chemistry analogy."[6]

FULL-ON IMMERSION IN DEFEAT: THE INITIATION OF TRAGEDY

In the subjective mental terrain of a man convinced he can manipulate his universe, there is no clear foothold for the consideration that a larger nothingness holds sway over chemistry. So there's an unwitting double entendre in Walt's sweeping characterization of reality ("revealed" through a misreading we can effect by inserting a simple comma and perhaps ellipses: "There's nothing here, but chemistry..."), which makes chemistry a caveat to the nothingness. Certainly my reading reflects a Buddhist bias: Mahāyāna Buddhists conceive of reality as being premised in śūnyatā or emptiness, which is inseparable from impermanence and all that brings unease (duḥkha) in our lives, but also consider reality to be endowed with soteriological features that free us from the extremes of nihilism and eternalism. Embracing emptiness, impermanence, and defeat has a strong and stable role in Indo-Tibetan Buddhism. The eleventh- to twelfth-century Tibetan teacher Langri Thangpa distilled the root principle of the so-called lojong (in Tibetan, "blo sbyong," or mind training) tradition into this aphorism:

> No matter what profound scriptures I open, I find none that do not suggest that all faults are one's own, and that all higher qualities belong to brother and sister sentient beings. Because of this, you must offer all gain and victory to others and except all loss and defeat for yourself. I have found no other meaning.[7]

Tolkien, too, wrote repeatedly of what seems to comprise the basic existential and historical geography of his worldview, a so-called long defeat, in both his Middle Earth fiction and his private correspondence. In a letter to his friend Amy Ronald in 1956, he wrote:

> Actually I am a Christian, and indeed a Roman Catholic, so that I do not expect 'history' to be anything but a long defeat – though it contains (and in a legend may contain more clearly and movingly) some samples or glimpses of final victory.[8]

Tolkien puts similar words in the mouths of other characters who vocalize this view, in particular Galadriel in *The Fellowship of the Ring*, who actually speaks of having "fought the long defeat."[9]

Tolkien's cautious theological realism stands in sharp contrast to the hubris of Walter White. Many moments in the show speak of off-the-charts hubris, even in the face of grave risk: from a chilling flashback scene, pre-cancer, of the day that he and Skyler view a house which they cannot afford while he encourages her to "Live a little," to the gambling addiction cover story the couple tell Hank and Marie (poignantly too close for comfort to his actual addiction to his meth cooking and its attendant adrenaline). The fundamentalism here is overconfidence in the power of the intellect.

Tolkien is valuable to any discussion about the value of examining defeat over gross expressions of ecstasy or triumphalism. Philosophers from Plato to Heidegger and Levinas have been wary of the latter, and appropriately so; modern evangelical exponents of the "prosperity gospel" sink to a new low in proclaiming their high, and anyone who has experienced or witnessed unbearable suffering can only wonder, "What is he smiling so much about?" But for a religious writer like Tolkien, who invests authorship with some order of divine creation, there is a continuum of considerable time and investment between creator and creation. I tentatively call this the "Dramaturgic Continuum" from creator to viewer. Despite Gilligan's agnosticism and Tolkien's Catholicism, the two artists can be compared *vis-à-vis* both the scope and the meticulous level of detail they impart to their respective visions. In the case of Tolkien, the impression that the author has memorialized every word ever spoken and mapped every square inch traversed or fought over represents acts of visionary historiography beyond the work of most historians. As for Gilligan, he commented on the visual work of *Breaking Bad* in an interview two years ago:

> With giant, wide TVs, you get to frame and emulate John Ford or Sergio Leone and, in the case of *Breaking Bad,* you can place characters in an endless expanse of Mexico prairie which gets to look very painterly and cinematic. That's a wonderful development.[10]

The aesthetic demanded by Gilligan pulls the background into the foreground as part of the dramaturgy—a visual movement akin to musical scoring, but at a multigenre, multisensory, nigh-synaesthesic level—immersing viewers in the experience of the story. It is my argument that cinematography of this order is at the core of the Dramaturgic Continuum.

A MORAL AESTHETIC AND "THE MONSTER" OF THE IMAGINATION: A SETTLEMENT BETWEEN SECULAR AND RELIGIOUS ETHICS

Philosopher of religion and theologian Friedrich Schleiermacher (1768–1834) argued that religious experience is closely akin in its quality to the appreciation of a work of fine art or music. In a representative passage from *On Religion:*

Speeches to its Cultured Despisers (*Über die Religion: Reden an die Gebildeten unter ihren Verächtern*), Friedrich Schleiermacher in many ways anticipates the Neo-Kantian innovations in the philosophy of religion of John Hick, who dared to suggest (when Kant would not) that the noumenal realm could be accessed subjectively in the lived ritual experience of the religious individual. Since Schleiermacher himself was heavily influenced by Kant, this extension of the Kantian championing of the human universe through individual subjectivity might also broadly complement Tolkien's notion of the author or artist as a sub-creator. But it's also an important remedy to the voice of Walter White, who finds it plausible to approach the whole world as an experiment to be dealt with objectively and empirically—and without recourse to the wisdom of the each of us as a human subject. Schleiermacher writes:

> ...[T]he piety of each individual, whereby he is rooted in the greater unity, is a whole by itself. It is a rounded whole, based on his peculiarity, on what you call his character, of which it forms one side. Religion thus fashions itself with endless variety, down even to the single personality. Each form again is a whole and capable of an endless number of characteristic manifestations. You would not have individuals issue from the Whole in a finite way, each being at a definite distance from the other, so that one might be determined, construed and numbered from the others, and its characteristics be accurately determined in a conception?
>
> Were I to compare religion in this respect with anything it would be with music, which indeed is otherwise closely connected with it. Music is one great whole; it is a special, a self-contained revelation of the world. Yet the music of each people is a whole by itself, which again is divided into different characteristic forms, till we come to the genius and style of the individual. Each actual instance of this inner revelation in the individual contains all these unities. Yet while nothing is possible for a musician, except in and through the unity of the music of his people, and the unity of music generally, he presents it in the charm of sound with all the pleasure and joyousness of boundless caprice, according as his life stirs in him, and the world influences him. In the same way, despite the necessary elements in its structure, religion is, in its individual manifestations whereby it displays itself immediately in life, from nothing farther removed than from all semblance of compulsion or limitation. In life, the necessary element is taken up, taken up into freedom. Each emotion appears as the free self-determination of this very disposition, and mirrors one passing moment of the world.[11]

Although Schleiermacher takes too many intellectual liberties segregating spiritual pursuits from scientific ones, I maintain that his writing does draw our attention to a fruitful cross-section of art and religious ideas—that mysterious thing called "inspiration"—to make sense of our human predicament.

From the same period as Scheleirmacher, and like *Breaking Bad*, Mary Shelley's *Frankenstein* is a narrative that both celebrates the power of inspiration and the imagination, yet admonishes us mercilessly of their dangers. Shelley grasps the moral lesson that must temper the primordial forces of creativity if we are to build a decent life and world. The novel shows us that there is nothing wrong with Promethean inspiration, unless and until it crosses certain limits. But limits hold little appeal for its central character Victor Frankenstein, whose zeal for chemistry follows the passions of the ancient alchemists as well as their reputation for the folly of excess.

Similarly, Gilligan and his team offer a glimpse of what happens when creativity is first not acknowledged—White is an overqualified and underpaid teacher, but also an ingenious inventor who has been cheated out of the rightful fruits of his inspiration by unscrupulous partners—and then unleashed in the wrong direction. Like Frankenstein, Walter White roughly fits the primal heresy of not respecting mortal limits: he is the modern heretic alchemist. It seems no accident that the color of White's proprietary crystal meth is blue, the archetypal hue of sadness.

From episode to episode, Gilligan makes us feel something in what seems to many of us like a soul, but may only be chemistry. Complementing the consistently realistic and moving depictions of the ensemble cast, Gilligan's cinematographic painting in the yellows, reds, and browns of the American Southwest and his endless experiments with composition and perspective drill to the core of emotional possibilities. Those colors also coalesce strangely and memorably in a pizza pie lingering on the roof of the White home, an image that has joined the iconic plastic bag of the film *American Beauty* as a sort of postmodern Technicolor question mark, asking "What does it all mean?" That query embodies a cosmic rhetorical question that sums up the series.

As hard-nosed and scientifically rigorous as Walt is, his downfall certainly lies in overreaches of a Promethean order. Perhaps the movement of Romanticism can be distilled down to one word: presumption (a close sibling to "Promethean"). Percy Bysshe Shelley's excesses (and mental instabilities) kept his poor wife and family running from debtors and living in misery. (White would not necessarily appreciate being likened to a Romantic poet, but there does appear to be common ground in grand pronouncements that do not always consider the cosmic caveats.) Another brilliant Romantic poet, John Keats, famously equated truth and beauty in his signature work "Ode on a Grecian Urn."

One can only wonder how a more seasoned and mature Keats, whose life was snuffed out at the age of 25 by tuberculosis, might have refined the assertion that truth is beauty, beauty truth. We do know the two must have something to do with one another, but surely they cannot be identical. We know that the Nazis were preoccupied with aesthetics; under Hitler's vision, fashionable uniforms and a Third Reich that promoted all of the arts were not entirely detached from Nazi ideology. There is also a parallel account of sartorial attention in the life of Philippine first lady Imelda Marcos, whose seamstress allegedly went blind following her aesthetic dictates.

Strategies for Not Succumbing to Reduction

Elliot Wolfson, a philosopher of religion centered in Judaic studies, has specialized in longitudinal efforts by Jewish thinkers over the past several centuries to avoid theological and philosophical idolatry by rooting out even the most subtle anthropomorphizing language from their efforts to know God. Wolfson provocatively calls this phenomena "theomania." When that arguably incurable human tendency is applied to theology—and indeed, even to apophatic theology, whose entire enterprise is premised in not making positive declarations about deity—the ensuing problems imperil the basis for one's entire work.

Wolfson's recent book *Giving Beyond the Gift* centers on this problem in the thought of four twentieth-century Jewish philosophers: Hermann Cohen, Martin Buber, Franz Rosenzweig, and Emmanuel Levinas. He also examines the way that two other, even more radical apophatic philosophers, Jacques Derrida and Michael Wyschogrod, brought their strategies of deconstruction and denegation to bear on this concern. Wolfson's meditation on Heidegger's use of the terms "gift" and "givenness," in a significant contrast to Jewish and Christian theological constructs around those words, rounds out the book.

Because Wolfson is also a gifted poet (and someone who knows the world-creating risks of poetry), the following passage from his book may help us shed light on our antihero and his commitment to "empire building":

> Apocalyptic hope is cast in post-Heidegerrian terms as the *legein* of *alētheia*, the gathering of truth, the disconcealment concealed in the nothing of the future revealed as the event that is always to come, the promise of the not yet inundating the present with anticipation of what cannot be anticipated except as unanticipated, the calculation of the incalculable that releases one from the sense of futurity dictated by the temporal density of the past. To attend the invocation of this promise—the promise fulfilled in the abeyance of its fulfillment—one must be awakened to the fact that there is no gift to receive but the gift of discerning that there is no gift other than the giving that gives with no will to give and no desire to be given.[12]

With this, we have unquestionably moved into discourse about a postmodern universe in which both Werner Heisenberg and Walter White/Heisenberg can hold court. Quantum mechanics, as paradigm-shattering moment in human knowledge, means that linear models of the universe, including and perhaps especially religious narratives, begin to look more like quaint artifacts than valuable tools on which we can depend.

There is much in the telling of Walter White's story that decenters not just a reliable God from the scope of what is certain, but any kind of final linearity or certainty. Newtonian physics continue to operate: in *Breaking Bad*, a bullet shot will still predictably pierce flesh with the reliable formulae, constants, and coefficients of standard ballistics. But two passenger jets colliding in the sky directly over the house of the man who, not immediately but beyond any doubt, brought about their destruction *is either how our world works or it isn't*. White is not prepared for the uncertainty and non-linearity he has ushered in. In an unexpected moment in Season Three's "Green Light," Walt attempts to throw a large potted plant through Ted Beneke's office window as revenge for Beneke sleeping with his wife Skyler, and the pot unceremoniously glances off with no impact: perhaps one of the most anticlimactic moments ever captured in cinema or TV. Equally strangely, the rising drug kingpin of Albuquerque seems to be a magnet for the repeated destruction of his car's windshield.

Most thoughtful people who observe the world as it actually functions—especially the fast-paced version of that world of today, when daily life contains statistically more variables—will recognize the intrusion of mystery, strangeness, antiteleology, and non-linearity into what seemed predictable and sure. We tend to expect gifts that we have no claim to, and ignore the blessings and gifts immediately in our midst. Ironically, our Heisenberg, a man who should be comfortable with uncertainty if he is to live up to his namesake, does not seem to recognize its *a priori* status in his world. He adapts to it better than most would, but surely does not seem to expect it.

We might take a different path than Walter White does. Even if God does not play dice (as Einstein remarked in some vexation over the implications of quantum mechanics), dice nonetheless somehow are certainly being played all the time. In a universe that permitted the Holocaust to take place, one ripe for environmental, nuclear, societal, or myriad other collapses or apocalypses, surely new conceptual vocabularies, languages, and strategies for living are warranted.

WALTER BLANCO, METÁSTASIS, AND HUGH EVERETT'S MANY WORLDS INTERPRETATION (MWI) OF QUANTUM MECHANICS

Unlike their Yankee analogue soap operas, the *telenovelas* of Latin America last only a number of months and then end. In a project fully endorsed by Vince Gilligan, producers from Sony and Univision's subsidiary, UniMás, filmed *Metástasis*, a mostly shot-by-shot recreation of *Breaking Bad* set in Bogotá, Colombia. The show packed the equivalent of five seasons of our familiar story into daily episodes from June through September of 2014. Meeting popular and critical acclaim, the "doppelganger series" instantly raised the bar for *telenovelas*.

Much of the work of transposing *Breaking Bad* to *Metástasis* is fairly literal—for example, Walter becomes Walter Blanco and Skyler is Cielo (literally "Sky"). But because Walter's initials are now "W.B.," the climactic story arc around the inscription from Gale Boetticher/Guido Bermudez must accordingly be a book written by an author other than Walt Whitman: the writers chose William Blake. Drug dealing is a more culturally sensitive subject in Columbia, so there is also more finesse in how it is handled, according to Colombian actor Roberto Urbina, who plays José Miguel Rosas, the Jesse Pinkman of this alternate universe.

In a universe in which we see *agnosis* not as an inherent problem but rather as a description of the meeting point of epistemology and ontology in the lived world, Hugh Everett's Many Worlds Interpretation (MWI) of quantum mechanics should not be barred from application in literary analysis (or philosophical speculation that finds common cause with it) and the qualitative questions asked in a poetics aiming for contemplation and truth rather than eristic. Addressing not *Breaking Bad*, but literature as a whole in an essay that examines quantum mechanics (and in particular Everett's MWI), Dr. Serpil Oppermann writes:

> Exploring the quantum world of infinite possibilities, a world of entangled agencies, and meaningful symmetries between modern science and the humanities, the essay focuses on how literature and quantum physics intersect in the interpretation of a physical reality whose essential ontology remains elusive. Since both the physicists and the literary scholars ask the same question of how to make this ontology meaningful for the general cultural imaginary, and since they both rely on metaphoric perception and hermeneutic processes in their accounts, I argue that the borders that separate the two disciplines are more porous than vigorous. The complementarity of these "two cultures", in other words, offers a viable framework for meeting the universe halfway.[13]

To the extent that an author really is a sort of sub-creator or demigod, per Tolkien, might there be some valuable aesthetic meaning in a universe that contains *both* a Walter White in Albuquerque, New Mexico, and a Walter Blanco in Bogotá, Colombia, two more or less identical men in largely—but not wholly—identical social environments? (We do know that there are real-life doppelgangers; this seems to be a matter of genetic probability and statistics.) Can physicists preaching the Many Worlds Interpretation extend the vision of an infinitely branching universe into the sphere of literary or filmic narrative? If not, why not? And to the extent that such a universe is possible, how do its mechanisms of differentiation and unification differ from the archetypes proposed by the Swiss psychiatrist C.G. Jung? How do such mechanisms differ from the Platonic form system, scarcely remembered by modern people as anything but a quaint artifact of a noble but less-informed people?

Can a universe in which Gus is at least something like a demigod be the same universe as that of an even bigger God who does indeed play dice? God as a gamer certainly might enjoy making two Walter Whites with nearly identical lives and only slight differences that add cultural flair. The story world of Gilligan's *Breaking Bad* is sufficiently unsettling, strange, and even putatively bordering on magic realism to provoke such inquiries. Gilligan outlines his own main spiritual stakes for his story:

> If there's a larger lesson to *Breaking Bad*, it's that actions have consequences....If religion is a reaction of man, and nothing more, it seems to me that it represents a human desire for wrongdoers to be punished. I hate the idea of Idi Amin living in Saudi Arabia for the last 25 years of his life. That galls me to no end....
>
> I feel some sort of need for biblical atonement, or justice, or something.... I like to believe there is some comeuppance, that karma kicks in at some point, even if it takes years or decades to happen. My girlfriend says this great thing that's become my philosophy as well. "I want to believe there's a heaven. But I can't not believe there's a hell."[14]

John Hick delineates a framework for discussing the existence of God or supernatural realities that challenge common beliefs by asserting that whether God is or is not a "fact" transcends mere linguistic usage. I invoke Hick here, because I think his discussion opens up a space or site where our qualitative meditation on poetics and literary concerns aptly can take up residence. He writes:

> ...[I]t may be suggested that the common core to the concepts of "existence," "fact," and "reality" is the idea of "making a difference." To say that x exists or is real, or that it is a fact that there is an x, is to claim that the character of the universe differs in some way from the character that an x-less universe would have. The nature of this difference will naturally depend upon the character of the x in question. And the meaning of "God exists" will be indicated by spelling out the past, present, and future difference which God's existence is alleged to make within human experience.[15]

Hick's understanding of God opens the door for a subjective, interior experience swayed by the phonic, imagistic, and archetypal values that stem from poetics, aesthetics, and literary concerns. Literary critic Harold Bloom's long career has covered much territory in these areas. But there are two themes for which he is best known, and which some of his greater works have fused into a single thesis. First is his early Freudian theory, on the one hand, of an "anxiety of influence" that all emerging great authors feel relative to a looming father figure whose shadow and influence must be overcome. The second is a preoccupation with the different expressions of Gnosticism (up to and including his proposition, set forth in a book of the same name, that "The American Religion" is a set of modern Gnostic sects), the range of ancient religions spanning alternative Jewish, Christian, and other Near Eastern soteriologies centered on a savior figure who stands in contrast to a wicked father of a God, a Demiurge. Bloom's case that this archetype is such a resilient one has much support. Bloom is dispositionally fixated on affirming Shakespeare as the greatest father figure—not an evil force, but a universally domineering one—in Western literature and thought (Shakespeare is "a spirit that permeates everywhere, that cannot be confined" whose spiritual "freedom made Dr. Johnson nervous and Tolstoy indignant"). Yet Bloom has much to teach us about spiritual–artistic influence, even if we choose not to quite literally worship his particular human deity.[16] For example, we might consider that Walter White's refinement of his proprietary blue crystal methamphetamine into an unprecedented and quality product transmutes his criminal alias, Heisenberg, into a *bona fide nom de plume,* beyond mere crime. The craft and care he applies to his creation surpasses the concerns of a mere artisan and blurs the line between scientist and artist.

To the degree that Gus Fring indeed became close enough to an omnipotent, all-knowing, "Darth Vader" figure whom Gilligan and his fellow writers had to make conscious efforts to rein in and humanize, he certainly qualifies as a Demiurge. Fring's meticulous aesthetic is not pestered or interrupted by mere morality, but he does unequivocally make crime a fine art, arguably a masterpiece. By quite literally destroying and overthrowing him—after we have watched Gus's new skeletal form making certain to straighten his tie, keeping with his impeccable aesthetic, before he dies—Walter emerges as the new ruling criminal artist of record in the region, the newly crowned Demiurge ("Face Off").

From Art to World: Breaking the Demiurge Cycle

But then, we, too, must destroy the Demiurge Heisenberg to claim our own lives and get them back, so thoroughly has Walter White's astonishing and, for television, unprecedented, tragic arc of Mr. Chips-to-Scarface wended its way, like some spirochete, into our consciousness. Anna Gunn's potent and jarring op-ed published in *The New York Times* just before the show concluded its final episodes, supports the principle of a Dramaturgic Continuum. Again, the establishment of some level of measurable vicarious identification is a sign that art has worked, and has been successful *as* art. But great art—and I maintain that *Breaking Bad* is a good example of this class— permeates life and sweeps its audience into a world-forming, quasi-religious creative space much as Bloom characterizes the spirit of Shakespeare doing.

Anna Gunn writes of her haunting legacy as a hated impediment to beloved Walt/Heisenberg:

> Could it be that [the angry fans] can't stand a woman who won't suffer silently or "stand by her man"? That they despise her because she won't back down or give up? Or because she is, in fact, Walter's equal? It's notable that viewers have expressed similar feelings about other complex TV wives—Carmela Soprano of "The Sopranos," Betty Draper of "Mad Men." Male characters don't seem to inspire this kind of public venting and vitriol. At some point on the message boards, the character of Skyler seemed to drop out of the conversation, and people transferred their negative feelings directly to me. The already harsh online comments became outright personal attacks. One such post read: "Could somebody tell me where I can find Anna Gunn so I can kill her?"[17]

Through high art made accessible to the masses, and in part due to the nearly literal worship of celebrity in modernity, we have entered a realm of religious hatred that is at least adjacent to Christian literalists blowing up abortion clinics, or Wahhabi Muslims embracing jihad. The "prophetic clout" of Bryan Cranston's portrayal, and his partnership with the ensemble cast and Gilligan and the crew, is so compelling that the audience must take conscious measures not to get pulled into the orbit of something whose psychic gravity can be the phenomenological likeness of a planetary body.

An incursion into our consciousness such as that Walter White embodies might—or perhaps *should*—give us pause to reflect on charismatic people with obsessive agendas in our own world. I am not condemning all such persons *prima facie* as some measure of charisma and tenacity of mission and values must be necessary in any successful leader. But ours is an age in which a realistic political consciousness may be able to challenge power differentials driven by charismatic reductionists who, indeed, paper over the lives of entire classes of people and reduce them to mere talking points: rhetorical bullets. We must recognize the allure of the Walter White archetype in its manifold iterations, both within us and all around us, to dethrone the Demiurge that defines its own safety by imperiling the safety of others. I point to the important feminist theologian Elisabeth Schüssler Fiorenza in extending intersectionalist feminism to address not only classical power divides between white women and women of color, but which encompass all people, men and women alike. In articulating the concept of a "kyriarchy" (from Greek kyrios, "lord") or complexly oppressive hierarchical dynamic, Schüssler Fiorenza compellingly addresses how men and women can be empowered individuals in one context and disenfranchised in another. Arguably, it is mainly thinkers equipped with both the robust empiricism and often durable methodologies of science *and* philosophical discernment informed by poetics and aesthetics who may finally be able to view clearly the way we sacralize scriptures, political narratives, and cults of personality alike to our own detriment, and by affording ourselves a renewed and more clear view, work to break the "Demiurgic cycle" and be more free.

In particular, we have an opportunity to challenge as irrational, unholy, and unscientific our theological inheritance from the Puritans of self-reliance to the extent of gratuitous martyrdom and self-destruction, a "Protestant work ethic" anchored in a psychopathology whose creed is "idleness is a sign of the devil." But this "ethic" brings about little but catastrophic mental and physical health consequences in an entire citizenry—not to mention drug addiction and the absurdist and ineffective drama of the "War on Drugs," the basis conceit of *Breaking Bad* and much more poignant, real-life stories. Such immediacies can be the premises for a philosophical poetics and a political philosophy to unite and form an argument, a dramaturgy, of better dreams.

NOTES

1. J. J. R. Tolkien, *Tree and Leaf: Smith of Wootton Major—The Homecoming of Beorhtnoth* (London: Unwin Paperbacks, 1977), 45.
2. Interview by Casey Carpenter, *The Cult*, last modified November 15, 2010. Web.
3. Guenther, *From Reductionism to Creativity: RDzogs-chen and the New Sciences of Mind* (Boston: Shambhala, 1989), 1.
4. Kornfield, *Teachings of the Buddha* (Boston: Shambhala, 2007), xiii
5. Samuel Beckett, *Waiting for Godot: Tragicomedy in 2 Acts* (New York: Grove, 1982), 28.
6. Interview by Jovana Grbić, *ScriptPhD*, last modified April 13, 2010. Web.
7. Gźon-nu-rgyal-mchog, Dkon-mchog-rgyal-mtshan, and Thupten Jinpa, *Mind Training: The Great Collection* (Boston, MA: Wisdom Publications, in Association with the Institute of Tibetan Classics, 2006), 106.

8. J. J. R. Tolkien, Humphrey Carpenter, and Christopher Tolkien,*The Letters of J.R.R. Tolkien* (Boston: Houghton Mifflin, 1981), 255.

9. J. J. R. Tolkien and Douglas A. Anderson, *The Lord of the Rings* (Boston: Houghton Mifflin, 1994), 348.

10. Interview by John Blistein. *Rolling Stone*. Last modified January 7, 2014. Web.

11. Friedrich Schleiermacher, *On Religion: Speeches to its Cultured Despisers*, trans. John Oman (Cambridge: Public Domain Digital Edition, 2006), 51–52.

12. Elliot R. Wolfson and Project Muse. *Giving Beyond the Gift: Apophasis and Overcoming Theomania* (New York: Fordham University Press, 2014), 260.

13. Serpil Oppermann, "Quantum Physics and Literature: How They Meet the Universe Halfway," *Journal of English Philology* 13 (2015): 87.

14. David Segal, "The Dark Art of Breaking Bad," *New York Times*, last modified July 6, 2011. Web.

15. John Hick, *Philosophy of Religion* (New York: Pearson, 1989), 106.

16. Harold Bloom, *The Western Canon: The Books and School of the Ages* (New York: Harcourt Brace, 1994), 52.

17. Anna Gunn, "I Have a Characters Issue," *The New York Times*, last modified Aug. 23, 2013. Web.

PART 4

"I Did It for Me": Morality, Mastery and Meth

CHAPTER 10

Recovering Lost Moral Ground: Can Walt Make Amends?

James Edwin Mahon and Joseph Mahon

Is it possible to recover lost moral ground? In the closing episodes of *Breaking Bad* it becomes clear that Walter White believes that the correct answer to this question is an affirmative one. Walt believes that he can, and that he has, recovered lost moral ground.

Breaking Bad may be said to explore two distinct and incompatible ways of attempting to recover lost moral ground. The first way is *revisionist*. This is to rewrite the script of what, morally speaking, has occurred, so that it appears that nothing wrong was done. Since no moral ground has been lost, there is no moral ground to recover. The second way is *restorative*. This is to admit to morally wrongful behavior, but to attempt to make amends for it. While we concede that it is possible to recover lost moral ground in both of these ways, we deny that Walt is able to do so in both of these ways. At best, Walt can only hope to recover lost moral ground by attempting to make amends for his past misdeeds.

Before looking at these two kinds of attempts to recover lost moral ground in Walt's case, however, two defenses against accusations of moral wrongdoing will first be considered, since Walt also avails of these defenses. The first is the *justificatory* defense, that of seeking to justify the moral wrongdoing, so that it is no longer morally wrong. The second is the *mitigatory* defense, that of seeking to excuse the moral wrongdoing, so that the person is no longer responsible for the moral wrongdoing. As will be seen, it is not possible, ultimately,

J.E. Mahon
Lehman College, City University of New York, New York, NY, USA

J. Mahon (✉)
NUI Galway, Galway, Ireland

© The Author(s) 2017
K.S. Decker et al. (eds.), *Philosophy and Breaking Bad*,
DOI 10.1007/978-3-319-40343-4_10

to defend Walt against accusations of moral wrongdoing in either of these two ways, beyond a few cases.

Defending Yourself from Blame

J.L. Austin famously argued that when you are accused of acting in a way that is wrong, bad, or even just inept, there are two avenues of defense. You may accept full responsibility for the action, but deny that it was wrong, bad, or inept. This is the justification defense. You accept that you performed the action, but you attempt to justify the action by attempting to demonstrate that it was, in fact, the right thing to do. The second route is to agree that the action was wrong, bad, or inept, but to deny that you were responsible—either fully or partially—for the action. This is the excuse defense. You attempt to excuse the action by attempting to reduce or eliminate your responsibility for the action.[1]

In the criminal law, almost every crime may be said to have two elements: the first is the forbidden behavior, known as the *actus reus* ("guilty act") which can involve failing to do something as well as doing something. The second element is the state of mind of the individual engaging in the behavior, which includes both the knowledge of what one is doing and the choice of doing it; these are known collectively as the *mens rea* ("guilty mind"). The forbidden behavior must be voluntary in the basic sense that one is in control of one's behavior; one is not, for example, hypnotized, sleepwalking, or drugged.[2] The required state of mind can vary in degree. It can be *intentional*, as the crime of murder (killing "with malice aforethought"), such as when Todd Alquist shoots Andrea Cantillo on her front porch within view of Jesse Pinkman ("Granite State"). It can be merely *knowing*, as in the crime of voluntary manslaughter—for example, killing someone when provoked, such as when Spooge's wife tips the stolen ATM on his head because he is verbally abusing her ("Peekaboo"). It can be merely *reckless*, as in the crime of (so-called) "involuntary manslaughter," such as running a red light and killing someone crossing the street as a result; something like this could have happened when Walt was running red lights while driving his car out to the Tohajiillee Indian Reservation to save his money from being torched by Jesse ("To'hajiilee"). Or it can be merely *negligent*, as in the crime of criminally negligent manslaughter, as seems possible in the case of the negligent error made by flight traffic controller Donald Margolis—a result of his depressed state—that led to Wayfarer 515 colliding mid-air with JM 21 over Albuquerque, killing 167 passengers[3] ("ABQ"). In each case, however, it must be true that the person knew, or should have known, what was happening, and that the person chose, or failed to choose, to act.

Defenses by justification and excuse accept that the person committed the "guilty act" and that the person had the requisite "guilty mind." Nevertheless, they insist that the person is not to be found guilty of criminal or moral wrongdoing. The justification defense says that there is nothing wrong with the "guilty act," and that it should not be condemned. The excuse route says that even though there is something wrong with the "guilty act," and even though the person had a "guilty mind," nevertheless, the person should not be condemned.

JUSTIFYING OR EXCUSING YOUR ACTIONS

The justification defense is more straightforward than the excuse defense. It can be understood in terms of a choice between two evils; that is, the "guilty act" may be performed because it is the lesser of two evils. The idea is that, in the particular situation, it would be a lesser evil to violate the moral rule, or break the law, than it would be to abide by the moral rule or to obey the law.[4] For example, in Season Three's "One Minute," when Walt's brother-in-law, Drug Enforcement Agency (DEA) agent Hank Schrader, is shot at by Marco and Leonel Salamanca while in his car, he reverses his car into Leonel, severely injuring him, and then shoots Marco as Marco is about to behead him with an axe. Hank's injuring and killing the two assassins (cousins of drug king-pin Tuco Salamanca, whom Hank had killed earlier in a shoot-out in Season Two's "Grilled") was justified because it was in self-defense. There was nothing morally wrong or criminal in what he did. The same can be said of Skyler White slicing Walt's hand with a kitchen knife when she refuses to run from the police with Walt, believing that he may have killed their brother-in-law, Hank ("Ozymandias"). What she did was justified because she was acting in self-defense as well as in defense of her children. There was nothing morally wrong or criminal in what she did. In both cases, Hank and Skyler know full well what they are doing, and choose to so act, but the behavior is permissible and not to be condemned, because it can be said to be a lesser evil to harm an aggressor than to suffer harm from an aggressor.[5]

The excuse defense is more complicated than the justification defense. For behavior to be excused, it must be the case that the person knows or should know what he or she is doing, chooses to act, and yet is not blamable or not *as* blamable. That is, even though the person has a "guilty mind," nevertheless, he or she is not as morally or legally blameworthy. These cases may be a matter of the person having a diminished capacity: examples include immaturity due to young age, mental illness, or the existence of duress or coercion.[6] For example, in Season Two's "Mandala," when 10-year-old Tomás Cantillo shoots and kills Christian "Combo" Ortega on orders from the two unnamed drug dealers working for Fring, he is not as morally or legally blameworthy for the killing, because he is merely a child. Or take Season Five's "Granite State," in which Jesse agrees to remain as a prisoner and cook methamphetamine for Jack Welker, after one of the White Supremacists, Todd, kills his former girlfriend, Andrea, and threatens to kill her only remaining son, Brock. In this situation, Jesse is not as morally or legally blameworthy for cooking for the gang because he is being coerced into doing so.

Although insanity is also a moral and legal excuse, it should be noted that being a homicidal maniac is not a case of insanity. Nor is engaging in anti-social and/or criminal behavior the same as being mentally ill. To quote the Model Penal Code, "the terms 'mental disease or defect' do not include an abnormality manifested only by repeated criminal or otherwise anti-social conduct."[7] For example, it would not be possible to excuse Tuco from being less blameworthy for his killings on the basis that he is a homicidal maniac, which he clearly is.

"He'll Kill Your Entire Family If You Let Him Go"

Given justification or excuse as the two possible avenues of defense, it is difficult to see how Walt could ever avail himself of the latter defense. He is not immature due to young age. He is not insane. He is not suffering from any mental illness. He was not coerced into entering a life of crime and becoming "Heisenberg," the leading manufacturer of crystal meth in the southwest. It is also difficult to see any of the killings he commits as coerced. If anything, Walt may be said to be guilty, morally if not legally, of coercing others into helping him with his life of crime. For example, he only gets small-time drug dealer Jesse to agree to work with him and make crystal meth after he threatens to turn him in to the DEA in the pilot episode.

It may be possible, however, for Walt to avail himself of the justification defense. In "To'hajiilee," when Walt is driving out to the Indian reservation to stop Jesse from burning his buried money, he shouts at Jesse on the cell phone: "Open your eyes. Can't you see that I needed you on my side to kill Gus? I ran over those gang-bangers, I killed Emilio, and Krazy-8. Why? I did all of those things to try to save your life as much as mine. Only you're too stupid to know it." This could be interpreted as Walt claiming that was acting in self-defense, and/or in defense of Jesse, and hence, that his behavior was justified.

In the pilot episode, Walt kills drug-dealer Emilio Koyama, and gravely injures another drug dealer, Domingo Gallardo "Krazy-8" Molina. The two drug dealers had Walt and Jesse at gunpoint, and were about to kill them, but Walt told them that he would show them how to make crystal meth in his makeshift Winnebago lab, in return for their lives being spared. Instead, he adds phosphorous to boiling water, producing a deadly phosphine gas and locks them in the vehicle with the gas. Walt does so because he does not trust the dealers not to kill them once they know how to make crystal meth his way. It is possible to see this killing and injuring as justified because it is a case of self-defense (Walt) and defense of others (Jesse) against aggressors. It is plausible to believe that the drug dealers cannot be trusted to keep their agreement once they know how to make crystal meth Walt's way.[8] The same could be said of Walt's attempt to poison Tuco with ricin after Tuco kidnaps Walt and Jesse and is holding them hostage until he can transport them to Mexico to cook crystal meth for him ("Grilled). Walt was acting in self-defense, and in defense of an innocent other.

However, it is more difficult to justify the rest of Walt's behavior in general, and his killings in particular, on the basis of the defense of self and others. His killing of Krazy-8 fails to be a case of legally justified killing, since Krazy-8 is not currently a threat, tied up as he is in the basement of Jesse's house ("… And the Bag's in the River"). It would be possible, by contrast, for Walt to turn himself in and have Krazy-8 arrested. Morally, Walt wrestles with his conscience in deciding whether or not to "murder" Krazy-8, citing in his pro and con list many reasons to let him go. However, when he knows that Krazy-8 is planning to kill him with a shard of a broken plate once he is freed, he kills Krazy-8.[9] If this killing—of an admittedly murderous drug-dealer, who cannot be trusted—cannot be morally justified, then Walt's later killings for the sake of protecting his crystal meth empire certainly cannot not be justified.

Even if the killing of Krazy-8 could be morally justified, it is hard to see how Walt's subsequent killings are morally justified, such as his killing of the two "gang-bangers" in Season Three's "Half Measures." As mentioned in the last section, these two drug dealers, working for Gus Fring, ordered Tomás Cantillo, the son of Jesse's girlfriend, to kill Jesse's friend Combo. After all, Combo was dealing Walt and Jesse's crystal meth on their turf. After Jesse convinced Gus to stop using kids to do his dirty work, Gus's dealers kill Tomás in order to cover their tracks. Enraged, Jesse gets a gun and confronts them— even though they are armed, experienced killers. Before they have a chance to kill Jesse, Walt runs them over in his Pontiac Aztek, killing one instantly. He then gets out and shoots the other point-blank in the head, shouting at Jesse, "Run!" Neither drug dealer was posing a threat to Jesse—or Walt—before Jesse went after them. Even if Jesse is entirely right to be outraged at their killing of Tomás, his attempt to kill them is a case of revenge-seeking rather than bringing them to justice. Walt does save Jesse from certain death at their hands, but Jesse was in peril only because of his own actions. For that reason, this fails to be a case of defending an innocent person. Walt's own life was never in danger either, and hence this fails to be a case of self-defense. As much as Walt may be motivated by his concern for Jesse's life rather than merely the prospect of losing his partner, and as much as the two drug dealers are beyond doubt ruthless murderers, Walt's killing of them in order to protect Jesse fails to be a case of justified killing, either legally or morally.[10]

It's also worth noting that Walt did not himself kill Gus Fring. Walt provided Gus's mortal enemy, wheelchair-bound Hector "Tio" Salamanca, an opportunity and means to kill Gus. Years before, Salamanca had murdered Gus's original business partner and presumed lover, Max Arciniega, as seen in a flashback in "Hermanos." Walt provides Salamanca with a powerful bomb that allowed him to kill Gus, Gus's assistant, Tyrus Kitt, as well as himself, in Season Four's "Face Off." Nevertheless, it was Walt's idea to convince Hector to kill Gus, and Walt only enlists Hector's help after he fails to kill Gus himself with the bomb. While it is true that Walt believes Gus wishes to kill him sooner or later and to have Jesse take over the lab, nevertheless, Gus is not currently a threat to Walt. Walt has the opportunity to turn himself in to the DEA with the rest of his family, inform on Gus, and escape. He chooses not to do so, instead opting to kill Gus with Hector's help. Killing Gus is therefore not a case of self-defense. It is also not a case of justified killing, either legally or morally. While it is true that "none of the dead were innocent. Salamanca, Gus, and Tyrus are all killers, wrapped up in the drug trade,"[11] none of them was currently threatening Walt's life, which establishes the relevant meaning of "innocent" when considering whether killing them was justified.

Walt's many other killings—for example, when he lets Jane Margolis, Jesse's girlfriend, choke to death on her own vomit ("Phoenix"), or when he shoots Gus's former hitman, Mike Ehrmantraut ("Say My Name"), or when, with an M60 mounted in the truck of his car, he mows down the White Supremacist gang led by Jack Welker who are holding Jesse prisoner ("Felina")— cannot be classified as cases of defense of self or others either, and hence are not justified killings, either legally or morally. Much as the killing of that gang of murderers might be thought to be a fitting end to their lives and a service to the world, Walt could have freed Jesse and turned them in to the police without killing any of them.

Neither of the two possible defenses—justification or excuse—can, therefore, absolve Walt of his moral blame. If he wishes to escape moral blame, his remaining options are to revise the account of what occurred, so that he is blameless, or to admit wrongdoing and attempt to make up for it.

REWRITING THE PAST

Revisionism consists in recovering one's lost moral ground by denying that anything wrong was done. Since one has not wronged anyone, no moral ground has been lost, and there is no moral ground to recover. Walt's efforts to recast his actions in a more honorable light are many and varied, but his last phone call to his son, Walt Jr. ("Granite State"), represents a particularly poignant attempt: "Son, the things that they're saying about me... I did wrong... I made some terrible mistakes... but the reasons were always... things happen that I never intended... I never intended...," he pleads.

Walt offers two different denials that he intended for any of the bad things in his career of crime to happen. Since he did not intend for any of the bad things to happen, he cannot be held guilty of moral wrongdoing. But he also seems to tell Walt Jr. that he had anything except the best reasons for acting in the way that he did, even if he did intend for some or or all of the bad things to happen. Do any of these exculpate him?

Walt could mean, first, that he never imagined that any of the bad things that happened would, in fact, happen, such as the killing of Hank Schrader by Jack Welker, in "To'hajiilee." Such things, he could be saying, were unforeseen by him when he embarked on his journey of manufacturing methamphetamine. If that is what he is claiming, then he is attempting to escape blame by appealing to the idea that he cannot be held responsible for bad things that happen as a result of what he did just in case he never imagined that they would happen.

He would be embracing the legal and moral standard of requiring a *mens rea*, and arguing that in order for him to be held liable for such bad things, he must have had a "guilty mind"—something that he denies having.

In embracing the standard of requiring a *mens rea*, Walt would be rejecting the standard of strict liability, or "faultless" liability, a standard used extremely rarely in the criminal law, and even more rarely (if ever) in morality, in which you are held criminally liable for what happens as a result of what you do (or do not do), even though you lacked any criminal intent, or knowledge of breaking the law, and were not reckless, or even negligent, in your behavior. An example would be getting a minor intoxicated by serving them alcohol, even if you had taken reasonable steps to ensure that they were of legal age.[12]

The simple problem with Walt's attempt to escape blame by denying he had a *mens rea*—intent, knowledge, recklessness, or negligence—to be held culpable, is that it is simply false that he never imagined any of these bad things could happen. He was fully aware of the risks of people being harmed as a result of what he was doing. As noted above, Walt killed a number of people himself; he also ordered the killing of ten former associates of Mike's in their jail cells. While he could attempt to argue that these killings were not, in fact, wrongful actions, because the victims were murderers, this would be a very different kind of defense (it would be an attempt to *justify* these killings, as discussed earlier). It would also fail to absolve him from blame for other bad things that he did, such as letting Jane die or ordering Jesse to kill Gale. Neither Jane nor Gale is a murderer. As other commentators have said, "But Walt's ordering Jesse to kill Gale under the threat of Walt's own demise, due to Walt's own actions, makes Walt complicit, and morally guilty for Gale's death perhaps as much as if he had himself pulled the trigger."[13] And these acts of violence do not even take into account the enormous amount of harm that he knowingly caused by manufacturing and selling the highly addictive and destructive crystal meth to people all over the country.

Walt did indeed possess the requisite *mens rea*, therefore, to be held culpable for these and many other bad things that happened. Even if it were true that there were some bad things that Walt never could have imagined—such as the deaths of the 167 people aboard flights Wayfarer 515 and JM 21—it is not clear that Walt can be absolved of blame for these, at least morally, on the basis that to hold him responsible would be to hold him to the standard of strict liability. It was Walt who let Jane choke to death on her own vomit, and it was her death that sent her father into a depression, which, it's not unreasonable for us to assume, led to the error and the deaths of the passengers, as well as his subsequent suicide. If this is what happened, then Walt may be held morally responsible for the deaths of those passengers, even if he cannot be held legally responsible, because he did something morally wrong in letting her die, and his moral wrongdoing ultimately led to their deaths.[14] The same can be said about Hank's death, and that of his partner Steve Gomez, at the hands of Jack Welker and his gang. Hank would never have met up with Jack Welker and his gang in the To'hajiilee Reservation if he had not been chasing Walt to bring him into custody for manufacturing and selling crystal meth. Walt does bear the moral responsibility for their deaths, because his decision to make crystal meth, and especially, to continue to make it after so many people were harmed, was morally wrong. As another commentator has said, "For the first time, the reality of what his descent into Heisenberg truly means hits Walt. He collapses, knowing that his deeds finally led to the ultimate sin. A family member is dead because of him."[15]

Embracing the standard of requiring a *mens rea*, therefore, will not absolve Walt of moral blame.

Collateral Damage

In saying to Walt, Jr., that "things happen that I never intended... I never intended...," Walt could mean something weaker than simply that he lacked the requisite *mens rea* to be blamed, morally or legally. He could mean that, although he believed either initially or eventually that these bad things would happen, nevertheless, he did not *intend* that any of these bad things would happen. He could be saying, simply, that he never intended to harm anyone—that he never intended for anyone to get hurt.

If this is what Walt is claiming, then he may be attempting to escape moral blame (if not legal blame) by implicitly appealing to the Doctrine of Double Effect (or the Principle of Double Effect), according to which an action that has both good and bad effects may be morally permissible. According to this doctrine, so long as I am intending some significant good, it is sometimes morally permissible to do something bad as a foreseen side-effect (the double effect), even if it would be morally impermissible to intend that same bad thing.[16] For example, in fighting a just war, it may be morally permissible to bomb a munitions factory in a nighttime bombing raid, injuring and even killing civilians asleep in their beds near the factory, as a side-effect of the factory bombing (so-called collateral damage), even if it would be morally impermissible to bomb those same civilians for the sake of winning the war. So long as I act in a way that is in itself morally praiseworthy, or at least not morally wrong (blowing up the enemy's munitions factory), only intending the good effect (the destruction of the enemy's arsenal, and ultimately, the defeat of the enemy), and not intending the bad effect, which I nevertheless foresee (injuring and killing nearby civilians), then my action is blameless, and may be praiseworthy. There are a few caveats to this: the bad effect I produce cannot be a means to the good effect (injuring and killing nearby civilians is not a means of destroying the arsenal or defeating the enemy), and the good effect must be sufficiently proportionately good that it compensates for the bad effect (the destruction of the enemy's arsenal, and ultimately, the defeat of the enemy, is sufficiently proportionately good that it compensates for the injuring and killing of nearby civilians). Such a doctrine may be said to be behind, for example, the morally permissible prescription of certain pain-relieving drugs like morphine that shorten life expectancy, or the removal of a cancerous womb from a pregnant woman (a hysterectomy), which kills the fetus.

According to some interpretations of the Doctrine of Double Effect, self-defense (and likewise the defense of innocent others) may be justified in this way: I perform some morally neutral, or morally praiseworthy, action, with the intent to defend myself (a good effect), and I merely foresee harming another person (bad effect).[17] If this were correct, then it could be argued that, for example, when Walt poisons Emilio Koyama and Krazy-8, his would-be killers, he does something that is morally neutral (mixing compounds and producing a gas) for a good effect (saving his life), and merely foresees their deaths as a result.

But it is highly doubtful that self-defense can ever be justified by appealing to the Doctrine of Double Effect. In self-defense, I do, in fact, intend to harm the other person who is about to harm me: this is the means to saving my life.[18] Self-defense is justified because you are justified in intending to harm someone who intends to harm you. That other person is a current threat, and not an innocent person. But even if Walt's acts of self-defense can somehow be justified by appealing to this doctrine, there are many other things that Walt does that cannot be justified by appealing to the doctrine. An example is when Walt (presumably) poisons Brock Cantillo—the son of Andrea, Jesse's girlfriend—with enough Lily of the Valley to make him ill, but not enough to kill him, and blames it on Gus Fring. Walt intends to harm an innocent boy (a morally wrong act), as a means to save his own life (a good effect). But intentionally committing a morally wrong act, even for a good end, is completely prohibited by the Doctrine of Double Effect. Walt cannot avoid blame for poisoning Brock Cantillo by appealing to this doctrine. The same can be said about Walt's ordering Jesse to kill Gale. Even if Walt believed that Gus was going to replace him with Gale and kill him, Gale himself was innocent. Walt intended to harm an innocent person (a morally wrong act), as a means of saving his own life (a good effect), something completely prohibited by the Doctrine of Double Effect. None of this can be considered collateral damage.

This is even more true with respect to Walt's making and selling of crystal meth. Walt produces very large quantities of an illegal, highly addictive substance for which there is a huge commercial demand. He does so, as he says, to provide for his family, and to cover his expenses for his cancer treatment. But the good effects of making large profits don't remotely compensate for the bad effects of the distribution and sale of crystal meth over a vast territory by criminal gangs. Moreover, those good effects could have been achieved by other means, had Walt been prepared to swallow his pride and accept the money offered by his fabulously rich former partner, Elliott Schwartz, and Walt's former girlfriend (now Elliott's wife) Gretchen Schwartz.

Appealing to the Doctrine of Double Effect, therefore, will not allow Walt to escape moral blame.

For Good Reasons

There is a third way of understanding what Walt is saying to Walt, Jr. when he says, "I never intended…" He might be restating his previous claim that "I did wrong… I made some terrible mistakes… but the reasons were always…" If this last sentence is finished with "good," then Walt would be admitting that he acted in morally wrong ways, but for good reasons—he had good intentions. Here it is important to note that the word "intention" is ambiguous. It can mean both *why* Walt does what he does—the end or goal for which he acts—as well as *what* Walt does. The first meaning of intention (as in claiming that someone acted with good intentions) is equivalent to the *reason* or *motive* for doing something; the second meaning (as in claiming that it was someone's intention to do this rather than that) is equivalent to the (intentional) *action* itself.[19] It is the first meaning that is relevant here.[20] Understood in this way, Walt is attempting to reduce or eliminate his blameworthiness for what he has done by saying that his reasons or motives for acting were always good. As he says in Season Three's "I.F.T.": "I've done a terrible thing, but I've done it for a good reason. I did it for us."

This is by far the weakest way for Walt to attempt to escape moral blame. To begin with, it would not absolve him from any blame in the eyes of the law. Granted that a person knows what he is doing (that is, has the requisite *mens rea*), and granted that he or she is not mentally ill or under duress, the reason or motive behind someone's criminal behavior is completely irrelevant: "Hardly any part of penal law is more definitely settled than that motive is irrelevant."[21] If a person intentionally kills another who is not a current threat to him—that is, if he commits murder—then it is irrelevant, as far as the law is concerned, if he murdered the person for revenge, for money, as a dare, to impress a girlfriend, for fun, to save himself, or to save other people.[22] For Walt to argue that, although he intentionally did things that were wrong, he did them for good reasons, is simply for him to argue that he is not a bad person despite the bad things that he has done.

Right up until the day he dies, Walt repeatedly tells his wife Skyler that the reason for all his actions—the reason why he manufactured crystal meth, protected and sold his product, and ultimately killed and harmed various people who got in the way—was to make enough money to take care of his family since he was going to die from cancer. This is what Walt means when he says to Walt, Jr., "but the reasons were always [good]." Indeed, when Walt begins to have scruples about his breaking bad and its fallout, he is talked back into staying the course by Gus, on this very basis, in Season Three's "Más":

> **Gus**: Why did you make these decisions?
> **Walt**: For the good of my family.
> **Gus**: Then they weren't bad decisions.
> **Gus**: What does a man do, Walter? A man provides for his family.
> **Walt**: This costs me my family.

Gus: When you have children, you always have family. They will always be your priority, your responsibility. And a man... a man provides. And he does it even when he's not appreciated, or respected, or even loved. He simply bears up and he does it, because he's a man.

The problem with this attempt to avoid blame, however, is that on the day that he dies, Walt finally admits that taking care of his family was not his reason. As he says in his final exchange with Skyler, he did it for himself:

Walt: You have to understand...
Skyler: If I have to hear, one more time, that you did this for the family–.
Walt: I did it for me.
Skyler: [Looking surprised].
Walt: I liked it. I was good at it. And... I was... really... I was alive.

Although it may be possible to reduce or eliminate Walt's moral blame-worthiness for what he did by establishing that he did it all selflessly, in order to take care of his family, it is hardly possible to reduce or eliminate his moral blameworthiness by claiming that he did it all because it made him feel alive.

Given that none of the three possible revisionist avenues for Walt will work, he cannot exonerate himself by availing of this approach to moral wrongdoing. Walt's repeated attempts to rewrite (and stage-manage the rewriting) the script of what has happened cuts no ice. There is lost moral ground to recover, a great deal of it. It follows that Walt has no option, in seeking redemption, other than attempting to make amends for his wrongful behavior.

Before considering this final option, however, it is worthwhile to address the question raised by Walt's final admission that his motivation was self-interest. Was he lying to Skyler, and Walt Jr., and Jesse, all along? Or was he deceiving himself?[23]

IN DENIAL

The best explanation of why Walt never previously admitted his true reason for pursuing a career as a drug kingpin is that he could not even admit it to himself. Quite simply, he was in denial about his own motivation. Walt's capacity for self-deception is almost as impressive as his capacity for deceiving others. Throughout his short-lived criminal career, he refused to morally evaluate his actions in a negative way or to acknowledge his true motivation, despite accumulating plenty of evidence to the contrary.

In the pilot episode, Walt frames his denial unequivocally. He declares in his speech to his family for the video-recorder: "No matter how it may look, I had only you in my heart." Accused by his wife of being a drug dealer in "No Más," he replies "I'm a manufacturer, not a dealer...." "I am not a criminal, that is not me," he tells Gus Fring in the same episode. "I can't be the bad guy," he repeats in the subsequent episode, "Caballo Sin Nombre." He acknowledges having made "a series of very bad decisions" ("Más"). "I never saw this coming," he blurts out in the episode "One Minute." "Sometimes compromises have to be made, for the best reasons," we are told in "Half Measures." In Season Four's "Box Cutter," he asserts "I didn't want any of this to happen," and in "Bullet Points," he reminds his wife that "I was and am providing for my family." "I alone should suffer the consequences of those choices," he maintains in the episode "End Times." "What we do we do for good reasons; there's nothing to worry about," he advises Jesse in Season Five's "Live Free or Die." "Now that we're in control, no one else gets hurt," he continues. "I'm sorry about Brock," he says to Jesse in "To'hajiilee," "but he's alive, isn't he?" As he might have said, Walt did make mistakes, but he never did anything wrong.

Walt is, then, in denial, or as Jean-Paul Sartre would say, he is guilty of bad faith.[24] It beggars belief that someone who arguably understands the chemistry and manufacture of methamphetamine better than anyone else alive could have no understanding of its impact on the bodies and minds of those who consume it. Walt is not ignorant of the ravages of drug addiction. When he goes searching for Jesse, following the death of Jane, he locates him in a fetid, squalid drug den strewn with lacerated, semi-comatose bodies. He even refers to the downstairs of Jesse's house, following a drug party, as "Skid Row." He is also not oblivious to the *modus operandi* of the drug cartels and the criminal underworld. Nor can Walt claim to be ignorant of the effects that his criminal career has on his family and associates, not to mention the people he kills and orders to be killed. Nevertheless, Walt somehow manages—or chooses—to ignore all of this. Although Sartre allows that to practice bad faith is to "to lie to oneself," he insists that "we distinguish the lie to oneself from lying in general."[25] In lying to others, I intend to deceive them, that is, to get them to hold as true what I know or believe to be false. But in lying to myself, the person who deceives and the person who is deceived are one and the same; this means, Sartre says, "that I must know in my capacity as deceiver the truth which is hidden from me in my capacity as the one deceived."[26] Bad faith or lying to oneself is not a state. It is not something that befalls you. On the contrary, "consciousness affects itself with bad faith. There must be an original intention and a project of bad faith."[27] Sartre concludes that it is a project rather than a condition or a state because the self-deceiver "must know the truth very exactly in order to conceal it more carefully."[28]

What is interesting about Walt's particular form of self-deception is that it takes the form of professionalism about his illegal drug manufacturing. This assumption of professionalism clouds his judgment from the very outset and remains embedded in his psyche. It is captured in the refrain that what he does is "just chemistry." Jesse knows "the business," while Walt knows "the chemistry." Walt is in charge of the cooking, because the chemistry is his realm. He even refuses to accept the accolade of its being art. After his first cook in the pilot episode, Jesse exclaims "You're a goddamn artist. This is art, Mr. White!" Walt replies, "Actually, it's just basic chemistry, but thank you, Jesse, I'm glad its acceptable." (Indeed, drug-dealer Emilio, whom he later strangles to death, also calls Walt an artist when he meets him). The chemistry, however, that Walt practices is state-of-the-art: "We will produce a chemically pure and stable product that performs as advertised." Above all, Walt insists, "the chemistry must be respected!" But Walt does more than rigidly respect the chemistry. He also produces and arranges for the distribution and sale of a substance which, when "burned," will turn so many users into zombies. He kills people to maintain his growing empire, despite having made more money than his family could possibly need. He has been seduced by the charms of professionalism, and this, in part, is what enables him to endure.

Walt's self-deception is also facilitated by Gale, who works as his assistant in the lab. Gale supplies Walt with, as he calls it, a "libertarian" justification for his breaking bad. Not everything that constitutes crime deserves to be criminalized, he asserts in Season Three's "Sunset": "There's crime, and then there's crime, I suppose." As Gale sees it, they supply goods for a market, and if they didn't supply them, someone else would. Moreover, the product they supply contains no toxins or adulterants. Their customers are getting exactly what they paid for. These same customers are consenting adults, deciding for themselves what to do with their lives, and "consenting adults want what they want." So, as producers and suppliers, Walt, Gale, and Gus are expanding the realm of freedom, the range of choices available to adult individuals. They are also fulfilling their contractual obligations. After that, what befalls drugs users is their own fate. They bring it on themselves. As free agents, they could always turn their backs and walk away. But Gale conveniently ignores the fact that their product is highly addictive, thus severely limiting, and perhaps even erasing, the libertarian freedom he speaks of. He also ignores the fact that the distribution and sale of that same product is illegal, and that the state does not condone these kinds of consensual activities.

While Walt's self-deception can be explained, it cannot be defended. The consequences of drug addiction are foreseeable and well documented. As a gifted chemist, Walt is in a prime position to know what these consequences would be for his customers. His involvement in the drug trade, from his encounters with Emilio and Krazy-8, not to mention Tuco, to Gus, and his dealers, exposed him to the ruthless, homicidal behavior commonplace throughout the criminal underworld. Even if he could not have known in advance who would be killed, or when, or where, or how, he could not have been blind to the fact that these things happen, and he knew from the start just how nasty they could be.

REFLECTIONS ON THE GUILLOTINE

The French existentialist author Albert Camus favored life imprisonment with hard labor over capital punishment for even the very worst murderers. He believed that imposing the death penalty on a person deprived her of the opportunity of making amends, and no one should be denied the opportunity of making amends. In the closing stages of his essay on the death penalty,

"Reflections on the Guillotine," Camus is concerned with the fate of those he calls "major criminals whom all juries would condemn at any time and in any place whatever. Their crimes are not open to doubt, and the evidence brought by the accusation is confirmed by the confessions of the defense."[29] He gives the example of a young man who, annoyed by a remark made by his father about his coming home late, killed both his parents in cold blood with an axe, then "undressed, hid his bloodstained trousers in the closet, went to make a call on the family of his fiancée, without showing any signs, then returned home and notified the police that he had just found his parents murdered."[30] While his "odd indifference" was abnormal, his reasoning power remained untouched, and the medical experts asserted he was responsible for his actions, as opposed to concluding he was suffering from a mental illness or acting under duress.

Such "monsters," notes Camus, evoke the most extreme response from society's guardians: "Apparently the nature or the magnitude of their crimes allows no room for imagining that they can ever repent or reform. They must merely be kept from doing it again, and there is no other solution but to eliminate them."[31] Camus, for his part, begs to differ. Everyone, he holds, is capable of making amends, and not just those with a beneficent disposition: "Deciding that a man must have the definitive punishment imposed on him is tantamount to deciding that a man has no chance of making amends."[32]

There are two parts to Camus' argument here. First, there is the claim that everyone is capable of making amends. Second, there is the claim that everyone has amends to make. The latter proposition is true because "we have all done wrong in our lives even if that wrong, without falling within the jurisdiction of the law, went as far as the unknown crime."[33] To make sure that we do not miss or underestimate the importance of this point, Camus adds, provocatively, "There are no just people - merely hearts more or less lacking in justice."[34] Allowing even the worst criminal to continue living is, for Camus, essentially a matter of giving precedence to the principle of equality: it is giving him, or her, the same opportunity to make amends as is given to everyone else. So it comes about that "the lowest of criminals and the most upright of judges meet side by side, equally wretched in their solidarity. Without that right, moral life is utterly impossible."[35]

Camus has a more abstract and complex concept of making amends than that found in common usage. To make amends, as the phrase is commonly used, means to restore to another, or to others, what you have taken from them; alternatively, it means to compensate others for the harm you have caused them. But for Camus, it means adding good things to the sum of good things you have done, which in turn augments the universal sum of good things done, which in turn will help atone or compensate for all the bad things you have done: "Living at least allows us to discover this and to add to the sum of our actions a little of the good that will make up in part for the evil we have added to the world. Such a right to live, which allows a chance to make amends, is the natural right of every man, even the worst men."[36] Whereas in common usage making amends means restoring to other people, or compensating them, for

Camus it means restoring an equilibrium between aggregates of good and evil. Thus, even Camus's preferred alternative to capital punishment—life imprisonment with hard labor—is capable of providing a person with the opportunity to exercise his or her right to atone, since, even under the gruesome conditions of penal servitude during the postwar period, a prisoner could have behaved badly or well toward other prisoners and warders. In any event, Walt, by contrast with Camus's prisoner, manifestly does have the resources to make some reparation to some of those he has harmed, as well as to the wider society.

Making Amends

Walt, who has been characterized as "a hapless passive-aggressive chemistry teacher" who mutates into "a hapless passive-aggressive meth cook,"[37] has also been characterized as a chemistry teacher who has not just broken *bad*, but "broken *evil*"—just as evil, indeed, as Gus Fring—and as someone who has "taken his wife down this path too, corrupting her, involving her in a conspiracy, and endangering his family and friends,"[38] not to mention converting his partner Jesse into a murderer. Walt has a lot of moral ground to recover. The question is whether and how much of this moral ground can be recovered by making amends for past wrongdoing, in Camus' sense.

It is conceded here that Walt does make some amends for his past misdeeds. The good things that he does in his final days, as depicted in the series' final episode, "Felina," add to the universal sum of good things achieved by all human agents. Walt himself believed he could make amends by way of direct compensation. He rescues Jesse from his imprisonment at the hands of Jack Welker and his gang, ending their crystal meth production, and in so doing removes the remaining threat to his family. He even hands Jesse a gun to give him the opportunity to kill him for all that he had put him through. He devises an elaborate benefaction scheme to finance Walt, Jr.'s college education with $9.72 million that he gives to Elliott and Gretchen Schwartz, so that they can set up an irrevocable trust fund for Walt Jr. on his eighteenth birthday. He also supplies Skyler with the GPS coordinates of the place where Hank and his partner Steve Gomez are buried, and tells her "Now you trade that for a deal with the Prosecutor. You'll get yourself out of this, Skyler."

It is true that, in order to do all of this, he has to shoot almost the entire gang—leaving Jesse to strangle his captor and tormentor, Todd—as well as poison Lydia, the mastermind behind the global distribution network for the blue crystal meth. He does not turn them into the authorities. He does not afford any of these murderers the opportunity for moral redemption. Nevertheless, even if these killings cannot be morally justified, the motivation behind wiping out a white supremacist gang, and shutting down global distribution network for the blue crystal meth, as well as that behind saving Jesse and protecting his family is more admirable than simply eliminating the competition. His killings could even be said to add to the sum of good in the world, even if his actions cannot be morally justified.

It has been said that "More importantly, there is no redemption for Walt in 'Felina.' None of what he does in that final episode excuses what he did in the 61 prior. None of it made him a hero in the end. He does not make up for his lies and crimes. He does not wash away poisoning children and destroying families and being a vile manipulator of people he claimed to care about."[39] While it is true that Walt's final actions do not excuse his previous moral wrongdoing, and do not elide his previous sins, and while it is true that these final actions do not "make up" for all his crimes and mistreatment of people, nevertheless, it is possible to believe that Walt does make some amends in his final days, and that in general he is right to think that it is possible for moral wrongdoers to recover lost moral ground. To some extent, Walt does recover lost moral ground toward the end of *Breaking Bad*. How much moral ground he has recovered is a probably a moot point. Suffice it to say that in the concluding scenes Walt appears a sad, depleted, ashen, forlorn, tragic figure, but he is no "monster." Some moral reputation has been restored.

NOTES

1. J. L. Austin, "A Plea for Excuses: The Presidential Address," *Proceedings of the Aristotelian Society* 57 (1957): 1–30.
2. See Mark C. Murphy, *Philosophy of Law: The Fundamentals* (Oxford: Blackwell, 2007), 113f.
3. For more on the prosecution of air traffic controllers for criminal negligence and negligent homicide, see Sofia Michaelides-Mateou and Andreas Mateou, *Flying in the Face of Criminalization: The Safety Implications of Prosecuting Aviation Professionals for Accidents* (Farnham, Surrey: Ashgate, 2010).
4. Murphy, *Philosophy of Law: The Fundamentals*, 133–134. See also Larry A. Alexander, "Lesser Evils: A Closer Look at Paradigmatic Justification," *Law and Philosophy* 24 (2005): 611–643.
5. Harming and killing in self-defense is morally and legally permissible, but not obligatory. One could permissibly choose to allow oneself to be harmed or killed by an aggressor, rather than harm an aggressor. It is a further question as to whether harming and killing in order to save (innocent) others is ever morally (and even legally) *obligatory*, such that it would be morally (and even legally) *impermissible* to refuse to harm or kill aggressors. For the argument that there is a "moral obligation to kill or seriously harm in defense of others," see James P. Sterba, "Introduction: Justice for Here and Now," in *Social and Political Philosophy: Contemporary Perspectives*, ed. James P. Sterba (London: Routledge, 2001), 22.
6. Murphy, *Philosophy of Law: The Fundamentals*, 139.
7. Quoted in Murphy, *Philosophy of Law: The Fundamentals*, 138.
8. David R. Koepsell and Vanessa Gonzalez have said that "Killing in self-defense is a well-known and widely recognized legal and moral justification or excuse" and "Killing Emilio would have likely been seen as justified or excusable legally" ("Walt's Rap Sheet," in *Breaking Bad and Philosophy*, ed. David R. Koepsell and Robert Arp (LaSalle, IL: Open Court, 2012), 6–7. However, self-defense is never an *excuse*. It is only a justification.

9. Eric San Juan has said "Walt eventually kills the remaining dealer, but only out of self-defense," in *Breaking Down Breaking Bad: Unpeeling the Layers of Television's Greatest Drama* (Eric San Juan, 2013), 15. But it is not self-defense if the other person is not currently aggressing. Pre-emptively killing Krazy-8, because he knows that Krazy-8 will attempt to kill him if he releases him, is not self-defense. Perhaps, however, San Juan is only referring to the final struggle, in which Krazy-8 is attempting to stab Walt with the shard of broken plate. Koepsell and Gonzalez have written about the final struggle that "Arguably, Walt's actions now amount to valid self-defense, but his moral blameworthiness for killing Krazy-8 seems greater than for Emilio" ("Walt's Rap Sheet," 6).

10. Koepsell and Gonzalez ask about this case "Is [Walt's] killing of two non-innocents to prevent the death of another non-innocent justifiable? Jesse surely wouldn't have been in the position of weighing to murder Gus but for Walt, so Walt's own actions and intentions are partly responsible for Jesse's intent to murder, and thus his targeting for murder... because Walt himself has helped create the situation Jesse is in, his saving Jesse is perhaps morally justifiable based on Walt's active responsibility, and given their special relationship and Walt's *relatively* honorable intentions" ("Walt's Rap Sheet," 10). Even if Walt feels partly responsible for Jesse's targeting of the two drug dealers, however, this only goes some way toward explaining why Walt kills them. It does not *justify* his killing them.

11. Koepsell and Gonzalez, "Walt's Rap Sheet," 12.

12. Murphy, *Philosophy of Law*, 143 n. 1.

13. Koepsell and Gonzalez, "Gus's Rap Sheet," 12.

14. Koepsell and Gonzalez have said that "it's a stretch to hold Walt morally responsible for these deaths. Although his actions are complexly implicated in the two related events of the Wayfarer crash and Donald's suicide, and some of Walt's decisions helped lead to them, they seem far too remote to *blame* upon Walt. He's a cause, but not the *proximate* or immediate cause of these deaths. His actions and decisions created their *possibility*, but did not make them inevitable" ("Walt's Rap Sheet," 13–14). However, moral responsibility does not require that one be a proximate cause, as is the case with legal responsibility in tort law. One may be held morally responsible for remote bad things if they happen as a result of one doing something morally wrong.

15. Eric San Juan, *Breaking Down Breaking Bad*, 88.

16. For the official Catholic Church account of the doctrine, see F. J. Connell, "Double Effect, Principle of," *New Catholic Encyclopedia*, vol. 4 (New York, NY: McGraw-Hill, 1967), 1021.

17. See Thomas Aquinas on self-defense in Alison McIntyre, "Doctrine of Double Effect," *Stanford Encyclopedia of Philosophy*, last modified September 23, 2014. Web.

18. For this reason, it seems, Augustine held that self-defense was *never* justified. See McIntyre, "Doctrine of Double Effect."

19. See James Edwin Mahon, "Doing the Wrong Thing for a Good Reason," in *The Good Wife and Philosophy*, eds. Kimberly Baltzer-Jaray and Robert Arp (LaSalle, IL: Open Court, 2013), 89–99.

20. When Koepsell and Gonzalez talk about "Walt's *relatively* honorable intentions" ("Gus's Rap Sheet,"10), and when Eric San Juan says "Skyler gave the money to Ted Beneke. She did so with the best of intentions" (*Breaking Down*

Breaking Bad, 59), they are all using "intention" in the sense of reason or motive.

21. Hall, 1960, quoted in Whitley R. P. Kayfman, "Motive, Intention, and Morality in the Criminal Law," *Criminal Justice Review* 28 (2003): 317–335.

22. In the famous British case of *The Queen v. Dudley and Stephens* (1884), it did not matter that the two shipwrecked sailors, Tom Dudley and Edwin Stephens, who were in the lifeboat with the sick cabin boy, Richard Parker, were starving to death, and that they killed and ate Parker, and shared the flesh with a third sailor, in order to survive. They were both convicted of murder. See Neil Hanson, *The Custom of the Sea: A Shocking True Tale of Shipwreck, Murder, and the Last Taboo* (New York, NY: John Wiley & Sons, 1999).

23. As Eric San Juan has pointed out, "It's a testament to Walter's amazing ability to lie (and Bryan Cranston's amazing ability to deliver those lines) that even in the final week of the show many viewers still believed he was motivated by a desire to provide for his family, even though it was clear that he *liked* indulging in crime" (*Breaking Down Breaking Bad*, 84).

24. See Jean-Paul Sartre, *Being and Nothingness*, trans. Hazel Barnes (London: Methuen, 1958), 47–70, and *Existentialism and Humanism*, trans. Philip Mairet (London: Methuen, 1965), 30–31.

25. Sartre, *Being and Nothingness*, 48.

26. Ibid., 48.

27. Ibid., 49.

28. Ibid.

29. Albert Camus, "Reflections on the Guillotine," in *Resistance, Rebellion, and Death* (New York, NY: Vintage, 1995), 218.

30. Ibid., 219.

31. Ibid., 219.

32. Ibid., 220.

33. Ibid., 221.

34. Ibid.

35. Ibid.

36. Ibid.

37. Dan Miori, "Was Skyler's Intervention Ethical? Hell, It Shouldn't Even Be Legal," in *Breaking Bad and Philosophy*, 27.

38. Koepsell and Gonzalez "Walt's Rap Sheet," 14.

39. Eric San Juan, *Breaking Down Breaking Bad*, 99.

CHAPTER 11

(Im)Morality in Action

Travis Dyk and Adam Barkman

Marcus Aurelius once said, "Injustice is not always associated with action. Usually it is an inaction."[1] This statement raises the question: "do we have a moral obligation to help those who are suffering?" Conversely, it may seem straightforwardly correct to say that it is morally wrong to actively harm others, but *Breaking Bad* asks its viewers to consider whether is it wrong to know of suffering and do nothing. Is it possible that allowing someone to die could be morally equivalent to the act of killing? *Breaking Bad*'s characters are often put into unique situations in which they are forced to choose between helping someone or leaving them to deal with the consequences alone. The most prominent depiction of this conflict within *Breaking Bad* is whether Walt's decision to allow Jane to die ("Phoenix") is just as immoral as his killing Mike ("Say My Name"). The way in which obligations seem to be measured throughout *Breaking Bad* is through civil law, results of actions, the intentions of an action, and the ability of the person to act in light of their choices.

Before jumping into moral obligations, it has to be established whether or not people, in this case the characters in *Breaking Bad,* live in a deterministic or libertarian world in regards to free will.[2]

In a deterministic world, a person has no ultimate control over what they may do. Determinists believe that the events of the past have built up so that whatever action a person commits, it is the only action they were ultimately able to commit. In contrast, a libertarian world is a world in which a person is

T. Dyk
Redeemer University, Hamilton Ontario, CA

A. Barkman (✉)
Redeemer University College, Ancaster, Ontario, Canada

© The Author(s) 2017
K.S. Decker et al. (eds.), *Philosophy and Breaking Bad,*
DOI 10.1007/978-3-319-40343-4_11

able to will against compelling causes. Libertarians believe that a person can genuinely choose between two or more options.

Aurelius certainly sounds like a libertarian since he believes that without the ability to choose one's actions, morality is meaningless. He believed if people were only able to do one thing in every choice situation—the one thing that the causal structure of the universe set up for them—their actions could not be moral or immoral, they would simply *be*. *Breaking Bad* toys constantly with the concept of free will, going back and forth about whether or not it exists in a robust or meaningful sense.

The first instance in support of a compatibilist world in the *Breaking Bad* universe comes when Walt and Jesse flip a coin. The coin is tossed to decide who has to deal with Krazy-8 and who has to dissolve his cousin Emilio's body in sulphuric acid ("Cat's in the Bag..."). Whoever loses the flip is in charge of getting rid of Krazy-8, a task which neither party particularly wants. If a coin decides what they do, neither Jesse nor Walt has control over what happens; they just have to act on what probability has decided from the result of the flip. To further this point, Jesse calls the toss "sacred," and despite Walt's struggle to decide if killing Krazy-8 is right, Jesse constantly asks him if he's done it yet, never asking if he intends to go through with it. This lack of options Jesse presents means he believes Walt does not have an option in the matter. Walt then proceeds to make a list of options to determine if killing Krazy-8 is the moral thing to do. The only objection Walt has to killing him at this point is that there is a probability that Krazy-8 will come after his family for revenge. Some of the principles that Walt has against killing Krazy-8 are for the "sanctity of life" and that "murder is wrong" ("...And the Bag's in the River"). It becomes clear that Walt thinks he has made the moral decision to let Krazy-8 go. As fate would have it, he ends up having to kill Krazy-8 in self-defense, nullifying all of his planning and his decision. This suggests that no matter how much Walt took morality into the equation, he had no choice but to follow a certain path toward killing Krazy-8.

The concept of a "sacred" coin toss is raised on two more occasions throughout the series. The next time it is mentioned is when Walt and Jesse are first planning to meet Saul, and they are deciding who should go ("Better Call Saul"). Walt loses the flip and once again is forced to do things that he has no desire to do. Again this shows that he has to follow the path set out before him. The final instance of the sacred coin flip is much different than the first two, and will be discussed later.

Breaking Bad again suggests that its characters live in a world in which they have to follow the single path that lies ahead; when a fly gets into the meth lab under Gus's industrial laundry, Walt spends an excruciating amount of time trying to kill the fly so that it doesn't "contaminate" their cook. When he can't kill it, he breaks down and tries to explain to Jesse how the world is just a bunch of subatomic particles moving around, completely at random, and he has no way to control it ("Fly"). While this is a good reference to why he chose his nickname, Heisenberg,[3] it also shows two important things about Walt's worldview.

First, Walt believes everything about life is out of his control, and in fact is determined by material causation on a grand scale. This is demonstrated in a flashback conversation between him and Gretchen Schwartz ("...And the Bag's in the River"). The two are trying to determine the full chemical makeup of a human being. After determining all the elements and the percentage of the body they make up, they realize that despite it all being there, they only ended up with 99.888042 percent of the total body mass. While trying to figure out what they are missing, Gretchen asks about the soul. Walt laughs and tells her that they are working on chemistry, and there is no such thing as a soul. This, we should note, is in stark contrast to Marcus Aurelius, who identifies the soul *as* the human; for him, the human soul is that which is most perfectly connected with higher Nature.[4] According to Aurelius, at least, Nature intended for human souls—those who are capable of higher knowledge and acting on this higher knowledge—to live morally pure lives.

A second scene in which the characters appear to have no control over their lives is when Walt finds out his tumor has shrunk by 80 percent. To most people this news would be more than they could have hoped for. For Walt though, this news is devastating. Ever since Walt received his diagnosis of lung cancer, everything he did was about trying to control his own life. He had everything planned out, including passing away in a few months. When he finds out that even his plan to die would be thwarted, he was livid, as shown by him furiously punching a hand drier in the bathroom ("4 Days Out"). Walt's frustration shows that he feels that he has never really had the opportunity to control his own decisions. He, at this point, believes in the deterministic worldview, that he has absolutely no control over what happens in his life.

This idea of lack of control comes up again when Huell Babineaux and Patrick Kuby, Saul's bodyguards, go to Ted Beneke's house to try and force him to pay the taxes he owes ("Live Free or Die"). While they are there, Ted tries to make a run for it, but ends up tripping, hitting his head on a desk, and receiving serious injuries. Saul calls up Skyler and tells her what happened, and says they were not responsible because "it was an act of God." This implication that things were completely out of their control and God orchestrated events to be how he wanted also adds to the show's deterministic argument. Adding acts of God to the show's premise enhances the shows deterministic view because if God controls people's actions, Huell and Patrick could not be held morally responsible for harming Ted. Since God determined what would happen, no matter how Huell and Patrick acted, Ted would have been injured.

Despite the characters' lack of control of their lives that *Breaking Bad* occasionally presents, it also displays instances in which they have complete control over their own lives. This begins when we get the final "sacred" coin toss. Unlike the first two that were discussed previously, where the characters follow what the coin determines, this time the character decides to go against the results. This occurs when Skyler becomes afraid of who Walt is becoming, grabs their daughter Holly, and flees town. She arrives at the corner of where Colorado, Utah, Arizona, and New Mexico meet, where she then flips a coin to decide which state to run to ("Cornered"). The first flip lands in Colorado, and unhappy with this, Skyler flips the coin again. Once again it lands in Colorado. Skyler takes her foot and nudges the coin into New Mexico, and she turns around and drives back home. Skyler makes her own choices. The "sacred" coin toss told her she had to go one way, but she decided not to follow it. This begins to suggest a more libertarian view of the *Breaking Bad* universe: one where the characters are free to make their own decisions.

However, the two differing ideas about freedom represented by determinism and libertarianism clash when Walt encounters a man who is also waiting at the cancer treatment center ("Hermanos"). Both of these men have cancer, but they view the fact in very different terms. The man Walt sees there not only believes that he has no control over the events of his life, he also seems to find comfort in it. He tells Walt that "Man makes plans, and God laughs." What he is implying is that no matter how much we try and control our lives, in the end our plans don't matter. After the incident with Krazy-8, it would make sense for Walt to believe this to be true. Walt had spent days figuring out if he should let Krazy-8 go, but after all his planning, he had to reverse his original decision. However, Walt immediately challenges the man on this concept, and tells the man that only he has control over his life. According to Walt, every life ends in death, but until he hears the news that that time has come, he will control every aspect of his life. Walt summarizes it with "Who's in charge? Me." Walt is saying that no matter what happens in his life, he is fully in charge, and nothing really matters besides that. Life can throw anything his way, but it does not matter, because he will have a hand in the outcome. It is at this point that Walt has rejected determinism.

Ironically, Walt contradicts himself by saying that every life ends in death. Walt can believe that he has full control over his own life, but with the possibility of death at any moment, he loses full control. This idea of full control also lends itself to a kind of moral subjectivity. For someone to have full control of their own life, they would have to also be able to control what morality is to them. To the extent to which a person's morality can be decided by outside factors like social mores or fear of the law, this would mean that they had less than full control. If these outside forces began to shape a person's moral compass, that would mean that social mores and a fear of the law are aspects of that person's life.

The idea of controlling your own morality is brought up once more when Jesse is at his recovery meeting ("Problem Dog"). The counselor of the group tells people that to recover from their addictions they simply need to accept who they are and stop hating themselves. The implication of this way of life is that the things you have done are only weighing you down because you feel they are wrong. If you could just accept that you have done them, they would not seem so bad. After being told this theory several times, Jesse begins to question this way of thinking. He finally asks the counselor, "If you just do stuff and nothing happens, what's it all mean? What's the point?" If you can just act terribly, Jesse thinks, and think there is nothing wrong with that, and if there are no consequences to actions, does anything one does really matter? If there are no consequences to our actions, then what we do would have no bearing on anyone else because despite our best efforts, other people could simply negate our actions. They would then be able to carry on without your actions influencing them. For a person to have full control over their own life would mean that other people's actions would not influence them. This is where *Breaking Bad* begins to steer away from the libertarian idea of having complete control over one's life.

Toward the finale of the show, Walt ends up rejecting this concept of complete control as well. After everything he has done, all the work he's put into covering up his actions, the Drug Enforcement Administration still finds out he is cooking meth. Walt still ends up, by himself, in a lonely cabin in the middle of a forest ("Granite State"). He has only a portion of the money that he had, and his family despises him. He calls the DEA from a bar, to turn himself in, but while he's waiting for the police to arrive, he hatches a plan on how to get the money to his family. He hides in a snow covered car and waits for the police officers to go inside the bar. While waiting, Walt utters a quick prayer "Just get me home, just get me home, and I will do the rest." Whether Walt is praying to God, or just asking fortune for a favor, he has finally realized that he's not entirely in control of his own life. Some of life is left up to chance, or a divine plan. There is a combination of control and chance. Yet, Walt is still in control of what happens, in this instance, after he gets home.

This view of the world, where life is controlled both by people and fortune, is the sort espoused by Machiavelli, who writes, "Nevertheless, not to extinguish our free will, I hold it to be true that Fortune is the arbiter of one-half of our actions, but that she still leaves us to direct the other half, or perhaps a little less."[5] This line of thinking goes along perfectly with how Walt's life is portrayed. Walt's life spirals out of his control when he is diagnosed with cancer and realizes he's going to pass away, leaving his family nothing. He takes things into his own hands to make money for his family, and plans to go out with a bang. He makes the most of the opportunity to make money and keep his family safe, but again his plans are ruined by the remission of his cancer. The entire series is a struggle between what fortune throws at him and how Walt ends up responding to what appears to be fate. While fate has such a heavy influence, the characters still have the free will to attempt to control their circumstances. Therefore, in the *Breaking Bad* universe, people can still control some of their own actions, and so according to Marcus Aurelius' thinking about moral responsibility, morality does play a factor in the lives of these characters.[6]

Now that we know that moral standards apply to action in the *Breaking Bad* universe, it needs to be determined whether a failure to act can be immoral. If inaction in some circumstances is immoral, then according to Aurelius, the just thing, and therefore what we should do, is respond with the correct action.

This supports the idea of there being moral obligations toward action. We see a strong depiction of this when Walt is teaching his chemistry class about "chirality" to his students (from the Greek word *chiral,* meaning "hands"). The hands are mirror images of each other, and so, chirality in chemistry refers to mirror molecules. Walt gives the chemical example of flutamide, which when ingested prevents pregnant women from getting morning sickness. He then mentions that the chiral compound of flutamide (dimethylamine) had been used for the same purpose until people realized that it was causing babies to be born with birth defects ("Cat's in the Bag...").

While the mention of dimethylamine is a nice foreshadowing of Walt's future plans, this concept of mirrors can be paralleled to action versus inaction. Walt goes so far as to say that the mirror chiral compounds can be seen as "active, inactive; good, bad." This suggests that being active is good, and being inactive is bad. If you come across someone you know needs help, you are obliged to help them because being inactive in that situation would be, as Walt hints, bad.

Is this always the case though? Is allowing someone to die, someone who you could have saved, always wrong? Walt faces this question when he breaks into Jesse's apartment ("Phoenix"). He is trying to help him get over his drug addiction, and in turn, get him back into cooking meth. When Walt gets into the apartment, he finds Jesse and his girlfriend, Jane, unconscious, and high on heroin. Walt tries to wake Jesse up, to talk to him, but with no avail. He is about to give up and leave, when Jane starts to choke on her own vomit. Walt moves in to try and save her, but then hesitates, leaving her to die. According to our application of his own idea of chirality, his inactivity would be considered wrong.

To counter this argument that Walt's inaction is immoral, one could claim that according to our civil law, it is not clearly wrong for Walt to leave her to die. While murdering someone is clearly in defiance of the laws in place, many countries have nothing in their laws about not trying to save a life. *Breaking Bad* makes it clear that "positive" or politically enacted laws do not demand the same thing as moral laws.

In fact, one of the themes that gets brought up repeatedly throughout the series, most notably in the first season, is how arbitrary positive law can be at times. In "A-No-Rough-Stuff-Type Deal," Walt and his DEA brother-in-law, Hank, are sitting in Walt's backyard. Hank offers Walt a Cuban cigar, which at this time is illegal in the United States. Walt points out that it's odd where lawmakers draw the line. He notes that, if they had been drinking the alcohol they had with them in the 1930s, they would be breaking the law. He then begins to ponder what will be legal next year, and Hank mentions that meth used to be an over-the-counter drug commonly sold in drug stores. What this scene is pointing out is that laws can be based almost entirely on how people of a particular time period think. Moral theorists point out that this constant change and fluctuation means that one can't base a consistent moral standard of right and wrong on a country's laws. If one did, then what is morally right in one country could be considered wrong in another country. This goes back to Jesse's argument with his rehab counselor, but on a larger scale.

At a Parent-Teacher Organization meeting with DEA agents at Walt's school, the viewer is again asked to consider the differences between social injustice and moral injustice. At the front of the meeting is a white board with the words "Meth=Death" ("A No-Rough-Stuff-Type Deal"). What this message is suggesting is that these two things are somehow equal, but are they? They do get equated in some situations in the show, with the morality of each being judged seemingly by the consequences that come about. Two situations in particular involve Gale Boetticher and Todd Alquist's Uncle Jack. Both of these men find themselves in situations in which the results will be the same whether or not they commit the crimes they are asked to do. Gale, who is Walt's new cooking partner in Season Three, is a brilliant chemist ("Sunset"). He received his B.S. and M.S. in chemistry, and could likely have gotten a job anywhere in the chemistry field. So why did he choose the life of crime? Walt wonders the same thing and asks Gale why he started cooking meth. Gale's response is that he believes "consenting adults" should be able to get what they want, including, presumably, drugs. In fact, Gale believes he is helping society because the meth that he and Walt create is purer, and therefore less harmful than other products. By making meth in the proper way, less damage is done to human health in the long run. If meth is going to be on the street whether they cook it or not, why not cook it right and make it the best meth possible?

Uncle Jack is put into a similar situation. No matter how he acts, the outcome will be exactly the same. This occurs when Walt is looking for someone who can simultaneously murder all of Mike's men in prison. Walt goes to Jack and tells him his plan, to which Jack replies how difficult a job it is going to be. Walt tells Jack, "It can be done, the question is, are you the one to do it?" ("Gliding Over All"). Jack gets put into a position in which Walt implies Mike's men will be killed whether or not he is the one to do the deed. Jack executes the plan, and does it quite successfully.

In both these cases, whether Gale or Jack chooses to act, the end results would very likely have been the same. So from this perspective, it does appear that "Meth=Death." However, there is a major difference between these characters and their situations. Throughout the show, Gale is portrayed as a largely innocent character. His death is portrayed to the viewer as tragic and unnecessary. Even Jesse wished he did not have to kill him because he believed that Gale had done nothing wrong. On the other hand, Jack is one of the show's most heinous characters. One of the reasons that Gale is portrayed as a more sympathetic character is because he was merely involved in political injustice. While Gale just broke a law of the land, Jack, by contrast, clearly broke moral laws by murdering multiple people. The contrast of these two characters shows that "meth" does not equal "death." The series suggests that the person cooking the meth is less heinous than the other character. It also shows that results of being active or inactive are not a firm basis to ground moral obligations. While Gale and Jack both took the path of action in their respective scenarios, if they had chosen the path of inaction, the outcome would have been the same.

A similar argument could be used to say that Walt did not have an obligation to help Jane while she was overdosing. Had Walt never been in Jesse's apartment, Jane still would have died. Walt's inaction can be seen as inconsequential, as the aftermath would have been the same, had he not been present. Like Gale and Jack, it did not matter whether Walt chose action or inaction.

One of the other reasons that Gale is perceived as less heinous than Jack is because of his intention. While Gale seems to be trying to help, Jack is killing people solely to make himself wealthy. Typically, we think that intention matters in morality—at least Aurelius seems to think so when he says, "In talk, mark carefully what is being said, and when action is afoot, what is being done. In the latter case, look at once to see what is purposed; and in the other, make certain what is meant."[7] He claims that when someone acts, we should try and understand why the person really did it, and when someone says something, we should figure out what they truly meant. Aurelius believed that the best way for humans to flourish was to help each other. This implies some obligation to provide assistance when one is able to.

Breaking Bad flirts with this concept as one of the main premises of the show, mostly in posing the question, "Why is Walt cooking meth?" Throughout the show he constantly tries to convince everyone, including himself, that he is doing it for his family. He does not want them to be left in crippling debt after he passes away. The viewer even hears from Walt that intentions play a huge role in what makes an action right or wrong, especially when the intentions are for the well-being of family. Walt says, "When we do what we do for good reasons, we have nothing to worry about. There's no better reason than family" ("Hazard Pay"). This is a noble intention, and near the beginning of the show, Walt is in fact portrayed as a man of morally outstanding character, even as he breaks the law for his family. We are told that Walt "wouldn't know a criminal if he was close enough to check [him] for a hernia" ("Crazy Handful of Nothing"). The show drives this point home, as Walt Jr. (Flynn) tells the news agency that his dad "always does the right thing" ("ABQ"). However, when it starts to become more apparent that Walt might be cooking for other reasons, his depiction shifts to a morally corrupt character, while Jesse begins to take the forefront in moral correctness. Eventually, Walt admits to Skyler that he did it because he "liked doing it, [he] was good at it, it made [him] feel alive" ("Felina"). This is where it becomes clear that Walt was no longer doing it solely for his family, but more out of selfish desire. The same can be said when Walt allows Jane to die. Walt intentionally allows Jane to die, as he hopes it will bring Jesse back under his control. Jesse had stopped cooking meth with him so that he could spend more time with Jane, and Walt believed that with her gone, Jesse would come back to him. Because of Walt's selfish motives, we are prodded to hold him morally accountable for Jane's death.

The idea that consequences matter less than intentions can be seen when Jesse disposes of his brother's drugs. As Jesse is crashing at his parent's place for a few days, their housekeeper finds a joint, and Jesse's parents kick him out, presuming the joint belongs to him. While Jesse is waiting for a cab to leave, his brother, Jake, comes out and admits that the joint was his. Jake thanks him for taking the fall, and asks for his drugs back. Jesse proceeds to throw it on the pavement, and crushes it with his foot, telling his brother that it was "skunk weed anyway" ("Cancer Man"). Despite the fact that he plays this action off, Jesse is trying to steer Jake down the right path. Yet, despite Jesse's efforts to keep his brother clean, Jake's initial ability to obtain drugs in the beginning meant that he would likely be able to get them again. This implies that even with Jesse's single effort to stop him, the results could have been exactly the same, with Jake getting more drugs down the road. The viewers never find out if Jake does get more drugs, because he is never shown or talked about in the series again. So despite our not knowing how effective Jesse was in stopping his brother from using drugs, Jesse's action is still portrayed as the right thing to do, because his intentions were morally correct. This once again displays the show's inclination toward portraying intentions as the moral guide over consequences.

Another factor *Breaking Bad* uses to determine moral obligation is the emotional impact actions have on others. If characters become emotionally distraught because of an action that could have been avoided, the show suggests that acting and preventing that action from occurring would be the just course of action. When Walt lets Jane die, only two people seem to be emotionally affected by her passing: Jesse and Jane's father, Donald Margolis.

Jesse is clearly upset about what happened to Jane. He believes that it is his fault, and that he should have done something to save her. Jesse is so distraught that he stays in a crack house until Walt is able to convince him to check into rehab ("ABQ"). Even while at the rehab center, Jesse's suffering continues, and he believes that he deserves everything that's happened to him.

Donald is also afflicted by the death of Jane. After seven weeks of mourning, Donald finally goes back to work as an air traffic controller. His co-workers ask him if he is ready to be back at work, and he tells them that there is only so much he can take of just sitting at home by himself. While directing some planes, Donald accidentally calls one of the planes "Jane" instead of "Julia" ("ABQ"). He then loses focus for a moment, and two planes collide in mid-air. The viewer learns this crash killed 167 people ("No Más"). This grander scale of emotional suffering—with the families and friends of the crash victims now involved—convinces the viewer that Walt should have acted to save Jane. While Jesse's state of mind provides very little evidence of the emotional consequences of Walt's action, the airplane crash presents the evidence clearly. The consequences of Walt's inaction affect not only Jesse and Donald, but also hundreds more, both directly and indirectly down the line. At a nearby school, students are asked to share how they are feeling. Many students can't sleep because of the crash, and we hear from one girl who is even questioning her faith in God. Walt might not admit it, or even realize, but the plane crash negatively affects him too. This is because "what is no good for the hive, is no good for the bee."[8]

Up to this point, *Breaking Bad* suggests that moral obligation is not based on political laws or upon consequences of actions. It places high value on the intentions behind actions, as well as accounting for the emotional repercussions on a small and large scale. However, according to Aristotle there is more to morality than this. In fact, according to Aristotle there are situations in which trying to save someone's life would be unjust. One of Aristotle's cardinal virtues is courage. He believed that courage was important because it would allow a philosopher to stand up for what he deemed to be right, even in difficult situations. As with all of the Aristotelian virtues that are understood as expressing a "mean," courage has a deficient form, as well as an excessive one. Courage's deficiency is cowardice, while its excess is rashness. Cowardice is failure to stand up to do the just thing in the right situation. However, rashness complicates things in the moral obligation argument. According to Aristotle, acting in a "courageous" manner becomes rash when it puts oneself or others in unnecessary peril.[9] This would apply in cases where there is little chance of saving a person, or in cases where action would put one's own, or others' lives in danger. For example, imagine you saw someone fall into a river, and begin to head toward a waterfall. If you do not know how to swim, it would be considered extremely rash if you tried to swim out and save them. Even if you were able to swim, it would be smart to weigh the options: How close are they to the falls? Do I have enough time to reach them, and if so, will I be strong enough to swim back? Therefore, trying to save a life in a rash manner is typically seen as a non-virtuous way to live, no matter how good your intentions may be.

The next thing to contemplate is whether or not someone has a moral obligation to help when they have no control or knowledge of a situation. This concept comes up in *Breaking Bad* when Marie blames Steve Gomez and George Merkert (head of the DEA) when Hank gets shot by the Mexican cartel. She blames Merkert for suspending Hank and taking his gun away when he needed it, and she blames Steve for not being there to support his partner. She eventually also blames Walt, because without him, Hank would have never heard of Jesse, assaulted him, and gotten his gun taken away. Little does Marie know that the cartel members were originally there to kill Walt out of revenge for Tuco's death. All three men, Steve, Merkert, and Walt, feel extremely guilty for what they feel is their part in Hank's injuries. However, these three also had something in common that made it impossible for them to help Hank, and that was lack of knowledge. Aurelius would argue that due to this lack of knowledge, none of them should feel guilty. When discussing why people feel guilty about different circumstances, Aurelius says, "'Because there is an insuperable obstacle in the way.' In that case, do not worry; the responsibility for inaction is not yours."[10] The "insuperable obstacle" in this case was not knowing an attack was coming. Since such a thing did not seem plausible for Walt, Merkert, and Steve, the men had no obligation to investigate whether or not an attack would take place. In fact, when Walt anonymously calls in that there is going to be another attack on Hank, the DEA is more than willing to do its part to keep their people safe. They send multiple units to guard Hank, for as long as they deem necessary. This shows that both parties, had they been armed with the proper knowledge, would have acted to the best of their ability to protect Hank. Therefore, since they had no ability to prevent the first attack due to an "insuperable obstacle," they are not morally responsible for Hank's injuries.

The final argument for morality that's raised in *Breaking Bad* is that doing something to help others should be done to the best of your ability. This coincides with the old saying that "anything worth doing is worth overdoing." This idea is portrayed in a conversation between Mike and Walt, when Mike tells Walt to take "no half measures" ("Half Measures"). But this view of morality is tainted by its uses in the show. Mike uses it to refer to a time where he should have killed a man, and Walt uses it to justify killing two people. Despite the seemingly immoral examples, the moral intention that it conveys still stands. When helping people, it is not enough to only put in a partial effort. If someone were hanging by a rope over a cliff, it is not just to pull them up halfway when you are able to pull them up all the way. Someone cannot claim that what they did was right simply because they helped a little. Of course, there may be people who only had the strength and endurance to pull the person up halfway, and those people could be seen as having done the right thing, because they put forth their best effort, despite not fully getting the victim out of their predicament. *Breaking Bad* tells the viewers through Mike and Walt, that if they perform an action, they must perform it to the best of their abilities.

Breaking Bad presents a variety of approaches to determining a person's moral obligation to act. The show strongly encourages the viewer to consider if a character has the right intentions. They also need to determine if that character has the ability to act, and also if that action puts themselves or others in harm's way. Finally, he must consider if they are causing or stopping other's emotional suffering, and if they are acting to the best of their abilities. Aurelius would want to present one final criterion as well. How does an action or inaction impact the person who is performing it?

> Of any action, ask yourself, 'What will its consequences be to me? Shall I repent? Before long I shall be dead and all will be forgotten; but in the meantime, if this undertaking is fit for a rational and social being, who is under the same law as God himself, why look for more?'[11]

The "consequences to self" Aurelius is referring to are similar to the emotional consequences discussed previously. They do not entail any form of personal gain that the agent might receive, but rather look at whether the action is good for the soul. As people living according to how God/nature intended us to live, we should strive to do right by them. If a person is inactive, they should ask themselves if such a life is morally right in accordance with the needs of the soul. As humans with souls, this means we do have a moral obligation to help ease others' sufferings.

Since *Breaking Bad* and Aurelius both express the variety of our moral obligations, the question remains: Is allowing someone to die equivalent to killing someone? For this question, the same criteria for moral obligation can be used. In the case of Walt allowing Jane to die compared to actually pulling the trigger on Mike, the answer is, "Yes, they are equivalent." In both cases, Walt was motivated by selfish concerns. In the scenario with Jane, it was to gain control over Jesse. Walt was fully capable of saving Jane without any chance of putting his own life or the life of anyone else in peril. In Mike's case, it was so Walt could kill Mike's men in prison without having to worry that Mike would come after him. Here, Walt had the choice to act in a way that would not put anyone in peril. Yet, in both cases, he chose the course that caused the most damage, both physically and emotionally.

The emotional suffering that stems from both Walt's actions and inactions is visibly present throughout the show, as well as implied. Following Jane's death, the emotional suffering that people went through was extremely apparent, displayed by Jesse, Jane's father, and the mourning town. With Mike's death, the emotional suffering is less measurable and more implied. He had a very close relationship with his granddaughter, and they both loved each other deeply. While his granddaughter is never shown after his death, it can be assumed that she went through emotional suffering caused by the disappearance of her grandfather. Since all of the criteria for judging moral obligations are equally fulfilled in both cases, allowing someone to die can be morally equivalent to murdering someone. Of course, the equivalence in this situation does not mean that all choices to let someone die or allow someone to experience suffering are equal to every action of murdering someone, or causing them suffering. One scenario in which action and inaction are not equivalent is when it would be rash to attempt to prevent suffering. "If you are neutral in situations of injustice, you have chosen the side of the oppressor."[12] *Breaking Bad* and Marcus Aurelius would argue that in times where you have the ability to prevent the suffering of others and you choose not to act, you are still held morally accountable for that decision.

NOTES

1. Marcus Aurelius, *The Meditations*, trans. G. M. A. Grube (Indianapolis: Hackett Publishing, 1983), 217.
2. Since *Breaking Bad* is a TV show and the characters have no mental life outside the script, this is merely an argument as to whether they are portrayed as having free will and to what degree.
3. The Heisenberg Uncertainty Principle, coined for its theorist, Werner Heisenberg, essentially proves how subatomic particles can move, but also says that their speed and position can't be determined during the same moment of observation.
4. Marcus Aurelius, *The Meditations*, 100.

5. Nicolo Machiavelli, *The Prince* (London: Encyclopedia Britannica, 1988), 35.
6. It could be the case, though we will not argue it, that fortune or God merely allowed Skyler the belief that she was making her own choices. The same could be said for Walt.
7. Marcus Aurelius, *The Meditations*, 105.
8. Ibid., 104.
9. Aristotle, *The Nicomachean Ethics*, trans. W. D. Ross (Oxford: Clarendon Press, 1925), 35.
10. Aurelius goes on to explain that if you make a mistake that is unfixable, and life is just not worth living anymore, you should just simply end your life. While he is filled with many great insights into the world, we would not follow him here. Walt seems to agree with us in this scenario. When he is diagnosed with cancer, it seems that he has hit an "insuperable object" that is impossible to overcome. However, we find out later the cancer was in fact treatable. Even when the cancer comes back again, Walt is still able to make the most out of it and leave his family several million dollars.
11. Marcus Aurelius, *The Meditations*, 121.
12. Robert McAfee Brown, *Unexpected News* (Westminster: John Knox Press, 1984), 19.

CHAPTER 12

The Transformation of Walter White: A Case Study in Bad Faith

Leslie A. Aarons

It is best to choose and to examine one determined attitude which is essential to human reality and which is such that consciousness instead of directing its negation outward turns it toward itself. This attitude, it seems to me, is *bad faith*.[1]

The concept of "bad faith" (*mauvaise foi*) is one of the most intriguing and complex concepts in the philosophy of Jean-Paul Sartre (1905–1980). Sartre defines bad faith as the ultimate self-deception whereby people are able to convert themselves into being what they are not. Remarkably, a person living in bad faith is not necessarily someone with an uneasy conscience. Sartre is careful to differentiate the act of "lying" from the act of bad faith. In its traditional sense, the act of lying supposes that the liar is aware of the truth and chooses to be intentionally deceptive. "The essence of the lie implies in fact that the liar actually is in complete possession of the truth which he is hiding."[2] Because of complex psychological operations, Sartre explains, a person who is living in bad faith does not realize her own self-deception, making it the perfect existential crime:

It follows first that the one to whom the lie is told and the one who lies are one and the same person, which means that I must know in my capacity as deceiver the truth which is hidden from me in my capacity as the one deceived.[3]

In *Breaking Bad*, we witness Walter White transition into a poster child for Sartre's concept of bad faith. At the outset, White is a mild-mannered, benign chemistry teacher. Upon being diagnosed with Stage III A inoperable lung cancer, he

L.A. Aarons (✉)
City University of NW-LaGuardia Community College, New York, NY, USA

© The Author(s) 2017
K.S. Decker et al. (eds.), *Philosophy and Breaking Bad*,
DOI 10.1007/978-3-319-40343-4_12

undergoes a radical existential transformation. Through Walter White's transformation into the drug lord Heisenberg, the show's protagonist becomes the ultimate antagonist, giving new meaning to the phrase "breaking bad."

The catalyst for White's astonishing change is intriguing and multifaceted. Initially, White rationalizes that he needs to make fast money in a big way, in order to finance his cancer treatments and to provide his family security in the probable case of his death. Using his skills as a chemist, he masterminds a remarkably high-quality methamphetamine with the help of his former student Jesse Pinkman, aka "Captain Cook." Upon closer scrutiny, we see that White's terminal diagnosis propels him to confront his own frailness and vulnerability as he comes face to face with his own mortality. At the age of 50, he has led an unremarkable life and he plummets into a bleak existential crisis. In this, we may recognize Sartre's philosophical theory that claims that the nature of human existence is revealed in the immanence of one's own death. The consequences of human responsibility that brings about "anguish," "abandonment" and "despair" drive Walter White to flee himself by negating himself. White finds incredible new vitality as Heisenberg. His total conversion into a ruthless, power-mongering drug lord is his escape from the pitiful predicament named Walter White. And here we find a stellar case study of Jean-Paul Sartre's bad faith.

"…WON'T BE ABLE TO LIVE WITH YOURSELF…YOU ARE NOT A MURDERER…"

Walter White sits on the toilet, pants down at his ankles, composing a pros versus cons list. Walt is in a dilemma as to what to do with Krazy-8, who remains chained by the neck with a bicycle lock in Jesse Pinkman's basement. Conventional wisdom holds that drawing up a list of pros and cons makes apparent the possible foreseen consequences of an impending choice. In this way, seeing the contrasting arguments for and against a contemplated action is thought to offer a helpful, graphic illustration of what the best choice may be. And generally speaking, the column with the longer list is supposed to prevail in this exercise. Walter White's list is composed of two courses of action: "Let him live" and "Kill him." Under the first column, Walter lists eight reasons to let Krazy-8 live:

- It's the moral thing to do
- Judeo/Christian principles
- He may Listen to Reason
- You are *Not* a murderer
- Sanctity of Life
- Post-Traumatic Stress
- Won't be able to Live with yourself
- Murder is Wrong!

On the second column he lists only one reason to kill Krazy-8: "He'll kill your entire family if you let him go." As it turns out this pros versus cons list is just another exercise in futility that brings Walter neither relief nor resolution.

White is struggling with a monstrous existential crisis that grows exponentially by the hour. A short time ago, he was just an ordinary guy: a family man, a humble scientist—a good man. But now faced with the traumatic cancer diagnosis and the threat of his impending death, he is undergoing a spectacular metamorphosis, a process of becoming what he is not. No longer being who he is, he is largely unaware of the existential processes driving this fantastic transformation. Sartre describes this process as follows:

> In bad faith there is no cynical lie nor knowing preparation for deceitful concepts. But the first act of bad faith is to flee what it cannot flee, to flee what it is. The very project of flight reveals to bad faith the inner disintegration in the heart of being, and it is this disintegration which bad faith wishes to be.[4]

Now, a matter of months later, Walter is a renegade outlaw extraordinaire! He has found himself manufacturing and distributing an illicit and highly addictive, menacing drug—methamphetamine; he must continually evade law enforcement; he has committed robbery, larceny, money-laundering; he has murdered men, destroyed evidence (including desecrating human corpses) and he's now kidnapped a man and is holding him prisoner. And this is just *some* of what is happening outside of his family life.

In order to compensate for his hasty, radical change of lifestyle, Walter struggles to maintain normalcy with his family. Walter's life with his pregnant wife, Skyler, and his teenage son, Walt Jr., was a relatively wholesome, dedicated and loving one before his diagnosis and his resultant criminal behavior. Previously, mere conversations about the "Wonder Bra" at the breakfast table, or his brother-in-law Hank's occasional risqué comments and behavior were enough to send his wife Skyler into a tizzy. But now Walter White is fraught with anxiety, fear and the burden of his denial and duplicity. He loves his family, and in the beginning, he truly believes that the grave risks that he is taking are an altruistic sacrifice for their benefit.

In the beginning of the pilot episode, Walter White is utterly panicked, terrified that the sirens he hears approaching him in the desert are law enforcement coming to get him. His meth lab/camper with what he believes are two dead bodies in it is in clear sight, as the one road in this New Mexican desert offers no means of camouflage or escape. In absolute desperation, he gets a video recorder from the camper in order to record what seems to be his last will and testament to his family. He says: "To law enforcement entities: this is not an admission of guilt." Sweating, choking and crying he continues, "I am speaking to my family now." Visibly hysterical, he covers the lens of the camera to try to gain some composure. "Skyler, you are the love of my life. I *hope* you know that. Walter Jr., you're my big man." Hyperventilating, his voice cracking, "There are going to be some things that you'll come to learn about me in the next few days. I just want you to know that no matter how it may look, I only had you in my heart. Goodbye."

Throughout most of the series, White steadfastly justifies his depraved behavior by arguing that he is doing it to provide financial protection for his family. This consequentialist argument stands as an attempt to transform his unethical actions into a noble mission. At his 50th birthday party, his brother-in-law Hank, a DEA agent, inadvertently demonstrated to Walter how lucrative the illegal drug industry could be. Awed by the amount of money that was seized at one of the DEA's drug busts, the seed was planted for Walter White to break bad, and Sartre's theory of bad faith offers a compelling means to analyze Walter White's wild transformation.

"It Disturbs me No More To Find Men Base, Unjust, or Selfish Than To See Apes Mischievous, Wolves Savage, or The Vulture Ravenous."[5]

Sartre theorizes that the human situation is fundamentally divided into what he calls "facticity" and "transcendence." For Sartre, facticity refers to all the situated facts about a person: an individual's physical characteristics, such as height and skin color; also an individual's psychological, social and historical attributes, such as one's array of desires and beliefs; one's race, class and national origin; as well as a person's past actions and family history. Facticity represents the contingency of human existence and belongs to "being-in-itself," the same sort of existence that humans share with the rest of nature and our inanimate surroundings. According to Sartre, the facticity of human existence does not determine or limit our freedom, but is the springboard from which we exercise our freedom ("being-for-itself"), namely, by transcending our facticity. Sartre writes, "Being is. Being is in-itself. Being is what it is,"[6] and that "we shall see that the being *for-itself* is defined, on the contrary, as being what it is not and not being what it is."[7] For Sartre, human reality is constantly contending with facticity and transcendence. Living authentically for Sartre is to transcend our facticity (i.e. the "in-itselfness" of existence), specifically because we *are* freedom, and we must therefore accept our indefinability, as well as our insurmountable responsibility.

Sartre empathizes with the arduous existence represented by this picture of human reality, this process of being condemned to having to create ourselves. We must persevere as free, all the while being fully aware of our finitude, and thus knowing that we have but a brief time to figure everything out and become all that we might want to be. Of course, what each of us may desire to become is itself an agonizingly elusive question. The person as being-for-itself will never adequately discover his or her own zenith. There is neither a destiny to be realized nor a determined legacy to fulfill. Man is freedom, and as such, we find ourselves in a predicament, not unlike Sisyphus. In his acclaimed book, *The Myth of Sisyphus*, Albert Camus (1913–1960) quantifies the value of life and determines that a man's life is ultimately an absurd predicament, as death will ultimately nullify all meaning and purpose. This famous existential sentiment clearly resonates with the unremarkable first half-century of Walter White's existence. Camus writes:

Likewise and during every day of an unillustrious life, time carries us. But a moment always comes when we have to carry it. We live on the future: "tomorrow," "later on," "when you have made your way," "you will understand when you are old enough."…But simultaneously he situates himself in relation to time. He takes his place in it. He admits that he stands at a certain point on a curve that he acknowledges having to travel to its end. He belongs to time, and by the horror that seizes him, he recognizes his worst enemy. Tomorrow, he was longing for tomorrow, whereas everything in him ought to reject it.[8]

Finding oneself in such a predicament results in our anguish. Sartre does not just claim that our self-conscious finitude makes us *feel* anguish. He states:

The existentialists say at once that man is anguish. What that means is this: the man who involves himself and who realizes that he is not only the person he chooses to be, but also a lawmaker who is, at the same time, choosing all mankind as well as himself, cannot help escape the feeling of his total and deep responsibility.[9]

Further, for Sartre, human freedom is ontologically inescapable. Man is condemned to freedom and therefore must perpetually choose himself—create his own essence, without any *a priori* guidance. This results in the existential emotion of "abandonment." Sartre writes:

If existence really does precede essence, there is no explaining things away by reference to a fixed and given nature. In other words, man is free, man is freedom. On the other hand, if God does not exist, we find no values or commands to turn to which legitimize our conduct. So, in the bright realm of values, we have no excuses behind us, nor justification before us. We are alone, with no excuses.[10]

In Sartre's atheistic paradigm, humanity is denied the comfort provided by an omnipotent, omniscient and omnibenevolent governor of the universe. Humanity is left, instead, in an absurd situation in which we chronically crave confirmation and legitimacy for our existence, but there ultimately is none to be found. And if these existential trials weren't enough, no matter how determined we are to persevere in the inescapable project of creating our essence, we are doomed to realize that the universe will not conform to our will, because there is only human reality and beyond that, nothingness. Sartre refers to this realization as "despair." Sartre writes, "The moment the possibilities I am considering are not rigorously involved by my action, I ought to disengage myself from them, because no God, no scheme, can adapt the world and its possibilities to my will."[11]

Not surprisingly, contending with our human predicament as Sartre views it often results in our desire *to escape* these burdens of our existence. Sartre describes these attempts to "flee" from our freedom and responsibility as inauthentic, irresponsible and futile. The many ways that we are capable of lying to ourselves, and of denying and distorting the extent of our free will and accountability, is what Sartre calls bad faith. Bad faith or inauthenticity can assume two primary forms: one that denies freedom or transcendence (e.g. "I can't do anything about it") and another that disregards the factical component of a situation (e.g. "I can do anything by just wishing it"). Both of these forms of bad faith offer temporary relief from our angst, and so there is an intoxicating allure that bad faith offers—like the irresistible call of sirens beckoning us to treacherous shores. In order to appreciate Sartre's concept of bad faith, it is necessary to understand the unique psychological, spiritual and behavioral outcomes that may manifest in attempting to escape the consequences of our absolute human freedom.

"This Line Of Work Doesn't Suit You Man. Get Out Before It's Too Late"

Walter is in a quandary as to what to do with Krazy-8. He has been agonizing over the apparently logical conclusion that a guy with a name like Krazy-8 lacks a reliable moral compass. In the first three episodes, Walter has ruminated over the improbable prospect that he may be able to reason with him, and that perhaps by freeing him and letting him live, Krazy-8 would show his relief and gratitude and let bygones be bygones. But to anyone watching this predicament, it is readily apparent that Walter White is not struggling over the right thing to do with Krazy-8, but rather how to work his way up to killing him. He is tormented with two incongruent self-realizations. On the one hand, Walt knows that he must murder this man and he grasps that it is within his ability to commit premeditated murder. Simultaneously, he is repulsed by the prospect of physically killing a man, and of the torturous existential consequences that this action will have on his conscience and on his existence.

By interpreting this situation through Sartre's theory of bad faith, we may view this scenario as a "magical" false dilemma, an elaborate scheme, choreographed by a desperate man. "We can see the use which bad faith can make of these judgments which all aim at establishing that I am not what I am."[12] Walter White knows the solution—ironically, one that will require his own dissolution—and this will springboard his incredible transformation. Walter White describes this process of "solution, dissolution and transformation," in his introductory lecture on chemistry in the pilot episode of the series. Quite poetically, Walter conjectures that chemistry is the study of "change." This is the only moment that we witness in which he seems authentically inspired and passionate about his otherwise dull and impotent career as a chemistry teacher. And this description has many fruitful parallels to his own dramatic existential conversion.

A compelling example of Walter's bad faith in this case can be found in a conversation he has with Jesse. Walter begins to pepper Jesse with questions about Krazy-8 in a desperate and impractical attempt to re-characterize this violent drug lord as a "reasonable businessman." The day before, Krazy-8 and his cousin Emilio were going to kill both Walt and Jesse, but their plan was foiled by Walter's chemical ingenuity, a response that resulted in Emilio's death. Krazy-8 managed to barely survive and is now the source of Walter White's dilemma. Walter pleads for Jesse's accord:

> **Walter**: What I'm trying to say is that he's a *business man*, he's a *man—of—business*. It would therefore seem to follow that he is capable of *acting* out of mutual self-interest! *Yes?*
> **Jesse:** What?
> **Walter**: Do you think he is capable of listening to reason?
> **Jesse:** What kind of reason? You mean like: Dear Krazy-8, hey listen, if I let you go, will you promise not to come back and *waste* my entire family—No Colombian Neckties! You mean *that* kind of reason? No man, I can't say as I have high fuckin' hopes where that's concerned.

It doesn't take a genius to concur with Jesse's insights regarding Krazy-8; everyone can easily see the obvious absurdity in attempting to characterize this crazy, violent criminal as an ethical businessman. Sartre writes, "To be sure, one that practices bad faith is hiding a displeasing truth or presenting a truth as a pleasing untruth."[13] If Walter can succeed in converting Krazy-8 into a reasonable man in his own mind, maybe he can escape the horrible prospect of becoming his murderer.

But, in fact, White is not hoping to reason with Krazy-8 at all. Rather, he is reckoning only with himself and his own difficult options. "Better yet I must know the truth very exactly *in order* to conceal it more carefully…" (Sartre's emphasis).[14] Here, Sartre might say that Walter is attempting to flee his predicament by distorting a truth he actually realizes, that is, by denying the complicated facticity of the situation to himself and by seeking to transform this present problem into something more easily tenable.

In Sartre's treatise on existential psychology,[15] he theorizes that humans often use their emotions to flee in bad faith from the burden of the factical determinism of the world. He writes, "This world is *difficult*" (Sartre's emphasis).[16] Sartre speaks of this "difficulty" as a real quality of the world. "This notion of difficulty is not a reflective notion which would imply a relationship to me. It is there, on the world; it is a quality of the world which is given in perception…"[17] For humans, life is always a challenge; our existence is filled with demands—places to go, people to deal with, obligations to satisfy—and all of this bears down upon us with our concurrent awareness of our finitude. The exigencies of our lives are constant and interminable, and bad faith offers us "magical" opportunities to escape, even if this escape is inauthentic, fleeting and ultimately ineffectual. Here too we find Walter White, attempting to convert his predicament into a situation that is more bearable to deal with. Sartre writes:

> It is a transformation of the world. When the paths traced out become too difficult, or when we see no path, we can longer live in so urgent and difficult a world. All the ways are barred. However we must act. So we try to change the world, that is, to live as if the connection between things, and their potentialities were not ruled by deterministic processes, but by magic.[18]

Desperate times call for desperate measures. At this point Walter White has very few options, and these range only from bad to worse. So, he attempts to "transform the world" and the facticity of his predicament instead. Sartre's existential emotion of despair makes itself apparent to human consciousness just at the moment it is realized that the universe will not conform to our desires and expectations. And when this happens, Sartre recommends the following advice: "The moment the possibilities I am considering are not rigorously involved by my action, I ought to disengage myself from them, because no God, no scheme, can adapt the world and its possibilities to my will."[19] To this Sartre adds, "When Descartes said, 'Conquer yourself rather than the world,' he meant essentially the same thing."[20]

As the segment concerning Krazy-8 winds to its conclusion, we see Walter doing all kinds of uncanny things to avoid killing the drug lord, including actually catering to him and seeking camaraderie with him. Once Walter White realizes that Krazy-8 absconded with a shard of the plate upon which Walter served him his sandwiches—with the crusts removed, as requested—he knew he had to kill him. The scene of Walter White killing Krazy-8 is brutal and graphic. Choking a man to death demands incredible force and intimate proximity to the victim. Walter is highly emotional and remorseful; crying, he futilely apologizes to the red, black and blue corpse. As the show progresses we see that Walter White shall also shed any sense of remorse, repentance or doubt in his indelible rise to power.

"But If I Am What I Wish To Veil, The Question Takes On Quite Another Aspect."[21]

In the episode "Green Light," Walter White is growing more despondent. He is utterly oblivious to the fact that he is sitting in front of his students assembled in his chemistry class. The students gaze at him, bewildered by his seeming catatonic state. He is lost in a fit of abstraction, wholly distracted, as if he is in deep meditation. The cinematography of this scene depicts White's emotional state, and the clock seems to tediously struggle to move from one second to the next. Drips of water hang in the balance from a faucet spout, as if struggling to resist their inevitable fall, as White's sitting image stares vacuously, appearing fuzzy and distant in the background. White's finger tapping monotonously on the lab table emits a slow, muted echo, as he insentiently sips a steaming beverage from a cup that ironically reads: "World's Best Teacher." Expressionless, Walter White is transfixed on himself, entranced by his own thoughts in front of his filled classroom.

To explain White's latest odd behavior we may take insight from Sartre's theory of emotions and bad faith. He states, "We shall try to place ourselves on the grounds of signification and to treat emotion as a *phenomenon*" (Sartre's emphasis).[22] This phenomenon of human emotion is a significant part of Sartre's treatise on human nature, his existential psychology and is central to his theory of bad faith. Sartre uses vivid examples of characters involved in an elaborate orchestration of self-manipulation. In this project of bad faith, an individual acts to avoid culpability for an action or situation by converting themselves into what they are not, and by simulating not being what they actually are: that is, absolutely responsible for their actions and their own predicament. By this transfiguration, Sartre writes, "I am on a plane where no reproach can touch me since what I really am is my transcendence. I flee from myself, I escape myself...."[23] By shifting our conscious awareness and "becoming" emotional, an individual (as being-for-itself) who is inescapably free and continually self-conscious is suddenly capable of denying the reality of their freedom and responsibility. This is enacted by the ability we have, according to Sartre, to negate our self-awareness, and concurrently transform ourselves (i.e. as transcendent being-for-itself) into an objectified in-itself, and by converting the facticity of the world, and our relation to it, into something resembling a theatrical production. For example, there is Sartre's well-known example of the waiter in the café. He writes:

> His movement is quick and forward, a little too precise, a little too rapid. He comes toward the patrons with a step a little too quick. He bends forward a little too eagerly; his voice, his eyes, express an interest a little too solicitous for the order of the customer. Finally there he returns, trying to imitate in his walk the inflexible stiffness of some kind of automaton while carrying his tray with the recklessness of a tight-rope walker by putting it in a perpetually unstable, perpetually broken equilibrium which he perpetually reestablishes by a light movement of the arm and hand.[24]

According to Sartre, the waiter transforms himself into an automated prototype of a waiter. His behavior models that of a consummate server—doting, attentive and servile. He objectifies himself and thus flees his transcendence; by doing so, he temporarily evades having to be self-conscious regarding his servitude or whether or not he is the author of his own meaningful destiny. After all, "He was a good waiter," is not how many of us would like to be memorialized. So to be able to momentarily avoid the self-loathing that may arise in recognizing himself as a servant of sorts, dedicating his life to serving food, he takes refuge by becoming a character playing the part of a consummate waiter. In doing this, he is provisionally relieved of the obligation to make meaningful choices that will define who he is. He has rendered himself inert in the role that he has adopted. Now, as anybody would do, he abides by the mechanistic laws that guide the expected pattern of the behavior of a waiter. "In short, the affected subject and the affective object are bound in an indissoluble synthesis."[25] He has, however ephemerally, become predetermined. He has become what he is not.

The project of bad faith involves an inherent contradiction. This magical transformation of the waiter is only achievable *because* the waiter is a being capable of complete transcendence, of being a for-itself. It is the very nature of his transcendent existence that allows him to choose to adopt such a scheme. Thus, the freedom of the for-itself is a prerequisite for the project of bad faith, which in turn denies it. Sartre writes, "The human being is not only the being by whom *négatités* are disclosed in the world; he is also the one who can take negative attitudes with respect to himself."[26] In bad faith, the actor is able to transfigure himself as an in-itself by adopting a false representation of himself to himself. It is a lie contracted by and to oneself that provides a tenuous escape from an uneasy conscience or a seemingly irremediable predicament. "Thus the duality of the deceiver and the deceived does not exist here. Bad faith on the contrary implies in essence the unity of a *single* consciousness."[27]

"You either run from things, or you face them, Mr. White"

Midway through the series, the vacillations of Walter White's character grow more intense. So why does Walt seem increasingly disturbed as he becomes better and more successful in his drug enterprise? At one point, Walter White watches as Jesse's girlfriend Jane chokes to death on her own vomit while Jesse lays unconscious bedside her. White stood over her, calculating her liability to his plans and intentionally neglected to try to save her—an act that simply required turning her petite body over so that her windpipe would not be blocked as she writhed and choked to death from an overdose.

And then we find Walter White at another moment turning down methamphetamine dealer Gustavo "Gus" Fring's lucrative offer of three million dollars for just three months of White's time. Here, Walter is visibly contrite, claiming that, "I'm making a change in my life…and I'm at something of a crossroads. And it's brought me to the realization: I am not a criminal—No offense to any people who are but—This is not me." White's contention that he is "not a criminal," and that "this is not me," defies the actual truth. In fact, Walt is now a hardcore, certifiable criminal, and in addition most of his criminal acts have been viciously premeditated. Further, he has continuously justified himself by his obvious lust for power and money. He tells Jesse, for example, "Jesse, you asked me if I was in the meth business or the money business. Neither. I'm in the empire business."

But at this moment, Walter White has agreed to meet Gus at Los Pollos Hermanos. He now claims that he has not come to discuss further cartel business, but that he has decided to rescind his partnership with Gus and quit any life of crime—because "it is not him." In this scene, Gus appeared uncharacteristically affable, and opened their discussion by telling White, "I have an offer that I think will be of interest to you." Responding, White interjects, "I'm here because I owe you the courtesy, and respect to tell you this personally. I'm done. It has nothing to do with you personally." Like most of the viewing audience at this point, Gus does not seem to take Walter White's confession too seriously, and responds, "I'd like you to hear my offer notwithstanding." Remonstrating, Walter White responds, "It won't change my mind. I'm sorry." Gus then proposes the profitable offer for White to work for just three months in a state-of-the-art lab that will be provided to him, producing his signature blue product in exchange for a three million dollar payment. But, at least for this brief moment, Walter White remains resolute in his vow to return to being a law-abiding citizen, this sweet deal notwithstanding.

There are questions that immediately arise from viewing this scenario: Are we witnessing an authentic epiphany on Walter White's part—a difficult, yet triumphant maneuver of his character to choose good over evil? This seems truly unlikely given his characteristic behavior thus far, including his seeming addiction to money and power. Thus, it seems more likely that if we view it from Sartre's perspective, we may be witnessing a classic example of bad faith. Sartre writes:

> I can in fact wish "not to see" a certain aspect of being only if I am acquainted with the aspect which I do not wish to see. This means that in my being I must indicate this aspect in order to be able to turn myself away from it; better yet, I must think of it constantly in order to take care not to think of it. In this connection it must be understood not only that I must of necessity perpetually carry within me what I wish to flee but also that I must aim at the object of my flight in order to flee it.[28]

Sartre contends that in order for a person to hide or deny their own true character, it is necessary to be *consciously* and *intimately* familiar with that part of themselves in the first place. A fascinating aspect of bad faith that is remarkably complex is this conscious effort to deny one's own actions, personality, beliefs or desires convincingly—not only to others, but also to oneself. Accordingly, the person acting in bad faith is attempting to flee the psychological and spiritual burdens that authentic self-actualization would likely bring about. Sartre would say that in this way they are attempting to flee their anguish. "This means that anguish, the intentional aim of anguish, and a flight from anguish toward reassuring myths must all be given in the unity of the same consciousness."[29]

But Walter White *is* a criminal—on many levels. He knows it, and we know it too. To be able to own up to this odious self-realization at this point is something that he is apparently not willing to do. This would require, at a minimum, great courage and fortitude in order to break with most of the directives that have conditioned his moral outlook and behavior for several years. Being a "criminal" in the ways in which he has *actually chosen* is "breaking bad" in the worst way! A good man is not a murderer; a righteous man cannot be a felonious drug kingpin; a true family man cannot be a corruptor of youth, a diabolical liar and thief. Walter White is in denial, and he wishes to make this denial real, both to himself and to everyone else. But this desire to not be what he is is ultimately impossible, and its pretense—like with all acts of bad faith will eventually fail—sooner rather than later.

"WE HAVE SEEN THAT HUMAN REALITY, FAR FROM BEING CAPABLE OF BEING DESCRIBED AS LIBIDO OR WILL TO POWER, IS A *CHOICE OF BEING*...."[30]

There is an important point that needs to be emphasized that distinguishes Sartre's view of human reality from other classic psychoanalytic views in order to clarify his distinctive concept of bad faith. Although indebted to

Freud and many of the concepts born from traditional psychoanalysis, he ultimately rejected many of the interpretations and mechanisms postulated by what he referred to as "empirical" psychoanalysis. One of the most crucial distinctions that Sartre emphasized was underscored by his thorough disagreement with Freud's deterministic concept of the libido as an irreducible, psycho-biological given.

> They differ fundamentally in that empirical psychoanalysis had decided upon its own irreducible instead of allowing this to make itself known in a self-evident intuition. The libido or the will to power in actuality constitutes a psychobiological residue which is not clear in itself and which does not appear to us as being beforehand the irreducible limit of the investigation.[31]

Sartre's point here highlights his idea of the absolute freedom of the for-itself, and reveals a much more holistic interpretation of the totality of consciousness for human reality. Accordingly, Sartre poignantly underscores both the inescapable freedom and inexorable responsibility of human choices, and negates any excuse or escape from our accountability. By rejecting the Freudian idea that individuals are a mere collection of characteristics, and by viewing each person as an individual, Sartre claims, "Our concern here is to understand what is individual and often even instantaneous. The method which has served for one subject will not necessarily be suitable to use for another subject or for the same subject at a later period."[32] Sartre therefore rejected the notion of the unconscious, and indeed disavowed any and all theories that conjectured deterministic forces driving an individual to behave in a certain way. Instead, Sartre not only insisted that there are only conscious acts, he claimed that the for-itself continually acts as a holistic unity. "It is a demand based on a preontological comprehension of human reality and on the related refusal to consider man as capable of being analyzed and reduced to original data, to determined desires (or 'drives'), supported by the subject as properties by an object."[33]

Consequently, when an individual acts in bad faith they are attempting to escape the burden of their inherent responsibility and the consequences of their own conscious acts. Sartre claims, "But the first act of bad faith is to flee what it cannot flee, to flee what it is. The very project of flight reveals to bad faith the inner disintegration in the heart of being, and it is this disintegration which bad faith wishes to be."[34] Therefore, according to Sartre, the project of bad faith is ultimately an exercise in futility. Sartre writes, "In a word, I flee in order not to know, but I cannot avoid knowing that I am fleeing; and the flight from anguish is only a mode of becoming conscious of anguish. Thus anguish, properly speaking, can be neither hidden nor avoided."[35]

"YOU—ARE TROUBLE. …YOU ARE A TIME-BOMB. TICK, TICK, TICKING…"

In Season 5's "Madrigal," Walter and Jesse go to visit Mike Ehrmantraut at his home. Somehow, Walter has talked Jesse out of yet another of his existential breakdowns and has seemingly once again rejuvenated Jesse's allegiance. They intend to re-start the manufacture of their product, and wish to enlist Mike's partnership in their business. Sitting at Mike's kitchen table, Walter explains to Mike that they will continue to handle the manufacturing end of the business. But Walter explains that they still need someone to handle "…distribution, support and logistics," and that they think Mike would round out the partnership perfectly. Stone-faced, Mike listens for a couple of minutes, and responds, "Thanks. But no thanks." Just as Walt had done with Jane Margolis, Mike has realized that Walter White is a volatile liability and he wants little to do with him. He realizes that Walt is a loose cannon, that his lust for power is no doubt doomed to crash and burn, and Mike "wants nothing to do with the boom."

Walt seems undeterred by Mike's rejection of his proposal. Ironically, he responds in a way strikingly similar to the way Gus Fring's did in Los Pollos Hermanos. But now Walt has become the proposer, and believes, as Gus did, that the money involved in their enterprise will seduce Mike. He explains to Mike, "There's no denying the popularity of our product. There's a market to be filled and currently no one to fill it." But, unlike Walter White, Mike is not a megalo-maniac, and does not have interest in becoming too involved. He'll ultimately get in and out quick for a good sum of money to help his daughter-in-law and granddaughter, but that's where it will end. Mike is well seasoned in both the law enforcement and the law-breaking enterprises, and this has earned him a cer-tain intuition about the risk management associated with both kinds of ventures. Walt appears smug in response to Mike's refusal. Here, as elsewhere, we witness a conspicuous, mounting, arrogant self-confidence from Walter White. With a noticeable smirk, Walt ends their conversation by saying to Mike, "Well—sleep on it. Maybe you'll reconsider. In the meantime, we're pressing on."

"WHATEVER HE BECAME—THE SWEET, KIND, BRILLIANT MAN WE ONCE KNEW—LONG AGO—IS GONE".

By the end of the series, Walter White has receded into seclusion, but the pristine wilderness of "Granite State" offers him no consolation. Feeling trapped, agonizingly isolated, morbidly depressed and vanquished, he is pro-foundly tortured that the outcome of all his efforts was in the end, for nothing. So much horrific torture, death, destruction and violence, orchestrated by his vicious obsession for power and money—was in vain. With his family gone and the millions of dollars he collected now largely depleted, he mourns over the utter loss of his envisaged empire. Now, he is just a pathetic fugitive without glory to justify the mayhem, pain and suffering that he has caused. Heisenberg is dead, and Walter White has killed him.

He blackmails his once good friends, Elliot and Gretchen Schwartz, and demands that they create an irrevocable trust for his son Walt Jr. on his upcom-ing eighteenth birthday. Befuddled, they ask Walter why he does not give the $9,720,000 of drug money to his son himself, and White responds, "My children are blameless victims of their monstrous father." Walter White has planned his finale that has inevitably come with the disintegration of his grand charade of bad faith.

Walt then pays a last visit to his estranged wife, Skyler. When she asks why he has come, he replies, "It's over and I needed a proper goodbye." Finally, on his fifty-second birthday and after five seasons and 62 episodes of justifying his actions on false pretenses, Walter White reveals the truth he has always known about himself: "Skyler…Skyler—All the things that I did…I did for me. I liked it. I was good at it—And I was—really—I was alive." Sartre would agree that we all have the potential of being just like Walter White. It is a chronic condition of the nothingness that remains in the heart of our being. He writes, "If bad faith is possible, it is because it is an immediate, permanent threat to every project of the human being; it is because consciousness conceals in its being a permanent risk of bad faith."[36] So ends the tale of Walter White, and the question as to whether he was ultimately a protagonist or an antagonist remains. But, it is best not to judge him too harshly, as we may not be that different from him after all.

NOTES

1. Jean-Paul Sartre, *Being and Nothingness: An Essay on Phenomenological Ontology*, trans. Hazel Barnes (London: Methuen, 1958), 48.
2. Ibid.
3. Ibid., 49.
4. Ibid., 70.
5. Sartre is paraphrasing from French play writer Moliére's play *The Misanthrope, Scene 1, Act 1*: "And it's no more a matter for disgust that men are knavish, selfish, and unjust, than the vulture dines upon the dead, and wolves are furious, and apes ill-bred." From *The Misanthrope*: A Comedy in Five Acts. (1666) Translated by Richard Wilbur.
6. Sartre, *Being and Nothingness*, lxvi.
7. Ibid., lxv.
8. Albert Camus, *The Myth of Sisyphus* (New York: Knopf, 1955), 5.
9. Jean-Paul Sartre, "The Humanism of Existentialism," in *Essays in Existentialism*, ed. Wade Baskin (New York: Citadel Press, 1965), 38.
10. Ibid., 41.
11. Ibid., 46.
12. Sartre, *Being and Nothingness*, 57.
13. Ibid., 49.
14. Ibid.
15. Jean-Paul Sartre, *The Emotions: Outline of a Theory* (New York: Citadel Press, 1975).
16. Ibid., 58.
17. Ibid.
18. Ibid., 58–59.
19. Ibid., 48.
20. Ibid.
21. Sartre, "The Origin of Nothingness," in *Essays in Existentialism*, ed. Wade Baskin (New York: Citadel Press, 1965), 143.
22. Sartre, *The Emotions*, 21.

23. Sartre, *Being and Nothingness*, 57.
24. Ibid., 59.
25. Sartre, *The Emotions*, 52.
26. Sartre, *Being and Nothingness*, 47.
27. Ibid., 49.
28. Sartre, *Being and Nothingness*, 43.
29. Ibid.
30. Ibid., 602.
31. Jean-Paul Sartre, *Existential Psychoanalysis* (Washington, DC: Regnery Publishing, 1981), 51–52.
32. Ibid., 55–56.
33. Ibid., 27.
34. Sartre, *Being and Nothingness*, 70.
35. Ibid., 43.
36. Ibid., 70.

CHAPTER 13

Breaking Bonds: White Lines of Love and Hate

Sara Waller

Television and films are full of partners and the tension between them. Famous pairs include Mulder and Scully of the *X-Files*, and Nick and Nora Charles of the *Thin Man*. Walt and Jesse make a powerful team, taunting and insulting each other as they produce the finest product and commit some big-time crimes. Like many other oddball-team dramedies, I argue that Walt and Jesse do not start out as friends, and while they approach friendship, ultimately the differences in their ethical principles tear them apart. Specifically, Walt portrays himself as a family man, as conscientiously providing for his loved ones and as willing to commit crimes to keep his family housed, fed and educated. Meanwhile, Jesse identifies himself as a partier and drug dealer, a criminal estranged from his family and a free spirit living out a very late adolescence without deep attachments or responsibilities. However, as the course of the *Breaking Bad* series reveals, Walt is "in the empire business" more than he is a family protector, and Jesse is devastated when he is unable to create a family with Jane, and later with Andrea and Brock. The line that is cut between them is a line of care: Walt ultimately locks himself into rigid and uncaring roles, disregards intimacy in the name of paternalism and, while he enjoys power and control, realizes too late that he is also a poor ethical egoist.[1] Jesse discovers that he has close bonds with friends, is hurt by his rejection by his family and enjoys being a parent and a reliable and caring lover. The trajectories of our two protagonists cross as the series develops, and care-based ethics helps us to understand what lines are crossed. I use Held's notion of care ethics as a centerpiece. "We want what will be good for both or all of us together. We want our children and others we care for, and those who care for us, to do well along

S. Waller (✉)
Montana State University, Bozeman, MT, USA

© The Author(s) 2017
K.S. Decker et al. (eds.), *Philosophy and Breaking Bad*,
DOI 10.1007/978-3-319-40343-4_13

with ourselves, and for the relations between us to be good ones."[2] This is the standard of care Walt fails to achieve.

I begin with Aristotle's definition of friendship: mutual well-wishing among equals, *haplos*. For Aristotle, "Perfect friendship is the friendship of men who are good, and alike in virtue...,"[3] and I argue that what friendship they build is based on Jesse's mistaken interpretation of Walt's moral commitments.

Walt and Jesse do not start as friends, not even as friends out of utility. In the pilot, they do not wish each other well. Walt threatens to turn Jesse in to the DEA if he refuses to partner with Walt, and upon that premise, the partnership is built. Jesse is equally difficult, happily taking Walt's life savings in "Mas" and partying it away, narrowly gaining, through unscrupulous bargaining, the RV that Walt's money was intended to buy. Second, Walt and Jesse are not equals. Different in age, education and social status, Walt and Jesse do not easily relate to one another; Walt doesn't whoop it up and has a bit of disdain for the culture of his current and former students; Jesse finds Walt stodgy and dull—not enticing as a friend. They do not find each other wise at first. Jesse doubts Walt really has a deep commitment to becoming a criminal; Walt thinks Jesse is an aimless addict. Third, their entire relationship is based on business success, and is clearly not "without qualification" or contingency.

Worse, neither Walt nor Jesse seems to have many characterologically redeeming features at first. As much as we empathize with Walt's financial and family struggles and work frustrations, Walt presents as something of a wimp and a loser (in contrast to both Jesse and Hank), and Jesse, though sexy, charming and rebellious, appears to be nothing more than an impulsive, trivial hedonist. Walt's lack of initiative, self-doubt and low self-esteem has left him without a research career, working in a car-wash, old and overweight. Jesse's lack of ambition has left him estranged from his parents and younger brother, and without any job skills that might employ him in a respectable position. So the audience is presented with a rather pathetic pair of somewhat unlikeable people who have little reason to bond with each other. And bonds are necessary for a care ethic to emerge and be enacted and for characters to reveal how uncaring they might be.

Through hardship, they bond, with each one at times playing both mentor and mentee to the other, and at times playing family member-like roles for each other. Walt sees potential in Jesse—Walt is the teacher who once encouraged the student to "apply himself," and Walt still cares to educate and assist. While Walt already has a son, Flynn's disability causes Walt worry, anxiety and sadness—Walt feels unable to help improve Flynn's physical situation. Jesse, in contrast, has simply failed to achieve things in life, and sees his parents pouring their attention and care on his younger brother while shutting him out of the family. Walt finds in Jesse the benefits of a second son—an older, more conveniently corrupt son who does not need to be protected from the world or from Walt's criminal endeavors. Walt can fulfill his urge to teach and guide Jesse, because Jesse could do better. Walt feels both effective and not responsible for Jesse's failures or bad behaviors.

Jesse, in turn, finds a father figure who is willing to work with him—a father figure who does not condemn him for cooking meth, and Walt becomes someone from whom Jesse wants to learn more. Walt is someone safe for Jesse, because he is not his real father; Walt will help him solve the problems of leading a criminal life—he will protect him from the police and from competing meth sellers, he will help him cover up the meth lab in his basement and he will help Jesse in spite of (and perhaps *because* of) Jesse's illegal inclinations.

These tenuous reasons for our two men to bond with each other are strengthened by circumstance—in the pilot, they have crashed in the desert with an RV full of injured and dead bodies. Any mutual dislike must be overlooked until their immediate problems are solved. While they vow to part ways again and again (in "Pilot," "Cat's in the Bag," and" Full Measures," to name just a few), circumstances continue to keep them together (someone's life is nearly always in danger, or there is a pressing problem to be solved) and the constant contact allows a respect to form.

That mutual respect is fueled in part by the human predisposition to judge others to be similar to ourselves. Walt and Jesse mistake each other's moral values. Walt takes Jesse to be uncaring in that he is a criminal, with seedy friends like Brandon "Badger" Mayhew, Combo and Skinny Pete. Walt will not let Jesse use his cell phone to call Jane in "Four Days Out" because he believes Skylar will think he has been calling "some stripper," and continuously accuses Jesse of being willing and able to smoke everything they cook; Jesse appears to Walt as someone who is unable to have true, caring friendships, or keep business agreements. By Season 3, Walt's distrust of Jesse is so great that he bugs his car in "Bug." But as the series unfolds, we realize Walt is far more self-serving than Jesse.

Jesse, in contrast, admires Walt, calling him an "iron chef" and an "artist" when they cook together. While he expects Walt to give him "ballwinding" speeches about not using, being careful and doing things more conservatively, Jesse always lets his irritation pass and continues to work with, and learn from, Walt. Jesse seemingly mistakes Walt for a loving, caring father who just needs money for his family. Jesse perhaps remembers the end of his aunt's life all too well, and projects onto Walt the features of his caring aunt who gave him a house to live in at the end of her illness. Thus, being a caring person himself, one who wants to know his younger brother and wants to protect his friends, it is easy for Jesse to ascribe to Walt an ethic of care.

And Walt is not uncaring to Jesse. As much as Walt berates and expresses disgust for Jesse's choices, Walt saves Jesse on numerous occasions—placing a gas mask on Jesse in the pilot, pulling Jesse out of the crack/heroin house after Jane's death and bringing him to rehab, running down and shooting Gus's drug dealers at the end of Season 3 and finally saving Jesse at the conclusion of the series. Walt does defend Jesse and risk his life and living to protect Jesse— the caring bond is not merely in Jesse's imagination. In "Four Days Out," Walt even eats a *Funyun*.

Ethics of care has been characterized by a number of authors, including Held, Noddings, Gilligan and Fisher, and can be summed up, more or less, as a moral practice based on nurturing relationships, and being loving to others and self, in order to make life and world good, healthy and enriching for all. Quality of life is fundamentally determined by quality of relationships, and so maintaining relationships and the emotional and physical well-being of individuals that comprise them is paramount. Walt at first appears to be a sympathetic character, for Jesse, and for all viewers, because his plight can be easily understood, *prima facie*, through an ethic of care. No caring husband would want to leave his family in debt, burden them with his care during a prolonged illness and harm his relationships by ending them as a frail, sickly shell of the person he once was. And caring for others is complex. Sometimes we lie or deceive, or commit crimes and kill, in order to be loving. This is where the plot thickens.

Practicing an ethics of care is intricate and difficult. To keep our families close, we may not always be best advised to tell them everything. Banal white lies such as "you don't look fat in those pants" and "of course I like your mother" might be necessary to preserve and nurture some relationships. Walt, Hank, Skylar and Marie play poker together in "Krazy Handful of Nothin" and Hank successfully bluffs everyone in an exciting family game. To nurture family bonds, in some cases, playing poker is important, and poker demands some level of deception. We can sympathize with why Walt lies to his family about his meth cooking, and waits so long to tell them about his cancer.

At first, it seems that he lies *because* he values his loved ones so much—he does not want them to suffer the ugly truths of his illness or his criminal endeavors. Hank is a DEA agent, and knowing the truth would cause family strife as well as imprison Walt. He lies because his family's value system would condemn his actions. In Walt's words, "people sometimes do things for their families" ("A No Rough-Stuff Type Deal") but, in response, Skylar tells Walt that he doesn't want to find out what she would think or do if she discovered that Walt was immersed in illegal/immoral actions like Marie's thievery. *Prima facie*, Walt lies to his family because he knows they would be offended by his new endeavors, and he wants to protect and love them.

But Walt's lies and other actions can be explained by another, less care-based interpretation. When Jesse watches him collapse during a cook in "Krazy Handful of Nothin," and sees his radiation target, Jesse admonishes him, revealing his underlying ethics of care ideology—"I'm your partner man, you should have told me." No real reason is given as to why Walt didn't tell Jesse of his illness (if he had confessed, it would have explained Walt's erratic and questionable partnership with Jesse in the first place), and if we press further, Walt has no real reason to not tell his family his diagnosis either. Yes, they are a bit controlling, and the family meeting is unpleasant, if not combative, but his family, ultimately, wants Walt to live because they care about him (even if this results in them wanting to control his actions and press him to seek treatment against his will). I suggest that Walt is caught in rigid notions of appropriate roles for people, and his rigid roles erode the care he has for those close to him.

"In care ethics, people are not demarcated selves with clear responsibilities."[4] One should genuinely care for others and their well-being, though not at the expense of oneself, and respond to the needs of others in a fluid, non–role-based way. But Walt is governed by notions of what it is to be a "man"—a man must provide for his family, be strong and not show weakness, always have enough money, never take charity, etc. In "End Times," Walt isolates himself from family as well as criminal collaborators when he says "I alone should suffer the consequences of those {his} choices." These boundaries cause him to lie and pull away from his family, to not achieve the caring and being cared for ideal of ethic of care.

Indeed, Walt seems to subscribe to the notion of liberal individualism as critiqued by Kittay and Held. He cannot bear to accept charity from his friends—he must be the one who supports everyone, and it horrifies him to think of others having to support him in return. For him, a loving relationship is bound up in roles and role-playing—a man provides for his family. The family is provided for, and loving toward the man (perhaps as a result of the money provided). Only this structure of the universe allows Walt to feel relaxed and loved—this is why he initially does not want treatment—he can't bear to think of his family as burdened with his care, and of himself as not strong and capable. For Held, our interests are "intertwined" with people for whom we care—an action based in care is both not selfish and not unselfish. It is not individualistic—to care for and maintain relationships, the individual members must be maintained as well.

But Walt can't separate himself from his individualistic ideals and his roles. He must make the money, Skylar must make the home and his son must look up to him and not help him by building a website asking for money for his operation. Walt's rigid role-playing is exemplified in many ways. He constantly competes with Hank, twice buys sports cars for his son, is offended when Flynn receives driving lessons from a friend and not his dad, needs to be "the brains" in his operation with Jesse and gets an immense amount of pleasure from controlling Tuco by blowing up his office (As do we all. Control is sometimes appropriate under an ethic of care, and the Tuco-inspired explosion was enacted specifically in defense of Jesse). Walt's lust for control exceeds the boundaries set by a care ethic. Walt says to a fellow cancer patient in "Hermanos" "Never give up control. Live life on your own terms," which might at first seem inspiring, but when Walt stays in the house after Skylar tells him she is waiting for his cancer to come back, he's definitely not exhibiting loving behavior. He's in the empire business, and his family has become part of the empire.

Virginia Held might agree that the private home life of Walt and family is structured by male political power. Walt takes on the male responsibility of being the primary earner (he is upset when Skylar goes back to work, even though there are medical bills surrounding their other debt). More darkly, Walt does want to control his family. He moves back in to his house in "Hazard Pay" because he knows he can pressure Skylar into allowing it, and not because he is wanted; this results in his "beloved" wife walking into the pool in "Fifty-One."

Earlier, at the end of Season 2, when Walt stands over the choking Jane, we recognize both his urge to protect Jesse from a heroin-laced and uncertain future, and his urge to control Jesse and keep the partnership in tact for the sake of the business. Much later in the series, when Walt enjoys a few moments comparable to a restored family harmony, he continues to hide his cancer and chemotherapy from his family in "Blood Money," a secret that is now overwhelmingly unnecessary given that Skylar knows he cooks meth, and their money has been explained to Hank and Marie as gambling winnings. Walt lies, covers up and continues to distance himself from his family in order to control and maintain his idea of the *perfect family*: one that gets along, with a strong man at the helm, a man who has overcome cancer and who has provided for all. Walt fulfills his imagined "roles" using actions in stark contrast to an ethic of care, in which "At the foundation of moral behavior …is feeling or sentiment." Walt's emotions are connected to his imagined roles and not to real people. Walt loves the idea of his family, but is constantly put out by the real family members.

If Walt is so locked into these rigid roles, how is it then that he can kill as many people as he does? Playing the role of a loving father seems incompatible with being a murderer—how can Walt reconcile the two? Perhaps surprisingly, scholarship in care-based ethics has confronted murder on more than one occasion, allowing us to think that Walt might participate in care ethics after all. Noddings considers murder quite extensively, saying "To remain one-caring, I might have to kill."[5] Noddings goes on to describe that unpleasant situation as one in which a cornered person finds herself without any better choices—the most loving and protective choice is to kill a threat or aggressor. Noddings admits that this situation is horrible, and that it ultimately compromises the deep principle of being caring, and she asks her readers to judge the murder according to the intentions of the agent. If greed or personal interest motivated the murder, then it was not an act of care. But if the murderer was pressed into that position "by unscrupulous others who made caring impossible to sustain?" then this is a sad case of compromised, but still loving, care.

Walt does not diverge far from Noddings' description of the murderous caring one. In "And the Bag's in the River" Walt agonizes over the killing of Krazy-8 in a way much more reflective than his self-defense-based gas attack on Krazy-8 and Emilio in the previous episode. Confronted with a real person, not much older than his son, a member of the community and child of the local furniture store owner, Walt has a couple of beers with Domingo and searches long and hard for a reason to just let him go. Ethicist of care, Haydon argues that occasionally murderers in one context can become heroes in the next, and suggests that a care-based ethics would allow those who attained power through violence to, in some cases, stay in power if a peaceful and loving society would be the result.

Sadly, Walt's ethical considerations are not so sophisticated. Instead, Walt scrawls "Judeo-Christian values," "post-traumatic stress" and "murder is wrong" on a piece of paper, only to abandon these thoughts when it occurs to him that Krazy-8 may murder his entire family (something Jesse suggested to him earlier). So, Walt does not think of care or love or community building. Rather, he appeals to religious principles (a religion he probably feels little connection to as a practicing scientist), a simplistic, ungrounded (for Walt) notion that murder is an immoral and a selfish reason—that Walt doesn't want to be traumatized by recalling the murder later. His other reasons repeat these reasons: "won't be able to live with yourself" "you are not a murderer" and "sanctity of life." Walt hasn't studied philosophy, and is caught between accepted societal values and his own urges toward self-protection.

However, Walt really is protecting his family by killing Krazy-8. Is this Noddings' condoned version of murder, in which the unscrupulous Krazy-8 makes caring impossible to sustain? Perhaps yes. Krazy-8 is, after all, going to stab Walt with that broken piece of plate.

But after Krazy-8, Walt's kill count continues to rise. And while arguably the people who he kills are bad people, few of them are a direct threat to his wife and children, or to Jesse. Tuco's thug companions who suffered in the explosion had no clear or direct connection to anyone in Walt's life; while they would kill anyone if hired to do so, the threat was not proximate, especially given Walt's intent to supply Tuco with lots of product. And Brock's illness, while strategic, was probably not the only method Walt could have used to protect himself, Jesse and his family from Gus' wrath. Walt wanted to control Jesse and Gus, to ensure Gus would appear at the hospital to talk with Jesse, to keep Jesse from doing violence on his own and to prevent Jesse from cooking without him. Making Brock sick was an easy way to accomplish those things. We must convict Walter White of acting, as Noddings would say, out of greed and personal interest. "Unless he is an immediate threat to you or someone else, you must meet him, too, as one-caring."[6]

I offer a small footnote before closing. One might argue that Walt acted out of greed and personal interest because he recognized that the family he wanted to provide for, and the relationships he wanted to preserve, were gone. In the episode "Fly," a heavily drugged Walt confesses that he should have died much sooner, that he wishes Skylar had never learned the truth and that he wishes he had not seen Jane's death or its impact on Jesse. Walt reflects he has lived too long, and seems to regret many of his actions beginning with the death of Jane. The viewer is left to ponder what Walter will do with the rest of his life—a life without his loved ones, and without his idea of family. Perhaps the only thing left for him is the empire business. But in the end, even that fails for Walt. He comes to get Jesse, too late, because he does care for him. He comes to apologize to Skylar, too late, because he does care for her. But two years of uncaring actions cannot be healed in a few days. Walter dies too soon to reconstruct the relationships he has destroyed, and lives long enough to destroy them. He tries to be fully selfish, and fails, just as he tries to be caring, but is too locked into rigid roles and poorly thought-out ethical principles to truly nurture those around him.

NOTES

1. The claim that Walt is a failed ethical egoist is courtesy of Dr. George Sieg at University of New Mexico West. I thank him for his excellent comments.
2. Virginia Held, "The Ethics of Care as Normative Guidance: Comment on Gilligan," *Journal of Social Philosophy* 45, no. 1 (2014): 112.
3. Aristotle, *The Nicomachean Ethics*. Translated by W. D. Ross. Oxford: Clarendon Press, 1925, Book 1, Ch. 3.
4. Van der Heijdena, Karin, Merel Visseb, Gerty Lensvelt-Muldersb, and Guy Widdershovenc, "To Care or Not to Care: A Narrative on Experiencing Caring Responsibilities," *Ethics and Social Welfare* 10, no. 1 (2016): 55.
5. Nell Noddings, An ethic of caring, 711.
6. Noddings, "An Ethic of Caring," 706.

PART 5

Becoming Jesse James: *Breaking Bad*'s Challenge to Philosophy

CHAPTER 14

Hatred: Walter White Is Doing It All Wrong

Kevin Guilfoy

Hatred is an underrated virtue, and rightly so. No other virtue can go as tragically wrong when taken to the slightest excess. Walter White is a hate-filled person. Still, we sympathize with several of Walt's hateful and vindictive actions. Of the remainder, we are appalled by most, but amused by some others because, despite their fictional nature, they would be excessive in real life. This makes Walter White a perfect object for a study of hatred.

There are many different kinds of hate and there is a *prima facie* intellectual case against all of them. Simple hate is just an intense aversion to something. One can hate cloudy days, broccoli, or an annoying person without wishing harm on them. Simple hatred can become excessive and, even when moderate, can be a little weird. Moral hatred is a strong aversion to a person based on their proclaimed values, accompanied by a wish for our values to somehow triumph over theirs. At its best, this is what we feel for the self-identified Nazi. Unfortunately, we can also feel moral hatred for anyone with different values. I have little to say about these forms of hatred. Simple hatred is mostly harmless. Moral hatred is not a dominant theme in *Breaking Bad*, yet vindictive hatred is.[1] This species of hatred is aimed at a person in revenge for some action that has injured, harmed, or degraded a victim. This hatred brings with it a desire for vindictive malice. I shall argue that vindictive hate, under the right conditions, is virtuous. Walt gives us several virtuous examples of vindictive hatred. But hate is also dangerous. Walt's hate turns to resentment and fuels his lust for power. He takes this virtue to amazing excess. Still, until he destroys everything he loves, we find ourselves sympathizing and rooting for Walt.

K. Guilfoy (✉)
Carroll University, Waukesha, WI, USA

© The Author(s) 2017
K.S. Decker et al. (eds.), *Philosophy and Breaking Bad*,
DOI 10.1007/978-3-319-40343-4_14

A Brief Theory of Vindictive Hatred, with Examples

There are three clear examples of Walt acting hatefully and vindictively that viewers cheer. In the pilot, Walt and Skyler are clothes shopping with Walt Jr. For any teenage boy, mom fussing about with them in a store is potentially humiliating. Walt Jr. is particularly vulnerable, since he walks with crutches and his speech is slurred, the result of cerebral palsy. Noticing this, three other boys in the store mimic his gait, and stammer about buying "big boy" pants. Walt sneaks around to the front of the store and assaults the instigator. He causes the boy temporary pain and, one hopes, lasting humiliation. I contend he was right to do so. He was right in that, as a community, we can recognize this response as moderate and appropriate.

People who think Walt's actions were morally good will balk at calling them hateful and vindictive, but they are. The essential element of hate is a focus on another person with the intent to cause harm. I will present a theory of hate as an Aristotelian virtue, but even Aristotle is of two minds. Aristotle says, "No amount of malice is moderate."[2] However, Aristotle also says "The man who is angry at the right things and with the right people, and, further, as he ought, when he ought, and as long as he ought, is praised."[3] Negative emotions like hate, when vented through appropriate vindictive actions, can be virtuous. Jeffrie Murphy is one of the few to offer a qualified endorsement of hate. For Murphy, retributive and vindictive passions are part of human nature. They must be satisfied to secure moral goods.[4] Thomas Scanlon endorses the emotions that Murphy would call hate, and many actions that Murphy would call vindictive, but uses a different word: "blame."[5] Scanlon condones withholding social obligations or beneficial actions toward one who we blame, but not actively causing offense, harm, or injury. But I don't see a meaningful difference between an act and an omission when both are intended to cause harm or hurt to an individual. My discussion owes much to these two scholars. But throughout I will use the word "hate" to name the virtue I am describing because that word brings with it the necessary connotations of malice toward an individual.

We are uncomfortable with hate for many reasons. The most basic argument against hate is that controlling the desire to hurt other people is essential for remaining a member of a moral community. But the need to control an impulse does entail the need to eliminate it. One could argue from the lessons of our dominant religious traditions. These tell us to love our enemies, turn the other cheek, and forgive. However, theologians have devoted centuries of moralizing to making these absolutist claims more consistent with human nature. We could also hold up examples from *Breaking Bad*: Walt himself provides an image of the hateful person as irrational, obsessive, and self-destructive. In Nietzsche's phrase, Walt is like a scorpion turning its poisoned sting against itself.[6] However, Nietzsche's scorpion consumes itself with resentment because it is impotent to act, not because it hates.[7] Walt demonstrates that repressed hatred is soul-crushing. The *prima facie* intellectual case against hate has never been as powerful as it seems.

We may be uncomfortable admitting it, but hate is a profound feature of our culture. There is tension between our stated values and our actions and judgments. Leading politicians compete to be tougher on criminals and to prove they can torture and kill most terrorists. The criminal law and foreign policy we choose by electing these politicians does not reflect the value of forgiveness. Vengeance, and the vindictive infliction of punishment, may be second only to sex as the most popular trope in modern entertainment. Writers who need to generate connection to characters easily appeal to vindictive passions. As viewers of *Breaking Bad*, we may be appalled by the violence: Gus killing Victor, Todd shooting the child in the desert, anything Tuco Salamanca does. Yet, when each of these men dies horribly, we approve. In the pilot, we are surprised when Walt assaults the boy in the store, but I do not think anyone is appalled. We are meant to see Gus and Todd as cold and unprincipled. We are meant to see Tuco as insane and dangerous. But we are not supposed to see Walt as an explosive violent monster (not yet). As the boys leave the store, Walt Jr. smiles at Walt. Walt looks both scared and proud of himself. We are meant to see a man standing up for his son. The writers know they can appeal to this emotive judgment.

Walt's action in the store is one of hatred, but is it virtuous? My definition of virtue is mostly Aristotelian, with a Stoic twist. In general, a virtue must produce some moral good. It must be a habit or state of character. It must admit of excess and defect, with the mean respected as virtuous. These are basic Aristotelian concepts. The Stoic twist is that hate is an ancillary virtue. Wisdom is a virtue that is good in itself and secures some good. It is good to be wise, and wise people flourish. As an ancillary virtue, hate is not good in itself, but secures some good. So there are additional restrictions.

There are two moral goods secured by Walt's action in the store: Walt Jr.'s self-esteem and a reinforcement of community norms. Self-esteem is the recognition of one's proper value and place in a moral community. This moral good is required for human happiness and flourishing. Self-esteem can be diminished or reinforced by the actions of others.[8] Walt asserted Walt Jr.'s value as a person in the face of those who had tried to diminish and lessen him. He demonstrated that Walt Jr. was neither a lesser being nor a proper object of ridicule. Moderate retribution confirms Walt Jr.s moral standing. Adam Smith shares the ambivalence people have toward hatred (which he calls resentment), but endorses this justification of vindictive hatred:

> There is no passion, of which the human mind is capable, concerning who's justice we ought to be so doubtful, concerning who's indulgence we ought to so carefully consult our natural sense of propriety, or so diligently to consider what will be the sentiments of the cool impartial spectator. Magnanimity, or regard to maintain our own rank and dignity and society, is the only motive which can ennoble expressions of this disagreeable passion. This motive must characterize

our whole style and deportment ... When resentment is guarded and qualified in this manner it may be admitted to be even generous and noble.[9]

Hatred aimed at those who degrade us is justified, but must be enacted well and moderately. A little vindictive hatred creates an ancillary good by reinforcing social norms. To use a newly popular term in the philosophical literature, the boys who make fun of Walt Jr. are "assholes." They have an inflated sense of their own value and are dismissive and degrading to those around them.[10] Not long ago, a person with a disability would have been an object of shame and pity. The boy's behavior would have been dismissed as boys being boys. Yet, Walt's action clearly asserts that this is not the case here and now. As passive observers of Walt's reaction, we might have hoped for a less violent action in showing that their behavior puts them outside the moral community, but something needed to be done.

The second requirement is that the virtue have an excess, a defect, and a socially accepted mean. The excess of hate is easy to describe. As Smith notes, we often feel insults aimed at us to be worse than an impartial observer might judge. So we may hate disproportionately to the harm or hurt inflicted. We also can be excessive in our feelings about the amount of retribution required. If Walt believed that the boys deserved to experience life as Walt Jr. does, he might have beaten the instigators so badly that they, too, were mobility impaired for the rest of their lives. Or, we can hate too single-mindedly. Even when the person we hate merits hatred and the action we intend is moderate, we can still be consumed with desire for this revenge. Gus Fring is undone by this form of excessive hatred for Hector Salamanca.

No character in *Breaking Bad* exhibits the defect, too little hate, but examples are not very hard to imagine. Jean Hampton describes a rape victim who does not believe she has been violated.[11] In Hampton's example, this woman does not see herself as having sufficient value to be wronged by another person. Hampton recognizes this is a completely inaccurate sense of self-esteem. As independent observers, we hope that the community punishes her attacker through public recognition that he violated her dignity. The hate directed at a rapist is a basic human response to the violation of one's dignity. Someone who does not believe they are worthy of feeling this hatred is objectively wrong.

The mean, as Aristotle tells us, is different for each person, so self-esteem is a subjective good. Assuming a person has an appropriate sense of self-esteem, the response necessary to assert their moral worth, to their own satisfaction, will be different. As a parent, my advice to Walt Jr. would be that a virtuous response to teasing should make him feel proud of himself. I don't know what that would be for him, but finding it is crucial for developing and asserting his own sense of worth as a member of the community. This is the most significant point about virtuous hate: it is assertive, but not commensurate. Virtuous hate does not balance the scales of justice (in many cases, the scales cannot be balanced). Jeffrie Murphy provides a perfect picture of moderate hatred:

Speaking (as almost any Irishman can) from extensive personal experience as a rather vindictive person, I believe that I've often gotten even with people by actions that were moderate and proportional-perhaps involving nothing more than a few well selected (and hopefully hurtful) words or by actions no more extreme than no longer extending lunch invitations or rides to work with them … Rarely have I been dominated by my vindictive feelings. I often let them float harmlessly in the back of my mind until an appropriate occasion for their expression occurs.[12]

In fiction, hateful characters are deep and broody, vindictive actions are dramatic and violent. Hate in real life is not necessary like this. A witty remark or the withholding of a social nicety is often enough to assert one's value and signal that some behavior was inappropriate. In real life many people don't brood, as they have Murphy's proper disposition to act when the occasion arises.

The value of an Aristotelian virtue is judged by the role it plays in community standards of flourishing.[13] Here we get mixed messages. We are told that vindictive passions are harmful to our own flourishing. On the other hand, we live in a culture that encourages individuals to vigorously assert and defend their self-worth in a harsh and competitive environment. We are told to forgive. But we voraciously consume revenge stories in fiction and on social media. In the episode "Cancer Man," we meet Ken. Ken's license plate, "KEN WINS," tells us that Ken is an asshole. At the bank Ken loudly rates the attractiveness of the tellers. At a gas station he honks at an old woman who is moving too slowly. All the while he is on his phone, proclaiming himself to be the most awesome person in Albuquerque. Those who bear the brunt of his self-absorbed pronouncements are hurt and offended. Witnesses to his actions cringe. At the gas station, Walt pops Ken's hood, lays the squeegee across the battery terminals, and walks away as the car shorts out and catches fire. Ken is not amused. Everyone else is. This is only virtuous in fiction.

In fiction we appreciate the dramatic over the moderate; in real life, blowing up a car is extreme. This constant diet of fictional excess clouds our understanding of moderation. In real life, words, wit, and small actions have power. There are many moderate hateful responses to Ken. The bank teller could go on break when Ken gets to the front of the line. Ken's coworker could put his call on speaker, making Ken an object of ridicule for the office. These actions are malicious. They cause minor harm. If they were done to an innocent person, or if they were done to Ken because he is of a particular race or ethnicity, the person doing them would be condemned. We may not call these small actions "hateful" because we all do them and they don't rise to the explosive level of Walt's revenge as seen on television. But this reflects the lack of appropriate language for the virtue of moderate hate, not a lack of community standards for moderate hate directed at assholes.

The Stoic twist in this definition of virtue comes from Peter Abelard. The Stoic tradition holds that the virtues are unified. There is one virtue, usually justice or prudence, and all the other "virtues" are really just this one virtue expressed in different contexts. For Abelard the primary virtue is justice. The other virtues are ancillary virtues. Abelard argues, for example, that prudence is the ability to tell right from wrong. But this is only a virtue if one then chooses what is right. Similarly, many immoral actions display the qualitative elements of courage. Courage is only a virtue when the courageous person does what is right.[14] Walt displays great courage when he sets up Gale to be executed and confronts Gus as his only remaining option to stay in business. Yet in no way are Walt's actions virtuous. Hatred is an ancillary virtue of this kind. Hate is not good in itself, it is only virtuous when it secures other moral goods.

There is a difference between courage and hate. Courage is something we have to work hard to have. The virtuous persons must strengthen and increase their courage. Often the virtue is its own reward. The satisfaction received is simply from having had the courage to do what is right. Hate is something we have, but don't necessarily want. Because we are more likely to err in excess with hatred, virtuous hate does not require strength the way courage does. Instead, it requires a great deal of self-awareness and self-control. There is much hard work involved in developing virtuous hatred, but this is just a different kind of work.

People can reasonably balk at these examples, saying that assaulting the boys or blowing up Ken's car are not in fact virtuous acts because of Walt's violence. But there is one instance where Walt unequivocally exhibits virtuous hatred. Bogdan Wolynetz owns the car wash where Walt works a second job, the same business that Walt eventually buys as a money-laundering front. Bogdan never misses an opportunity to belittle Walt. He even refuses to sell the car wash to Skyler because Walt is not man enough to negotiate the offer himself. In "Cornered," Walt goes to get the keys after the sale and Bogdan tells him that the boss needs to be tough. He is not apologizing for his past behavior. He is intimating that Walt is too weak. He tells Walt to ask his wife for help. Walt is not bothered by the petty sexism here. Bogdan is a nasty man trying to degrade Walt. Believing he has sold an expensive problem to an unknowing Walt, Bogdan reminds him that the sale is "as-is" (Skyler has conned Bogdan into thinking the car wash has serious wastewater problems). On his way out, after insulting and privately gloating at having cheated Walt, he asks for the ceremonial framed first dollar that was left on the office wall. Bogdan is obviously hurt when Walt refuses to return this memento, reminding Bogdan that the sale was "as-is." Bogdan leaves. Walt puts the dollar into the vending machine and enjoys a particularly satisfying Diet Coke.

All the elements of virtuous hatred are here. Bogdan had been intentionally and knowingly degrading to Walt. Even in Season Four when we know of Walt's crimes and that he and Skyler have tricked Bogdan into selling the car wash, Bogdan is still an asshole. Since quitting the car wash, Walt had not been consumed with resentment or revenge fantasies. With respect to Bogdan, Walt does not even come close to the picture of a man consumed by hate. Keeping the framed dollar bill was mildly injurious to Bogdan (were this a prized possession Bogdan would have remembered to pack it, or maybe asked for it twice).

The injury to Bogdan is much less than that suffered by Walt, but Walt is satisfied. The virtuous hatred is assertive, not commensurate.

At this point it can be objected that Walt's action is morally permissible, but not virtuous. The objection reflects the *prima facie* argument against malice. Wouldn't it be better to just let it go? In the store with Walt Jr., Skyler says in the pilot, "Just ignore them, they don't matter." But this is just not true. The boys in the store and other assholes like Ken, and Bogdan *do* matter. If we are to live in a moral community of mutual respect, those who inappropriately degrade others cannot just be ignored. The objection, and Skyler's words, reflects a Stoic influence: feeling injured is a failure on your part. You allowed yourself to feel hurt. Vindictive passions are always inappropriate because they are always misdirected. The view has been influential as an ideal, but has never been widely practiced. The Roman Stoic philosopher Seneca describes how the wise man avoids insults:

> The wise man is slighted by no one because he is conscious of his own greatness, and assures himself that no one is accorded so much power over him; he does not need to overcome feelings of annoyance or distress he does not even experience them … The wise man can dismiss the proud, the arrogant, and those who are corrupted by prosperity—these are the people from whom insults come—by the noblest virtue magnanimity. He will understand that all other men are his inferiors.[15]

This line of thought is appealing when we think about established power hierarchies. Professors, for example, should not allow themselves to feel vindictive hatred toward a grumpy freshman. But on a larger scale, this Stoic view should not be held up as an ideal. In a diverse community of moral equals, there will always be conflict. A person who is so far above the fray that nothing others do is significant to him cannot be an equal member of a moral community.[16] Many people will feel it is beneath them to respond vindictively, even when a simple word like "asshole" would suffice. John Stuart Mill's advice in *On Liberty* for calling out fools applies to the kind of assertive confrontation I am advocating. "It would be well, indeed, if this good office were much more freely rendered than the common notions of politeness at present permit."[17]

WALT AND HANK

The most significant development of these themes can be found in the love/hate relationship between Walt and Hank Schrader. Walt both loves and hates his brother-in-law Hank. Hank loves Walt but hates Walt's meth-cooking alter ego Heisenberg. Walt takes his hate to dramatic and exciting excess. Yet Hank is more philosophically interesting. He is the deserving victim of hatred from both Walt and his coworkers in the DEA. In response, this character develops his character. In the end, Hank may be the only virtuous main character on the show.

When we first meet Walt and Hank, they could not be more different. Hank is big, brash, and loud. He is the kind of man that ignorant people think is manly. We first meet him at Walt's birthday party in the pilot. Actually, we first meet Hank's gun: whipping it out and holding it between his legs, Hank's first line of the series is: "Glock 22. That's my daily carry." Walt Jr. is impressed. Walt grumbles a bit as Hank gives Jr. the gun. When Jr. insists Walt hold the gun, he gingerly takes it, but is clearly uncomfortable. Hank laughs and says "That's why we [the DEA] hire *men*." He offers a few more insults, then toasts Walt's birthday, and takes Walt's beer. Walt is left impotently holding Hank's gun and watching Hank drink his beer. Hank then dominates the party with tales of his latest, huge drug bust.

Yet Walt is equally a caricature. The first meaningful thing we see of Walt's life is a wall plaque commending him for having led a research project in 1985 that resulted in a Nobel Prize. Twenty-five years ago, Walt had a chance to be somebody. For his fiftieth birthday, Skyler makes him a breakfast of soy bacon. She talks about selling things on eBay as a way to get a bit of extra money. He gets recognized at the car wash while cleaning some rich student's sports car. He has had a very bad day before coming home to a Hank-dominated birthday party. That night in bed, Walt is the recipient of a truly demeaning sex act.[18] This is all before we learn Walt has cancer and that his insurance won't cover treatment. The setup is clear: Walt is a nebbish; Hank is a big deal DEA agent who has very little respect for him.

Hank is the proper object of Walt's hatred, but most of Walt's vindictive responses go unrecognized by Hank. Walt takes obvious pleasure in knowing that he is the mastermind thwarting the tough-guy DEA agent. When Hank walks through Walt's chemistry lab to document the stolen equipment in "Crazy Handful of Nothin,'" Hank is dismissive of his naïve brother-in-law. As a result he unknowingly gives Walt great advice for getting away with his crimes. By allowing Hank to ignorantly demonstrate his perceived superiority, Walt is in fact treating Hank in a vindictive way. This is clearer if we strip away the criminal activity. Suppose a particularly arrogant coworker is incorrectly "mansplaining" some procedure important for their job. Yet the coworker is mistaken about what he should do; if he goes forward, he will suffer minor embarrassment. You could correct them, but this would involve a positive act that would benefit this person. You could also nod, smile, and watch from a safe distance. Intentionally omitting to act when you could have prevented their self-inflicted hurt from happening is a vindictive act. This can reinforce your subjective sense of self-esteem. A well-chosen word afterward can remind them that other people have value. Walt doesn't have that moment with Hank until much later in the series.

Walt Jr. is the pawn in Hank and Walt's personal relationship. As a teenager, he does not have full agency and he cannot be faulted for being overimpressed with Hank's bravado. Walt has an obligation to put up with him and to teach him. Hank, on the other hand, knows that he is overstepping his proper boundaries. In "… and the Bag's in the River," Marie takes Skyler's cryptic hints about drug use to mean that Walt Jr. is using marijuana. She calls Hank who is reluctant to intervene. Hank says rightly that this is his father's job, but then laughs and suggests Skyler would be the one to set Jr. straight.[19] When Marie says, "He respects you," her intonation makes her meaning clear. Walt is not respected by his son, Marie, or Hank. Later in "Gray Matter," Walt Jr. is arrested trying to buy beer and calls Hank to bail him out. This is where Hank draws the line. He makes it clear to Walt Jr. that he should have called his father. He also convinces Skyler to keep the incident from Walt. These issues continue at family gatherings, culminating with Walt Jr. vomiting tequila into the swimming pool in "Over." This party is to celebrate the remission of Walt's cancer. Hank is bragging about the incident in the desert with Tortuga the snitch (this time, we viewers know what really happened). Walt starts to seethe at Hank's meathead act and Walt Jr.'s admiration for it. Walt pours a tequila shot for his son, who shoots the tequila with predictable gasping and coughing. Hank ramps up the meathead act, now with stories of drunken exploits. Hank balks at the meaningful work of being a father, but is willing to dominate Walt Jr.'s alcohol-fueled rite of passage. He is culpable because he is aware he has been overstepping his boundaries. Walt pours another round. Hank gently puts his hand on Walt Jr.'s shoulder as he drinks. Hank knows this is going too far. He puts his hand over the cup. Walt pours a third round through Hank's fingers. At this point Hank wisely takes the bottle away. Walt stands and yells "My son! My bottle! My house! ... Bring it back!" His voice is a low-pitched growl. For the first time he stares down Hank. Before the confrontation can escalate, Walt Jr. vomits into the pool.

Walt's hatred is aimed at Hank. But he intentionally hurts his son in order to assert his role as father against Hank. There is not enough space in this chapter to list all the reasons this is wrong: Walt Jr. has done nothing blameworthy; Walt has an obligation to his son; it is wrong to use people as means to an end, *etc.* Walt's hatred is excessive. He has failed to respond to Hank's behavior for so long that he is on a hair trigger and finally explodes. This is how resentment does its nasty work. If Walt had the appropriate dispositions or habits, he would have responded effectively to Hank long ago. If Walt had exercised the virtue of moderate hatred toward Hank earlier, his resentment would not have built up. Ultimately Walt achieves neither of the moral goods secured by virtuous hatred. Walt is correct when he feels he is not respected by Hank. His actions do not assert his proper moral role. They demonstrate that he does not deserve the level of respect he is demanding. With regard to the ancillary good, Walt's actions only reinforce Hank's offending behavior, they do not shut it down.

Things could have been different. Hank actually responds well to virtuous hatred, as we see with the incident with Tortuga in the desert, a scene that is a key to Hank's moral development. Hank gets promoted to a more significant DEA office in El Paso. He has been called up from the minor leagues, but he's still Hank. He is rude, dismissive, and impatient with his new colleagues. He is disdainful of their coddling of the snitch Tortuga, and of their lack of aggression in general. In response, his new coworkers are simply nasty to him. They ridicule him in Spanish (which he inexcusably does not speak), and withhold all help and support as he self-destructs. His new coworkers respond to his ignorance, condescension, and arrogance vindictively, and Hank gets it. Tortuga is the second step in Hank's development.

The first step was Hank's killing of Tuco Salamanca. Killing Tuco is the kind of pseudo-manly act that Hank crows about. But Hank is deeply affected. He knows he killed another human being. He knows he was lucky, not powerful. When the turtle ambles up to the El Paso DEA agents with Tortuga's severed head attached, Hank has a panic attack and runs. His coworkers taunt him, but the turtle is a bomb. The metaphor is clear. Recognizing the humanity of even a "lowlife scumbag snitch" like Tortuga saves Hank's life. From this point in Season Two, Hank begins to change. He returns to the Albuquerque office, focuses on doing his own job, and is less of an asshole to his coworkers. The El Paso DEA agents hate Hank and this hatred secures the ancillary good: Hank's behavior changes and the social order is improved. Unfortunately, they get blown up by a turtle and are not around to enjoy the benefits.

In the end Hank is shot to death by white supremacists while Walt begs for Hank's life. Hank has changed for the better. By this point Walt has run his life so far off the rails that speculating about his side of the relationship is pointless. At Walt's birthday party in the pilot, Hank toasts Walt, saying "You've got a brain the size of Wisconsin, but we don't hold that against you." He follows it up with some "I love you man" bullshit and steals Walt's beer. At the end, in "Ozymandias," while Walt is begging for Hank's life, Hank tells him "You want me to beg? You're the smartest guy I ever met, and you're too stupid to see. He made up his mind ten minutes ago." Hank is courageous and self-composed. Hank at the end is not the same meathead who brags to children but can't handle real pressure. This is at least in part due to his reactions to the negative emotions and vindictive behavior aimed at him.

Hank merits one final note: he exhibits moral hatred for Heisenberg. If moral hatred is virtuous, he does it well. Hampton endorses moral hatred as she defines it: "An aversion to someone who has identified himself with immoral cause or practice, prompted by moral indignation and accompanied by the wish to triumph over him and his cause or practice in the name of some fundamental moral principle."[20] Malice is not an essential part of moral hate. Hank is close to obsessed with catching Heisenberg. But it's not personal. When Hank catches "Heisenberg," his actions are moderate and appropriate. As he puts the cuffs on Heisenberg, Hank's moral order has been set right. Hampton rejects ordinary hatred as self-destructive and immoral, but endorses moral hatred.[21] Conversely, I reject moral hatred. Moral hatred is incited when another person holds different values. To anyone with strongly held values, a person holding different values is immoral to some degree. It is easy to justify hatred of Nazis. But value conflicts also lead people to hate Mormons, homosexuals, and Yankees fans. Hank's moral order is set right, but many people believe that recreational drug use is a permissible moral choice, and that the war against drugs is an immoral waste of money. Moral hatred is damaging to the social order of a diverse society.

GRAY MATTER

The other main objects of Walt's hatred are his former partners, Gretchen and Elliot Schwartz. Walt was dating Gretchen when the three of them founded Gray Matter. After Walt and Gretchen broke up—under circumstances that are never explained—Walt sold his share of the business for $5000. The principles of the company were later awarded the Nobel Prize. At the time of our story, Gretchen and Elliot are married and the company is valued at $2.16 billion. I mentioned earlier that Walt has a plaque commemorating his role as project leader on the Nobel Prize winning discovery. It is on the wall next to an Award of Merit from the public school system. Oh how the mighty have fallen! Both are in front of Walt's stepper so he can stare at them each morning while he exercises. In leaving Gray Matter, he made a decision with terrible consequences and he is not happy with his life. Those negative feelings are misdirected at the Schwartzes.

Walt's contributions were crucial, and he missed out on a huge reward. His envy is natural.[22] However, there is absolutely no indication that Elliot cheated Walt, or that Gretchen had something to apologize for after their breakup. Both are eager to help Walt when he is diagnosed. They seem motivated by kindness, not guilt. The insult Walt feels is just not real. Walt has missed out on a tremendous benefit, but he was not wronged by the Schwartzes. Walt is finally pushed over the edge when he sees Gretchen on TV distance herself and the company from Walt, and announce a large donation to charity for methamphetamine treatment. This public relations stunt is insulting to Walt, but by any reasonable standard, he deserves it.[23] The Schwartzes are not the proper object of Walt's hatred.

Walt's unvirtuous hatred of the Schwartzes turns him into Nietzsche's scorpion stinging himself to death. In "Buy Out," Walt has the chance to walk away with $5 million but he refuses to sell the meth business. Jesse reminds him that initially he claimed he only needed $700,000. He tells Walt he can enjoy life, spend time with his family, and "no one else needs to die." Jesse brings Walt an excellent offer. Walt, in turn, tells Jesse about Gray Matter. He admits that he looks up the valuation of Gray Matter every week. He confesses his sin against himself, that he "sold his potential, and his children's birthright, for a few month's rent." In that too-brief moment, Walt may be aware that he should hate himself. Since we don't know what precipitated the sale of Gray Matter, we really can't say whether this self-hatred would be justified.[24] He may have undervalued himself. The sale may have been the only way out of a situation he created but is rightly embarrassed by. Alternately, the self-hatred may be unjustified. He may have made the best decision he could have at the time and was just unlucky. Either way, Walt's moment of self-reflection passes.

Walt's hatred blinds him to his present opportunity. To restore his sense of self-esteem Walt needs to lord his superiority over the world. Walt is "not in the drug business, or the money business, [he is] in the empire business." The fame, publicity, and wealth surrounding Gray Matter represents, for Walt, the whole world rubbing his degradation in his face. While self-esteem is a subjective good and the actions needed to assert one's value will differ from person to person, Walt's needs are contrary to the flourishing and happiness of himself and others. This is excessive.

His revenge against the Schwartzes is for them to deliver $9.72 million in cash with the instructions that they are to give it to Walt Jr. in an irrevocable trust. Any fees are to be paid from Walt's money. The Schwartzes are not to contribute a penny. Walt believes that they have cheated him, but he is using his power to prevent the Schwartzes from rectifying their wrongs. Walt's revenge doesn't reinforce his appropriate self-esteem, or assert his proper place in the moral community. It doesn't reinforce social norms. Instead, it shows that Walt has the power over the Schwartzes; he can reject their atonement. Walt tells them he has hired assassins. The scene ends with Walt standing behind the couple, the red dot of a laser on their chests. Walt explains:

> Whatever happens to me tomorrow [the assassins] will still be out there keeping tabs, and if, for any reason, my children do not get this money, a kind of countdown will begin. Maybe a day. Maybe a week, a year. When you were going for a walk in Santa Fe, or Manhattan, maybe Prague, wherever, and you're talking about your stock prices without a worry in the world, suddenly you hear the scrape of footsteps behind you. But before you can even turn around: POP. *(Walt jabs his index fingers into the back of their heads. They scream.)* Cheer up beautiful people this is where you get to make it right. ("Felina")

Walt's revenge fantasy gives the Schwartzes a choice: give Walt Jr. the money, or live the rest of their lives in constant fear. His resentment has eaten at him for years. Walt has not allowed himself a moment's happiness since the Schwartzes "robbed" him. They will now do what he wants or suffer equally, unable to enjoy any happiness for thinking of Walt. He has rationalized that it is just to inflict equal suffering on those he judges responsible for his own. This is brilliant revenge fantasy, but it is not virtuous.

How to Do Things with Bad Words

The last few pages have discussed hatred gone spectacularly wrong. I now turn back at the end of this chapter to a discussion of hate done well. I noted above that fictional vindictiveness is literally explosive. In the real world, words have great power. In the dark watches of the night, who hasn't thought about exercising Walt-like power over those who have "wronged" us? It can be pleasant to imagine fantastic ways of forcing Brian in the business office to stop questioning me and to approve my travel forms. We all have moments, usually shortly after an insulting encounter, when we think of the perfect witty response. These are often hateful and vindictive thoughts. Without saying the words aloud, we acknowledge to ourselves that we were wronged and deserved better. Although the words are never uttered, we can laugh at our own wit and, restored, go on with the day. Sometimes, a little self-reinforcement is all that is needed to confirm that you did not deserve the treatment you received.

Other times we need to take it a step further and express the thought to a friend. They will laugh appropriately, maybe praise us on our cunning plan, and that is all. A real friend will even tell us if we are wrong to feel injured in the first place. Either way, a friend will reinforce appropriate self-esteem; as always, the ancillary good is secured indirectly. If you are a jerk to a waiter, he really does think about doing nasty things to your food. That is why people who have waited tables make better customers. Having been abused, former waiters are more respectful. We focus a lot of thought on the incorrigible asshole. But these people are very rare. We are all occasional assholes, but we are capable of self-reflection, empathy, and improvement.[25]

Walt Jr. expresses the most effective hatred in the series. He secures both goods and uses only words. In "Granite State," Walt calls his son to tell him that he is sending money. Junior yells back, calling Walt an asshole and telling him to "just die already." This is significant moral development. He is no longer the youth being forced to drink tequila shots, or the teenager petulantly changing his name to Flynn. Teenagers lash out like this frequently. In this case, given all Walt has done, Walt Jr.'s actions are something he could be proud of. Calling someone an asshole or simply telling them you hate them is an aggressive act. Walt is hurt. That is exactly Jr.'s intention. The word "asshole" is hurtful merely in its use. There are many such words, but unlike most, "asshole" is a reflection of the content of a person's character, not their race or gender. "Asshole" is a powerful, and socially acceptable, expression of moderate hatred.[26] At this point Walt calls the DEA and waits at the bar to turn himself in. This is when he sees Gretchen on TV distancing the company from his crimes, and we get a much more exciting ending.

We have not yet discussed the central relationship in *Breaking Bad* between Walt and Jesse. Much of their conflict in the early seasons surrounds Jesse asserting his merit as a partner, demanding Walt recognize him as an equal. Jesse behaves towards Walt the way Walt should have behaved toward Hank. When Walt recognizes that Jesse is actually his equal, things get really bad. In Season Four, Gus and Mike test Jesse. Jesse had not made a good first impression. Gus and Mike are impressed and recognize that Jesse can replace Walt. Knowing that Gus is looking to replace him, Walt does everything he can to denigrate Jesse and destroy his confidence. When that fails, he poisons the son of Jesse's girlfriend and successfully frames Gus to get Jesse on side (at this point Jesse doesn't know that Walt allowed his previous girlfriend to die in order to maintain control over him). There can be no doubt that Walt is the proper object of Jesse's hatred. Except for trying to burn Walt's house down, Jesse handles his hatred pretty well.

Jesse is the easiest character to empathize with in *Breaking Bad*. He is provoked more than anyone would be in real life, but he is left to deal with it using only the tools the rest of us have. He has good intentions, at least when he thinks about it. He just has limited resources: intellectually, economically, spiritually, across the board. Jesse is not a genius mastermind. In his one attempt at video game-style vengeance, Jesse attempts to kill the drug dealers who murdered his girlfriend's brother in Season Four. This would have gotten him killed but Walt saves the day.[27] At the very end, after the shootout with the white supremacists, Walt slides his gun across the floor to Jesse, and tells Jesse to shoot. He wants to dictate Jesse's revenge. Jesse is tempted but tells him to do it himself. Jesse sees that Walt is wounded, but Walt shows no sign that the wound is severe. It would be wrong to say that Jesse is letting fate do the dirty work for him. We cannot conclude Jesse is a good soul who has risen above the insults he suffered—he has just finished strangling Todd. Jesse hates Walt. Outside, before Jesse drives the El Camino into the desert, Walt and Jesse look at each other and offer a slight terse nod. Actor Aaron Paul's assessment of this final parting supports my argument:

> I think they understand each other as true partners now. I don't think Walt considers himself as a boss to Jesse anymore. Maybe deep down, because Walt has a big ego, but I think Jesse sees himself as being equal to Walt.[28]

They are not Butch and Sundance. I doubt Jesse would ever want anything to do with Walt again. Just like Walt Jr., Jesse refuses to be Walt's tool. He could kill Walt. He could vent his anger and wound Walt leaving him to die slowly. He doesn't. Jesse's hatred is not commensurate to the wrong Walt has done to him, because no amount of Walt's suffering could ever compensate Jesse. Jesse's hatred is assertive. If Aaron Paul is correct, Jesse feels he is finally seen as Walt's equal. Thanks to Walt, Jesse is a damaged human being. His hatred and vindictiveness alone will not make him whole. But the assertion of his proper self-esteem is a start.

This is a fitting final comment. Virtuous hatred won't make a damaged person whole again. It may be an important first step. In responding to lesser injuries, we are so prone to dangerous and self-destructive excess that we have to question whether the benefit is worth the risk.

NOTES

1. See Jeffrie Murphy and Jean Hampton. *Forgiveness and Mercy*. Cambridge: Cambridge University Press, 1988. Chapters 2 and 3 define and discuss these kinds of hate.
2. Aristotle, *Nicomachean Ethics*, §1107a12.
3. Ibid, § 1126a5.
4. Murphy and Hampton, *Forgiveness and Mercy*, p. 88ff.

5. Thomas Scanlon, *Moral Dimensions: Permissibility, Meaning, Blame* (Cambridge, MA: Belknap Press, 2008), p. 122ff.
6. Friedrich Nietzsche, *Thus Spoke Zarathustra*, trans. R. J. Hollingdale (London: Penguin Books, 1961), V.
7. "Resentment itself, if it should appear in the noble man, consummates and exhausts itself in immediate action and therefore does not poison." Nietzsche, *On the Genealogy of Morals*, trans. Walter Kaufmann (New York: Random House, 1967), 39.
8. Some would disagree. Hampton argues that our value as human beings can never be diminished or raised by the actions of others; Murphy and Hampton, *Forgiveness and Mercy* 43ff. Clarence Thomas, arguing against homosexual marriage, concludes that nothing the state does (slavery, internment, Jim Crow, etc.,) can diminish human dignity because the state does not confer human dignity; *Obergfell v. Hodges* 576 U.S. 2015. Both are making claims about our metaphysical value as human beings. While they may be correct on that level, this is cold comfort when faced with the lived experience of degradation in a moral community.
9. Adam Smith, *Theory of Moral Sentiments*, ed. A.L. Macfie and D.D. Raphael (Indianapolis: Liberty Press, 1982), 38. Many other thinkers recognize the moderate satisfaction of vindictive passions as a basis for moral standing in a community. For Thomas Hobbes, moral equality is in part derived from the "ability of the weakest of us to kill the strongest." See Thomas Hobbes, *Leviathan*, § XIII. David Hume argues that we feel justice only applies to those who can "make their indignation known"; see David Hume, *Enquiries Concerning Human Understanding and Concerning the Principles of Morals*, ed. L. A. Selby-Bigge (Oxford: Clarendon Press, 1975), 152.
10. G. Nunberg, *The Assent of the A-Word* (Perseus: New York, 2012), 22; A James, *Assholes: A Theory* (New York: Anchor, 2014), 5; R. Sutton, *The No Asshole Rule*, 10.
11. Murphy and Hampton, *Forgiveness and Mercy*, 49–55.
12. J. Murphy, *Getting Even*, 24.
13. M. Nussbaum, "Non-Relative Virtues: An Aristotelian Approach," 242–270.
14. P. Abelard, *Collationes*, 136ff.
15. Seneca, *De Constantia*, §10.3–11.2. "Those corrupted by prosperity" may be Seneca's definition of "asshole."
16. The Stoic tradition is, of course, much richer and more nuanced. The trite Stoicism of Skyler's remark is not. The same could be said for the claim that the boys will be punished in some way by God or by Karma. The trite impulse acknowledges the harm, but turns God and Karma into vicarious, fantasy vindictiveness.
17. J.S. Mill, *On Liberty*, §IV, 75.
18. Skyler gives Walt a birthday hand-job while she is watching her auctions on e-bay. She becomes increasingly excited as her auction is bid up. The auction finishes before Walt and the scene ends awkwardly.
19. The relationship between Hank and Walt is infected with a stereotypical masculinity. This is an artifact of the show. A similar relationship could exist between Skyler and her sister-in-law. Walt's metafictional sister could demean Skyler in some stereotypically feminine ways. The Internet is full of mommy-shaming examples. Skyler's response would be hateful and vindictive but also feminine.

The lifetime Network's UnReal is a wonderful example of feminine hatred and vindictiveness.

20. Murphy and Hampton, *Forgiveness and Mercy*, 61.
21. Ibid., 149.
22. Some would even argue that envy can be a virtue when it inspires a person to achieve something. N. van de Ven, M. Zeelenberg, and R. Pieters, "Leveling up and down: The experiences of benign and malicious envy" *Emotion,* Vol 9:3 (2009), 419–429.
23. Even by the unreasonable standards of philosophers, like Augustine or Kant, who would prohibit all lying, it is not clear that Walt is hurt by Gretchen's lie.
24. Virtuous self-hatred is quite common. Everyone does things that they are not proud of, or are inconsistent with their appropriate self-esteem. Self-discipline or atonement can be seen as self-directed vindictive behavior.
25. This is a weakness in all the recent literature on assholism. Philosophers focus on how to respond to the vanishingly small number of complete assholes. Sutton (*The No Asshole Rule*) who is in business management, does offer advice on recognizing and correcting one's own behavior. His wife suggested he put some thought into this (96).
26. Nunberg, *The Assent of the A-word*, 16: "It is right to treat assholes as assholes because assholes have it coming."
27. Avenging murder is something that the state has rightly taken from the hands of individuals. Relatively minor insults and hurts are left to be dealt with through personal hatred. In contrast, people in illegal businesses are in Hobbes' sense outlaws. They lack the protection of the law and the access to these judicial institutions. Based on T. Hobbes, *Leviathan* §15, it seems reasonable to treat drug gangs as operating in Hobbes' state of nature.
28. Blair Marnell, "Aaron Paul 'Hates' Walter White on 'Breaking Bad.'" Crave Online.

CHAPTER 15

"We Are Responsible to All for All":
An Intersubjective Analysis of *Breaking Bad*

Sheridan Hough

Walter White is dying.

It is tempting to start the story here, since the series thus begins: except that the imminent death of Walter is *not* how the initial episode opens. The first filmic moment is desert glare, and a pair of twisted, legless chinos falling from a blazing sky.

So, Walter White is dying of inoperable lung cancer, and that's where we wish to begin the tale, since his illness is the engine that drives his choices and their consequences. In remembering the 2008 season opener, perhaps the sequence in the oncologist's office comes to mind: Walt, unable to hear the words being spoken to him, the death sentence uttered as he hears murmured sounds, seeing only a mustard stain on the oncologist's white coat. The face of Walter White, while hearing but not hearing that he must die, is one we will see again and again in the series on many different characters: Hank the DEA officer, knowing that Jack is about to execute him; Gus Fring, finally realizing why Hector Salamanca has called him to his nursing home; Lydia, in bed with "flu-like symptoms," hearing Walt's voice explain that there was ricin in her green tea; Gale Boetticher, opening the door to Jesse, and seeing the end of his life in Jesse's outstretched, shaking hand, clutching a gun.

Of course, this is also the face that every one of us sees, every day, in the morning mirror (to brush, shave), or the passing glance on the way to work (adjust hair, or tie), at night, preparing to let go of all of this grooming and tending, and simply curl up as a simulacrum of fetal breath and being. Each human face is (when we wish to so consider it) the imprimatur of its mortality; hence, the familiar keening pang of seeing a portrait—the Renaissance

S. Hough (✉)
College of Charleston, Charleston, SC, USA

© The Author(s) 2017
K.S. Decker et al. (eds.), *Philosophy and Breaking Bad*,
DOI 10.1007/978-3-319-40343-4_15

grandee, how ruddy and robust of flesh! Heroic nose, vivid eyes, yet all of it so much dust, so long ago. As such, "facing death"—that close-up of Walter White, hearing what he cannot bear to hear—is neither unique nor instructive.

Walter's face in close-up captures our attention because it vividly depicts the face each one of us wears. That face, however, is not—and cannot be, in the moment of self-dissolution's knowledge—looking in the direction of its own origin. We need to know how this person came to be.

Who is Walter White? Discovering who Walter is will require the camera to pan out considerably. It will, to use Walter's own words from the pilot episode, require chemistry—as he puts it, "the study of change…solution, dissolution, just over and over and over—growth, decay and transformation."

Again: who is Walter White? We viewers think we know the answer: Walt is highly intelligent (the plaque we glimpse commemorating his membership on a Nobel prize-winning chemistry team), initially browbeaten by life (mocked by his feckless high school students, berated by his overlord at the car wash, Bogdan), enamored of his wife and dedicated to his family, both his children and his in-laws (a "fact" about Walt that becomes mantra-shaped in its repetition, and one to which we will return). No, Walt's character seems clear, and his increasingly feral and murderous choices flow directly from his skillful determination to succeed in "providing for his family."

Ah, those choices, those depraved actions. What about them? Surely our interest here should be directed to some kind of ethical evaluation—after all, how far can thoughts about Walter's character take us? As Aristotle gamely points out in the *Poetics*, "Character gives us qualities, but it is in our actions—what we do—that we are happy or the reverse…the first essential, the life and soul, so to speak, of tragedy is the plot; and that the characters come second."[1] Walter's choices to act, or not to act, are center-stage. Series creator Vince Gilligan apparently agrees: "If there's a larger lesson to *Breaking Bad*, it's that actions have consequences…I like to believe…that karma kicks in at some point, even if it takes years or decades to happen."[2]

Gilligan's appeal to "karma" is of interest, because that notion (the Sanskrit word simply means "action") is an ontological claim. The "karmic world" is, and indeed operates, by means of causal laws: every action has a consequence, and each consequence is bound up with a dynamic nexus of other conditions and subsequent causes. This account of the absolute connection between cause, its conditions, and effect also necessarily denies the discrete or independent reality of the objects and persons within the causal structure: every thing—a rock, a cat, an airplane, a human being—is what it is because of the conditions that have created it; of course, each material state of affairs is constantly changing (in much the way that Walter White pictures our chemical reality). Hence, the Buddhist philosophical notion of "dependent arising": all things depend upon, and are the product of, a previous set of conditions; all things are aggregates only temporarily assembled, and constantly shifting in their construction. (Alteration can, of course, be brutally swift, and the *Breaking Bad* series has some breathtakingly gruesome illustrations of this principle: Victor, at one moment Gus Fring's assistant and henchman, the next a garroted corpse, the next—dissolved matter in a barrel of hydrofluoric acid; Gus, in his turn, adjusts his tie after Hector's suicide bomb, not yet aware that half of his face is now missing.) No thing, no person, has a stable identity, and the aggregate reality is always on the move.

To return to Gilligan's remark about the "larger lesson" of *Breaking Bad*: in adopting the concept of karma, Gilligan is asserting that his storyline reflects the way that things actually *are*. This point is important: storytellers reliably pander to our craving for comeuppance, and few moments of a filmed narrative are more visually satisfying than when the villain is caught, or destroyed, especially when that destruction is partly of their own making. Sure, it feels good to see the bad guy get what's coming: but just who is that bad guy, and are we entirely sure about what's coming? The thrills of justice and vengeance do not bespeak the deep truth of the karmic picture, and Gilligan seems to be pressing for a depiction with a greater kind of ontological heft.

The very notion of karma, however, depends on a more fundamental claim about the nature of reality, one that is a feature of thinking in both Eastern and Western philosophical traditions: the truth of intersubjectivity. Given what it means, the term intersubjectivity is itself problematic: an intersubjective ontology argues that persons are properly understood as social creations emerging from a shared linguistic, economic, and cultural terrain: we, as "subjects," are not (as the term suggests) discrete entities; instead, we are who we are because of others. The ontological claim of intersubjective reality thus points again to the question of Walt's identity, a question that will now take a different form: how does Walter understand his location in his human community?

INTERSUBJECTIVITY

Before we set out to investigate something as clinically distant as 'intersubjectivity,' we might ask ourselves the same question we asked of Walter White: who are we? More to the point: who am I?

An initial response probably reflects my ongoing sense of self—my fingers on the keyboard, my purposes and plans as I sit at my desk. And surely this consciousness of myself and the immediate (and wider) world that I inhabit is the source of my understanding of the world—and indeed the *world* as such. The self as a transcendent ego whose operations make the world manifest is the centerpiece of Edmund Husserl's phenomenological work; he claims, in a Cartesian mode, that we cannot doubt what we find in consciousness (my strokes on the keyboard, the pause for a sip of lukewarm coffee), but—unlike Descartes—Husserl will describe phenomena as they present themselves, rather than reason from them. This realm of subjective certainty involves a method of access; instead of merely taking for granted the contours of my office (and that now really unappealing half-cup of coffee), I am invited to abstain from epistemic judgments and observe what is available to me. This abstention, the so-called epoché, suspends the idea that a transcendent reality "explains" experience, and compels us to look at *consciousness* and its objects rather than the world and *its* objects. In other words, when we study phenomena we do not distinguish between mind and world, we merely attend to the "minded" objects in the world. The usual epistemic division of mind and world within the epoché disappears: within the epoché there isn't mind in world, but a world in which objects are manifested in consciousness.[3] As Merleau-Ponty (perhaps a better reader of Husserl than Husserl himself) says of the epoché: "it does not take us…from 'objective' to 'subjective'; rather, its function is to unveil a third dimension in which this distinction becomes problematic."[4] What now becomes apparent is that I cannot doubt the realm of appearances; I may doubt that that is a coffee cup in front of me, but I cannot doubt that I am having a "coffee cup appearance." Furthermore, consciousness is that which generates or manifests those appearances; they are created by consciousness. Evidently, in order to understand the constitution of appearances we must understand how consciousness works.

But here we should return to that intimate, important question: who am I? If the world, and its contents (and we've yet to speak of its other human inhabitants), is "manifested in consciousness"—namely, *my* consciousness—then it seems we have an immediate problem with other persons, who are also so constituting the world. Of course, this is one of the fundamental and enduring pleasures of cinema and television: we readily, happily give over to seeing the world and its contents through a character's unique experience. Our eagerness to see Walter White's environment solely through the lens of his ego (transcendental or otherwise) begins to consume that setting, its props, terrain, weather, traffic, and other persons (particularly his wife Skyler), in an effort to feed our sense of what things are like for *him*. Walter's fellow human creatures become mere obstacles or opportunities, and we join together in so seeing them.

It is this sort of reductive solipsism that Husserl devoted much thought and a great deal of ink to defeating. The problem lies in the very place where our "who am I?" question began: if the analysis of the world—that is, our investigation of the phenomena—starts with an individual's own consciousness, then it is hard to see how we can substantively retrieve another consciousness, the Other, in that analysis. As Dan Zahavi puts it, "If one is to speak meaningfully of a foreign subject, of an Other, it is evident that we are dealing with something that cannot be reduced to its mere givenness for me."[5] Indeed, Husserl consistently argues that the world, and our relations in it, are intersubjectively structured, and that this structure is the source of *all that there is*: "Concrete, full transcendental subjectivity is the totality of an open community of I's… Transcendental intersubjectivity is the absolute and only self-sufficient ontological foundation [*Seinsboden*], out of which everything objective…draws its sense and validity."[6]

So let us think more about an "open community of I's," and how that reality is forged. A first, most immediate, and undeniable intersubjective claim is that each person is shaped by, and shapes, others. The family—alembic of human identity, with all the struggle and turmoil that such primal relations entail—is a person's entrance into the world, a place where one is, at the same time, inevitably formed, actively or reactively, by the encounter with the Other. Loved, or bullied; called "egghead," deemed "lazy" or "athletic," rejected as "worthless"—every human is embraced, taunted, nurtured, and scarred by those who tend and educate her as she grows into personhood; her response to the treatment of others—accepting or denying these characterizations—in turn alters her social environment. Furthermore, and more broadly, a person cannot be who she needs to be, or do what she needs to do without the work of others. I cannot be a professor without students, or other faculty and colleagues, nor can I do my work without classrooms (and their manifold of equipment), or without the entire institutional structure of higher education (and so forth). Walter White cannot entertain becoming a meth kingpin without the immediate help of Jesse and his network of contacts, and—to pan further out—the whole vast tangle of the criminal drug culture, one made both absurdly lucrative and dangerous (to its practitioners, and to everyone else caught in the "crossfire"—hardly a metaphor!) by its illicit status. A person's projects do not stand alone: they are always already the projects of others.

So, family and the persons thus emerging into a wider world of shared projects and concerns constitute what we will call the "ethical" dimension of intersubjectivity, in that a person's character and the choices that a person finds viable and appealing are the product of those early, potent bonds, and lay the groundwork for the relations a person will construct and share in a wider social setting. A person's "location" in this cultural terrain depends on a vast, interconnected history of the choices of others, choices that build institutions, and choices that make particular ways of life possible.

We know very little about Walter White's familial past, but Walt has much to say about his own family, and his role in protecting and "providing" for them. In Season One, Walt provides a blunt account of where his family lies in his own moral reckoning when he and Jesse are taken hostage by Emilio and Krazy-8. Walt and Jesse escape when Walt concocts phosphine gas in the RV lab; Emilio is killed but Krazy-8 survives and winds up a prisoner in Jesse's basement. Now what does Walt do? Killing Emilio was an act of self-defense, but Krazy-8 is recovering, thanks to Walt's ministrations. Krazy-8 must surely die, but Walt cannot bring himself to do it. Two moments tip the balance. First, Walt makes a "pro and con" list: the "let him live" list contains the usual fare: "it's the moral thing to do," "Judeo-Christian principles," "You are not a murderer," "He may listen to reason," "Post-traumatic stress," "Won't be able to live with yourself," and—finally—"Murder is wrong!" In the "kill him" column? One item only: "He'll kill your entire family if you let him go." Still Walt continues to feed and tentatively "befriend" Krazy-8; the decisive moment comes when Walt realizes that Krazy-8 has managed to hide a shard of a broken plate, clearly intended as a weapon to kill Walt. The "let him live" list—a sad jumble of moral placards and pragmatic considerations—is no match for the encounter with the Other, especially one who is determined to defeat his opponent and survive. Walt's feeble attempts to soothe his own moral pangs are not in touch with the reality of a murderously angry prisoner; he is unable to imagine the view from Krazy-8's perspective, and, to make the more important Husserlian point, to see his own complicity in the current unfolding moment (he could, of course, turn himself and Krazy-8 in to the police. He does not).

Walt may think—and he certainly tells himself, and the viewer—that what he is doing (which now includes murder) is for his family's welfare. But how does he understand that family, and his place in it? When Walt collapses at the car wash, he is taken by ambulance to the hospital; on the way, the paramedic asks him if there is anyone he should contact. Walt instantly replies, "No, God, no." Why not? Surely his wife Skyler needs to know what has happened. "Family," for Walt, is both totem and emblem for his own will and self-rule. Walt understands himself as utterly autonomous—a term from the Greek meaning to establish the rule or law for oneself. Walt's "family" is for him a thing—codified through sentimentality, nurtured with reliable patriarchal homilies—that he can work for the benefit of, but only in a discrete and distant way; he will not tell Skyler the entire truth about what he has done, ever, even when they meet for the last time (he lies to her about the money that will soon come to Walt Jr. through Gretchen and Elliott). Walt reliably makes a plan, takes actions that suit that plan, and calculates, as best he can, how his choices will impact others—and yet he has no sense that his plans necessarily have origins outside of himself: that who he is, and what he wants, or *thinks* that he wants, is deeply heteronomous. The dizzying trajectory of choice—to lie, to pass on in silence, to murder—begins long before action is called upon, and ramifies long after each choice to act is made.

Walt does not see his own existential debts to his wife and children, to his wife's sister, to his brother-in-law, and indeed to the wider relational setting that has made him, and his work, possible. He may consider himself the sole, luminous point in a dark sky filled with other distant lights, but that view is intersubjectively false; it belies the "totality of an open community of I's." Walt can deny the ethical bonds that make him who he is, but the deeper chemical reality of the Other will always be made manifest.

In seeing one's debt to "the Other," one also sees a deeper *ontological* debt: I cannot be a person *as such* without what Hegel calls the "recognition" of my fellow creatures. In the *Phenomenology of Spirit's tour de force* section, "Lordship and Bondage," we see the encounter of two conscious beings who, in the presence of the other, become *self*-conscious: this is a primordial tale about the development of "selfhood," of how a self can come to be in the first place. What indeed are the conceptual pieces necessary for understanding selfhood?

In Hegel's telling, an individual consciousness—desirous, consuming, unreflectively altering its environment—becomes aware of itself in a new way when it encounters another like consciousness. Here is the fateful Hegelian announcement: "Self-consciousness exists in and for itself when, and by the fact that, it so exists for another; that is, it exists only in being acknowledged...Self-consciousness is faced by another self-consciousness; it *has come out of itself*."[7] I am aware of myself as I struggle to get what I want; the more recalcitrant the object, the more I become aware of my self as consumer. The ultimate recalcitrant object is surely another person: and in that person's resistance to my making use of him, manipulating him, bringing him under concepts, I become more aware of my own equally recalcitrant self; the consciousness has "come out of itself" and become a "self-consciousness." In this primordial conflict, each consciousness attempts to prevail as the ultimate subject, leading to a "fight to the death." For Hegel, our intersubjective condition is conceived in mortal conflict.

Here "recognition" isn't the social convention of acknowledging and respecting fellow humans (although this is, in part, its terminus); rather, Hegel argues that humans only become fully human when they encounter a like creature, one who also has a profound sense of its own potency, and one who desires to control and consume what it can in its immediate environment. The primordial collision of human with human creates the reflexively self-aware creature that each of us is: I have my own desires and designs, but I am truly made human when I encounter another, one like myself, and thus realize that other persons like me are also determined to impose their will on the world around them. This tale of human self-awareness as born in an encounter with another is one of fundamental *hostility*: as the Hegelian story goes, this primordial human, accustomed to making use of its surroundings—eating, fending off wild animals, making a shelter—is suddenly faced with a like creature that it cannot consume in this way. Certainly, each *can* attempt to kill the other in a struggle for supremacy ("I'm the ultimate consciousness around here!"), but the death of one combatant leaves the other without what it truly craved: recognition, from a fellow consciousness, an acknowledgment that is the nascent beginning of *self*-consciousness.[8]

Sartre takes Hegel's agonistic developmental account of human self-consciousness much further: for Sartre, our intersubjective condition is not fundamentally one of human co-constitution, but rather confrontation and sustained conflict. The Other-as-subject, argues Sartre, takes the world from me: when I encounter the Other, particularly when her gaze reaches me, the world around me becomes hers, not mine: "...the Other's look as the necessary condition of my objectivity is the destruction of all objectivity for me. The Other's look touches me across the world and is not only a transformation of myself but a total metamorphosis of the world. I am looked at in a world which is looked-at."[9]

The existence of other humans is, for Sartre, a contingent yet inescapable part of the world each person navigates: the encounter with the Other is always ontologically hostile. Of course, humans can, and typically do, work together as entities in choosing and establishing a common enterprise and goal. But how to explain this kind of cooperation in a way that both acknowledges this fundamental subjective hostility on the one hand, but steers away from an account of some "collective consciousness" from which we all emerge on the other? Sartre rejects Heidegger's analysis of *Mitsein*, the primordial "being-with" that characterizes *Dasein*. The image that Sartre offers in his critique of Heidegger, however, is wonderfully useful for our purposes here: Sartre describes our intersubjective condition as a ship's crew: "The original relation of the Other and my consciousness is not the you and me; it is the we. Heidegger's being-with is not the clear and distinct position of an individual confronting another individual; it is not knowledge. It is the mute existence in common of one member of the crew with his fellows, that existence which the rhythm of the oars or the regular movement of the coxswain will render sensible to the rowers and which will be made manifest to them by the common goal to be attained, the boat or the yacht to be overtaken, and the entire world (spectators, performance, etc.) which is profiled on the horizon."[10] Everyone on the ship coordinates oars and motion in keeping with the coxswain, but that shared project emerges from the consciousness of each person, each endorsing and pursuing—*for the moment*—a mutual undertaking.

The many motley and lethal "crews" at work in the five seasons of *Breaking Bad* (Jack and his neo-Nazi skinheads, Don Eladio Vuente's Mexican cartel, the DEA agents led, at times, by Hank) often operate as the "crew" of a farcically tragic version of this Sartrean ship. Perhaps the most jarring example of this kind of "teamwork" is in Season Five's "Dead Freight," when Walt plans to steal a freight tanker of methylamine. The skill and cooperation involved in such a heist demands the viewer's attention, even admiration: the water replacing the methylamine must be carefully calibrated, and every member of the team must be ready for the Other, those feckless, accidental incursions into a shared and utterly time-sensitive operation. The first of these is comic: Walt's crew manages to stop the train (and thus surreptitiously siphon off the chemical) by faking a breakdown of a dump truck on the railroad tracks, but a helpful passing driver offers to help them push the truck out of the train's way. Walt recklessly urges his team to keep pumping, making their getaway dangerously close: Jesse ends up on the tracks, letting the train pass over him, while Todd must jump from the trestle. Walt and his men have pulled off a difficult feat, without anyone on the train being the wiser, or even getting hurt: the viewer might feel a frisson of glee about this breathtakingly risky yet successful mission.

But this undertaking is not a mission, or a quest—it is theft grandly writ, and that composition's ugliness bursts on the scene when Todd kills a small boy on a dirt bike. The boy was out in the desert collecting insects, and he had seen the crew and waved at them; Todd decides that he must die, and cheerfully waves back at him before shooting him. Todd's "crew logic" is impeccable: he was told that no one can ever know about this theft, and the boy's existence potentially compromises their goal. Todd's distinctive Boy-Scout brand of psychopathy is seen again when he executes Jesse's girlfriend: as Andrea looks out of her front door for Jesse, Todd slips behind her and remarks, "Just so you know, this isn't personal."

This depraved calculus can only admit the shared purposes of the crew; for Todd, the killing of these innocents is not a slight against them—no personal grievance is involved—but impediments must be removed, and lessons meted out (Andrea is murdered to punish Jesse for trying to escape). Walter White is, of course, the chief adept of this "ship of (intersubjectivity-denier) fools" approach to human interrelations; his notions of "family" and "friend" are fluidly defined only by how they figure in Walt's voyage. Even as he begs Jack to spare Hank's life (with the cry "He's family!"), Walt avoids the awful truth that he himself has brought his brother-in-law to this remote death in the desert. When Skyler confronts Walt about Hank—after all, Walt is supposed to be in DEA custody—Walt says that he "negotiated." When Skyler asks, "What does that mean?" Walt tells her, "It means *we're* fine, okay?" She accuses him of killing Hank, and Walt shouts his reply: "No, no, no! I tried to save him," an "attempt" that even Hank, in his final moments of life, finds ridiculous.

Surely this kind of hostile and solipsistic intersubjective ontology is not what Vince Gilligan, at least by his own putative karmic lights, sets out to depict. Is there another story about our intersubjective relations here?

NARRATIVE

The action of *Breaking Bad* is a meticulously crafted narrative arc stretching over five years, 62 episodes, and roughly 46.5 hours of viewing time. Of course, Gilligan and his writing team faced the usual storytelling challenges: choices must be plausible, with cause and effect firmly in place. The unforeseen and untoward must be accommodated by some sense of how the world actually operates: in absurdist cinema, things can and do happen in a "reasonless" fashion; if, however, the *auteur* is committed to the view that "actions have consequences"—not as billiard-balls but as some kind of existential reckoning—then those plot-point choices need to reveal *how* this fundamental fabric is being woven. The hostility and solipsism reflected in our Hegelian/Sartrean intersubjective ontology point to a richer ontological account, one that is especially underscored by the action of season two.[11]

The second season's 13 installments have a comprehensive sense, a coherence made available in four of the episode titles: episodes 1 ("737"), 4 ("Down"), 10 ("Over"), and 13 ("ABQ"). Together, these form a chilling sentence, yet one that can't be uttered or understood until the final, horrific scene of a mid-air plane collision. These four episodes all begin in black and white, fore-illumining of what is to come, each one adding more detail to this pending disaster. In the first, a plastic eye is floating in the White family's swimming pool[12]; the next three openers amplify our sense of what is to come: men in Hazmat suits, evidence bags, a pair of glasses that look like Walt's. The only color in these four opening sequences is a pink and white, one-eyed bear, tongue out. In the third of these initial sequences, two body bags are carried to the front of the White's house; finally, in the last episode ("ABQ") we see the detached eye, the pink and white mutilated bear, a burnt book, a shoe, once again the two body bags: and then the camera pans out as the scene regains a livid color, two plumes of smoke staining the horizon.

How did we get here?

Consider a central storyline of Season Two: if the first season focused on Walt's family and the meth-cooking crew that he attempts to assemble, Season Two has much to say about the *neighbor*. And who is a "neighbor"? A family is constituted by bonds of consanguinity (ones that, as both Aristotle and Hume remind us, are profoundly deep), and the shared task of survival through shelter, food, socialization; but a "crew" or "team" is assembled and disassembled as the goal of the shared project shifts (is Mike, or Lydia, foe or friend? That depends). The "neighbor," however, seems conceptually distinct from both of these: it suggests a person in regular proximity, whether next door or down the street. Neighbors are, at the very least, potentially involved in maintaining a common environment; watering plants, taking in the mail, watching out for children playing in the street or suspicious characters loitering. One funny moment in the series' final season ("Blood Money") is the White's next-door neighbor's reaction to the sight of Walt in front of his former house, now fenced off and boarded up. Walt, who has become nationally infamous as the drug lord "Heisenberg," greets her with a smile and the usual friendly greeting: "Hello, Carol." Carol, terrified, drops the sack she's holding.

We may, and often do, feel a special kind of civic responsibility for the people we live among. If I see a neighbor struggling with their groceries, I may help out (open a door, carry the bag); the neighbor is a fellow dweller, and some sense of maintaining an orderly, even friendly, environment, is important. Again, proximity matters: I probably won't attempt to help a stranger in a different community with those groceries—my efforts might be misunderstood.

In Season Two, the crucial story about neighbors and their mutual care (or the disastrous abuse of it) is, of course, Jesse's arrival at Jane's duplex. Both are wounded creatures—Jane is in recovery from drug use, and Jesse is now estranged from his family. Jane is initially dubious about Jesse; Jesse tells her that he "didn't meet his parents' expectations again" and that he just "needs a chance;" she relents and rents him the adjoining, identical apartment. These neighbors become friends and then lovers. Jane, like Jesse, is an artist, and their conversations provide a respite from Jesse's world of drug distribution. When Jesse assembles his team to describe their "sales protocol," the meeting is "clean"—soda, pretzels, and the warning that no drugs will enter, or be used, in his house (thus keeping his neighborly promise to Jane).

In this "duplexity," one side of the building houses a recovering addict, while its mirror-image, its conjoined "other," hides a drug dealer: which apartment will prevail in defining the neighborhood? Jesse's sense of himself and his environment begins to shift, but the terrors of selling meth are never far away. One of his distributors, his friend Combo, is gunned down in a territory dispute, and Jesse's horror and rage tip the balance. He tells Jane that he is going to smoke some meth, and that he wants her to leave. She replies, "You could come with me to a meeting—" and reminds him that drugs won't help. Jesse insists that they will, and the next scene makes it clear that Jane is now using again. The fall from fragile grace is swift: Jane brings home a heroin kit and teaches Jesse how to inject himself.

Walter—who claims that he is trying to get out of the business—finds them both passed out when he breaks in to retrieve the 38 pounds of "product" that Jesse has stashed under the sink. The sale is made (and prevents Walt from being present when his daughter is born); Walt subsequently tells Jesse that he is keeping his half of the money until he stops using. When Jane discovers that Walt has Jesse's money, she blackmails him into returning it. Now Jesse and Jane can run off to New Zealand...but of course the temptation to have one last heroin binge is too much (indeed, it is what their lives together have become). Walt returns once more, and again finds them in a drugged stupor. He tries to wake up Jesse, but accidentally knocks Jane onto her back. She begins to choke on her own vomit, and Walt makes no effort to save her. She dies as Walt watches.

Before thinking about what kind of responsibility is at work here, and who bears what sort of blame, we should revisit the concept of the neighbor, this time in an existential mode.

Who is the neighbor?

Here we might fruitfully return to Husserl on intersubjectivity, an account that is much richer than my remarks have so far suggested. Husserl's attempts to get clear about our intersubjective condition culminate in his account of the *Lebenswelt*, the "lifeworld"—that non-objectively ramified, well-worn, and loved place from which we all originate. As he writes in his posthumous work, *The Crisis of European Sciences and Transcendental Phenomenology*, the objective account of the world provided by contemporary science has eclipsed our subjective reality, the sensuous and concrete environment from which we, and indeed the scientific pursuits that seek to reduce it to what can be measured and calculated, emerge. As he remarks in his "Vienna Lecture":

> Mathematical natural science is a wonderful technique for making inductions with an efficiency...unimaginable in earlier times.... As for the rationality of its methods and theories, however, it is a thoroughly relative one.... Since the intuitively given surrounding world, this "merely" subjective realm, is forgotten in scientific investigation, the working subject is himself forgotten; the scientist does not become a subject of investigation[13]

(It is worth noting that Walter White's commitment to the law-like purity of chemical reactions, regardless of the lawlessness and depravity that his use of chemistry's "methods and theories" constitutes, is an obvious example of Husserl's claim.) Husserl calls us to revivify the social and cultural dimension of human experience; hence, two aspects of the lifeworld are important: our norms and the traditions that embody them. We are, from birth, dwelling in a world filled with, and structured by, other people; the "self" that each of us experiences, and the world we thus apprehend is made possible by the practices and habits of a shared community, and our ongoing participation in, and anticipation of, those practices. We are who we are within the ongoing work and indeed presence of others—our debt (to make use of a Heideggerian notion) to these phenomenal structures is absolute:

Experiencing—in general, living as an ego (thinking, valuing, acting)—I am necessarily an "I" that has its "thou," its "we," its "you".... And equally necessarily, I am and we are, in the community of egos, correlates of everything to which we address ourselves as existing in the world...naming it, speaking about it, grounding our knowledge, and which as such is there for us, is actual, is valid for us in the community of conscious life *as a life which is which is not individually isolable but is internally communalized.*[14]

Emmanuel Levinas—whose own analysis of intersubjectivity is much indebted to Husserl's—deepens this account of the *Lebenswelt* by drawing out the existential and indeed ethical structures embedded in it. Levinas' writings often focus on 'the neighbor,' whom we are ontologically called to be responsible for (unlike the familiar New Testament exhortation to *love* the neighbor): "A being (*l'étant*) is a human being and it is as a neighbor that a human being is accessible—as a face."[15]

Recall that this essay began with a meditation on the fragile and mortal aspect of the human face; Levinas would urge us to consider a more profound revelation that a face can and should provide. "The face orders and ordains me," he remarks; furthermore, "...access to the face is straightaway ethical."[16] A face reveals the Other to me; once the Other is thus discovered, an intersubjective obligation always already in place must be acknowledged: "Responsibility in fact is not a simple attribute of subjectivity, as if the latter already existed in itself, before the ethical relationship. Subjectivity is not for itself; it is, once again, *initially for another*."[17] Our intersubjective reality is what makes possible our sense of ourselves as sovereign subjects. Here Levinas moves decisively away from Sartre's antagonistic analysis of the arrival of the Other: as he puts it, "And Sartre will say that the Other (*Autrui*) is a pure hole in the world—a most noteworthy insight, but he stops his analysis too soon."[18] What Sartre has stopped short of is what the Other's intrusion into the subject's domain signifies: the subject is fundamentally a *social* subject, and is thus bound up with the cares and concerns of the Other. The responsibility we bear for each other thus precedes all else: "...I speak of responsibility as the essential, primary and foundational mode of subjectivity. For I describe subjectivity in ethical terms. *Ethics, here, does not supplement a preceding existential base; the very node of the subjective is knotted in ethics understood as responsibility.*"[19]

Hence, Levinas' notion of the neighbor: we are all in primordial ethical proximity to each other, long before reflection comes on the scene: "The relation of proximity does not amount to any modality of distance or geometrical contiguity, nor to the simple 'representation' of the neighbor; it is already a summons of extreme exigency, an obligation which is anachronistically prior to every engagement."[20]

Fair enough: but who *is* the neighbor?

Our initial sketch had to do with ordinary human proximity, and the practical concerns that a shared environment create; so described, the "neighbor" is perhaps just a more stable version of the ship's crew. In order to fully appreciate the phenomenological heft of what Levinas is claiming, we should look to his nineteenth-century existential forbear, Søren Kierkegaard. Yet his Christian existential account of the human condition will find the "ship's crew" characterization of the neighbor radically insufficient; in fact, Kierkegaard argues: "...love... has only one single object, the neighbor, but the neighbor is as far as possible from being a one and only person, because *the neighbor is all people.*"[21]

Kierkegaard, unlike Levinas, does not shy away from the language of *love* for the neighbor; in fact, he thinks that "love" should be understood not as a preferential and intermittent affect, but as the hallmark of our existential need of the Other.[22] By recognizing our co-constituted condition, we see that the need and care of the Other reflects the careful tending of our own need that each of us provides for ourselves. In his meditation on Matthew 22:39 ("You shall love the neighbor as yourself") Kierkegaard remarks, "The concept 'neighbor' is actually *the redoubling of your own self...*"[23]

The literal "duplexity" of Jesse and Jane is echoed here. Each recognizes a kindred talent, suffering, and compassion, and each wants to help the other: both Jesse and Jane see their own humanity reflected in the other. Now, as Jane puts it, they are "partners" (she rejects the notion that Walt ever cared for Jesse's actual interests, and asserts that "*I'm* your partner"). But this "redoubling" of the self is not, in this case, enough, since this understanding of mutuality is not shared by any of their other neighbors: Jane's father, Donald, wants her simply to follow his orders; Walt certainly wants Jesse to follow his. In the darkly serendipitous meeting of Walt and Donald at a neighborhood bar, both complain about their children; Walt identifies Jesse as his "nephew." Donald, in describing his frustration with Jane, is on the way to the right idea when he remarks: "Family. You can't give up on them. Never. I mean, what else is there?" Kierkegaard reminds us that there *is* something else, the *neighbor*: had Walt seen Jane as a person, like himself, in mortal need, she would not have died—recall that Walt cries out "No, no, no" as she begins to choke. But, for Walt, a detached perspective prevails: Jane is better—for Walt—out of the way; it isn't, after all, his fault that she injected heroin on this occasion. Nonetheless, Walter weeps as she dies, perhaps recognizing that this act has finally banished him to a windowless, isolated cell of the self, with no means for seeing the absolute connectedness of all persons and events. Walt is sentenced to an endless round of his own desires and devices (much as he will actually be in the safe house in New Hampshire: he is safe from the authorities, but not from himself).

This network of connections is, of course, what Kierkegaard's "redoubled" neighbor recognizes. A person's joys and catastrophes, puzzles and pains, can only be understood in light of the *neighbor's* concerns, because the emerging situation, and the persons within it, is being mutually constructed from moment to moment. If Walt *had* rescued Jane—what then? The new narratives are unknowable, but one outcome is eliminated: the particular tableau given to us by Vince Gilligan, that day, and that moment, in which Jane's father Donald is too overcome with grief to do his job as an air-traffic controller, could not be.

The notion of ongoing "mutual construction" is a favorite existential theme in the novels of Dostoyevsky (a writer who also plays an important role in Levinas' account of intersubjectivity).[24] In *The Brothers Karamazov*, the character Father Zossima provides a sermon about our intersubjective condition, lessons he in turn learned from his brother, Markel. On his deathbed, Markel had an ontological insight: first, as he put it, "…every one is responsible to all men for all men and for everything."[25] In acknowledging how every choice we make alters the existential state of play, a person must take responsibility for the way that things now are. Father Zossima puts it this way: "…all is like an ocean, all is flowing and blending; a touch in one place sets up movement at the other end of the earth."[26]

Walt, after the airline collision, is quick to deny that he—or anyone else—is culpable for what happened. In "No Mas," Walt is asked to speak to a gymnasium filled with confused and grieving high school students. One girl asks, "I just keep asking myself, why did this happen? I mean, if there's a God and all… Why does he allow all those innocent people to die for no reason?" Walt tells the stunned assembly that they must "look on the bright side" (it's only the fiftieth worst air disaster in aviation history, and a "tie" at that), and reminds them that "People move on." Jesse asks Walt if he knows that Jane's father Donald is in fact the air traffic controller responsible for the mid-air crash; Walt answers, "*You* are not responsible…there are many factors in play there—I blame the government." Jesse, now better attuned to thinking about who he is and what he's doing (not necessarily for the better, as it happens), replies, "You either run from things or face them, Mr. White."

Mr. White is getting better and better at avoiding his place in these developing disasters, but Jesse has always had some sense of being the "existential neighbor." Father Zossima exhorts his listeners to be careful at all times, especially around children: "Every day and every hour, every minute, walk round yourself and watch yourself, and see that your image is a seemly one. You pass by a little child, you pass by, spiteful, with ugly words, with wrathful heart, but he has seen you, and your image…may remain in his defenseless heart. You don't know it, but you may have sown an evil seen in him and it may grow…"[27] Jesse is particularly careful with children: recall the filthy and untended boy in the care of Spooge and his addled wife. Jesse teaches the boy to play "peekaboo," and makes him a marshmallow fluff sandwich when he says "hungry." After the *Grand Guignol* demise of Spooge under a stolen ATM machine, Jesse makes sure that the boy is safely away from the scene, wrapped in a blanket, waiting for the police. "You have a good rest of your life, kid," Jesse tells him. Maybe he will.

But not Walt. In the series' final moment, as he collapses in a meth lab—faintly smiling?—and there is some relief in the camera giving us the longer view, with the police now swarming the compound. We wish to get further away from this face, still absorbed in whatever triumphs or setbacks Walt's last thoughts circle around. More panning back, perhaps in time, and now we can see the mural Jane painted on her bedroom wall: herself, floating in space, a pink teddy bear flying high above her.

It is good to want to get away from Walt's face filling the screen, since we haven't seen this face as we should. More to the point: we haven't wanted this respite *enough*. That sentence, composed of episode titles, can now be read: "737 Down Over Albuquerque." In the first episode of Season Two, surely the title "737" was a reference to Walt's calculation that he only needed $737,000 to get out of the meth-making business (the pun here is irresistible)? And those black and white opening sequences, each with a few more details: the White's own swimming pool, glasses that look like Walt's, two body bags in the driveway (surely Jesse and Walt!). We viewers are always looking out for the welfare, or fate, of our characters, until our own self-involved anticipation—*what will happen to our players?*—finally explodes in the sky. Those expectations, teased out of us by the plotting of Season Two, are revealing. Even though the action necessarily focuses on a set of characters, they too belong to a wider world. The actions of Jesse and Walt—and Gus, and Mike, and Jane, and Hank, and Skyler, and Elliot, and Walt Jr., and—*everyone*—are always in play, on the move, and, in each case, "all are responsible for all."

NOTES

1. Aristotle, *Poetics*, trans. Ingram Bywater (New York: Random House, 1941), 1460.
2. David Segal, "The Dark Art of *Breaking Bad*." *New York Times*, last modified July 6, 2011. Web.
3. Edmund Husserl, *Ideas: General Introduction to a Pure Phenomenology and to a Phenomenological Philosophy 2*, trans. F. Kersten (The Hague: Martinus Nijhoff, 1983), 55–61.
4. Maurice Merleau-Ponty, *Signs*, trans. R. McCleary (Evanston, Illinois: Northwestern University Press, 1964), 163.
5. Dan Zahavi claims that Husserl wrote more about intersubjectivity that any of the later phenomenologists. *Husserl's Phenomenology*, 109.
6. Ibid., 111.
7. G.W.F. Hegel, *The Phenomenology of Spirit*, trans. A. V. Miller (Oxford: Oxford University Press, 1977), 111.
8. Ibid., 113–115.
9. Jean-Paul Sartre, *Being and Nothingness: An Essay on Phenomenological Ontology*, trans. Hazel Barnes (London: Methuen, 1958), 360.
10. Ibid., 332. This illustration, I would argue, tells us far more about Sartre's own picture of intersubjectivity as essentially one of conflict than it does about Heideggerian *Mitsein*; Heidegger would no doubt point out that Sartre's focus on consciousness and its positing activity—the thematizing of 'goal to be attained'—begins in precisely the wrong place.
11. According to Vince Gilligan, Season Two is the only season that was plotted from end to beginning ("Vince Gilligan Walks Us Through Season Four of *Breaking Bad*," *AV Club* interview, October 10, 2011): the far-flung and wholly unanticipated consequences of actions is the signature of this set of episodes.

12. A pool, as James Meeks remarks, where no one is ever seen swimming, "but which will over time receive all kinds of substances (money, vomit, a false eyeball from an exploding plane)..." The pool, empty of water in the series' finale, has become a skateboard rink for kids breaking into the White's ruined yard. *London Review of Books*, January 3, 2013, 9.

13. Edmund Husserl, *The Crisis of European Sciences and Transcendental Phenomenology*, trans. David Carr (Evanston: Northwestern University Press, 1970), 295.

14. Ibid., 336, emphasis mine.

15. Emmanuel Levinas, *Basic Philosophical Writings*, 8.

16. Levinas, *Ethics and Infinity*, 97, 85.

17. Ibid., 96, emphasis mine.

18. Levinas, *Basic Philosophical Writings*, 60.

19. Levinas, *Ethics and Infinity*, 97, emphasis mine.

20. Levinas, *Basic Philosophical Writings*, ed. A. T. Peperzak, Simon Critchley, and Robert Bernasconi (Bloomington, IN: Indiana University Press, 1996), 81.

21. Søren Kierkegaard, *Works of Love*, trans. H. V. Hong and E. H. Hong (New York: Harper & Brothers, 1962), 55, emphasis mine.

22. As Jamie Ferreira points out, "Levinas' preference for the term 'responsibility,' rather than 'love' for the neighbor, is understandable. The word 'love' can too easily fail to portray what is at stake..." She goes on to argue that Kierkegaard's analysis of love for the neighbor adumbrates Levinas' notion of a responsibility that is recognized as an imperative that is absolute: "there is something severe in this love; this love is commanded." *Love's Grateful Striving: A Commentary on Kierkegaard's Works of Love* (Oxford: Oxford University Press, 2001), 48–9.

23. Kierkegaard, *Works of Love*, 21, emphasis mine. Levinas concurs: "In the impossibility of evading the neighbor's call, in the impossibility of distancing ourselves—perhaps we approach the other in contingency, but henceforth we are not free to distance ourselves from him or her...my responsibility for everyone can manifest itself while also limiting itself." *Basic Philosophical Works*, 95.

24. Levinas remarks, "I am I in the sole measure that I am responsible, a non-interchangeable I...It is in this precise sense that 'Dostoyevsky said, "We are all responsible for all men before all, and I more than all the others."'" *Ethics and Infinity*, trans. Richard A. Cohen (Pittsburgh: Duquesne University Press, 1985), 101.

25. Fyodor Dostoyevsky, *The Brothers Karamazov*, 344. Levinas concurs: "In the impossibility of evading the neighbor's call, in the impossibility of distancing ourselves—perhaps we approach the other in contingency, but henceforth we are not free to distance ourselves from him or her...[in our] responsibility for everyone..." *Basic Philosophical Works*, 95.

26. Fyodor Dostoyevsky, *The Brothers Karamazov*, trans. Constance Garnett (New York: Random House, 1950), 383–4.

27. Ibid., 383.

CHAPTER 16

Theater of the Absurd: *Breaking Bad* as Edifying Philosophy

Kevin S. Decker

In his eponymous 1960 essay, critic Martin Esslin coined the term "Theater of the Absurd" to describe the drama of Samuel Beckett, Jean Genet, Arthur Adamov, and Eugene Ionesco, among others. In attempting to put his finger on the trigger of the mental anguish at the heart of these playwrights' postwar work, Esslin declared:

> Ours being, more than most others, an age of transition, it displays a bewilderingly stratified picture: medieval beliefs still held and overlaid by eighteenth-century rationalism and mid-nineteenth century Marxism, rocked by sudden volcanic eruptions of prehistoric fanaticisms and primitive tribal cults. Each of these components of the cultural pattern of the age finds its own artistic expression. The Theatre of the Absurd, however, can be seen as the reflection of what seems to be the attitude most genuinely representative of our own time. The hallmark of this attitude is its sense that the certitudes and unshakable basic assumptions of former ages have been swept away, that they have been tested and found wanting, that they have been discredited as cheap and somewhat childish illusions. The decline of religious faith was masked until the end of the Second World War by the substitute religions of faith in progress, nationalism, and various totalitarian fallacies. All this was shattered by the war. By 1942, Albert Camus was calmly putting the question why, since life had lost all meaning, man should not seek escape in suicide.[1]

While Camus is the great poet of absurdity in works such as *The Stranger* and "The Myth of Sisyphus," his equation of absurdity with meaninglessness can be philosophically deepened by adding to it insights from fellow existentialists

K.S. Decker (✉)
Eastern Washington University, Cheney, WA, USA

© The Author(s) 2017
K.S. Decker et al. (eds.), *Philosophy and Breaking Bad*,
DOI 10.1007/978-3-319-40343-4_16

Simone de Beauvoir and Jean-Paul Sartre, as the first part of this chapter will show. In all three thinkers, absurdity can be understood in terms of the acknowledgment of contingency in human relationships to the natural and social worlds. Inauthenticity, then, becomes the lack of acknowledgment of contingency and the ignorance of absurdity.

Contingency is brought to the fore in the work of Richard Rorty in his *Philosophy and the Mirror of Nature, Contingency, Irony and Solidarity*, and a number of essays. Rorty gives us a new vocabulary for coping with the absurd, a vocabulary tied to treating the recognition of contingency as the primary reason for the "loss of all meaning in life" that Esslin offers.

In his work, Rorty offers novel and controversial interpretations of three thinkers who he sees as the most important philosophers of the twentieth century. Rorty writes of John Dewey (1859–1952), Ludwig Wittgenstein (1889–1951), and Martin Heidegger (1889–1976):

> All three make it as difficult as possible to take their thought as expressing views on traditional philosophical problems, or as making constructive proposals for philosophy as a cooperative and progressive discipline. They make fun of the classic picture of man, the picture which contains systematic philosophy, the search for universal commensuration in a final vocabulary. They hammer away at the holistic point that words take their meanings from other words rather than by virtue of their representative character, and the corollary that vocabularies acquire their privileges from the men who use them rather than from their transparency to the real.[2]

Rorty's view of the significance of contingency is informed by his post-linguistic turn in the understanding of how words, sentences, and vocabularies are used to constitute a social reality. According to Rorty, the recognition of contingency as pervasive in the world is the central insight of naturalism, "the view that *anything* might have been otherwise, that there can be no conditionless conditions."[3] Through a look at Rorty's interpretation of certain absurd implications of these "thinkers of contingency" in the third part of this chapter, we'll see how the linguistic dimension of contingent relations calls for a rethinking of traditional philosophical concerns. In addition, we'll have framed a new understanding of the value of freedom in an absurd and contingent universe, an understanding that draws from the tradition of existentialism.

Breaking Bad adopts a darkly, playful attitude toward our comfort level with contingency, which is typically quite low. There are several senses of the term "contingency," but only two that concern us here. First, Rorty's understanding of contingency encompasses the idea that there is no certainty in events, while at the same time asserting that "we are nothing save the words we use,"[4] and the words we use are themselves contingent upon a mixture of history and relatively free choices of individuals. The other philosophically interesting sense of "contingency" is less philosophically weighty but closer to common sense:

that all future events are possible but cannot be anticipated except with varying degrees of certainty, not certainty itself.

This becomes important in the second season of *Breaking Bad*, for example, when episodes such as "Seven Thirty-Seven" and "Down" begin with flash-forwards of the infamous pink teddy bear, workers in hazmat suits, and body bags—all of which, as it turns out, are recovered from the White's pool and property. As the main plots of Season Two converge with the flash-forwards of the aftermath of the crash of Wayfarer Flight 515 with a charter plane, the unpredictable series of causes and effects that led to the crash are slowly revealed. The failure of air traffic controller whose distracted depression caused the crash, Donald Margolis, can be traced back to Walt's decision not to save Margolis' daughter, Jane, as she chokes on vomit during a drug overdose. We, the audience, are clearly supposed to consider the tragedy in the air yet one more episode of violence to be laid at Walt's feet. In the third part of this chapter, I use Sartre's phenomenological analysis of human action to illustrate why we might want to question this conclusion and what that tells us about contingency and the absurd.

In the fourth and final part, I return to *Breaking Bad* as a latter-day Theater of the Absurd, overshadowed as it is by Walter White's ongoing confrontation with his obsessions and his own mortality. Walt's absurd, five-season journey begins with him understanding the resonances of the thought that everything one is and everything one has accomplished must finally be negated by death. But how do we spend the time between now and then? The eternally rock-rolling protagonist of Camus' "Myth of Sisyphus" provides a metaphor for Walt's career as a methamphetamine cook and drug kingpin who acknowledges the absurdity of both the form of, and the manner in which he sets out to leave a legacy for his family.

ABSURDITY, OR THE MYSTERY IN BROAD DAYLIGHT

Many of us are familiar with the post-mortem plight of Sisyphus and his stone; in the one task given to him to make eternity meaningful, both Sisyphus and the stone cannot rest. But equally interesting are the conditions that brought Sisyphus to this point. First is the character's own insouciance: Camus cites Homer that "Sisyphus was the wisest and most prudent of mortals. According to another tradition, however, he was disposed to practice the professional of highwayman."[5] Camus sees no contradiction between the two. Sisyphus courted danger by joking about the gods and was reputed to have stolen their secrets; he put Death in chains.

This is all in stark contrast to Walter White: in the pilot, he's "apparently watching his cholesterol" and subjected to veggie bacon. His chemistry students at the high school are listless and unengaged, despite his enthusiasm in teaching; he works part-time at a car wash where he's belittled by his know-nothing boss, Bogdan.

When it comes to the absurdity of existence, there is no difference between the life of Sisyphus and that of Walter White. They are both "absurd heroes" as much through their passions as through their torture.[6] Camus explains that we know nothing about the mental or emotional states of Sisyphus in the underworld, rolling his rock, only that "if this myth is tragic, that is because its hero is conscious. Where would his torture be, indeed, if at every step the hope of succeeding upheld him?"[7] On the other hand, the entirety of *Breaking Bad* is Walter White's reaction, complex and often subtle, to his diagnosis of lung cancer. With a son who has cerebral palsy and a new daughter on the way, Walt finds it inconceivable that his family can go on without even his paltry school district salary. He needs cash and fast. So he looks up former student Jesse Pinkman:

> **Walt:** Short speech. You lost your partner today. What's his name? Emilio? Emilio is going to prison. The DEA took all your money, your lab. You got nothing. Square one. But you know the business. And I know the chemistry. I'm thinking maybe you and I could partner up.
> **Jesse:** You want to cook crystal meth? You? You and, uh and me?
> **Walt:** That's right. Either that or I turn you in. ("Pilot")

In some ways, Walt is successful in his goal to provide for his family after his impending death (albeit by a bullet, not by cancer): they secure about $10 million from Walt's machinations against Elliot, the co-founder of Gray Matter.[8] The irony is that this amount isn't part of the $80 million that Walt had in the storage unit ("Felina"). As show creator Vince Gilligan paraphrases Saul Goodman's advice about the futility of the entire enterprise in the penultimate episode: "You'll never get it past the cops, and if somehow you manage to get to your family, the cops will find out about it and they'll seize it because it's drug money. And if miracle of miracles, you manage to get it past the cops, your family is not going to take it because it's from you and they hate you. Especially your son, who is primarily the one you're doing this for, so it's an impossibility."[9] Seen in this way, all Walt's efforts, his threats, his violence, and even his death are meaningless in a larger context—that is, they are absurd.

Yet Walt's diagnosis and his decision to "break bad" are a particularly intriguing example of Sartre's notion that we are "condemned to be free." This implies that only the refusal to choose for oneself—which is the same, for Sartre, as *choosing oneself*—is an abdication of freedom. We are condemned to be free, not (as the pessimist might have it) to fail and not (as the optimist might claim) to succeed. "Success is not important to freedom," Sartre explains. "The discussion which opposes common sense to [views of] philosophers stems here from a misunderstanding: the empirical and popular concept of 'freedom' which has been produced by historical, political, and moral circumstances is equivalent to 'the ability to obtain the ends chosen.' The technical and philosophical concept of freedom, the only one which we are considering here, means only the autonomy of choice."[10] And despite five years of deaths, violence, losses, and setbacks, it's clear that Walt has embraced this autonomy when he tells Skyler in the final episode, "I did it for me. I liked it. I was good at it. And I was really—I was alive."

The absurdity-as-meaninglessness of Walt's humdrum existence before his drug enterprises seems to be contrasted with the danger and intrigue in assuming the mantle of "Heisenberg." This street pseudonym is significant in our context for two reasons. First, it's meaningless to both drug lords like Tuco and Hank Schrader and the DEA; in the latter case, decoding the significance of the name as that of a prominent physicist might have brought Hank to confront Walt much earlier. However, the name "Heisenberg" is popularly associated with the "uncertainty principle" that says that the momentum of a particle and its position in space cannot both be precisely measured at the same time. The essential duality of the two basic physical properties of the particles constituting all matter is analogous to Walt's duality as law-abiding family man, on the one hand, and meth cook and dealer, on the other. But Heisenberg's uncertainty principle also seems to be confirmation that there is something irrational at the core of the universe, something absurd—that is, it offers the notion that indeterminacy is the basis for all further physical determinations. Of course, this is the central doctrine of quantum mechanics, of which Heisenberg was the originator.[11]

Ultimately, Walt's words to Skyler in the final episode about "doing it for himself" reveal that it is only through willing himself free—through wit, violence, and force of will—that he has found self-realization. For Sartre and Simone de Beauvoir, Walt's recognition of this signals his acknowledgment of the *transcendence* of his subjectivity. The individual who, like Camus' Sisyphus, sees their world and their place in it as absurd, confronts a *double negation*: first, the complex and potentially infinite world, organized as it is in terms of series of causes and effects, is nonetheless without the impress of a creator and therefore lacks an ultimate purpose. Yet humans—as the origin of nothingness in Sartre's work—are precisely the sort of questioning creatures that philosophers have seen them to be since Thales and Socrates. "...[T]he questioner, by the very fact that he is questioning, posits himself as in a state of indetermination; he *does not know* whether the reply will be affirmative or negative," Sartre says.[12] Furthermore, the effort to gain knowledge through questioning points to a negation at the heart of every knowing subject: the search for true knowledge is an admission of a *lack of being* in the questioner. "It would be in vain to deny that negation appears on the original basis of a relation of man to the world," Sartre continues. "The world does not disclose its non-beings to one who has not first posited them as possibilities."[13] As the kind of creatures whose intentional consciousness is itself a negation (and as such, our "selves" are not constituted by an unchanging essence or spirit), consciousness—as Husserl pointed out—is always consciousness *of* something. Consciousness is always pointing away toward something that is its object: a thing in the world, a memory, an anticipation of future events. In this activity, we are constantly transcending our subjectivity, a process we can see played out on our screens, especially in the first two seasons of *Breaking Bad*, as Walt is confronted by situations that draw from him responses as surprising to his enemies as they are to the audience. One of the most memorable of these scenes occurs in "Crazy Handful of Nothin'" after Jesse fails to make a deal with Tuco and is beaten for his troubles. Then Walt arrives at Tuco's building:

> **Tuco**: What's your name?
> **Walt**: Heisenberg.
> **Tuco**: Heisenberg. Okay. Have a seat, Heisenberg.
> **Walt**: I don't imagine I'll be here very long.
> **Tuco**: No? Alright, be that way. It's your meeting. Why don't you start talking and tell me what you want.
> **Walt**: Fifty thousand dollars.
> **Tuco**: (*laughs*) Oh man, fifty Gs? How you figure that?
> **Walt**: Thirty-five for the pound of meth you stole and another fifteen for my partner's pain and suffering.
> **Tuco**: Partner? (*puts out cigarette on his tongue*) Oh yeah, I remember that little bitch. So you must be daddy.
> **Tuco**: Let me get this straight. I steal your dope. I beat the piss out of your mule boy! And then you walk in here and you bring me more meth? (*laughs*) Whew, that's a brilliant plan, *ese.*
> **Bodyguard**: Brilliant.
> **Walt**: You got one part of that wrong. (*picks up one of the crystals*) This is not meth. (*Walt turns around quickly and throws it toward the ground. The crystal explodes, shooting things out of the windows*).
> **Tuco**: Are you fucking nuts?!
> **Walt**: You wanna find out?
> **Tuco**: No, no, Gonzo, calma, calma, calma. You got balls, I'll give you that. Alright, alright, I'll give you your money. That crystal that your partner brought me…it sold faster than $10 ass in TJ. Let's say you bring me another pound next week.
> **Walt**: Money up front.
> **Tuco**: Alright, money up front. Sometimes you gotta rob to keep your riches. Just as long as we got an understanding.
> **Walt**: One pound is not gonna cut it. You have to take two.
> **Tuco**: (*laughs*) Orale. Hey, what is that shit?
> **Walt**: Fulminated mercury. With a little tweak of chemistry.

One of the charms of *Breaking Bad* is that we can't easily predict where Walt's quest for transcendence will take him next. In exploring this concept of transcendence in her 1944 essay "Pyrrhus and Cineas," Simone de Beauvoir writes: "The paradox of the human condition is that every end can be surpassed, and yet, the project defines the end as an end. In order to surpass an end, it must first have been projected as something that is not to be surpassed. Man has no other way of existing."[14]

Fundamentally, Walt seeks control, while Jesse seeks connection in *Breaking Bad*. The absurdity of their efforts toward transcendence is that they, like all of us, strive to reach a stable equilibrium in which all their projects have come to fruition. But this can never be, Beauvoir tells us:

> Man can neither indefinitely reduce his being, nor expand it to infinity. He cannot find rest, and yet what is this movement that leads him nowhere? One finds the same antinomy in the realm of action as in that of speculation. Any stopping is impossible because transcendence is a perpetual surpassing. But an indefinite project is absurd since it leads to nothing. Here man dreams of an ideal symmetrical to that of the unconditioned God called for by speculative thought. He demands and unconditioned end for his acts such that it could not be surpassed, a term at once infinite and complete in which his transcendence would grasp itself anew without limiting itself. He cannot identify himself with infinity. But within his singular situation can he destine himself to do it?[15]

Sartre and Beauvoir both affirm the final question, albeit in very different ways. Beauvoir locates the source of authentic transcendence in our relationships with other people: "…[E]very man needs the freedom of other men and, in a sense, always wants it, even though he may be a tyrant," she writes. "The only thing he fails to do is assume honestly the consequences of such a wish."[16] For Sartre, however, our ethical obligations are not to others so much as they are to become the sort of person that others might want to be as well. In this way, Sartre takes seriously the notion of *facticity* as an obstacle, not to transcending our own subjectivity *per se*, but to transcending it in such a way as to make a moral or ethical connection with an other.

"Because I Say So"

In *Contingency, Irony, and Solidarity*, Richard Rorty offers interpretations of three different facets of contingency, at least as viewed from the perspective of post-linguistic turn philosophy. For Rorty, the key existentialist value of freedom is to be found in the recognition of contingency. Over the last two centuries of Anglo-European civilization, he claims, the centrality of imagination rather than reason has been found to be the key to freedom, and thus truth has been treated by many thinkers as "made" rather than "found." "The German idealists, the French revolutionaries, and the Romantic poets had in common," he writes, "a dim sense that human beings whose language changed so that they no longer spoke of themselves as responsible to nonhuman powers would thereby become a new kind of human beings."[17] As an anti-foundationalist and anti-essentialist in this same tradition, Rorty offers playful inversions of dependency relations that have structured much of Western philosophy; these are reversals of theories like Spinoza's, in which modes and attributes were dependent upon the concept of necessary substance, or Hegel's view that the transitory and historically contextualized forms taken by *Geist* are all dialectical outgrowths of the necessity of Spirit's full self-consciousness at the end of history.

So in pointing out the contingency of *language*, or how (supposedly time-less, unchanging) truth is dependent upon (historically variable) languages and their vocabularies, Rorty is rejecting the idea of a nonhuman—perhaps divine—"perfect" language in which truth might inhere necessarily:

> To say that the world is out there, that it is not our creation, is to say, with com-mon sense, that most things in space and time are the effects of causes which do not include human mental states. To say that truth is not out there is simply to say that where there are no sentences there is no truth, that sentences are elements of human languages, and that human languages are human creations. Truth can-not be out there—cannot exist independently of the human mind—because sen-tences cannot so exist, or be out there.[18]

Rorty is led to the conclusion that "the truth is *not* out there" by acceptance of two other premises: one is a thoroughgoing *holism* regarding language, in which the truth of each sentence depends upon the acceptance of the truth or falsity of other sentences, *ad infinitum*. The other is a premise that accepts that the potential verifiability or falsifiability of individual sentences has always been used as the paradigm of truthfulness as correspondence to independent reality, but that when we move to the level of vocabularies that make those sentences *meaningful*, we lose the track of truth as correspondence. "When we consider examples of alternative language games—the vocabulary of ancient Athenian politics versus Jefferson's, the moral vocabulary of Saint Paul versus Freud's, ... —it is difficult to think of the world as making one of these better than another, or the world as deciding between them."[19]

And he offers an interpretation of Wittgenstein on language that supports this thesis about the contingency of language: according to Rorty, the early, "unpragmatic" Wittgenstein—author of the *Tractatus Logico-Philosophicus*—held the presupposition in common with Russell, Frege, and others that the meaning of language was to be found in its power to reliably refer to features of objective existence. To make this view work, however, Wittgenstein and his fel-lows had to *reify language*—that is, to specify a set of terms that provide "their own conditions of linguistic accessibility," providing context and explanation (Rorty calls it "describability") to mere empirical truths.[20] However, because of a turn in his thinking between the 1921 *Tractatus* and the publication in 1953 of *Philosophical Investigations*, Wittgenstein had rejected such a theory of objective reference in favor of the idea that words and sentences gain their meaning through the roles they play in "language games," for Rorty "a set of indefinitely expansible social practices, not a bounded whole whose periphery might be 'shown'" by *a priori* terms providing their own conditions of linguis-tic accessibility.[21] The result is a thoroughgoing holism: words as elements of language games take their meaning from other words and other social prac-tices, not from some basic representing function.

Breaking Bad as a whole is indicative of this holistic view of language. Although he admits that "*Breaking Bad* ... is arguably the most profound, symbolically-rich program ever presented on the small screen," Pearson Moore, author of the show guidebook *Breaking Blue*, also points to the significance of Walt's admission to a student in the pilot:

> Chemistry is—well, technically, chemistry is the study of matter. But I prefer to see it as the study of change. Electrons change their energy levels. Molecules: Molecules change their bond. Elements: They combine and change into compounds. Well, that's all of life, right? ("Pilot")

Moore's study of symbolism in *Breaking Bad* highlights the fact that valid interpretation of the meaning of its various languages—colors, character behaviors, objects—may hold true for a season or merely an episode only. "A character's behavior and her entire value system may change radically in the course of a season or two. Wardrobe changes, even from one scene to the next, may carry tremendous, context-relative significance and value," Moore writes.[22]

We return to Rorty with the idea of the contingency of *selfhood*, or the way in which our concept of the (supposedly timeless, unchanging) core of our being, formerly identified with "soul" or "personality," is dependent upon (historically variable) causes and events. "Neither a constant external reality nor an unfailing interior source of inspiration forms a background for such dramas" of an individual human life, he claims.[23] Both familiar approaches to the self of "nature" and "nurture" fly from contingency to light upon some unchanging facts about human nature, and should be rejected. Self-knowledge is, rather, self-creation. Again taking up the perspective that language creates the only human reality, he says that "confronting one's contingency, tracking one's causes home, is identical with the process of inventing a new language— that is, of thinking up some new metaphors. For any *literal* description of one's individuality … will necessarily fail."[24] Rorty's explanation of what a literal description of one's individuality would entail is startlingly similar to one of the senses of "facticity" we looked at in the last section: individuality is by definition idiosyncratic or private, so any attempt to classify it as "a specimen reiterating a type, a copy or replica of something which has already been identified" must necessarily fail.[25]

Rorty recommends Martin Heidegger, along with Nietzsche, William James, and even the poet Philip Larkin, for offering a "pathos of finitude" that supports the idea of the contingency of selfhood. The "pragmatic" Heidegger of 1927s *Being and Time* states that "the person is not a Thing, not a substance, not an object," and thus eludes categorization and determination by "objectifying" sciences such as anthropology, psychology, and biology.[26] The character of authenticity of a person (or, more commonly in Heidegger, *Dasein*) explicitly involves negation, as the "mineness" of the self is found in its "hav[ing] lost itself and not yet won itself."[27] Sartre, deeply influenced by Heidegger's *Being and Time*, takes up the idea of the self as essentially a negation, resistant to *determination* by facticity and to *literal* description:

> The *self* therefore represents an ideal distance within the immanence of the subject in relation to himself, a way of *not being his own coincidence* of escaping identity while positing it as unity—in short, of being in a perpetually unstable equilibrium between identity as absolute cohesion without a trace of diversity and unity as a synthesis of multiplicity.[28]

Sartre's view helps answer a question, one that Rorty's theory leaves open, about how selves are changed by their recognition of contingency. Sartre would explain the freedom found in contingency by the fact that consciousness is not wholly free in one important sense. The self cannot overcome its form as negation, yet despite this it isn't constrained in its authentic engagement with the world or with itself when it adopts the questioning stance that is the "human evidence" of the negative nature of the self.

Walt, suffering from issues of self-esteem, resentment (particularly of Fring, of Skyler's choices, and his loss of a stake in Gray Matter Technologies), and control, is certainly one of the most reflective and questioning characters in contemporary television. His transformation from a mild-mannered chemistry professor fearful of the future to a self-assured narco kingpin demonstrates a radical fluidity of self. Yet, it is the dedication to which Walt applies himself to his freely chosen project of illegally making money for his family—a project that later turns into a personal quest for power and authority—that best illuminates the contingency of the self, at least as Sartre understands it. For Sartre, facticity, or the autonomous describings and redescribings of the world that are both outside human consciousness and yet impact the choices of that consciousness, may partially determine the course of my life (Walt's cancer is the obvious factical determinant here); however, Walt also has a Sartrean "fundamental project," that "original relation which the for-itself chooses with its facticity and with the world."[29] It concerns "my total being-in-the-world," ordering all my other ends and giving them internal coherence and meaning.[30]

In Sartre's view, however, human subjectivity (*"pour-soi,"* or "for-itself"), mediated by the body, exists in an environment: the *"en-soi"* (in-itself). The "in-tself" roughly coincides with what we consider to be the elements of objective reality, while the *pour-soi* represents a healthy subjectivity. The reason why these are only rough coincidences is that Sartre is not interested in creating new words for the subject/object distinction but rather wants to phenomenologically distinguish between two kinds of appearances that we distinguish, not cognitively but by the different moods and visceral and moral emotions they present us with. Their fundamental difference, however, is that freedom is a fact *about* and *present to* the *pour-soi*, while the concept of "freedom" is not one that applies to the world of the *en-soi* (note that this is different than saying the *en-soi* as the natural world is causally determined). Contrary to Rorty's sense of freedom as the ability to endlessly redescribe "reality," Sartre holds that there is a brute, alien, and unresponsive dimension to the world that resists any description whatsoever.[31] Beyond this, the Sartrean distinction between the in-itself (*en-soi*) and the for-itself (*pour-soi*) attempts to limn the difference between the factors in life we can control and those we cannot control, and therefore where our responsibilities lie. One of the most important influences Sartre's ontology has made on his fellow existentialists and phenomenologists is that reality has *value* fully, if invisibly, shot through it.

These views of the contingency of language and selfhood can be used to extend existentialist themes to contemporary criticism of philosophy and culture, including the criticism of popular culture like *Breaking Bad*. Rorty believes that if we recognize the contingency in our own use of language, our own selfhood, and our social environments, we discover the degree to which we are free to attempt to alter those parts of "human nature" that we formerly took to be unchanging and inflexible.

The Elusiveness of Facticity

However, this discussion about contingency and freedom may appear to be far-fetched when we apply it to the universe of *Breaking Bad*. Even if we ignored the fact that what occurs on our screens is fully determined by the writers, actors, and production team, and tried to wholly immerse ourselves in the lives and events of Walt, Jesse, Skyler, and Hank, it may seem as if they inhabit a universe in which subtle and not-so-subtle forces are constantly at work, allowing the appearance but not the substance of freedom. Or perhaps we believe—along the lines of the doctrine of original sin—that the free choices of those who came before us doom us to suffering "the sins of the father." Pat Robertson, an evangelical Christian and host of *The 700 Club*, infamously invoked this kind of reasoning when he blamed American iniquity (specifically, homosexual behavior and abortions) for the devastation wrought by Hurricane Katrina. "[H]ave we found we are unable somehow to defend ourselves against some of the attacks that are coming against us, either by terrorists or now by natural disaster?" Robertson asked his television audience. "Could they be connected in some way?"[32] And even with all the possibilities discussed by creator Vince Gilligan with the writers for the *Breaking Bad* finale in 2013, it seemed clear that an ending to the show that did not in some way engage with Walt's choices, offering up some form of redemption, salvation, or damnation, was going to be unsatisfactory to the audience.

Consider this crucial series of events from *Breaking Bad*, most of which happen in the episodes "Phoenix," "ABQ," and "No Más":

1. Jesse Pinkman rents an apartment from Jane Margolis.
2. Jesse and Jane become an "item."
3. Jesse and Jane enjoy crystal meth, pot and heroin speedballs together.
4. Because he's high, Jesse causes Walt to nearly miss a big meth deal with Fring and to miss the birth of Walt's daughter.
5. Walt withholds Jesse's share of the profits from the big meth deal.
6. Jane blackmails Walt into turning over Jesse's share.
7. Jesse and Jane enjoy heroin speedballs together.

8. Walt breaks into Jesse's apartment, finds Jesse and Jane strung out, and while shaking Jesse to wake him, Jane flips on her back.
9. Jane begins to asphyxiate on her own vomit from an overdose.
10. Walt thinks about saving Jane, but ultimately withholds action.
11. Jane dies of asphyxiation.
12. Jane's father, Donald, becomes depressed because of her death.
13. While at his job as a flight traffic controller, Donald's mind wanders to Jesse and he fails to notice two intersecting flight paths.
14. Wayfarer Flight 515 collides with a charter plane, killing 167 people.

Although many fans on *Breaking Bad* discussion boards point to Walt's decision in (10) as being the moment at which they stopped sympathizing with him, and while the audience in general was clearly supposed to reflect on the causal connection between (10) and (14), the moral responsibility that accrues to Walt for the air collision is far from beyond doubt. The set of circumstances in (1–14) above is but one contingent way of describing these events, and the interpretation of Walt's character that casts aspersions on his decision to let an innocent person die to "free" Jesse from her grasp is but one contingent description of Walt's self.

The language of freedom and responsibility granted to us by the materialist, Christian, liberal democratic society that is America in the twenty-first century is not particularly helpful in evaluating these last few claims. In *The Ethics of Ambiguity*, Simone de Beauvoir provides a different language:

> Every man is originally free, in the sense that he spontaneously casts himself into the world. But if we consider this spontaneity in its facticity, it appears to us only as a pure contingency, an upsurging as stupid as the clinamen of the Epicurean atom which turned up at any moment whatsoever from any direction whatsoever. And it was quite necessary for the atom to arrive somewhere. But its movement was not justified by this result which had not been chosen. It remained absurd. Thus, human spontaneity always projects itself toward something.[33]

Since in the last section we identified the objects of Walt's spontaneous choices in terms of his "fundamental project"—money for his family and power and control for himself—we can make sense of his decision not to save Jane within this context. On the other hand, as observers of Jane's death, we see Walt vacillate for minutes, turning slightly toward the bed and then away from it, again and again. Given this, *when* was it Walt's spontaneous choice to withhold action? As observers, the fact that Walt finally lands on allowing her to die is absurd—a "swerve" (clinamen) of his original intention in coming to talk sense into Jesse—and, as such, is fundamentally inexplicable. What happens to Donald Margolis afterward is equally absurd: while we could have anticipated (12) above as a plausible reaction by Donald to his daughter's death, we could not have predicted it—and certainly not (13). Sartre's phrase for the unpredictability of human choices is "what comes from the brute being of the for-itself."[34]

The conversation between two strangers, Jane's father, Donald Margolis, and Walter White in the bar before this scene reveals how the contingency of language produces a tragic, if darkly ironic result:

> **Walt:** So, any advice? Having a daughter. Any advice?
> **Donald:** (*shaking head*) No, not really. Just love them. Just—Yeah. I mean, they are who they are.
> **Walt:** Yeah. I've got this nephew. This nephew who is—I mean, he's an adult. But you can't infantilize them, you can't live their life for them. But still, I mean, there is that frustration. You know, that, God, that frustration that goes along with, you know: "Yes, as a matter of fact, I do know what is best for you, so listen." But of course, they don't. I mean, what do you do with someone like that?
> **Donald:** Family?
> **Walt:** (*hesitates*) Yeah. Family.
> **Donald:** You can't give up on them. Never. I mean, what else is there?

Donald's "you can't give up on them" sums up his troubled relationship with Jane, but at the same time suggests a valid interpretation of Walt's physical reaction: he thinks he must treat Jesse as a member of his own family and do what it takes to convince him that Walt knows what's best for him. The fact that Donald and Walt are ignorant of their hidden connection means that this instance of the contingency of language will pit their intentions directly against one another, with Jane caught in between.

In a sense, then, Donald's advice was a condition for Jane's death. Sartre was a pioneer in insisting that moral evaluations of free agents can neither be actualized or understood without grasping the "situation," or framing conditions of choice and action. "…[T]he *situation*, the common product of the contingency of the in-itself and of freedom, is an ambiguous phenomenon in which it is impossible for the for-itself to distinguish the contribution of freedom from that of the brute existent."[35] Impossible to *distinguish*, but not to *describe*, as individuals from Pat Robertson to fans on discussion boards distressed with Walt in "Phoenix," have discovered.

In the chronological list of events above, I deliberately included (1–7) as background to Jane's death and the mid-air collision. These events—some of which are choices made by Jesse and Jane and some of which, like the minor deviations in the flight paths of Wayfarer 515 and the charter plane, can only be put down to facticity—form the situation for Walt's choice to let Jane die and all the consequences that are conditioned by that event.

> …[T]he fact of not being able *not* to be free is the *facticity* of freedom, and the fact of not being able *not* to exist is its *contingency*. Contingency and facticity are really one; there is a being which freedom has to be in the form of *non-being* (that is, of nihilation). To exist as *the fact* of freedom or to have to be a being in the midst of the world are one and the same thing, and this means that freedom is originally a *relation to the given*.[36]

Without a given situation, Sartre insists, there is neither opportunity nor reason to exercise one's freedom. Walt did so in letting Jane die, and must accept responsibility for that—Sartre and Beauvoir will not allow us to separate our intention from our action in every case of free choice. But Walt is not morally responsible, on the existentialists' view, for the mid-air crash, and although other acts of violence in the show, including the deaths of Gale Boetticher, Hank Schrader, and Steve Gomez have been rather carelessly argued to be Walt's fault, the conditions for their deaths are as much down to the "given" of the factical situations as they are to the free choices of the *Breaking Bad* characters. An absurd conclusion, but that's rather the point.

EDIFYING PHILOSOPHY AS THERAPY FOR ABSURDITY

As you've been reading this chapter, Sisyphus has kept at it, rolling his stone up the hill over and over again, only to see it tumble back to where it started in each instance. Camus tells us, perhaps surprisingly, that "…Sisyphus is the absurd hero. He is, as much through his passions as through his torture. His scorn of the gods, his hatred of death, and his passion for life won him that unspeakable penalty in which the whole being is exerted toward accomplishing nothing. This is the price that must be paid for the passions of this earth."[37] The intervention of contingency into the best-laid plans of Sisyphus—that is, the justice of the gods—meant that in his repetitious task, Sisyphus would have to make his own truth, because the absurdity of his situation quickly revealed to him that there was none to be *found*.

"The pragmatist must avoid saying that truth will win," Rorty says, since we all share only mutual yet contingent starting points for justifying our actions, our thinking, and our ways of life.[38] But if philosophy isn't about finding truth (at least) or setting the conditions for better prediction and control of our lives (as applied sciences do), then what's it good for?

Philosophy shares with broad, deep artifacts of popular culture like *Breaking Bad* the potential to be *edifying* rather than truth-discovering. The practice of philosophizing, as asking questions and offering redescriptions of world and self that make the comfortable seem strange and the strange more comfortable, is for Rorty, as it was for the existentialists, a product of self-cultivation (*Bildung*) without a particular goal or endpoint in sight:

> To say that we become different people, that we "remake" ourselves as we read more, talk more, and write more, is simply a dramatic way of saying that the sentences which become true of us by virtue of such activities are often more important to us than the sentences which become true of us when we drink more, earn more, and so on. The events which make us able to say new and interesting things about ourselves are, in this nonmetaphysical sense, more "essential" to us … than the events which change our shapes or our standards of living.[39]

Seeking truth seems like a public project, while pursuing edification through philosophy and popular culture seems narrowly private. Yet edification is not about self-interest, but instead aimed at expanding the horizons of the self and its community. "…[A]ll human existence is a passion," Sartre writes, "the famous *self-interest* being only one way freely chosen among others to realize this passion." And as Beauvoir emphasizes in her assertions that freedom is social—that when I will my freedom, I will the freedom of all others—this edifying project need not be solipsistic or about navel-gazing. In fact, when the creative team behind challenging and thoughtful television programs like *Breaking Bad* share their passion with the world, they illustrate the ways in which absurdity and contingency, far from urging us toward a quietism about our own agency, can provoke edifying activity (I assume, after all, that is why you're reading this book). In the end, we did it for ourselves.

NOTES

1. Martin Esslin, *The Theatre of the Absurd* (Woodstock, NY: Overlook Press, 1973), 4–5.
2. Richard Rorty, *Philosophy and the Mirror of Nature*, 368.
3. Richard Rorty, "Wittgenstein, Heidegger, and the Reification of Language," in *Essays on Heidegger and Others* (New York: Cambridge University Press, 1991), 55.
4. Richard Rorty, "Heidegger, Contingency and Pragmatism," in *Essays on Heidegger and Others* (New York: Cambridge University Press, 1991), 37.
5. Albert Camus, *The Myth of Sisyphus* (New York: Knopf, 1955), 52.
6. Ibid., 53.
7. Ibid.
8. Dan Snierson, "'Breaking Bad': Creator Vince Gilligan Explains Series Finale," *Entertainment Weekly*, last modified September 30, 2013. Web.
9. Ibid.
10. Jean-Paul Sartre, *Being and Nothingness: An Essay on Phenomenological Ontology*, trans. Hazel Barnes (London: Methuen, 1958), 621–22.
11. See Roberto Torretti, *The Philosophy of Physics* (New York: Cambridge University Press, 1999), chapter six.
12. Sartre, *Being and Nothingness* 36.
13. Ibid., 38.
14. Simon de Beauvoir, "Pyrrhus and Cineas," trans. Marybeth Timmermann, in *Simone de Beauvoir: Philosophical Writings*, ed. Margaret A. Simons (Urbana, IL: University of Illinois Press, 2004), 113.
15. Ibid., 102.
16. Simon de Beauvoir, *The Ethics of Ambiguity* (New York: Citadel, 2000), 71.
17. Rorty, *Contingency, Irony, and Solidarity*, 7.
18. Ibid., 5.
19. Ibid., 4.
20. Rorty, "Wittgenstein, Heidegger and the Reification of Language," 55.
21. Ibid., 57.

22. Pearson Moore, "Breaking Down Breaking Bad," *Forum*, last updated January 15, 2015. Web.
23. Richard Rorty, *Contingency, Irony, and Solidarity* (New York: Cambridge University Press, 1989), 29.
24. Ibid., 27.
25. Ibid., 28.
26. Heidegger, *Being and Time*, 73/H48.
27. Ibid., 68/H43.
28. Sartre, *Being and Nothingness*, 123–24.
29. Ibid., 457.
30. Ibid., 480.
31. See Sartre, *Nausea*, trans. Lloyd Alexander (New York: New Directions, 2013).
32. *CNN*, "Pat Robertson Says Haiti Paying for 'Pact to the Devil'." CNN. Last modified January 13, 2010. Web.
33. Beauvoir, *The Ethics of Ambiguity*, 25.
34. Sartre, *Being and Nothingness*, 627.
35. Ibid.
36. Ibid., 625.
37. Camus, "The Myth of Sisyphus," 52.
38. Rorty, "Pragmatism, Relativism and Irrationalism," in *The Consequences of Pragmatism*, 173.
39. Rorty, *Philosophy and the Mirror of Nature*, 359.

BIBLIOGRAPHY

Abbot, J.I. 2013. There's nothing here but chemistry: *Breaking bad* and the philosophy of religion. *The Jerusalem Post*. Last modified October 8, 2013. Web.

Abelard, Peter. 2001. *Collationes*. Trans and eds. J. Marenbon and G. Orlandi. Oxford: Clarendon Press.

Abraham, Lyndy. 2001. *A dictionary of alchemical imagery*. Cambridge: Cambridge University Press.

Ainslie, George. 2001. *Break-down of the will*. Cambridge: Cambridge University Press.

Ainslie, George. 2005. Précis of *break-down of the will*. *Behavioral and Brain Sciences* 28: 635–673.

Ainslie, George. 2013. Money as MacGuffin: A factor in gambling and other process addictions. In *Addiction and self-control: Perspectives from philosophy, psychology, and neuroscience*, ed. Neil Levy, 16–37. Oxford: Oxford University Press.

Alexander, Larry A. 2005. Lesser evils: A closer look at paradigmatic justification. *Law and Philosophy* 24: 611–643.

Alexandra, Andrew. 1989. 'All men agree on this…' Hobbes on the fear of death and the way to peace. *History of Philosophy Quarterly* 6(1): 37–55.

Annas, Julia. 2011. *Intelligent virtue*. Oxford: Oxford University Press.

Arendt, Hannah. 1963a. *Eichmann in jerusalem: A report on the banality of evil*. New York: Penguin.

Arendt, Hannah. 1963b. *On revolution*. New York: Penguin.

Arendt, Hannah. 1971. *The life of the mind*. New York: Harcourt Brace.

Arendt, Hannah. 1972. On violence. In *Crises of the Republic*. New York: Harcourt Brace.

Arendt, Hannah. 1977. *Between past and future: Eight exercises in political thought*. New York: Penguin.

Arendt, Hannah. 1989. In *Lectures on Kant's political philosophy*, ed. Ronald Beiner. Chicago: University of Chicago Press.

Aristotle. 1925. *The nicomachean ethics*. Trans. W. D. Ross. Oxford: Clarendon Press.

Aristotle. 1941. *Poetics*. Trans. Ingram Bywater. New York: Random House.

Audi, Robert. 2005. Intrinsic value and meaningful life. *Philosophical Papers* 34: 331–355.

© The Author(s) 2017

K.S. Decker et al. (eds.), *Philosophy and Breaking Bad*,

DOI 10.1007/978-3-319-40343-4

Aurelius, Marcus. 1983. *The meditations*. Trans. G. M. A. Grube. Indianapolis: Hackett Publishing.

Austin, J.L. 1957. A plea for excuses: The presidential address. *Proceedings of the Aristotelian Society* 57: 1–30.

Baggini, Julian. 2005. *What's it all about? Philosophy and the meaning of life*. Oxford: Oxford University Press.

Baier, Annette C. 1994. *Moral prejudices: Essays on ethics*. Cambridge, MA: Harvard University Press.

Beauvoir, Simon de. 1949. *The second sex*. Trans. Constance Borde and Sheila Malovany-Chevallier. New York: Vintage.

Beauvoir, Simon de. 2000. *The ethics of ambiguity*. New York: Citadel.

Beauvoir, Simon de. 2004. Pyrrhus and cineas. Trans. Marybeth Timmermann. In *Simone de Beauvoir: Philosophical writings*, ed. Margaret A. Simons, 35–70. Urbana: University of Illinois Press.

Becker, Lawrence. 2001. *A new stoicism*. Princeton: Princeton University Press.

Beckett, Samuel. 1982. *Waiting for Godot: Tragicomedy in 2 acts*. New York: Grove.

Belliotti, Raymond. 2001. *What is the meaning of life?* Amsterdam: Rodopi.

Benhabib, Seyla. 2014. Who's on trial, Eichmann or Arendt? *The New York Times*. Last modified September 21, 2014. Web.

Bentham, Jeremy. 1995. *Panopticon*. London: Verso Books.

Bloom, Harold. 1994. *The Western canon: The books and school of the ages*. New York: Harcourt Brace.

Borges, J.L. 2000. *The aleph and other stories*. New York: Penguin.

Bourke, V.J. 1958. *Saint Augustine: The city of god*. New York: Doubleday.

Broadie, Sarah. 2012. *Nature and divinity in Plato's Timaeus*. Cambridge, MA: Cambridge University Press.

Brown, Robert McAfee. 1984. *Unexpected news*. Westminster: John Knox Press.

Brown, Lane. 2013. In conversation: Vince Gilligan on the end of *breaking bad*. *Vulture*. Last modified May 12, 2013. Web.

Brownstein, Henry H., Timothy M. Mulcahy, and Johannes Huessy. 2014. *The methamphetamine industry in America*. New Brunswick: Rutgers University Press.

Brueckner, Anthony L., and John Martin Fischer. 1986. Why is death bad? *Philosophical Studies* 50(2): 213–221.

Burbidge, John. 1981. Man, god, and death in Hegel's phenomenology. *Philosophy and Phenomenological Research* 42(2): 183–196.

Butler, Judith. 1990. *Gender trouble*. New York: Routledge.

Calkins, May Whiton. 1918. *The good man and the good*. New York: MacMillan.

Campbell, Joseph. 1949. *The hero with a thousand faces*. New York: New World Library.

Campbell, Joseph. 1988. *The power of myth*. New York: Anchor Doubleday.

Camus, Albert. 1955. *The myth of Sisyphus*. New York: Knopf.

Camus, Albert. 1995. Reflections on the guillotine. In *Resistance, rebellion, and death*, 215–240. New York: Vintage.

Caputo, John D. 1986. Hermeneutics as the recovery of man. In *Hermeneutics and modern philosophy*, ed. Bruce R. Wachterhauser, 416–445. Ithaca: Ithaca University Press.

Center for Behavioral Health Statistics and Quality. 2015. *Behavioral health trends in the United States: Results from the 2014 national survey on drug use and health* (HHS Publication No. SMA 15–4927, NSDUH Series H-50). Center for Behavioral Health Statistics and Quality. Last modified February 25, 2016. Web.

Churchill, Ward. 2001. 'Some people push back': On the justice of roosting chickens. *Cryptome*. Last modified September 12, 2001. Web.

Cirlot, J.E. 1971. *A dictionary of symbols*. Trans. J. Sage. London: Routledge.

CNN. 2010. Pat Robertson says Haiti paying for 'pact to the devil'. *CNN*. Last modified January 13, 2010. Web.

Cohen, Richard A. 2006. Levinas: Thinking least about death: Contra Heidegger. *International Journal for Philosophy of Religion* 60(1/3): 21–39.

Connell, F.J. 1967. Double effect, principle of. In *New catholic encyclopedia*, vol. 4. New York: McGraw-Hill.

Corbett, David. 2014. From Odysseus to Walter White: The antihero's journey. *Bright Ideas Magazine*. Last modified May 1, 2014. Web.

Couch, Aaron. 2015. *Breaking bad*: See iconic scenes Reshot for Spanish-Language remake. *The Hollywood Reporter*. Last modified June 6, 2015. Web.

Courdet, Allison. 1980. *Alchemy: The philosopher's stone*. Boulder: Shambhala.

Cottingham, John. 2003. *On the meaning of life*. London: Routledge.

Craig, William Lane. 2008. The absurdity of life without god. In *The meaning of life: A reader*, ed. E.D. Klemke, 40–56. Oxford: Oxford University Press.

Delgado, Richard, and Jean Stefancic (eds.). 2005. *The derrick bell reader*. New York: New York University Press.

Derrida, Jacques. 1976. *Of grammatology*. Trans. Gayatri Spivak. Baltimore: The Johns Hopkins University Press.

Derrida, Jacques. 2004. Plato's pharmacy. In *Dissemination*. Trans. B. Johnson, 61–172. New York: Continuum.

Dostoevesky, Fyodor. 1950. *The Brothers Karamazov*. Trans. Constance Garnett. New York: Random House.

Dostoevesky, Fyodor. 2012. *Crime and punishment*. Trans. Richard Pevear and Larissa Volkhonsky. New York: Random House.

Dostoevesky, Fyodor, *Crime and punishment*. Penguin, UK, 2014.

Draper, Kai. 2004. Epicurean equanimity towards death. *Philosophy and Phenomenological Research* 69(1): 92–114.

Ducasse, C.J. 1953. Demos on 'nature, mind, and death'. *The Review of Metaphysics* 7(2): 290–298.

Dworkin, Ronald. 2000. *Sovereign virtue. The theory and practice of equality*. Cambridge, MA: Harvard University Press.

Edinger, Edward. 1985. *Anatomy of the psyche: Alchemical symbolism in psychotherapy*. LaSalle: Open Court.

Edwards, Paul. 2008. The meaning and value of life. In *The meaning of life: A reader*, ed. E.D. Klemke, 114–133. Oxford: Oxford University Press.

Esslin, Martin. 1973. *The theatre of the absurd*. Woodstock: Overlook Press.

Ferreira, Jamie. 2001. *Love's grateful striving: A commentary on Kierkegaard's works of love*. Oxford: Oxford University Press.

Fiorenza, Elisabeth Schüssler. 1992. *But she said: Feminist practices of biblical interpretation*. Boston: Beacon Press.

Fischer, John Martin. 2006. Epicureanism about death and immortality. *The Journal of Ethics* 10(4): 355–381.

Frankfurt, Harry. 1982. The importance of what we care about. *Synthese* 53: 257–272.

Franz, Marie-Louise von. 2015. *Alchemy: An introduction to the symbolism and the psychology*. Toronto: Inner City Books.

Freud, Sigmund. 2010. *Beyond the pleasure principle.* Trans. James Strachey. San Francisco: Pacific Publishing Studio.

Gadamer, Hans Georg. 1989. *Truth and method.* Trans. Joel Weinsheimer and Donald G. Marshall. New York: Crossroad/Continuum.

Gatta, Giunia. 2014. Visiting or house-swapping? Arendt and jaspers on empathy, enlarged mentality, and the space in between. *Philosophy and Social Criticism* 40(10): 997–1014.

Gewirth, Alan. 1998. *The community of rights.* Chicago: University of Chicago Press.

Gilligan, Carol. 1982. *In a different voice: Psychological theory and women's development.* Cambridge, MA: Harvard University Press.

Gilligan, Carol. 1995. Moral orientation and moral development. In *Justice and care: Essential readings in feminist ethics*, ed. Virginia Held, 19–39. Boulder: Westview Press.

Gilligan, Vince. 2010a. Interview by Casey Carpenter. *The cult.* Last modified November 15, 2010. Web.

Gilligan, Vince. 2010b. Interview by Jovana Grbić. *ScriptPhD.* Last modified April 13, 2010. Web.

Gilligan, Vince. 2014. Interview by John Blistein. *Rolling stone.* Last modified January 7, 2014. Web.

Gilligan, Carol, and David A.J. Richards. 2009. *The deepening darkness: Patriarchy, resistance, & democracy's future.* New York: Cambridge University Press.

Glimcher, Paul W. 2009. Choice: Towards a standard back-pocket model. In *Neuroeconomics: Decision making and the brain*, ed. Paul W. Glimcher, 503–522. Amsterdam: Elsevier.

Goodman, Tim. 2015. 'Mad men': Tim goodman on pairing up and partnering off as change announces its arrival. *Hollywood Reporter.* Last modified April 27, 2015. Web.

Guenther, Herbert V. 1989. *From reductionism to creativity: RDzogs-chen and the new sciences of mind.* Boston: Shambhala.

Gunn, Anna. 2013. I Have a character issue. *The New York Times.* Last modified August 23, 2013. Web.

Gźon-nu-rgyal-mchog, Dkon-mchog-rgyal-mtshan, and Thupten Jinpa. 2006. *Mind training: The great collection.* Boston: Wisdom Publications.

Hanson, Neil. 1999. *The custom of the sea: A shocking true tale of shipwreck, murder, and the last taboo.* New York: Wiley.

Hatab, Lawrence J. 2005. *Nietzsche's life sentence: Coming to terms with eternal recurrence.* New York: Routledge.

Haydon, Graham. 1999. Right, wrong and murder. *Journal of Philosophy of Education* 33(1): 20–21.

Hays, G. 2002. *Marcus Aurelius: Meditations.* New York: Modern Library.

Hegel, G.W.F. 1977. *The phenomenology of spirit.* Trans. A. V. Miller. Oxford: Oxford University Press.

Heidegger, Martin. 1962. *Being and time.* Trans. John MacQuarrie and Edward Robinson. New York: HarperCollins Publishers.

Held, Virginia. 2005. *The ethics of care: Personal, political, and global.* Oxford: Oxford University Press.

Held, Virginia. 2010. Can the ethics of care handle violence? *Ethics and Social Welfare* 4(2): 115–129.

Held, Virginia. 2014. The ethics of care as normative guidance: Comment on Gilligan. *Journal of Social Philosophy* 45(1): 107–115.

Heyd, David, and Franklin G. Miller. 2010. Life plans: Do they give meaning to our lives? *Monist* 93(1): 17–37.

Hick, John. 1989. *Philosophy of religion*. New York: Pearson.

Hick, John. 2000. The religious meaning of life. In *The meaning of life in the world religions*, ed. Joseph Runzo and Nancy M. Martin, 269–286. Oxford: Oneworld Publications.

Hillman, James. 1981. Alchemical blue and the *Unio Mentalis*. *Sulfur* 1: 33–50.

Hillman, James. 2010. *Alchemical psychology. Uniform edition of the writings of James Hillman*, vol. 5. Putnam: Spring Publications.

Hitchcock, Alfred. 1954. *Rear window. Film*. Los Angeles: Paramount.

Hobbes, Thomas. 1994. In *Leviathan*, ed. E. Curley. Indianapolis: Hackett.

Hugo, Victor. *Les Miserables*. New York Modern Library, 1992.

Hugo, Victor. 2013. *Les Miserables*. Trans. Christine Donougher. New York: Penguin.

Huffington Post. 2013. *Breaking bad* dedicates premiere To Kevin Cordasco, 16-year-old who lost battle With cancer. *Huffington Post*. Last modified August 14, 2013. Web.

Hume, David. 1975. In *Enquiries concerning human understanding and concerning the principles of morals*, ed. L.A. Selby-Bigge. Oxford: Clarendon Press.

Hurka, Thomas. 1993. *Perfectionism*. Oxford: Oxford University Press.

Hursthouse, Rosalind. 2001. *On virtue ethics*. Oxford: Oxford University Press.

Husserl, Edmund. 1970. *The crisis of European sciences and transcendental phenomenology*. Trans. David Carr. Evanston: Northwestern University Press.

Husserl, Edmund. 1983a. *General introduction to a pure phenomenology*. Trans. F. Kersten. Hingham: Kluwer Boston, Inc.

Husserl, Edmund. 1983b. *Ideas: General introduction to a pure phenomenology and to a phenomenological philosophy 2*. Trans. F. Kersten. The Hague: Martinus Nijhoff.

Ingarden, Roman. 1973. *The literary work of art*. Trans. George G. Grabowicz. Evanston: Northwestern University Press.

Ingarden, Roman. 1989. *Ontology of the work of art: The musical work, the picture, the architectural work, the film*. Trans. Raymond Meyer and John T. Goldthwait. Athens: University of Ohio Press.

Jaggar, Allison M. 1995. Caring as a feminist practice of moral reason. In *Justice and care: Essential readings in feminist ethics*, ed. Virginia Held. Boulder: Westview Press.

James, A. 2014. *Assholes: A theory*. New York: Anchor.

Jung, C.G. 1956–1986a. *Aion: Researches into the phenomenology of the self*. Trans. R. F. C. Hull. In *The collected works of C.G. Jung*, vol. 9.2, eds. H. Read et al. Princeton: Princeton University Press.

Jung, C.G. 1956–1986b. *Alchemical studies*. Trans. R. F. C. Hull. In *The collected works of C.G. Jung*, vol. 13, eds. H. Read et al. Princeton: Princeton University Press.

Jung, C.G. 1956–1986c. *Archetypes and the collective unconscious*. Trans. R. F. C. Hull. In *The collected works of C.G. Jung*, vol. 9.1, eds. H. Read et al. Princeton: Princeton University Press.

Jung, C.G. 1956–1986d. *Development of personality*. Trans. R. F. C. Hull. In *The collected works of C.G. Jung*, vol. 17, eds. H. Read et al. Princeton: Princeton University Press.

Jung, C.G. 1956–1986e. *Freud & psychoanalysis*. Trans. R. F. C. Hull. In *The collected works of C.G. Jung*, vol. 4. eds. H. Read et al. Princeton: Princeton University Press.

Jung, C.G. 1956–1986f. *Practice of psychotherapy*. Trans. R. F. C. Hull. In *The collected works of C.G. Jung*, vol. 16, eds. H. Read et al. Princeton: Princeton University Press.

Jung, C.G. 1956–1986g. *Psychological types*. Trans. R. F. C. Hull. In *The collected works of C.G. Jung*, vol. 6, eds. H. Read et al. Princeton: Princeton University Press.

Jung, C.G. 1956–1986h. *Psychology and alchemy*. Trans. R. F. C. Hull. In *The collected works of C.G. Jung*, vol. 12, eds. H. Read et al. Princeton: Princeton University Press.

Jung, C.G. 1956–1986i. *Structure & dynamics of the psyche*. Trans. R. F. C. Hull. In *The collected works of C.G. Jung*, vol. 8, eds. H. Read et al. Princeton: Princeton University Press.

Jung, C.G. 1956–1986j. *The symbolic life: Miscellaneous writings*. Trans. R. F. C. Hull. In *The collected works of C.G. Jung*, vol. 18, eds. H. Read et al. Princeton: Princeton University Press.

Jung, C.G. 1956–1986k. *Symbols of transformation*. Trans. R. F. C. Hull. In *The collected works of C.G. Jung*, vol. 5, eds. H. Read et al. Princeton: Princeton University Press.

Jung, C.G. 1956–1986l. *Two essays on analytical psychology*. Trans. R. F. C. Hull. In *The collected works of C.G. Jung*, vol. 7, eds. H. Read et al. Princeton: Princeton University Press.

Kalmanson, Leah, and Sarah Mattice. 2015. The De of Levinas: Cultivating the heart-mind of radical passivity. *Frontiers of Philosophy in China* 10(1): 113–129.

Kant, Immanuel. 1999. *Practical philosophy*. Trans. M. J. Gregor. Cambridge: Cambridge University Press.

Kayfman, Whitley R.P. 2003. Motive, intention, and morality in the criminal law. *Criminal Justice Review* 28: 317–335.

Kekes, John. 2000. The meaning of life. *Midwest Studies in Philosophy* 24: 17–34.

Kerényi, Carl. 1996. *Dionysos: Archetypal image of indestructible life*. Trans. R. Manheim. Princeton: Princeton University Press.

Kierkegaard, Søren. 1962. *Works of love*. Trans. H. V. Hong and E. H. Hong. New York: Harper & Brothers.

Kierkegaard, Søren. 1980. *The sickness unto death*. Trans. H. V. Hong and E. H. Hong. Princeton: Princeton University Press.

Kierkegaard, Søren. 1981. *The concept of anxiety*. Trans. H. V. Hong and E. H. Hong. Princeton: Princeton University Press.

Kierkegaard, Søren. 1983a. *Either/or, vol. I*. Trans. H. V. Hong and E. H. Hong. Princeton: Princeton University Press.

Kierkegaard, Søren. 1983b. *Fear & trembling and repetition*. Trans. H. V. Hong and E. H. Hong. Princeton: Princeton University Press.

Kierkegaard, Søren. 1988. *Stages on life's way*. Trans. H. V. Hong and E. H. Hong. Princeton: Princeton University Press.

Kierkegaard, Søren. 1992. *Eighteen upbuilding discourses*. Trans. H. V. Hong and E. H. Hong. Princeton: Princeton University Press.

Kierkegaard, Søren. 1993. *Upbuilding discourses in various spirits*. Trans. H. V. Hong and E. H. Hong. Princeton: Princeton University Press.

Kierkegaard, Søren. 1997. *The essential Kierkegaard*. Trans. H. V. Hong and E. H. Hong. Princeton: Princeton University Press.

Kierkegaard, Søren. 1998. *The point of view*. Trans. H. V. Hong and E. H. Hong. Princeton: Princeton University Press.

Kierkegaard, Søren. 2009. *"The moment" and late writings*. Trans. H. V. Hong and E. H. Hong. Princeton: Princeton University Press.

Klemke, E.D. (ed.). 1981. *The meaning of life: A reader*. New York: Oxford University Press.

Klosterman, Chuck. 2011. Bad decisions. *Grantland*. Last modified August 2, 2011. Web.

Koepsell, David R., and Vanessa Gonzalez. 2012. Walt's rap sheet. In *Breaking bad and philosophy: Badder living through chemistry*, ed. David R. Koepsell and Robert Arp, 1–15. LaSalle: Open Court.

Kohlberg, Lawrence. 1981. *Essays on moral development, volume 1: The philosophy of moral development*. San Francisco: Harper & Row.

Kornfield, Jack. 2007. *Teachings of the Buddha*. Boston: Shambhala.

Kuo, Albert, and Michelle Wu. 2012. In hell we shall be free: On breaking bad. *Los Angeles review of books*. Last modified July 13, 2012. Web.

Lanham, Andrew. 2013. Walter white's heart of darkness. *Los Angeles review of books*. Last modified August 11, 2013. Web.

LeBar, Mark. 2013. *The value of living well*. Oxford: Oxford University Press.

Leopold, Todd. 2013. The new, new, new TV golden age. *CNN*. Last modified May 6, 2013. Web.

Levinas, Emmanuel. 1979. *Totality and infinity: An essay on exteriority*. The Hague: Martinus Nijhoff.

Levinas, Emmanuel. 1985. *Ethics and infinity*. Trans. Richard A. Cohen. Pittsburgh: Duquesne University Press.

Levinas, Emmanuel. 1996. In *Basic philosophical writings*, ed. A.T. Peperzak, Simon Critchley, and Robert Bernasconi. Bloomington: Indiana University Press.

Levine, Michael P. 1987. What does death have to do with the meaning of life? *Religious Studies* 23(4): 457–465.

Linden, Stanton J. 2003. *The alchemy reader: From Hermes Trismegistus to Isaac Newton*. New York: Cambridge University Press.

Lipstadt, Deborah. 2011. *The Eichmann trial*. New York: Schocken.

Locker, Melissa. 2013. Is Felina the secret to the *breaking bad* finale? *Time Magazine*. Last modified September 25, 2013. Web.

Machiavelli, Niccólo. 1988. *The prince*. London: Encyclopedia Britannica.

MacInnes, Paul. 2012. *Breaking bad* creator Vince Gilligan: The man who turned walter white from Mr. Chips into scarface. *The Guardian*. Last modified May 18, 2012. Web.

Magaldi, Kristin. 2015. White to Don Draper: The science behind our love of antiheroes. *Medical Daily*. Last modified March 26, 2015. Web.

Mahon, James Edwin. 2013. Doing the wrong thing for a good reason. In *The good wife and philosophy: Temptations of Saint Alicia*, ed. Kimberly Baltzer-Jaray and Robert Arp, 89–100. LaSalle: Open Court.

Marlan, Stanton. 2008. *The black sun: The alchemy and art of darkness*. College Station: Texas A&M University Press.

Marnell, Blair. 2013. Aaron Paul 'hates' walter white on *breaking bad. Crave Online*. Last modified May 18, 2013. Web.

Martens, Paul, and Tom Millay. 2011. 'The changelessness of god' as Kierkegaard's final theodicy: God and the gift of suffering. *International Journal of Systematic Theology* 13(2): 170–189.

May, Todd. 2009. *Death*. Stocksfield: Acumen Publishing Limited.

McIntyre, Alison. 2014. Doctrine of double effect. *Stanford Encyclopedia of Philosophy*. Last modified September 23, 2014. Web.

Merleau-Ponty, Maurice. 1964. *Signs*. Trans. R. McCleary. Evanston: Northwestern University Press.

Merleau-Ponty, Maurice. 2005. *Phenomenology of perception*. New York: Routledge.

Métall, Rudolf Aladár. 1969. *Hans Kelsen: Leben und Werk*. Vienna: Deuticke.

Metz, Thaddeus. 2013. The meaning of life. *The Stanford Encyclopedia of Philosophy*. Last modified June 3, 2013. Web.

Michaelides-Mateou, Sofia, and Andreas Mateou. 2010. *Flying in the face of criminalization: The safety implications of prosecuting aviation professionals for accidents*. London: Ashgate.

Mill, J.S. 1979. *On liberty*. Indianapolis: Hackett.

Milton, John. 1911. In *The tenure of kings and magistrates*, ed. William Talbot Allison. New York: Henry Holt and Company.

Milton, John. 1999. In *Aeropagitica and other political writings of John Milton*, ed. John Alvis. New York: Liberty Fund.

Milton, John. 2016a. The doctrine and discipline of divorce. *The John Milton reading room*. Last modified January 15, 2016. Web.

Milton, John. 2016b. *Paradise lost. The John Milton reading room*. Last modified January 15, 2016. Web.

Miori, Dan. 2012. Was Skyler's intervention ethical? Hell, it shouldn't even be legal. In *Breaking bad and philosophy: Badder living through chemistry*, ed. David R. Koepsell and Robert Arp, 27–40. LaSalle: Open Court.

Mitscherling, Jeff. 1997. *Roman ingarden's ontology and aesthetics*. Ottawa: University of Ottawa Press.

Mitscherling, Jeff. 2005. Concretization, literary criticism, and the life of the literary work of art. In *Existence, culture and persons: The ontology of roman ingarden*, ed. Arkadiusz Chrudzimski, 137–158. New Brunswick: Ontos Verlag.

Moore, Pearson. 2015. Breaking down breaking bad. *Forum*. Last updated January 15, 2015. Web.

Murphy, Jeffrie. 2003. *Getting even*. New York: Oxford.

Murphy, Mark C. 2007. *Philosophy of law: The fundamentals*. Oxford: Blackwell.

Murphy, Jeffrie, and Jean Hampton. 1988. *Forgiveness and mercy*. Cambridge: Cambridge University Press.

Mylonas, George E. 1974. *Eleusis and the Eleusinian mysteries*. Princeton: Princeton University Press.

Nietzsche, Freidrich. 1961. *Thus Spoke Zarathustra*. Trans. R. J. Hollingdale. London: Penguin Books.

Nietzsche, Freidrich. 1967. *On the genealogy of morals*. Trans. Walter Kaufmann. New York: Random House.

Nietzsche, Freidrich. 2006. *Human, all-too-human*. Trans. Helen Zimmern and Paul V. Cohn. Mineola: Dover Publications.

Noddings, Nell. 2013. An ethic of caring. In *Ethical theory: An anthology*, ed. Russ Shafer-Landau, 701–720. New York: Wiley.

Norman, Richard. 2006. The varieties of non-religious experiences. *Ratio*: volume 19, issue 4, 490–513.

Nozick, Robert. 1981. *Philosophical explanations*. Cambridge, MA: Harvard University Press.

Nunberg, G. 2012. *The assent of the A-Word*. New York: Perseus.

Nussbaum, Martha. 1993. Non-relative virtues: An aristotelian approach. In *The quality of life*, ed. M. Nussbaum and A. Sen, 242–270. New York: Oxford.

Nussbaum, Emily. 2013. The closure-happy 'Breaking bad' finale. *The New Yorker*. Last modified September 30, 2013. Web.

Oppermann, Serpil. 2015. Quantum physics and literature: How they meet the Universe Halfway. *Journal of English Philology* 13: 87–104.

O'Reilly, Mollie Wilson. 2013. Breaking bad #516: 'Felina'. *Commonweal.* Last modified September 30, 2013. Web.

Plato. 1997. *Phaedo.* Trans. G. M. A. Grube. In *Plato complete works*, ed. John M. Cooper. Indianapolis: Hackett Publishing.

Poole, Scott. 2014. *Monsters in America.* Waco: Baylor University Press.

Quinones, Samuel. 2015. *Dreamland: The true tale of American opiate epidemic.* London: Bloomsbury.

Rachels, James, and Stuart Rachels. 2007. *The elements of moral philosophy.* Boston: McGraw-Hill.

Railton, Peter. 1988. Alienation, consequentialism, and the demands of morality. In *Consequentialism and its critics*, ed. S. Scheffler, 93–133. Oxford: Oxford University Press.

Rawls, John. 2005. *A theory of justice.* New Delhi: Universal Law Publishing.

Rawls, J. *A theory of justice.* Havard U. Press 2009.

Rorty, Richard. 1979. *Philosophy and the mirror of nature.* Princeton: Princeton University Press.

Rorty, Richard. 1982. *The consequences of pragmatism.* Minneapolis: University of Minnesota Press.

Rorty, Richard. 1989. *Contingency, irony, and solidarity.* Cambridge: Cambridge University Press.

Rorty, Richard. 1991. *Essays on Heidegger and others: Philosophical papers*, vol. 2. Cambridge: Cambridge University Press.

Rumble, Wilfred E. 1985. *The thought of John Austin: Jurisprudence, colonial reform, and the British constitution London.* Dover: Athlone Press.

Runzo, Joseph, and Nancy M. Martin (eds.). 2000. *The meaning of life in the world religions.* Oxford: Oneworld Publications.

Russell, Daniel. 2009. *Practical intelligence and the virtues.* Oxford: Oxford University Press.

San Juan, Eric. 2013. *Breaking down breaking bad: Unpeeling the layers of television's greatest drama.* North Charleston: CreateSpace.

Sartre, Jean-Paul. 1958. *Being and nothingness: An essay on phenomenological ontology.* Trans. Hazel Barnes. London: Methuen.

Sartre, Jean-Paul. 1965a. *Existentialism and humanism.* Trans. Philip Mairet. London: Methuen.

Sartre, Jean-Paul. 1965b. The humanism of existentialism. In *Essays in existentialism*, ed. Wade Baskin, 1–45. New York: Citadel Press.

Sartre, Jean-Paul. 1965c. The origin of nothingness. In *Essays in existentialism*, ed. Wade Baskin, 140–175. New York: Citadel Press.

Sartre, Jean-Paul. 1975. *The emotions: Outline of a theory.* New York: Citadel Press.

Sartre, Jean-Paul. 1981. *Existential psychoanalysis.* Washington, DC: Regnery Publishing.

Sartre, Jean-Paul. 2013. *Nausea.* Trans. Lloyd Alexander. New York: New Directions.

Scalambrino, Frank. 2015a. *Full throttle heart: Nietzsche, beyond either/or.* New Philadelphia: The Eleusinian Press.

Scalambrino, Frank. 2015b. The temporality of damnation. In *The concept of hell*, ed. Benjamin W. McCraw and Robert Arp, 66–82. New York: Palgrave.

Scalambrino, Frank. 2015c. The Vanishing subject: Becoming who you cybernetically are. In *Social epistemology & technology*, ed. Frank Scalambrino, 197–206. London: Rowman & Littlefield.

Scalambrino, Frank. 2016. *Meditations on orpheus: Love, death, and transformation*. Pittsburgh: Black Water Phoenix Press.

Scanlon, Thomas. 2008. *Moral dimensions: Permissibility, meaning, blame*. Cambridge, MA: Belknap Press.

Schleiermacher, Friedrich. 2006. *On religion: Speeches to its cultured despisers*. Trans. John Oman. Cambridge: Cambridge University Press.

Searle, John. 1997. *The construction of social reality*. New York: Free Press.

Segal, David. 2011. The dark art of breaking bad. *New York Times*. Last modified July 6, 2011. Web.

Seneca. 1920. *De Constantia*. Trans. and ed. J. Basore. Heinemann: New York.

Shelley, Percy Bysshe. 1901. Ozymandias. In *The complete poetical works of Percy Bysshe Shelley*, ed. George Edward Woodberry. Boston: Houghton Mifflin Company.

Siegler, Elijah. 2015. Television. In *The Routledge companion to religion and popular culture*, ed. John C. Lyden and Eric Michael Mazur, 41–64. New York: Routledge.

Silverstein, Harry S. 1980. The evil of death. *The Journal of Philosophy* 77(7): 401–424.

Singer, Peter. 1993. *Practical ethics*. Cambridge: Cambridge University Press.

Smith, Adam. 1982. In *Theory of moral sentiments*, ed. A.L. Macfie and D.D. Raphael. Indianapolis: Liberty Press.

Smith, Quentin. 1991. Concerning the absurdity of life. *Philosophy* 66(255): 119–121.

Snierson, Dan. 2013. 'Breaking bad': Creator Vince Gilligan explains series finale. *Entertainment Weekly*. Last modified September 30, 2013. Web.

Stanford News. 2005. 'You've got to find what you love,' jobs. *Stanford News*. Last modified June 14, 2005. Web.

Stangneth, Bettina. 2015. *Eichmann before Jerusalem: The unexamined life of a mass murderer*. New York: Vintage.

Stein, Edith. 1989. *On the problem of empathy*. Trans. Waltraut Stein. Washington, DC: ICS.

Stein, Edith. 2014. *Self-portrait in letters: Letters to Roman Ingarden*. Trans. Hugh Candler Hunt and ed. Maria Amata Neyer. Washington, DC: ICS Publications.

Sterba, James P. 2001. Introduction: Justice for here and now. In *Social and political philosophy: Contemporary perspectives*, ed. James P. Sterba, 1–26. London: Routledge.

Suits, Bernard. 1967. Is life a game we are playing? *Ethics* 77(3): 209–213.

Sutton, R. 2010. *The no asshole rule*. New York: Hachette.

Taylor, Richard. 1970. *Good and evil*. New York: Macmillan.

Taylor, Richard. 1999. The meaning of life. *Philosophy Now* 24: 13–14.

Tolkien, J.R.R. 1977. *Tree and leaf: Smith of Wootton Major—The homecoming of Beorhtnoth*. London: Unwin Paperbacks.

Tolkien, J.R.R., and Douglas A. Anderson. 1994. *The lord of the rings*. Boston: Houghton Mifflin.

Tolkien, J.R.R., Humphrey Carpenter, and Christopher Tolkien. 1981. *The letters of J.R.R. Tolkien*. Boston: Houghton Mifflin.

Toretti, Roberto. 1999. *The philosophy of physics*. New York: Cambridge University Press.

Trisel, Brooke Alan. 2002. Futility and the meaning of life debate. *Sorites*: volume 14, 70–84.

Trisel, Brooke Alan. 2004. Human extinction and the value of our efforts. *The Philosophical Forum* 35: 371–391.

Van der Heijdena, Karin, Merel Visseb, Gerty Lensvelt-Muldersb, and Guy Widdershovenc. 2016. To care or not to care: A narrative on experiencing caring responsibilities. *Ethics and Social Welfare* 10(1): 53–68.

Van der Werff, Todd. 2013. *Breaking bad* ended the anti-hero genre by introducing good and evil. *A.V. CLUB*. Last modified September 30, 2013. Web.

Van de Ven, N., M. Zeelenberg, and R. Pieters. 2009. Leveling up and down: The experiences of benign and malicious envy. *Emotion* 9(3): 419–429.

Velleman, David. 1991. Well-being and time. *Pacific Philosophical Quarterly* 72: 48–77.

Velleman, David. 2005. Family history. *Philosophical Papers* 34: 357–378.

Vogler, Christopher. 1985. A practical guide to Joseph Campbell's *the hero with a thousand faces. Hero's Journey*. Last modified January 15, 1985. Web.

Voss, Karen-Claire. 1989. The Hierosgamos theme in the images of the *Rosarium Philosophorum*. In *Proceedings of the International Conference on the History of Alchemy at the University of Groningen*, April 17–19, ed. Z.R.W.M. von Martels, 140–158. Leiden: E. J. Brill, 1990.

Wachterhauser, Bruce R. 1986. Introduction: History and language of understanding. In *Hermeneutics and modern philosophy*, ed. Bruce R. Wachterhauser, 5–64. Albany: State University of New York Press.

Wanat, Matt, and Leonard Engel (eds.). 2016. *Breaking down breaking bad: Critical perspectives*. Albuquerque: University of New Mexico Press.

Wang, Hansi Lo. 2014. *Breaking bad* fans get their fix in Spanish. *NPR*. Last modified September 17, 2014. Web.

Wasson, R. Gordon, Albert Hofmann, and Carl A. P. Ruck. 2008. *The road to eleusis: Unveiling the secret of the mysteries*. Berkeley: North Atlantic Books.

Weber, Max. 2002. *The protestant ethic and the "spirit" of capitalism and other writings*. Trans. and ed. Peter R. Baehr and Gordon C. Wells. New York: Penguin.

Wielenberg, Erik. 2005. *Value and virtue in a godless universe*. Cambridge: Cambridge University Press.

Wolf, Susan. 2010. *Meaning in life and why it matters*. Princeton: Princeton University Press.

Wolfson, Elliot R. 2014. *Giving beyond the gift: Apophasis and overcoming theomania*. New York: Fordham University Press.

Zahavi, Dan. 2003. *Husserl's phenomenology*. Stanford: Stanford University Press.

Zimbardo, Philip. 2008. *The lucifer effect: Understanding how good people turn bad*. New York: Random House.

Zuntz, Günther. 1971. *Persephone: Three essays on religion and thought in Magna Graecia*. Oxford: Clarendon Press.

INDEX[1]

[1] Note: Page numbers followed by n denote footnotes

© The Author(s) 2017
K.S. Decker et al. (eds.), *Philosophy and Breaking Bad*,
DOI 10.1007/978-3-319-40343-4

CPSIA information can be obtained
at www.ICGtesting.com
Printed in the USA
LVOW03*2311071216
516330LV00038B/834/P